DEATH MAGICK ABUNDANCE AKASHA RABUT

Anthology Editions

New York

This book is dedicated to Sam Feather,
who inspired me to make photographs of New Orleans.
Thank you for being a dear friend.

FOREWORD

Sam Feather

When I first saw a second line, I was alarmed. Why had no one told me stuff like this happened in America? Are folks really doing this all the time down in New Orleans? Why don't people anywhere else learn how to party this way?

On a broken street, trumpet whistle bottle bell... drum slide step drop drag. A culture sprung from funerals: way uptown, way downtown, in the streets of New Orleans resides the essence of parade.

Act like it's your last day to live, or your partner's first day in heaven.

Death came. Dance. Death coming any time. Dance.

It is the fleeting nature of things that makes them so precious. The sun hums down steady and the clouds unroll above the street, which has become a dream of endless Sundays. Let's imagine together that this is all there is. A pulse has been passed down from way back that is foolish to talk about. It has survived by doing.

At a good second line, there will be teenagers dressed in fly new outfits; could be from the beauty shop or the boutique. There will be men sweating, pushing wagons full of two-dollar beer. Hot sausage and burgers for sale, maybe fried fish. There will be a hot-ass brass band playing traditionals and pop radio covers. There will be people of all ages buckjumping and strutting, climbing onto the tombs and electrical boxes to dance. Men in three-piece suits, women with two-inch fingernails, sculptural hair, custom "RIP" airbrush and iron-on. There will be big clouds of weed smoke, loud engines. T-shirts that tell exactly how the wearer is related to someone in the parade. There is an air of majesty about a young man on a horse, strengthened by the street fashions on the riders.

Second lines are a source of power. In a city where so much is oriented toward outsiders, the parade is not for sale, not advertised, not sponsored by corporations, not accompanied by souvenirs. Despite very tight budgets, you will see some of the most creative dressing in the world at the second line. It's a stage and a dance club and a neighborhood block party all walking by in the afternoon. It's a tiny economy.

Lot of eyes out here, lot of cameras, lot of friends, and a lot of familiar strangers. People become local celebrities, like the triple-snake man, or the man with the penny-farthing bicycle, the towel man who also sells whistles, the man with the electric wheelchair, and the chihuahua named Chichi. Everyone knows their face even if they don't know their name. How about Ms. Sue Da Lemonade Lady, or Mr. Valerie's Pralines? The Scooter Boyz, the Gamechangers, the Caramel Curves? We know them instantly when described, simply because they show up every Sunday and do their thing. This is a special feature of second line: the way the division between audience and spectacle dissolves. Sure, there are club members at the center riding on floats, but a lot of folks came for everyone else out here: I came for the cars, she came for the gossip, he came for the brass band, someone came for the fashion, someone came to dance for their family who just died. And all these people who came to see the parade—we are the parade.

Second line is a celebration of a spirit held fast:
a spirit of exuberance—*be joyful*
a spirit of continuity—*repetition with variation*
a spirit of improvisation—*do what you feel*
a spirit of regality—*know your worth*
a spirit of grief—*honor those lost*
a spirit of surrender—*be lost in the crowd, together*
a spirit of freedom—*your soul is still free.*
A declaration from the jaws of disaster or irrelevance: we're still here, still twinkling like a jewel.

A precarious place, the Big Easy, celebrates death, and in doing so overflows with life (or vice versa?). Destroyed and rebuilt from its beginning, New Orleans is at once grand and ramshackle, seductive and dangerous. Second lines integrate these seeming contradictions and reflect a native wisdom. Beauty and sadness are two sides of one coin; they are the light and shadow by which we define life. This coin has sharp edges—joy and pain—which ring out loud across New Orleans and cut through every blessed thing. Yet wherever you are in life, this tradition can hold you.

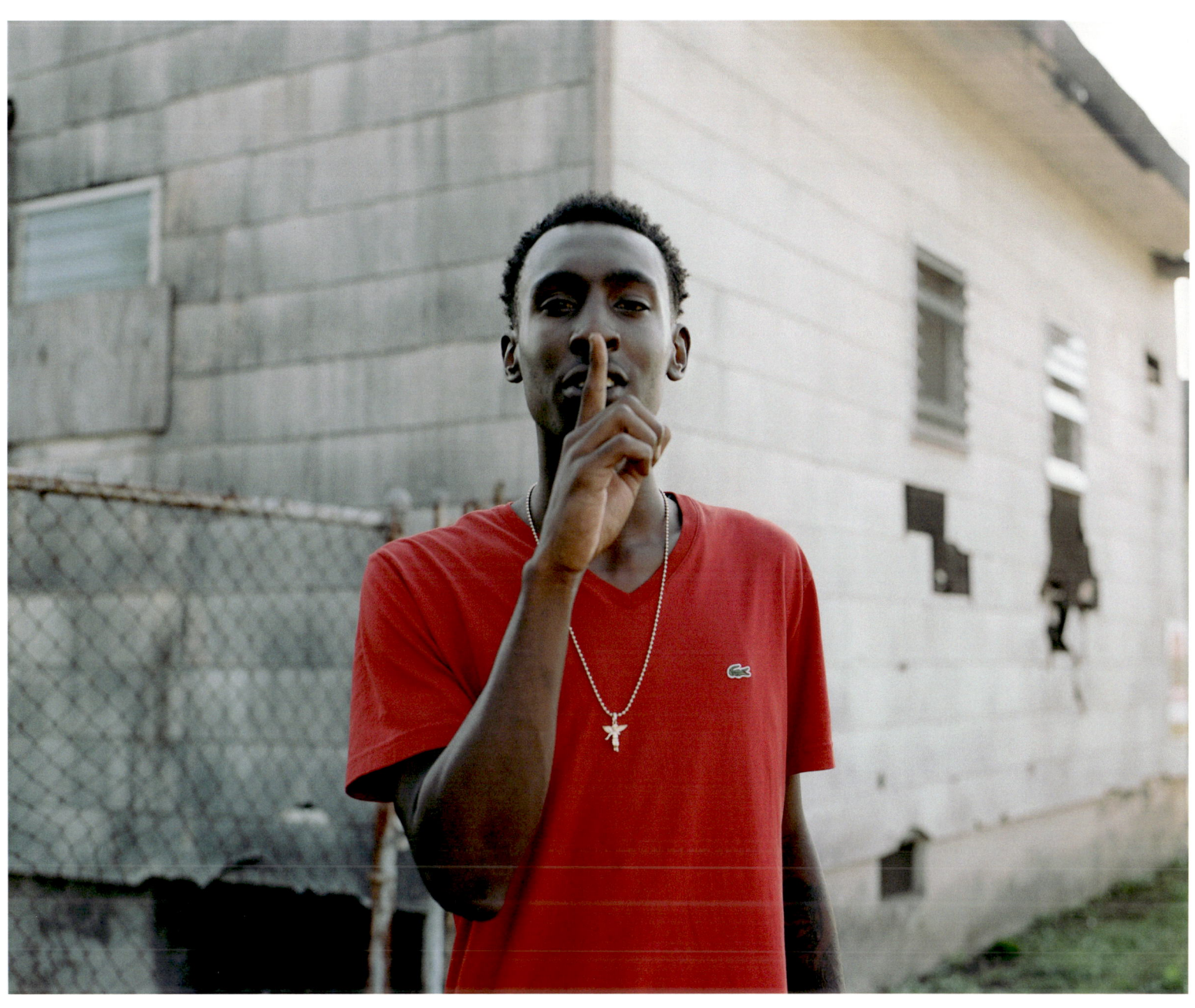

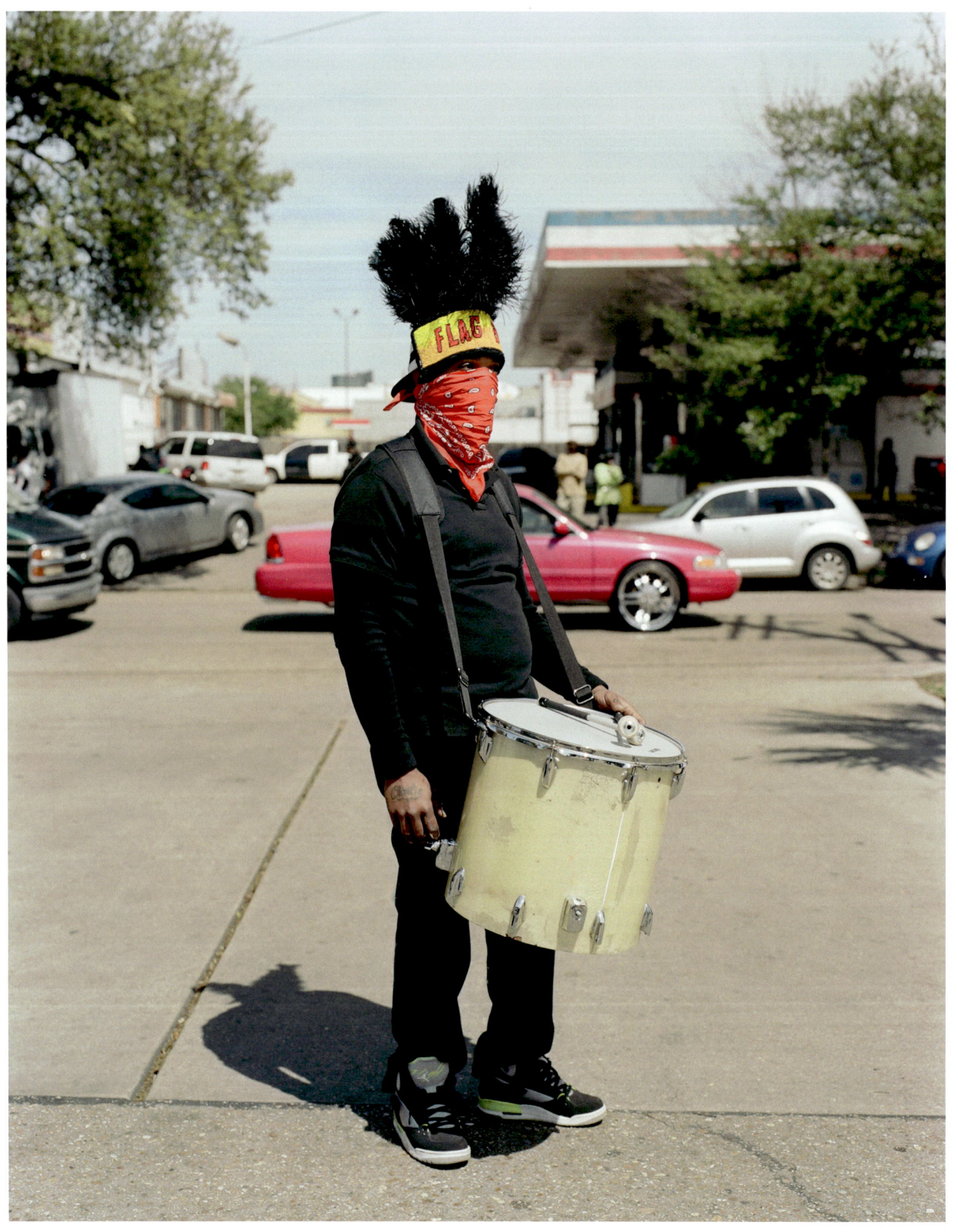

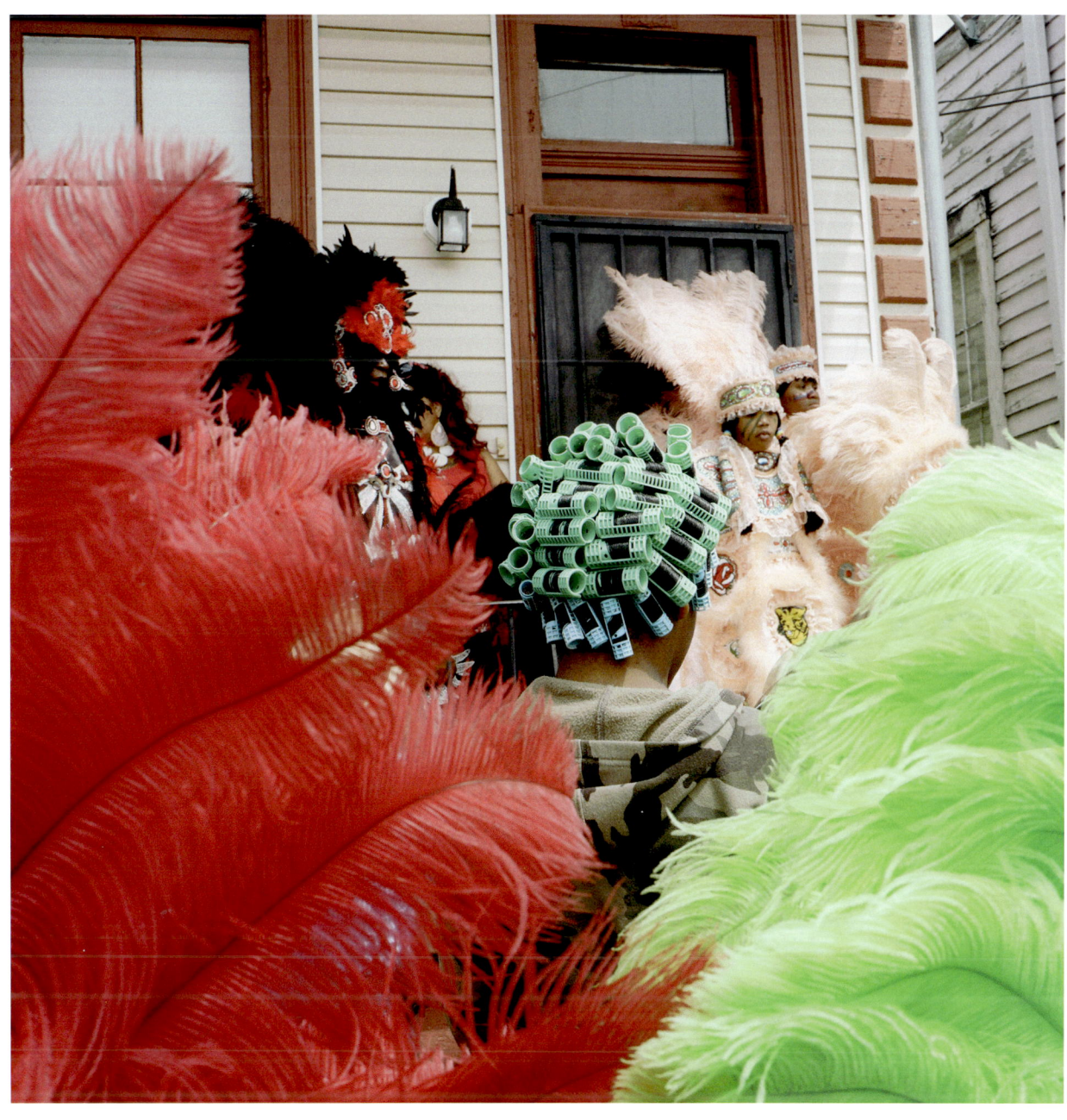

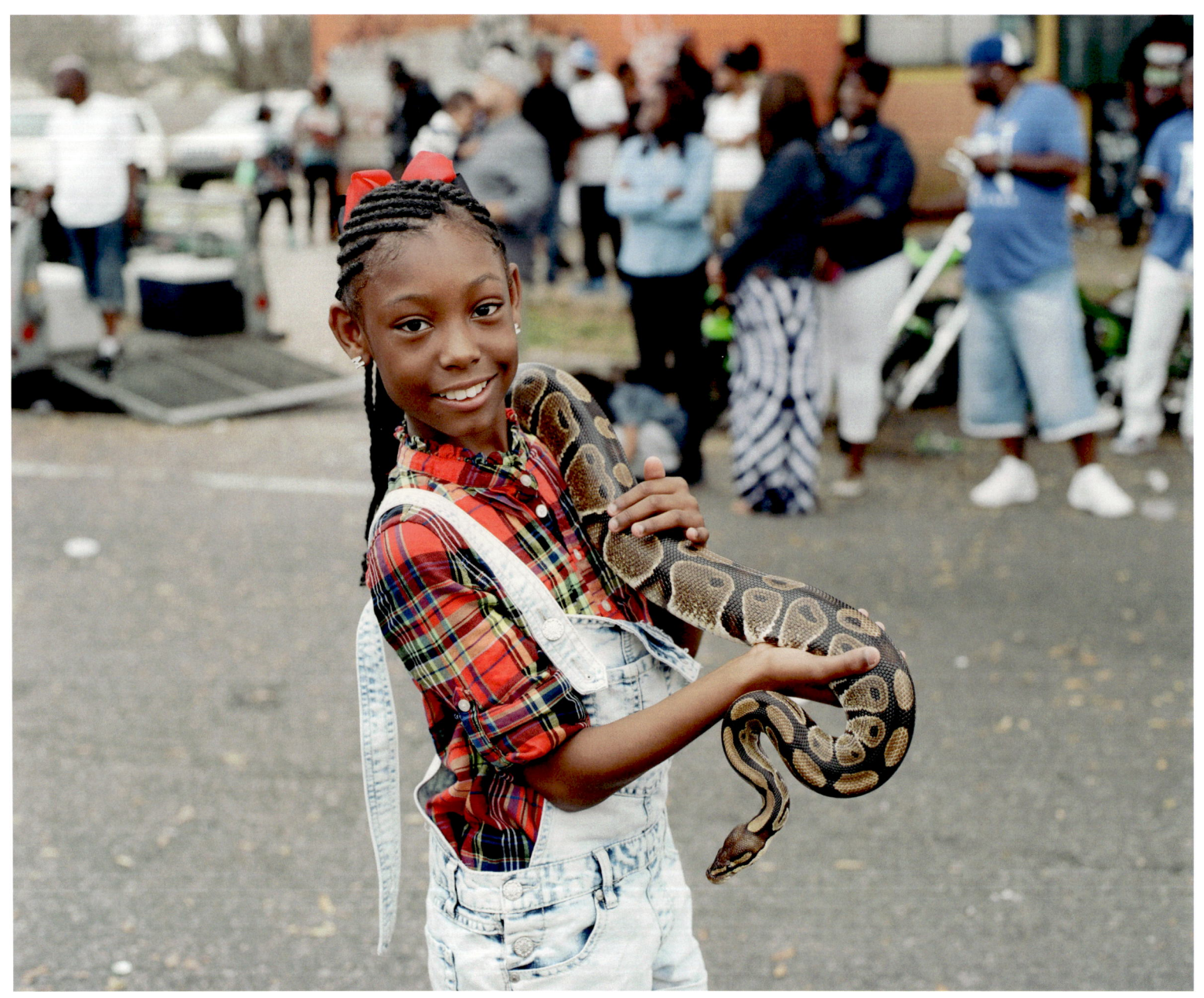

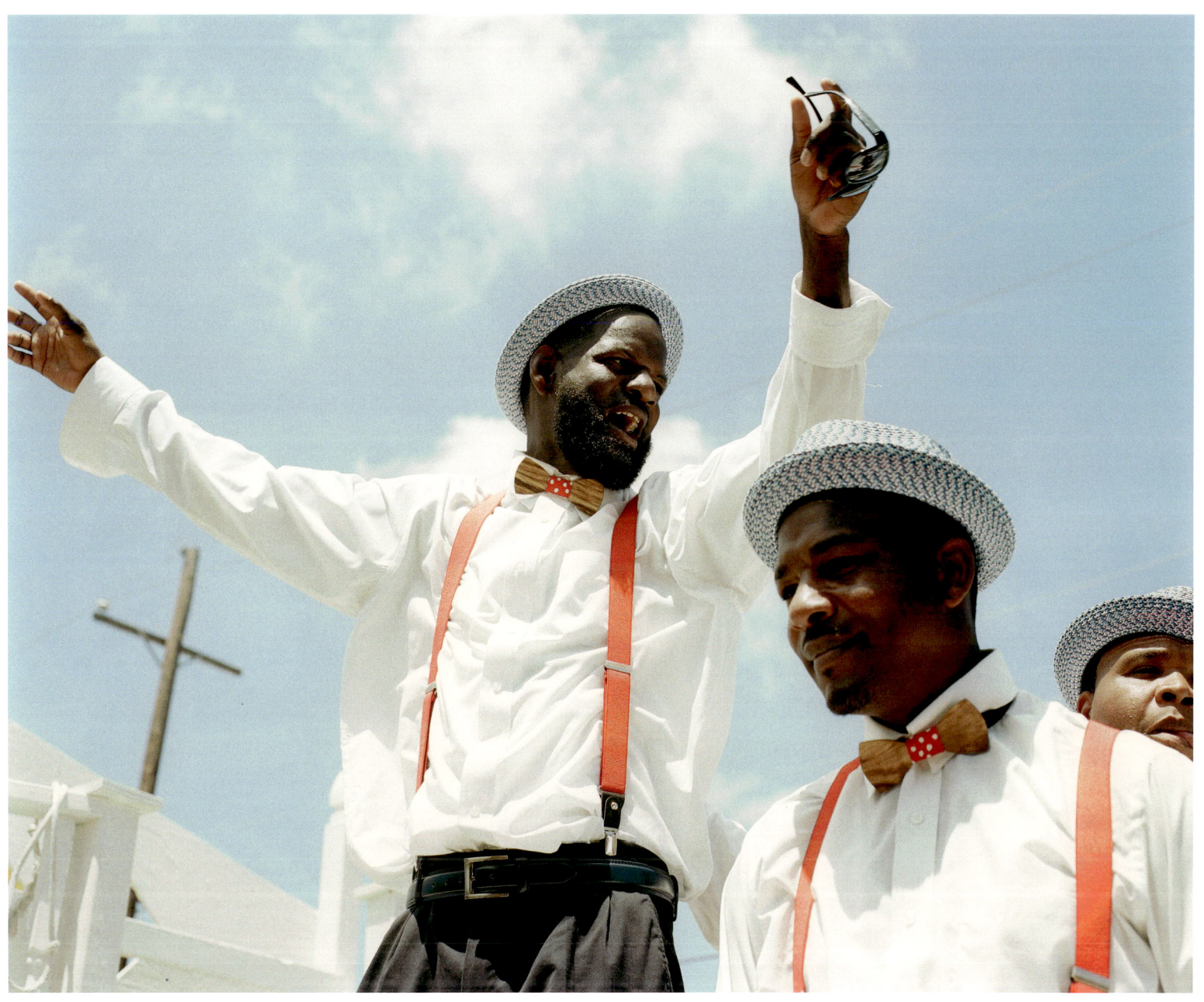

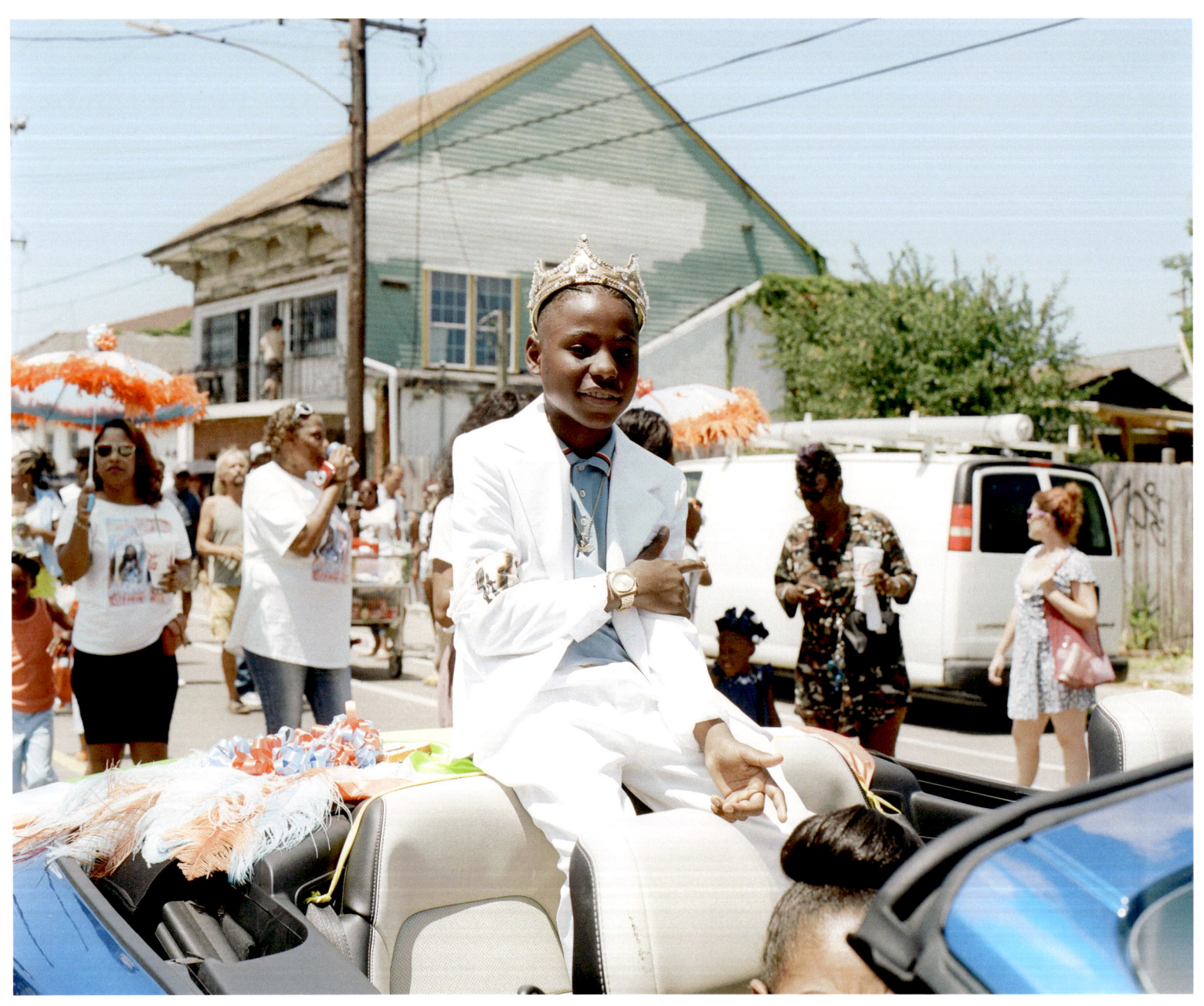

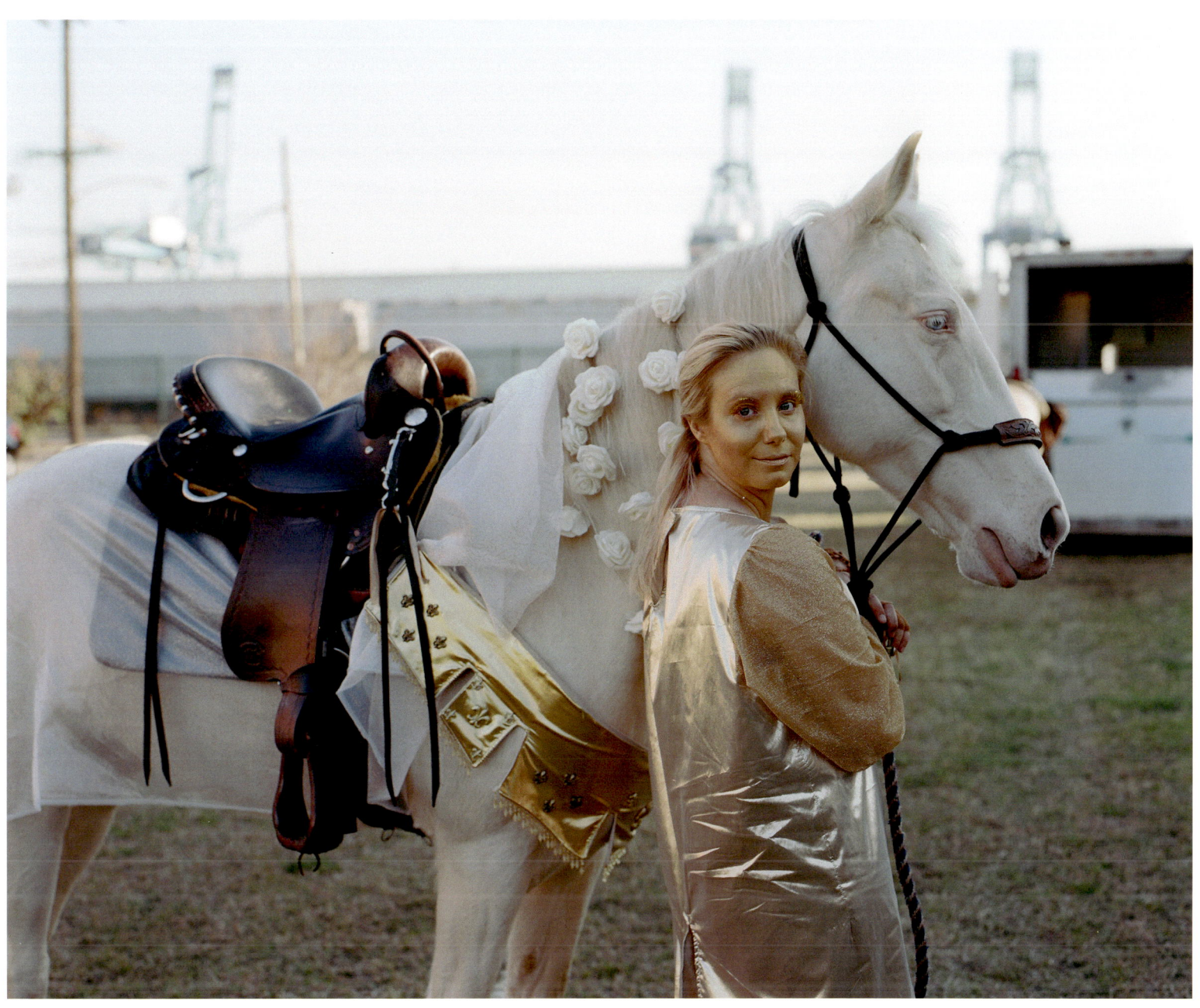

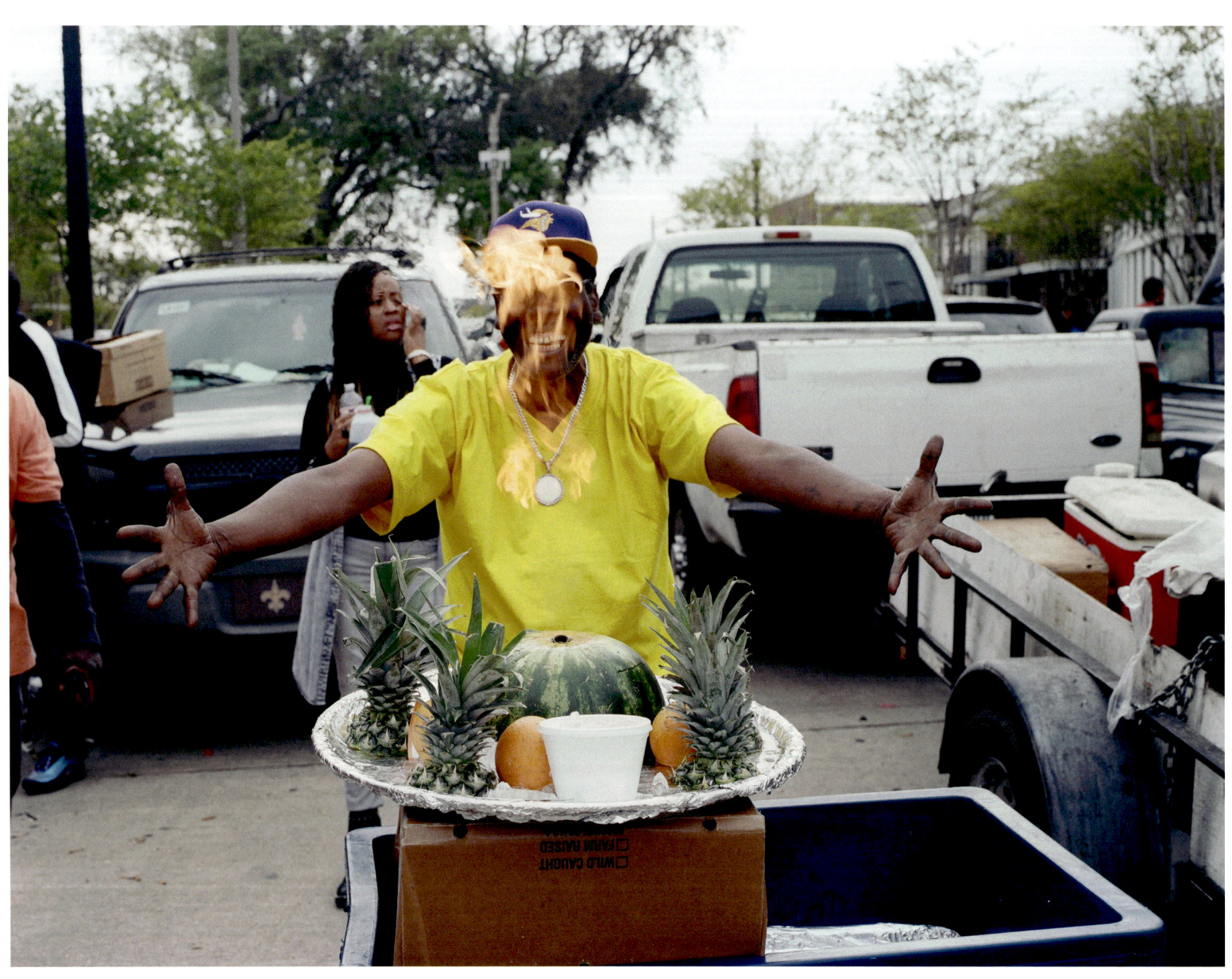

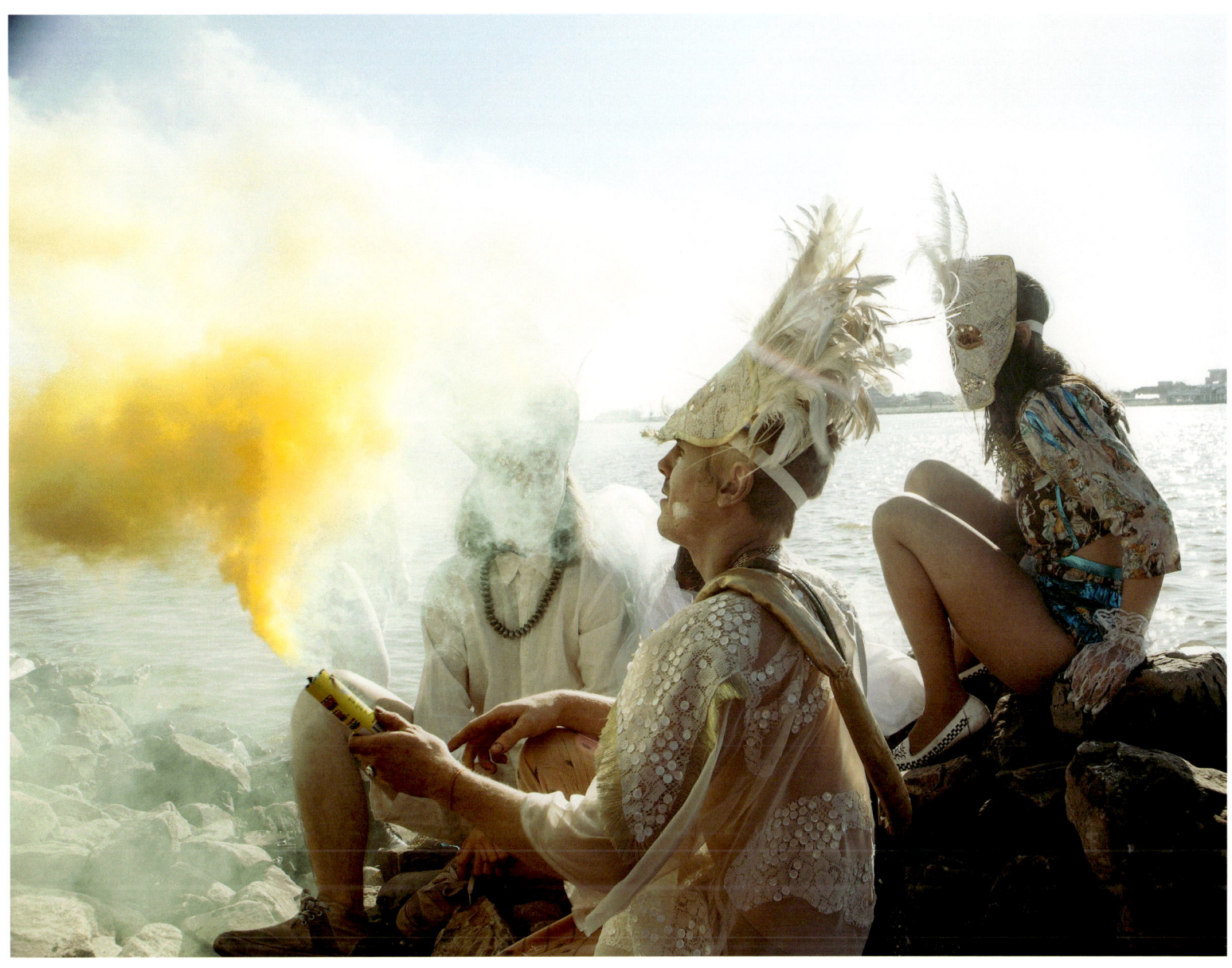

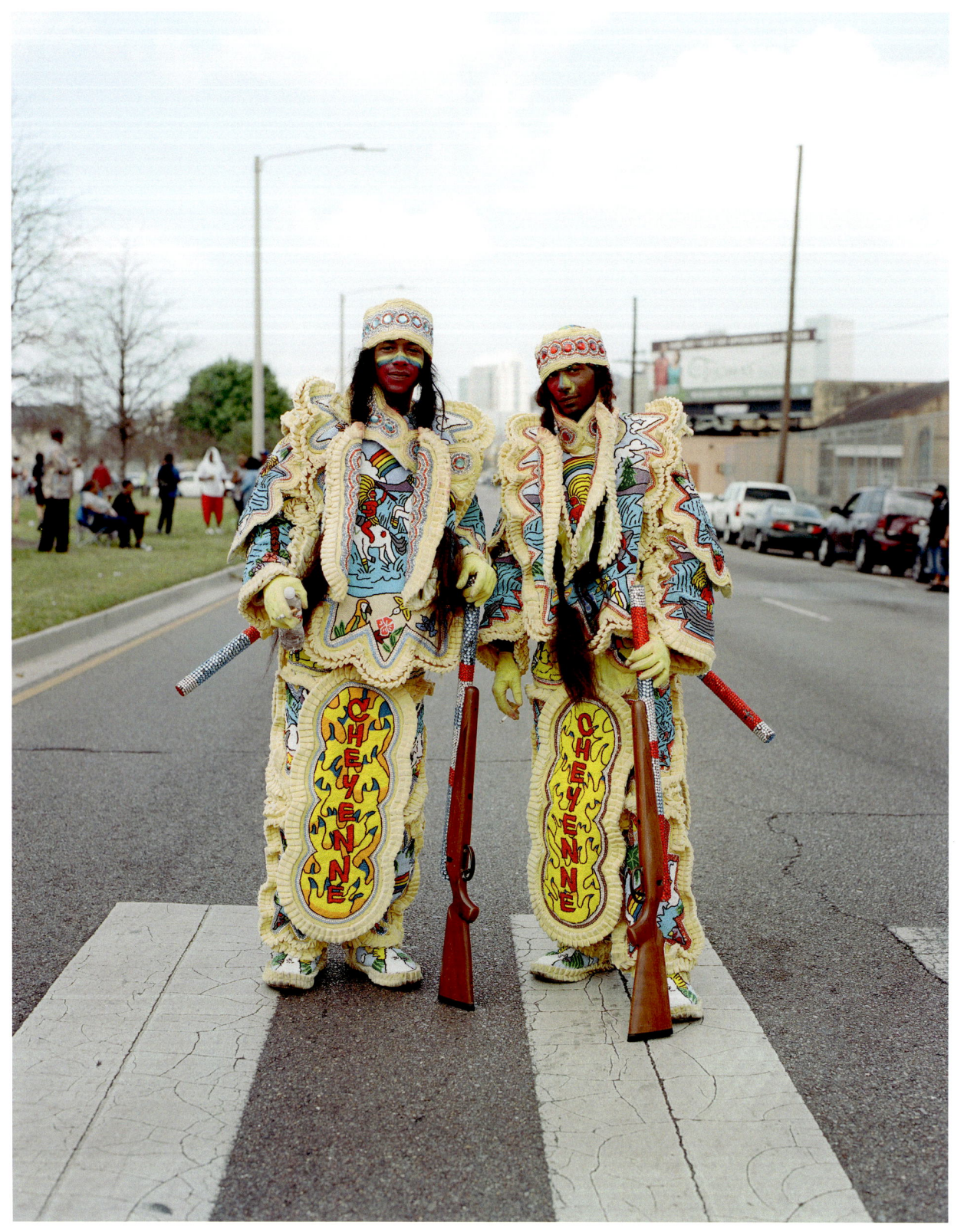

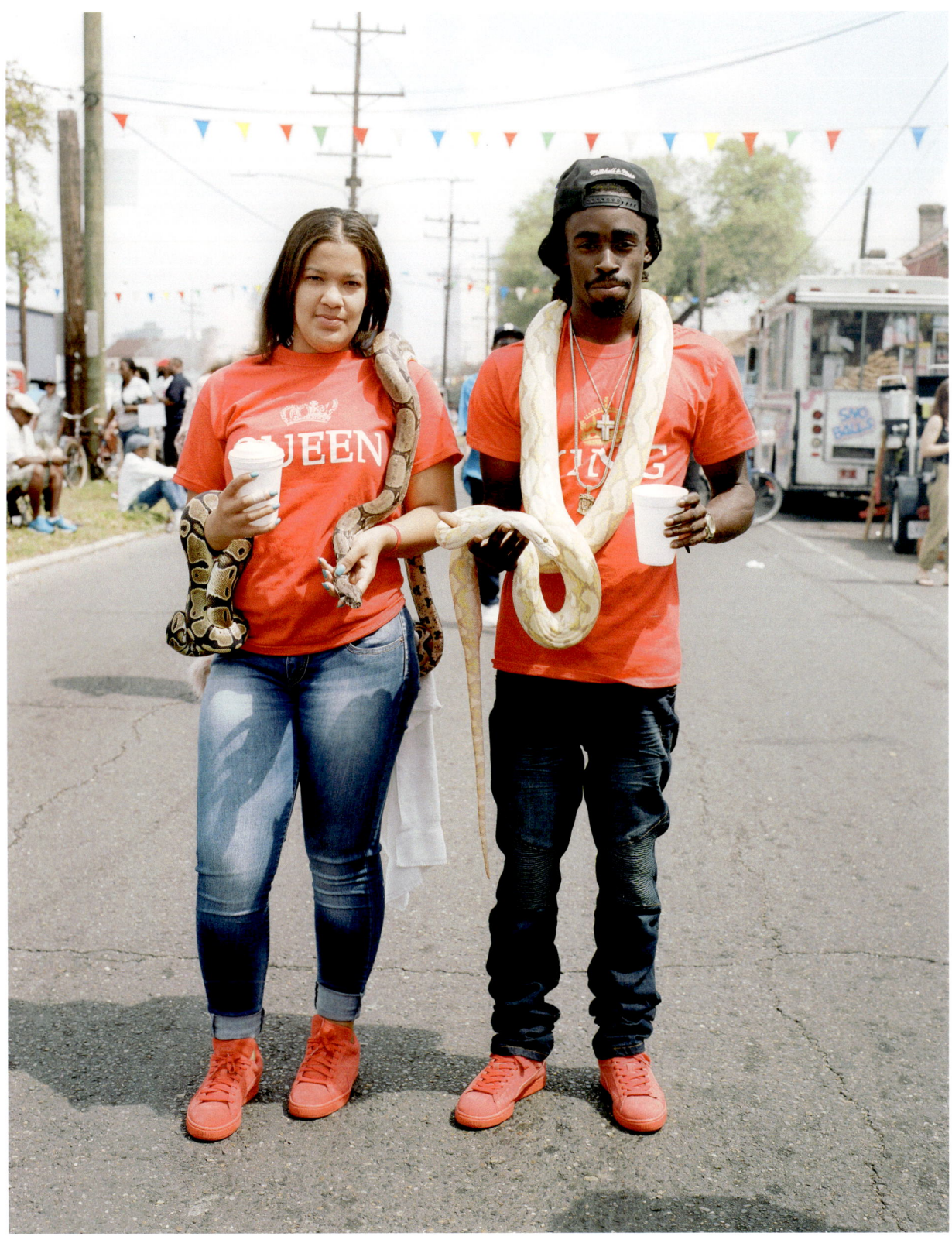

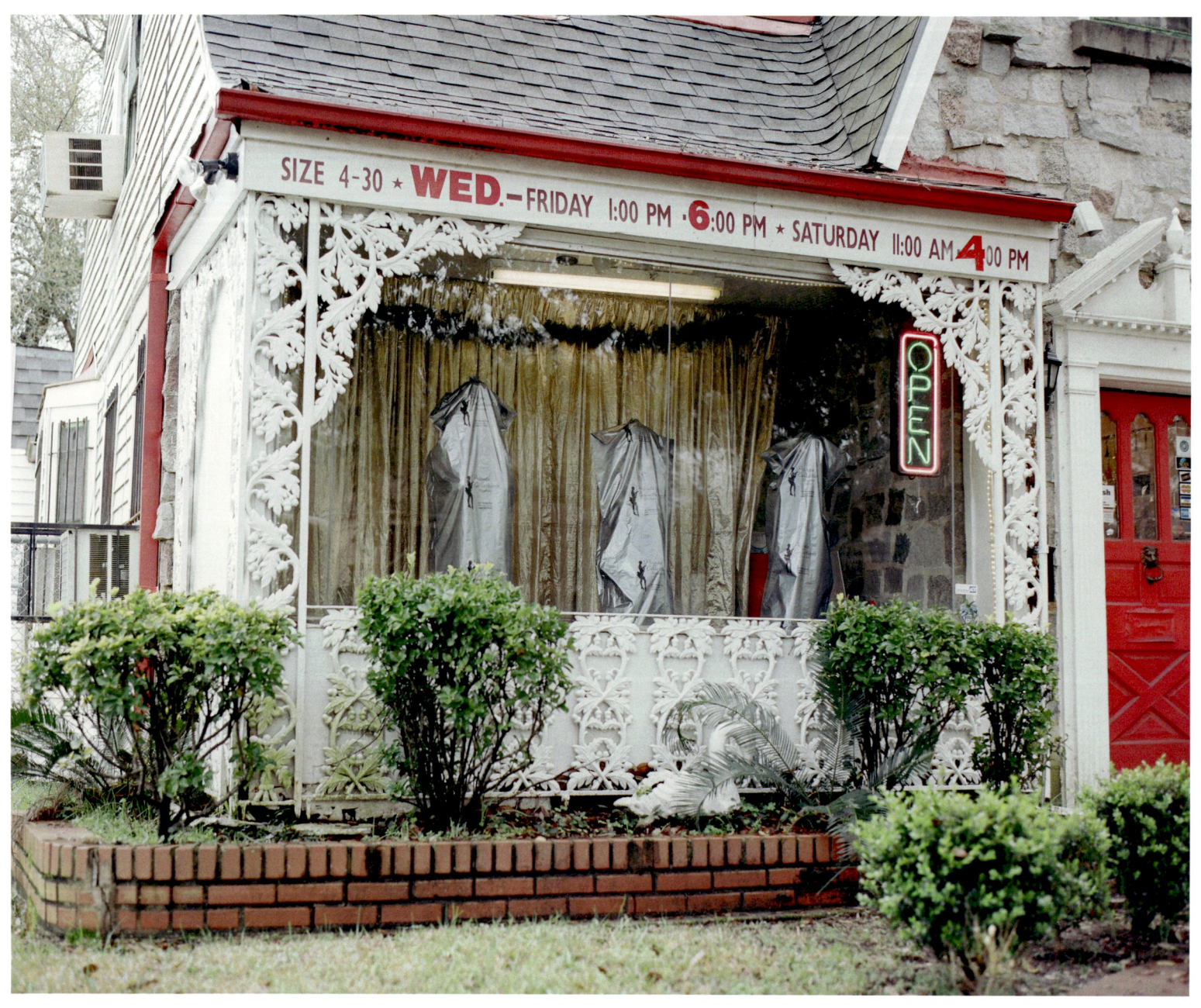

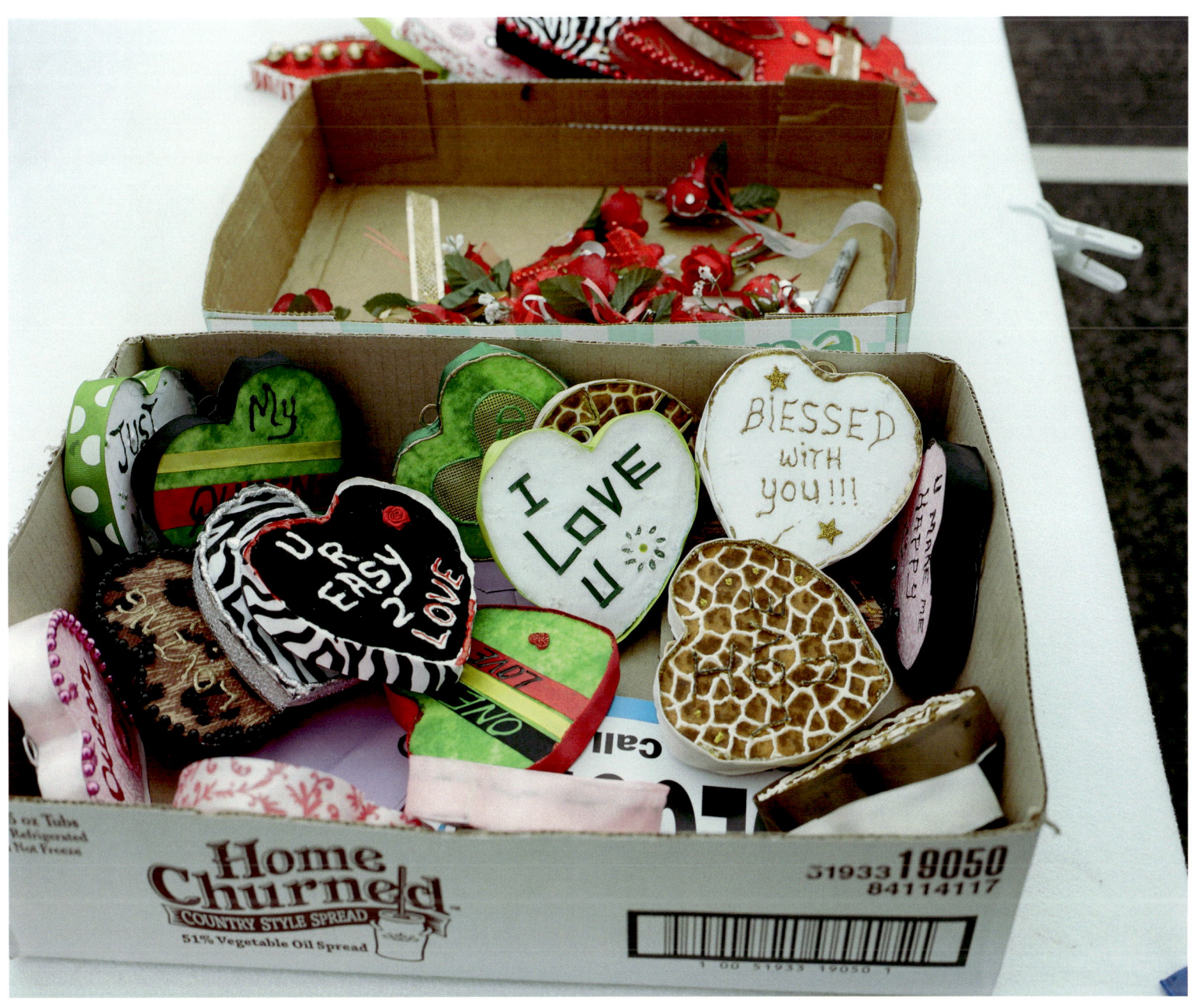

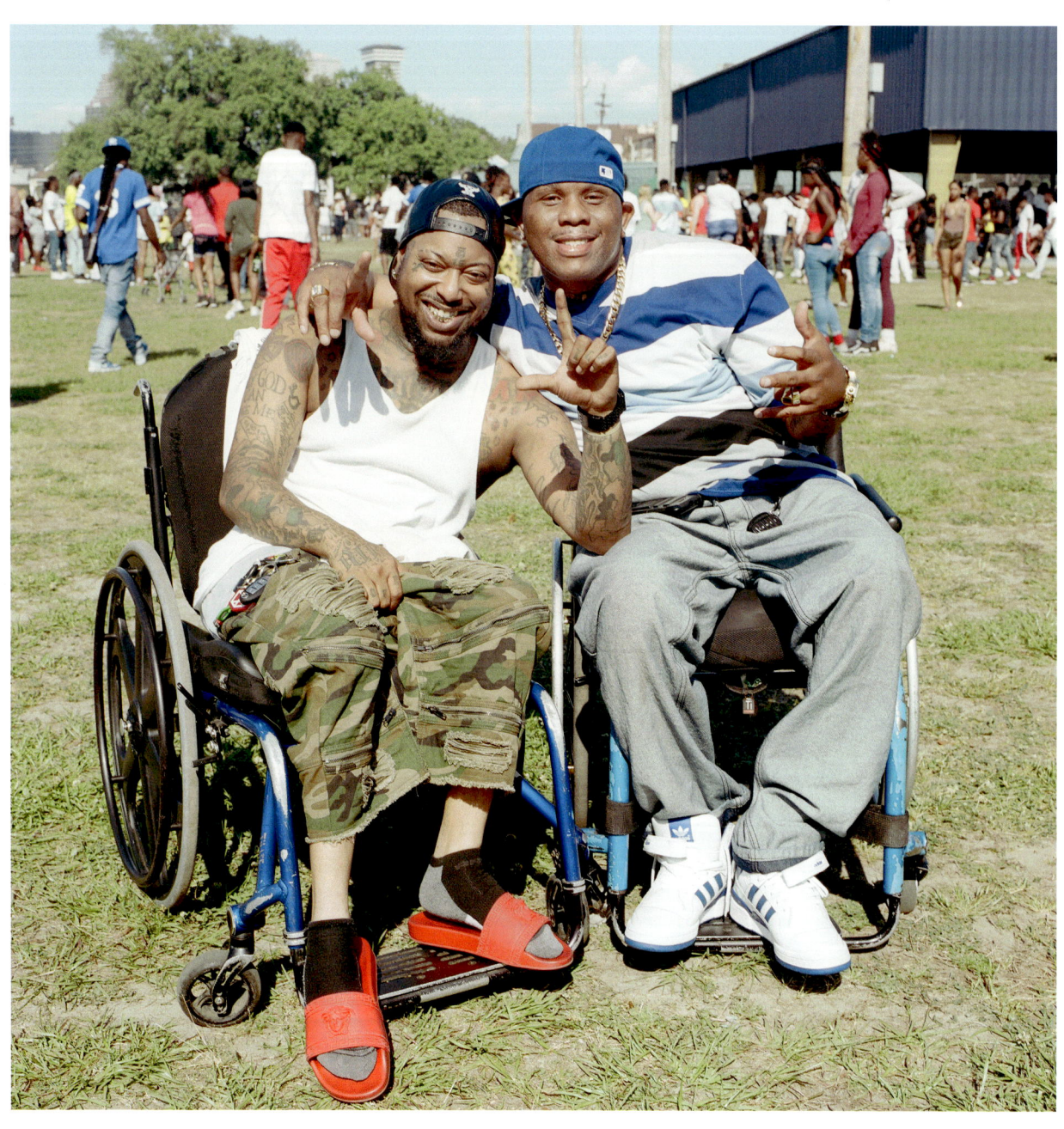

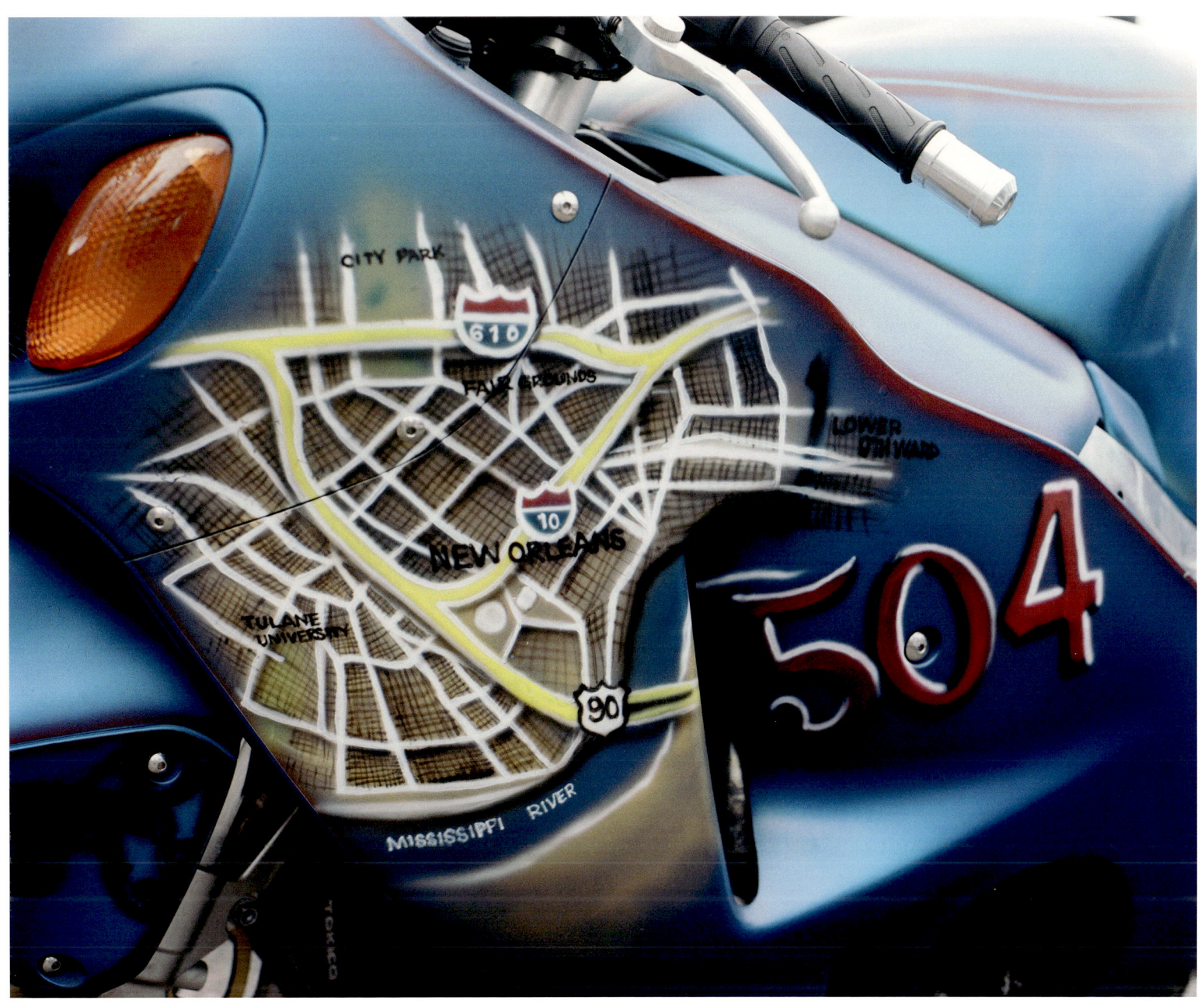

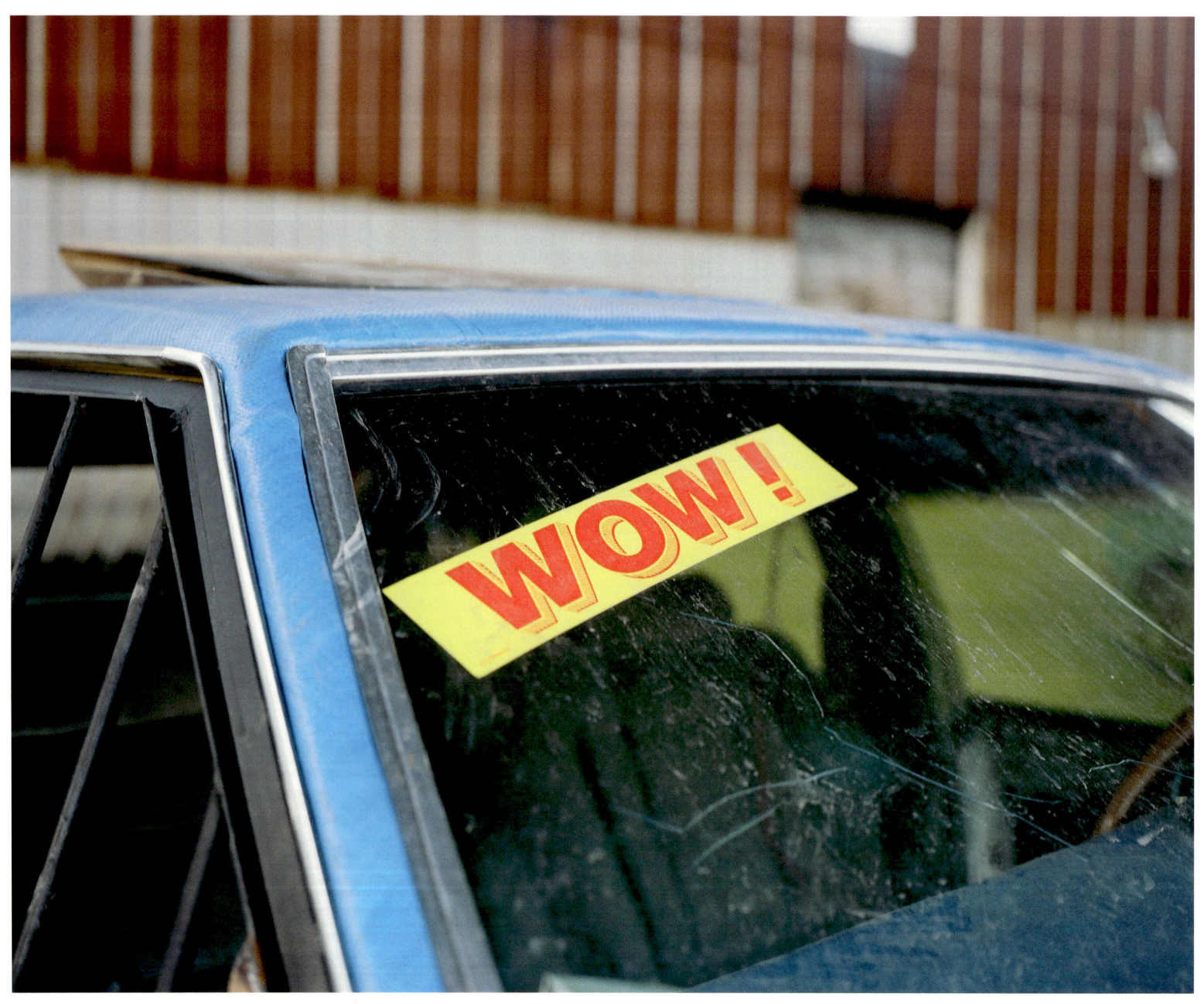

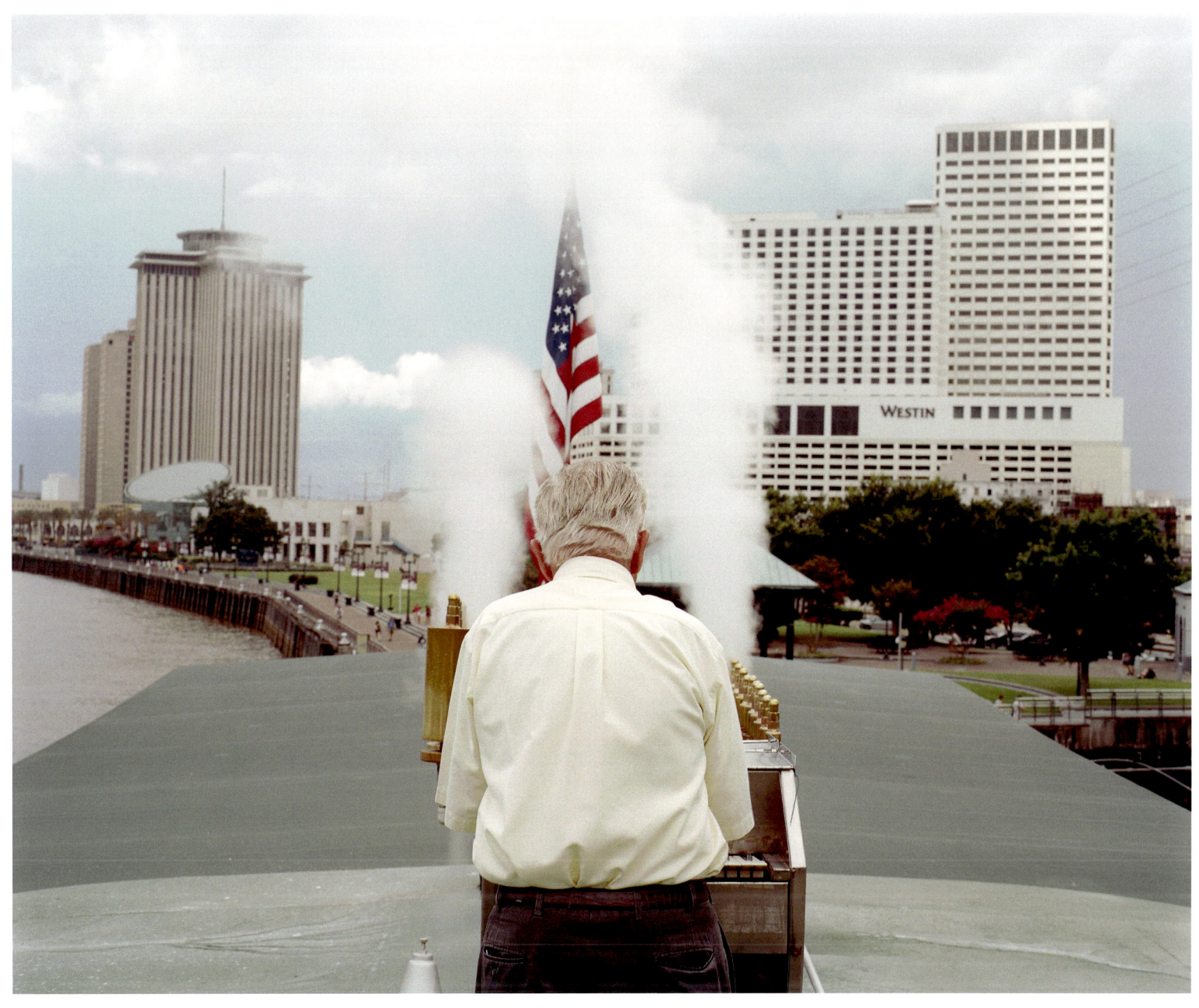

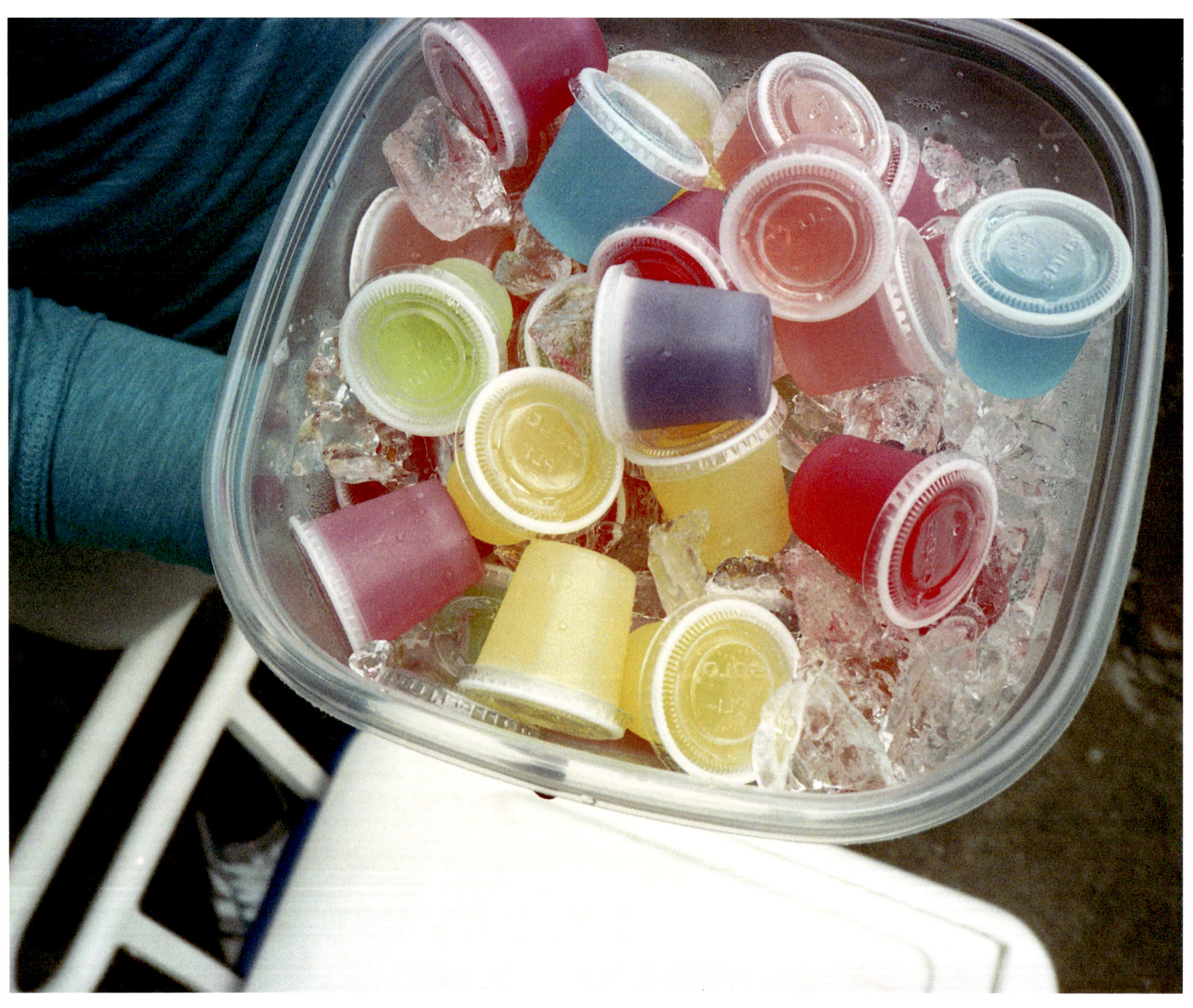

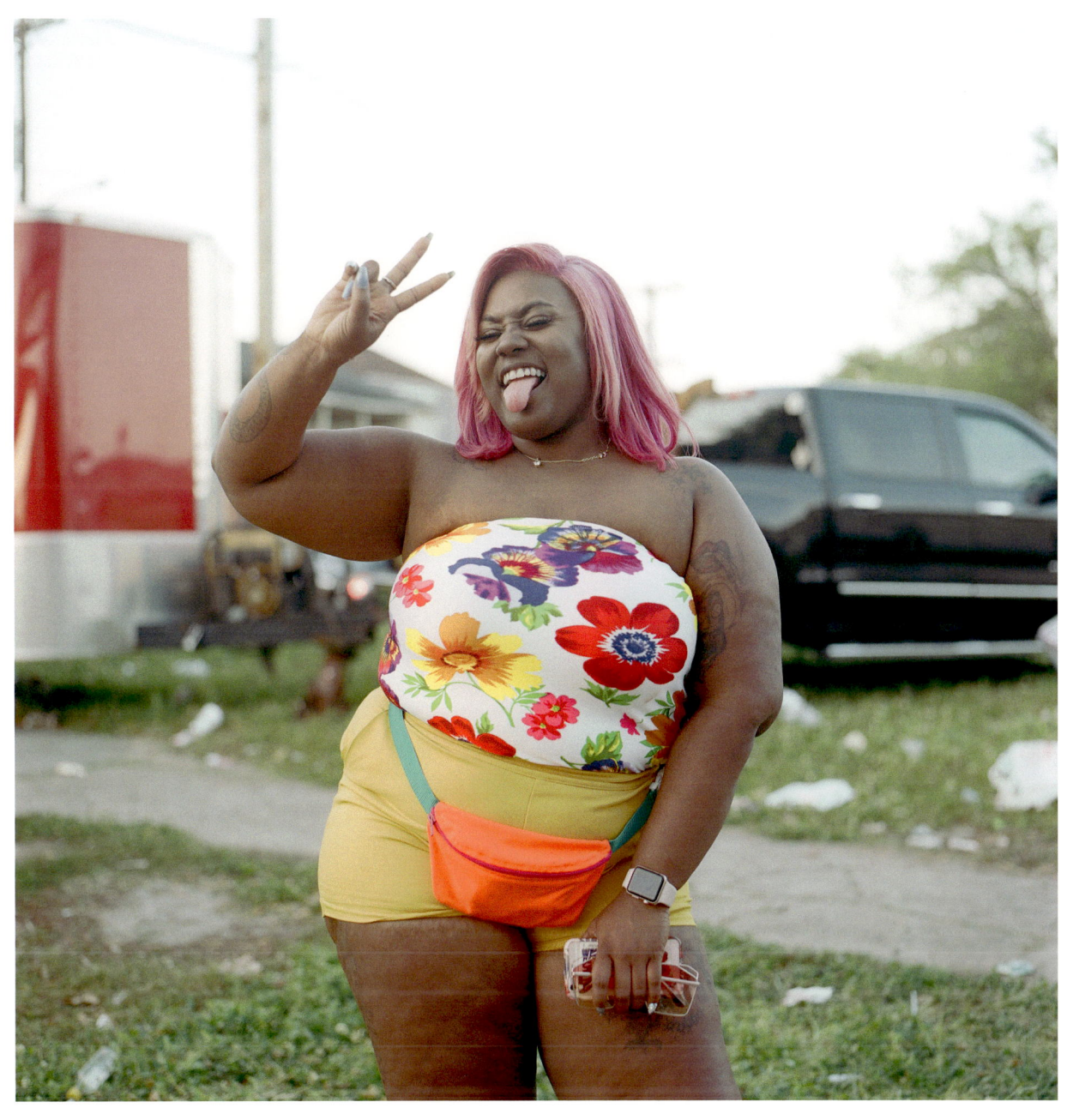

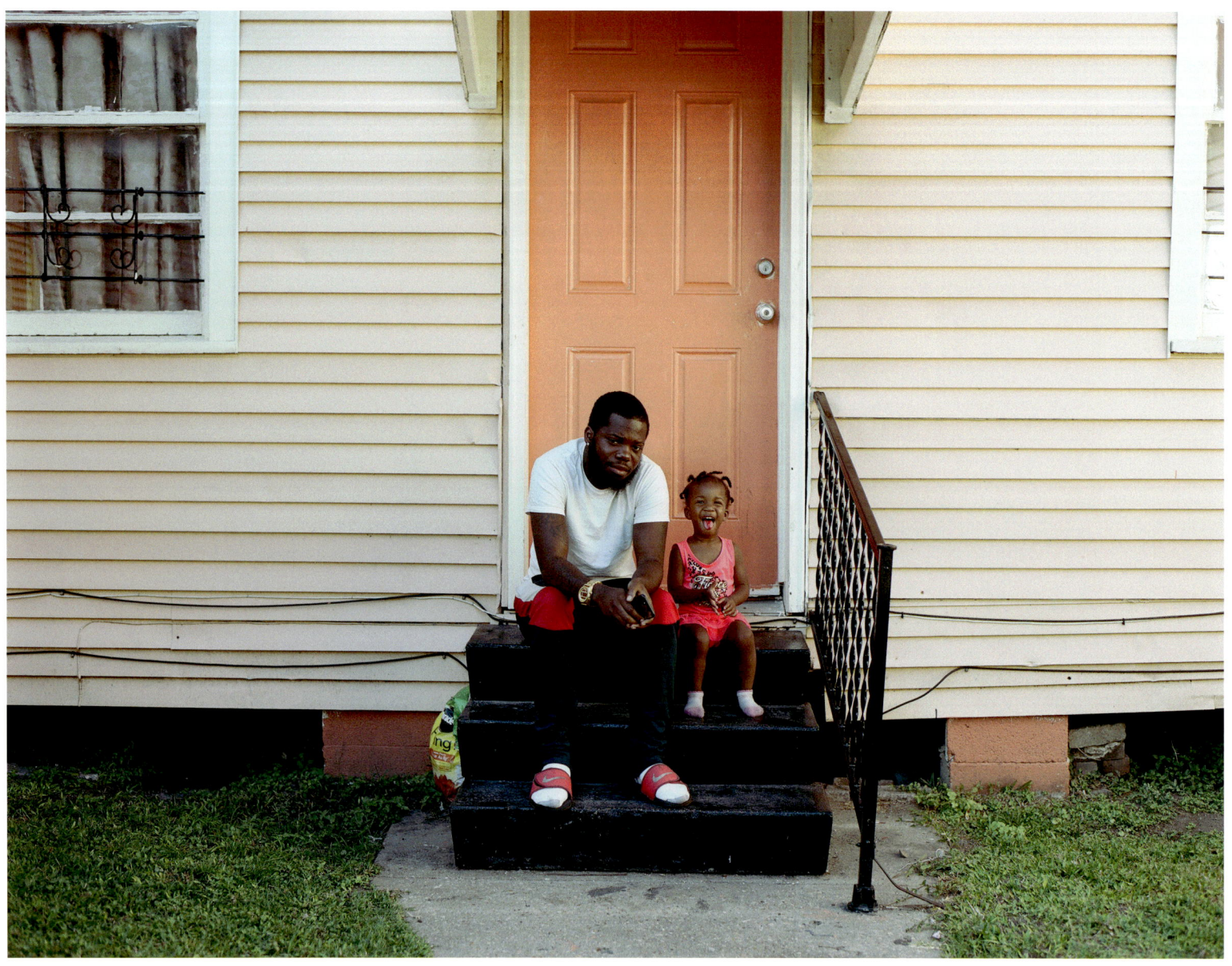

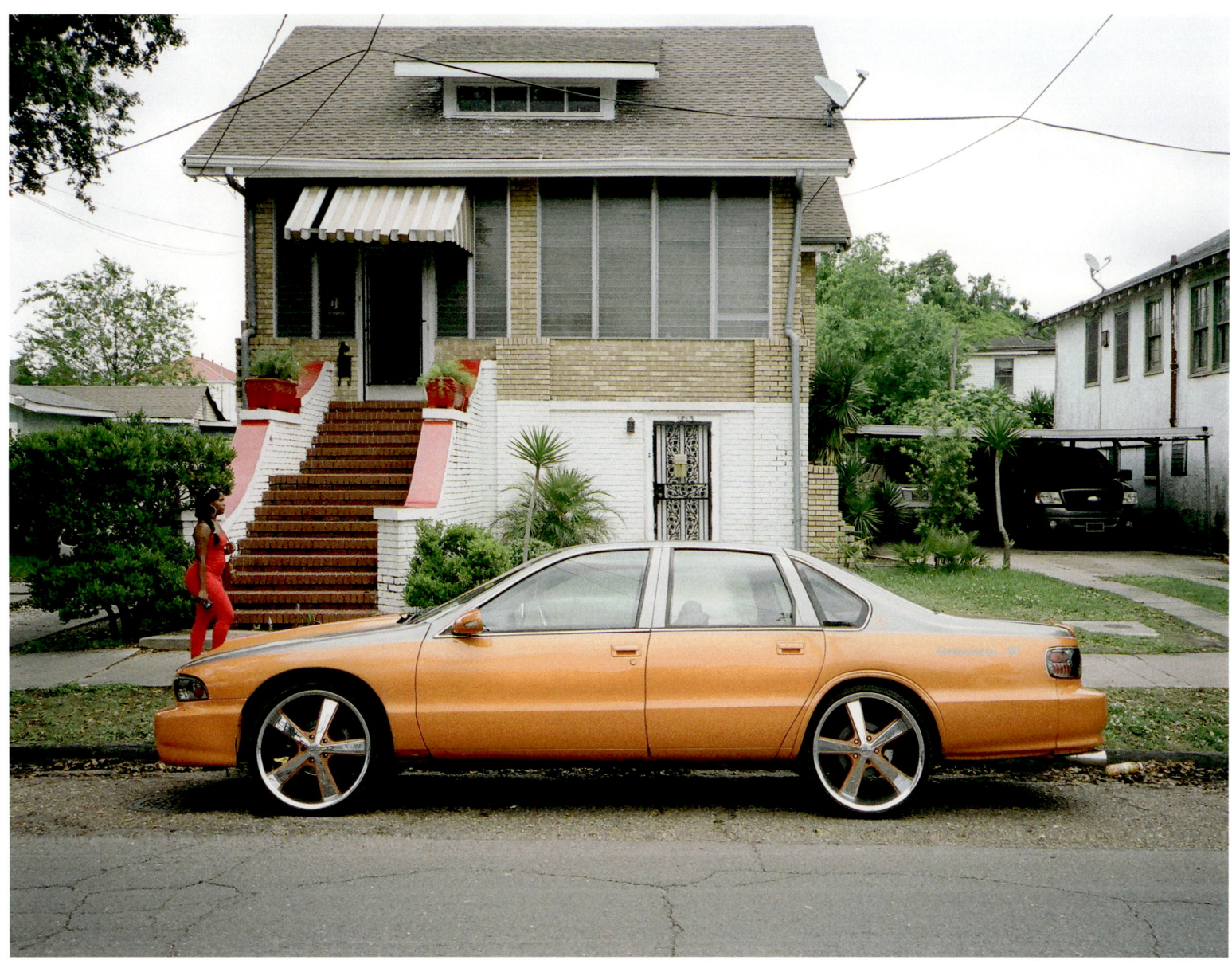

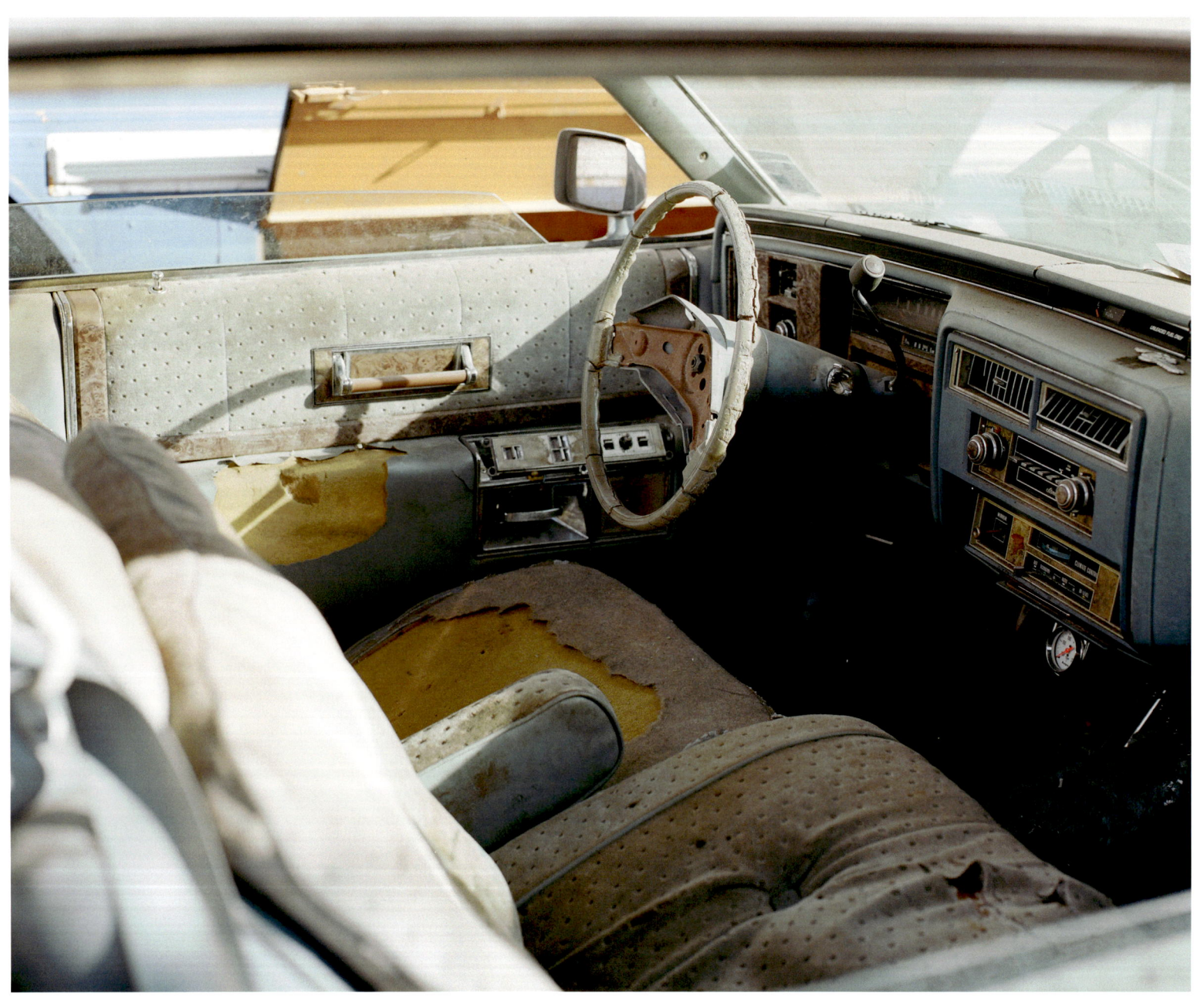

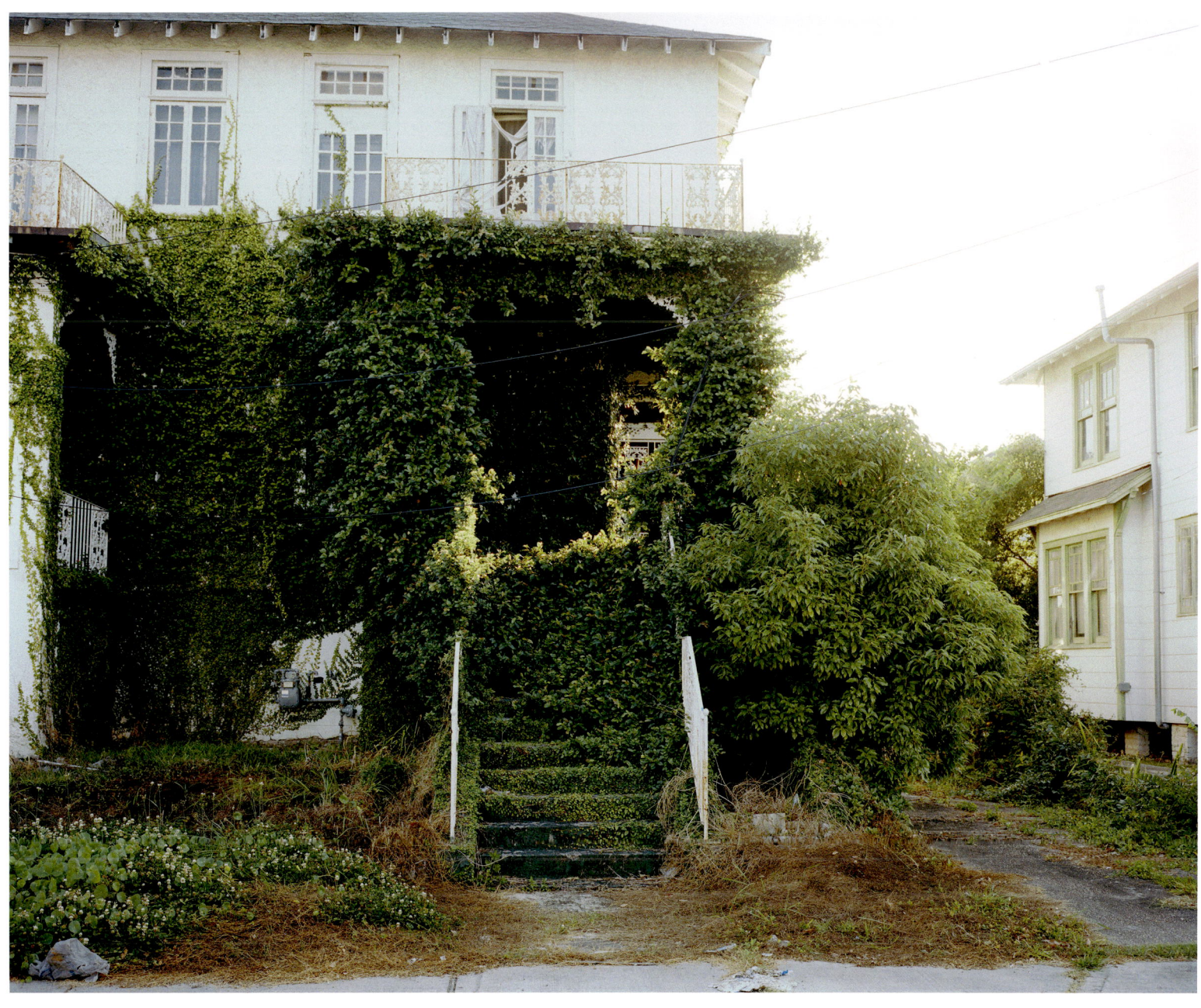

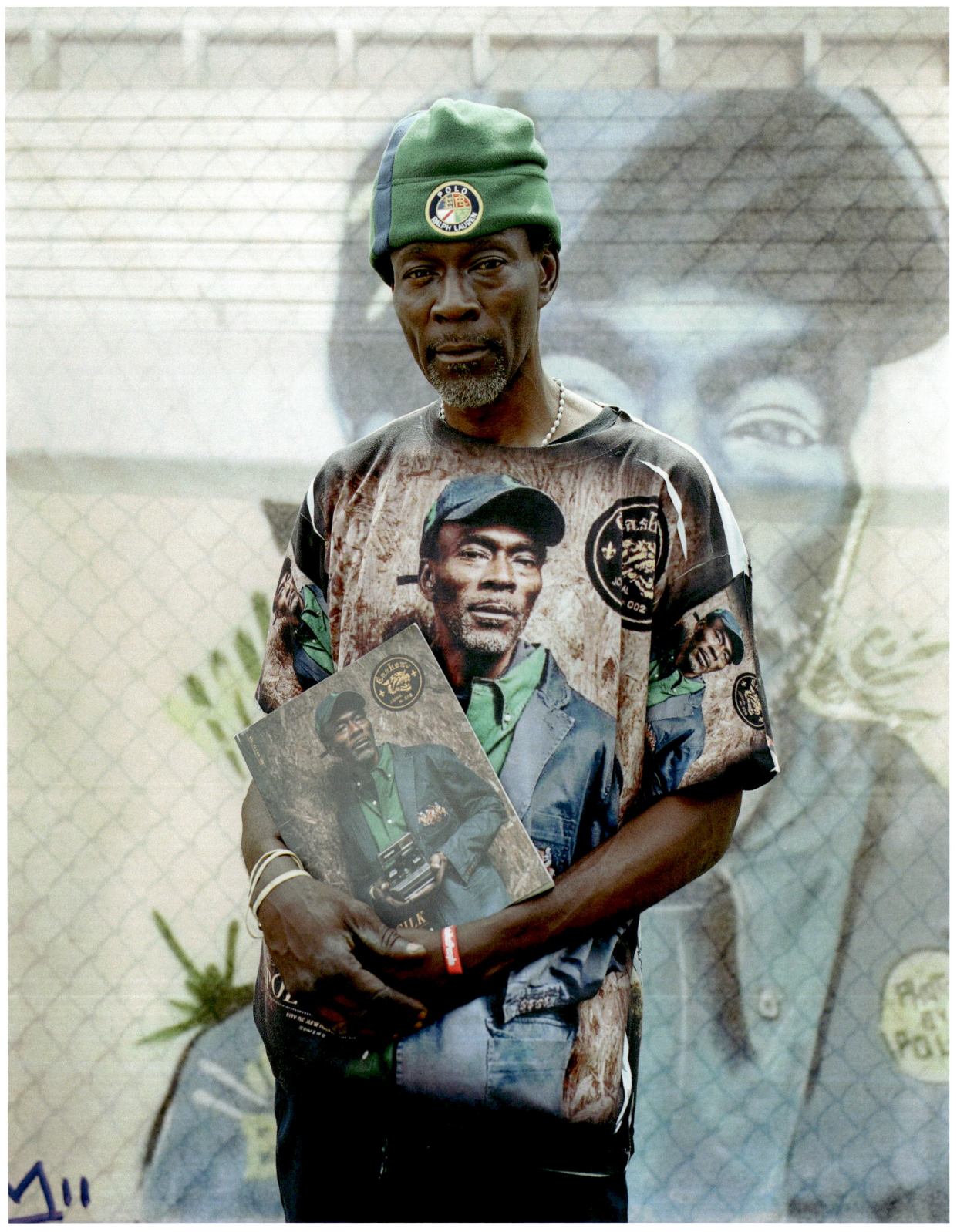

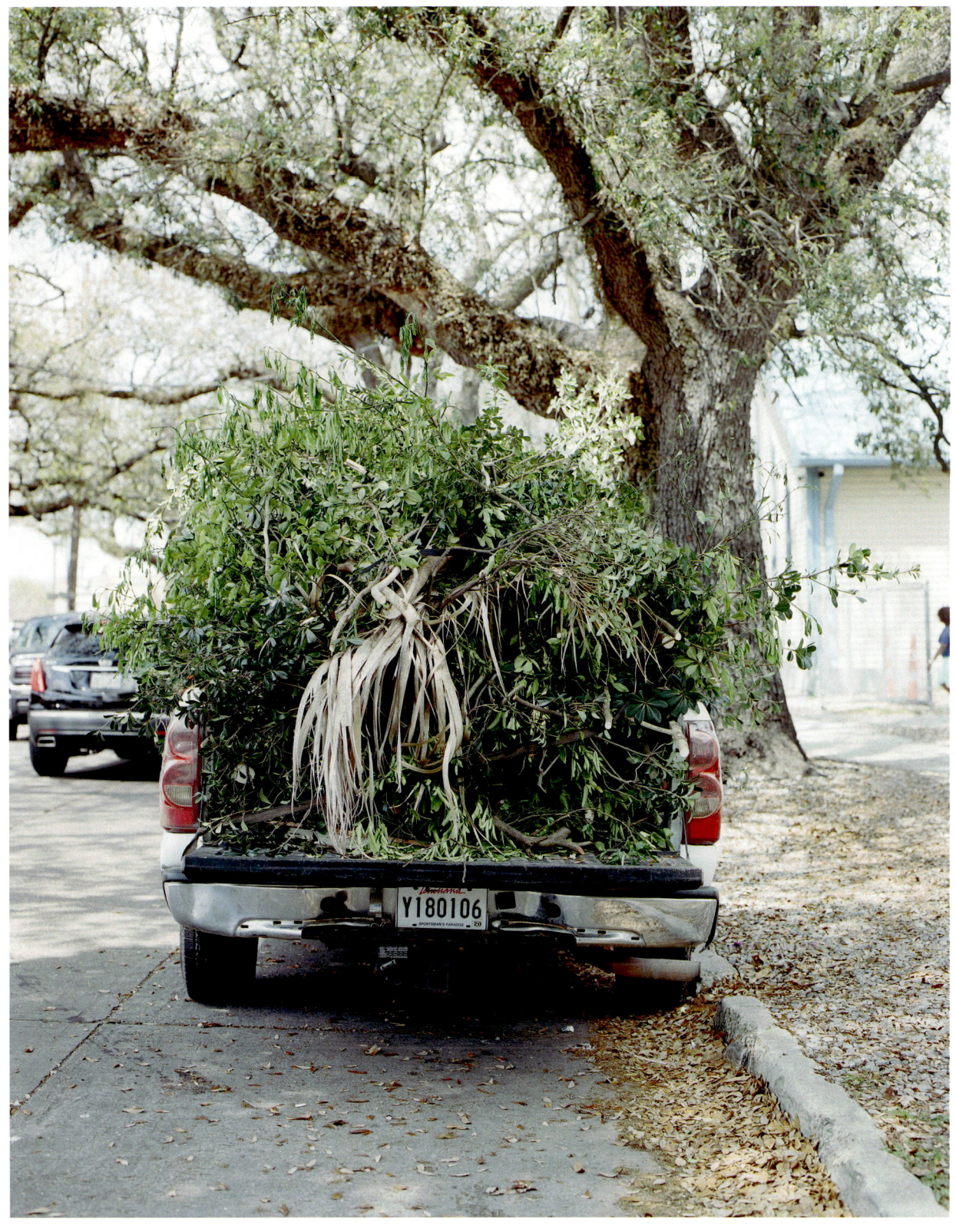

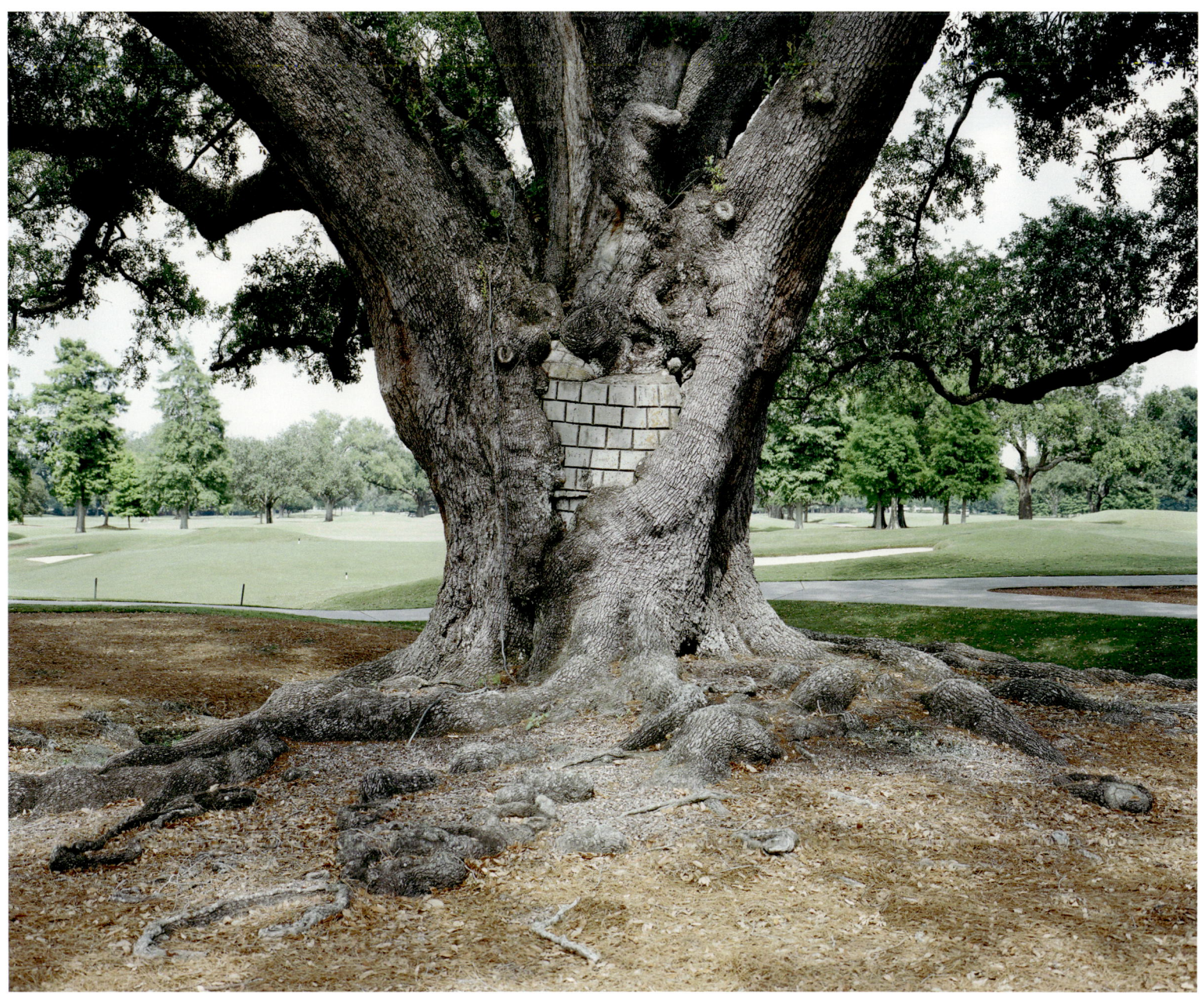

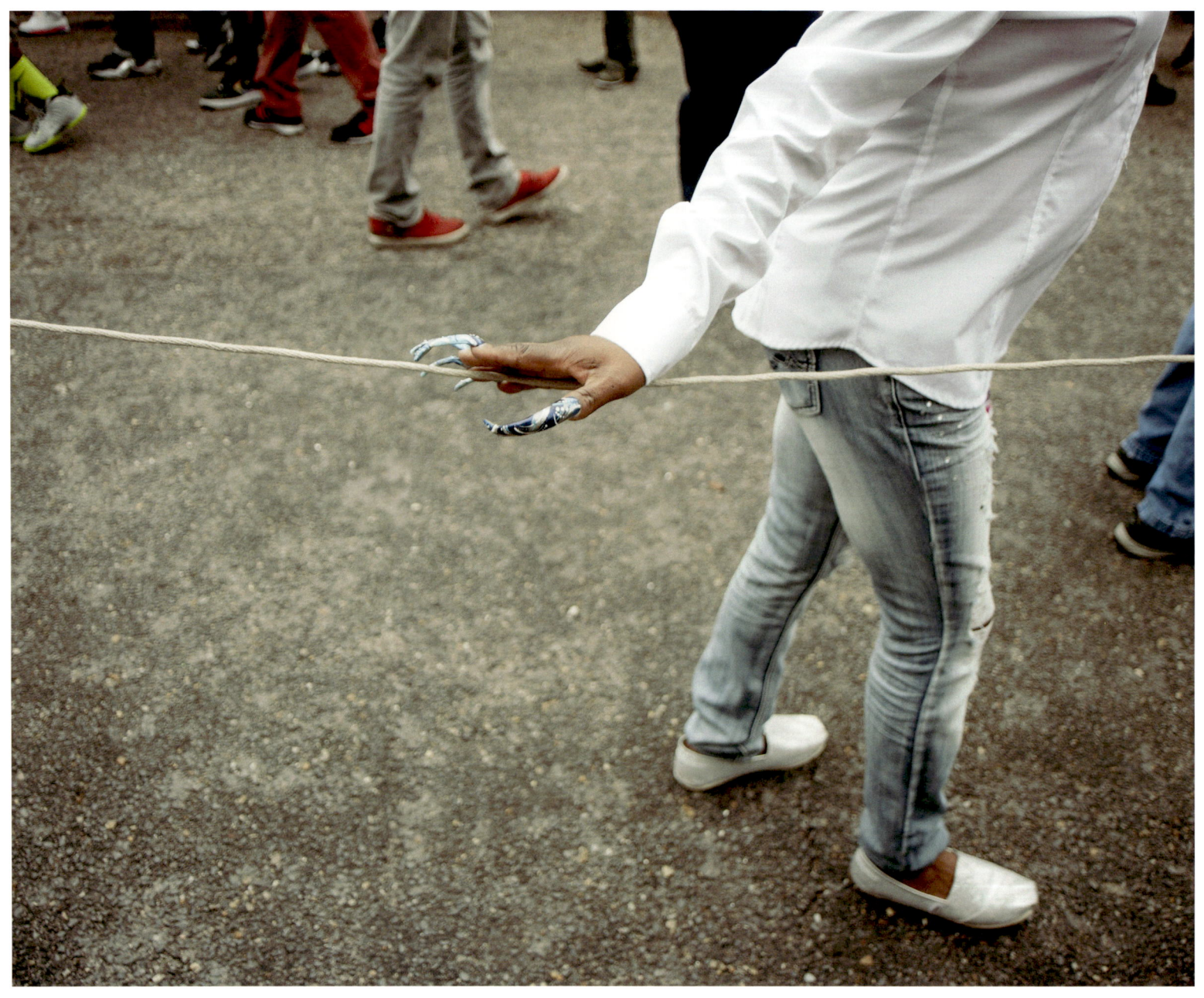

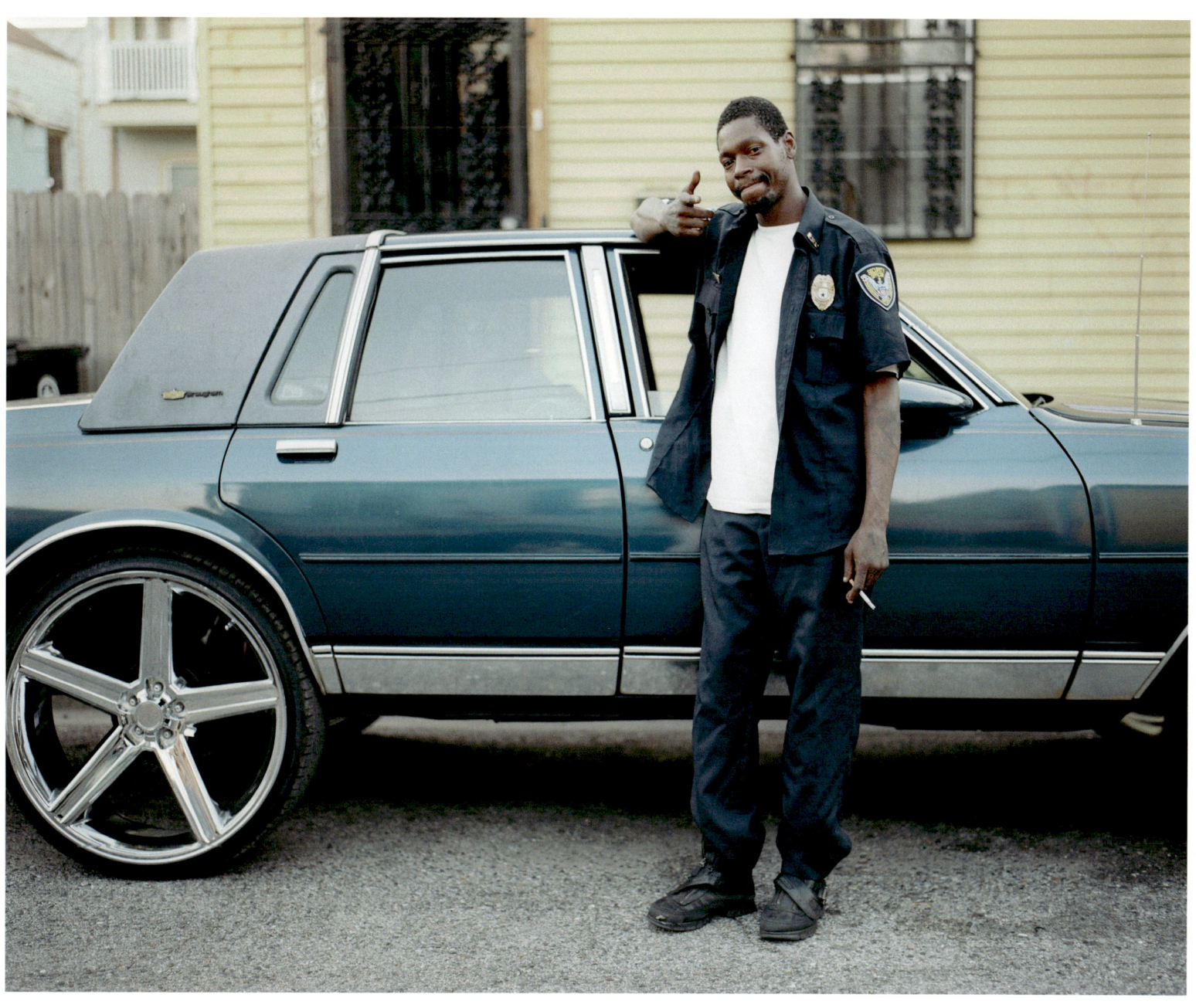

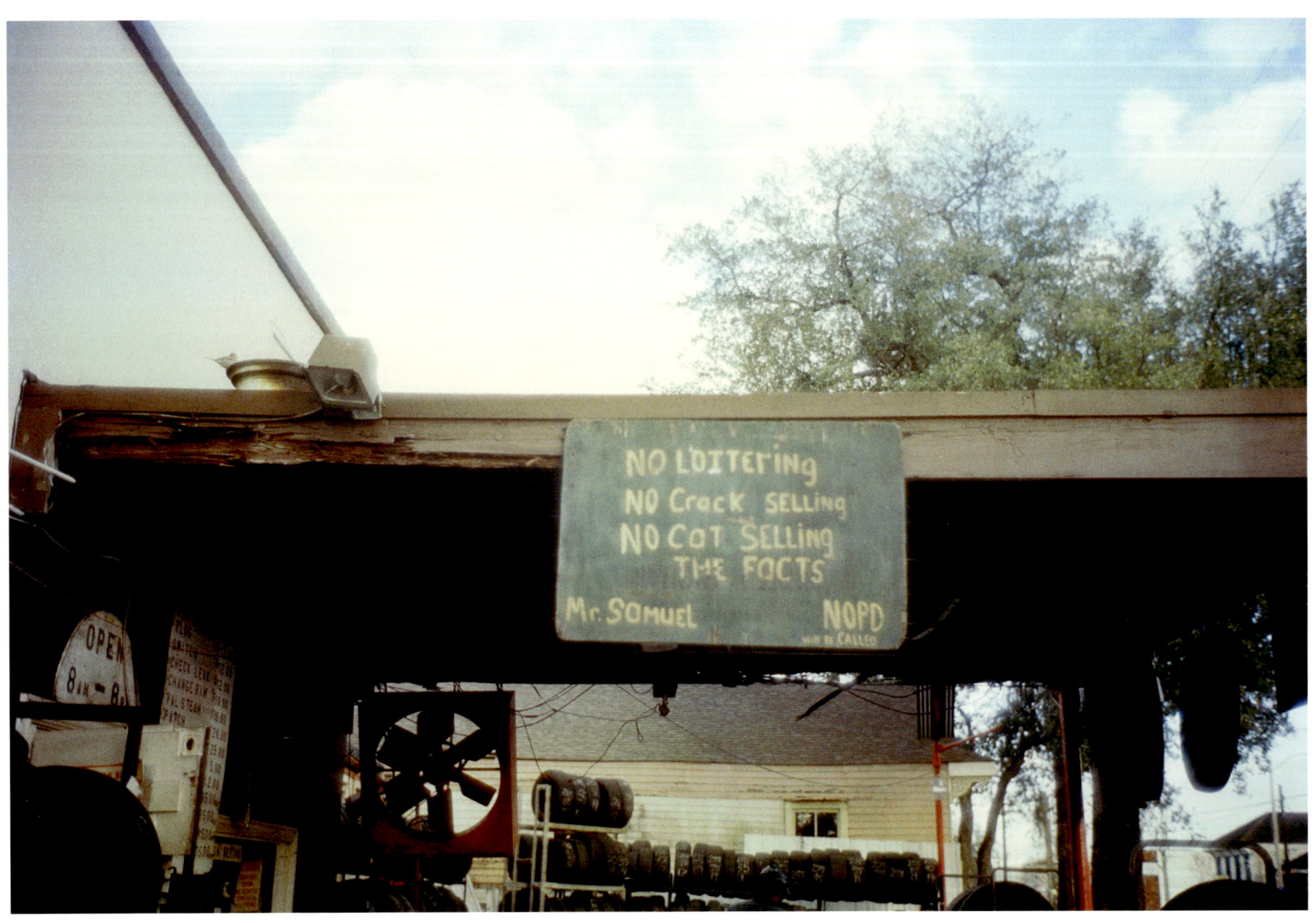

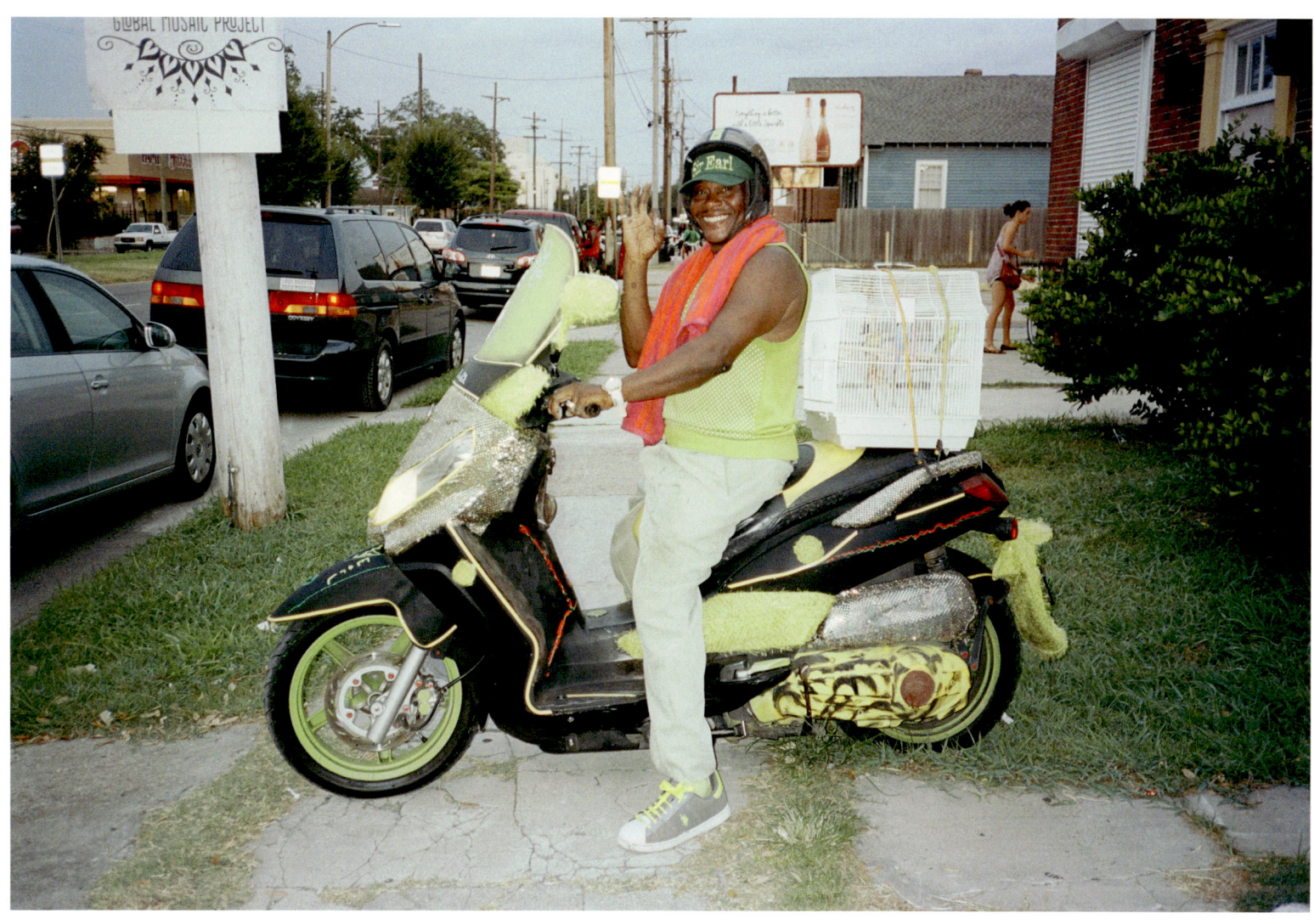

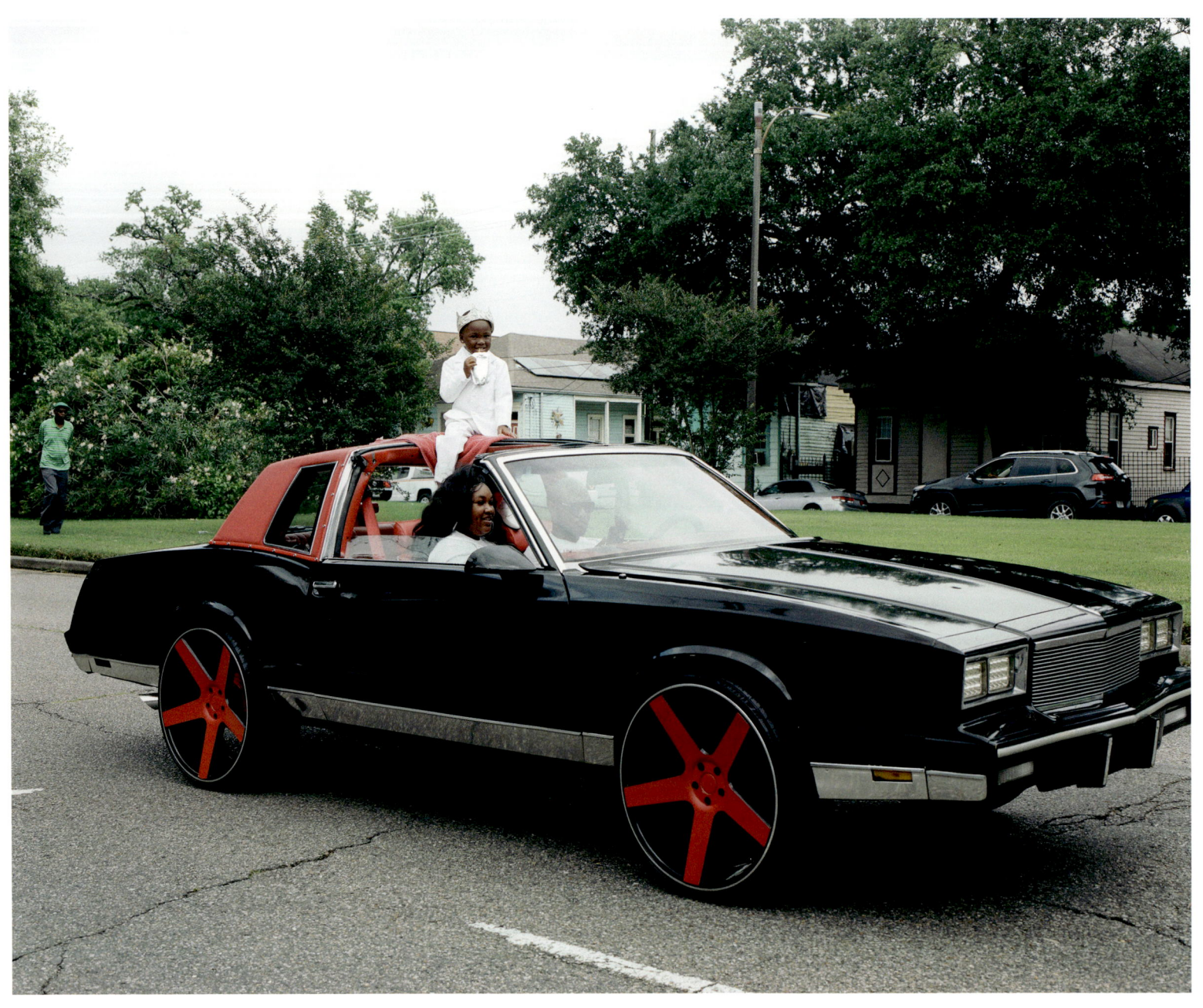

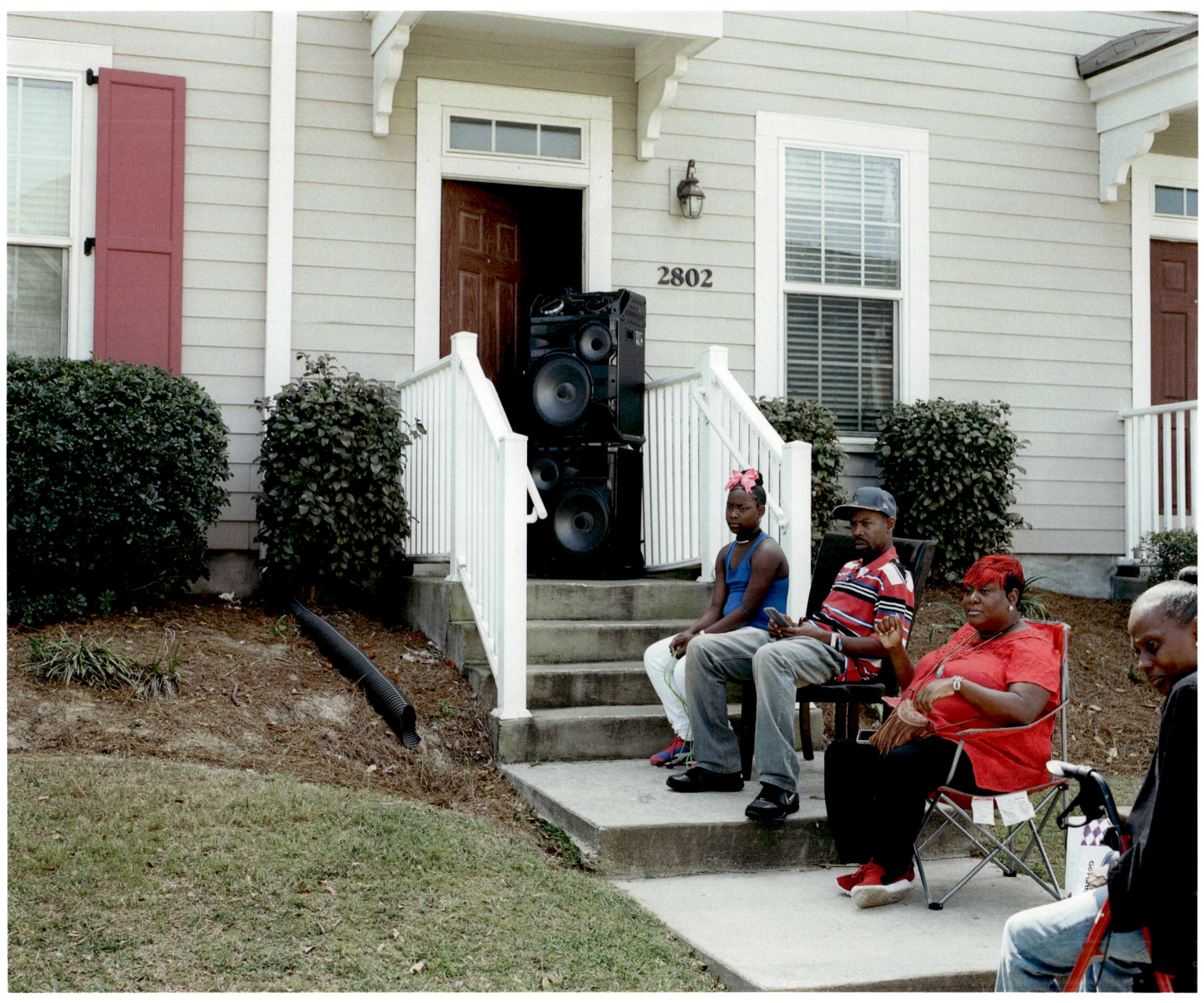

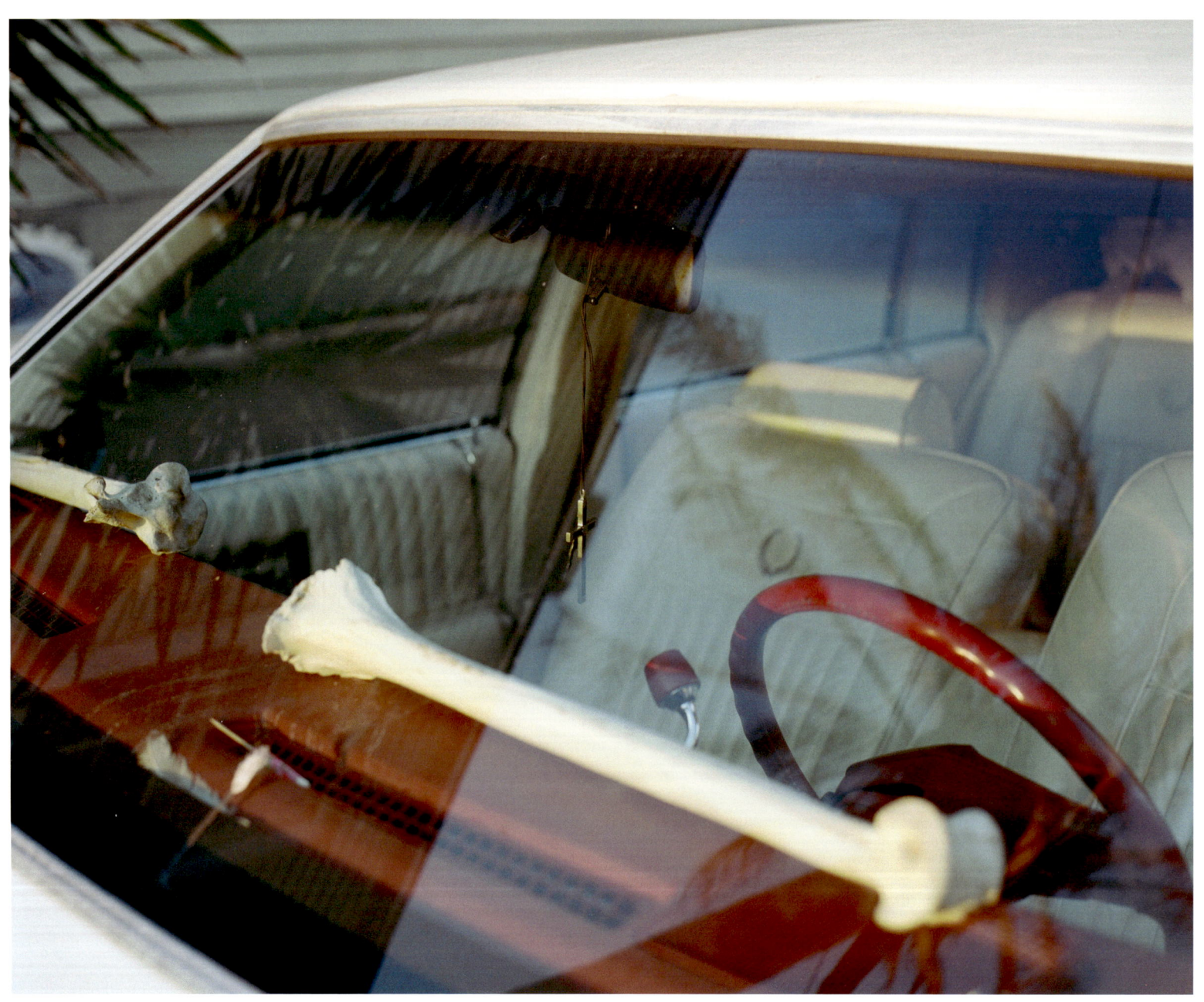

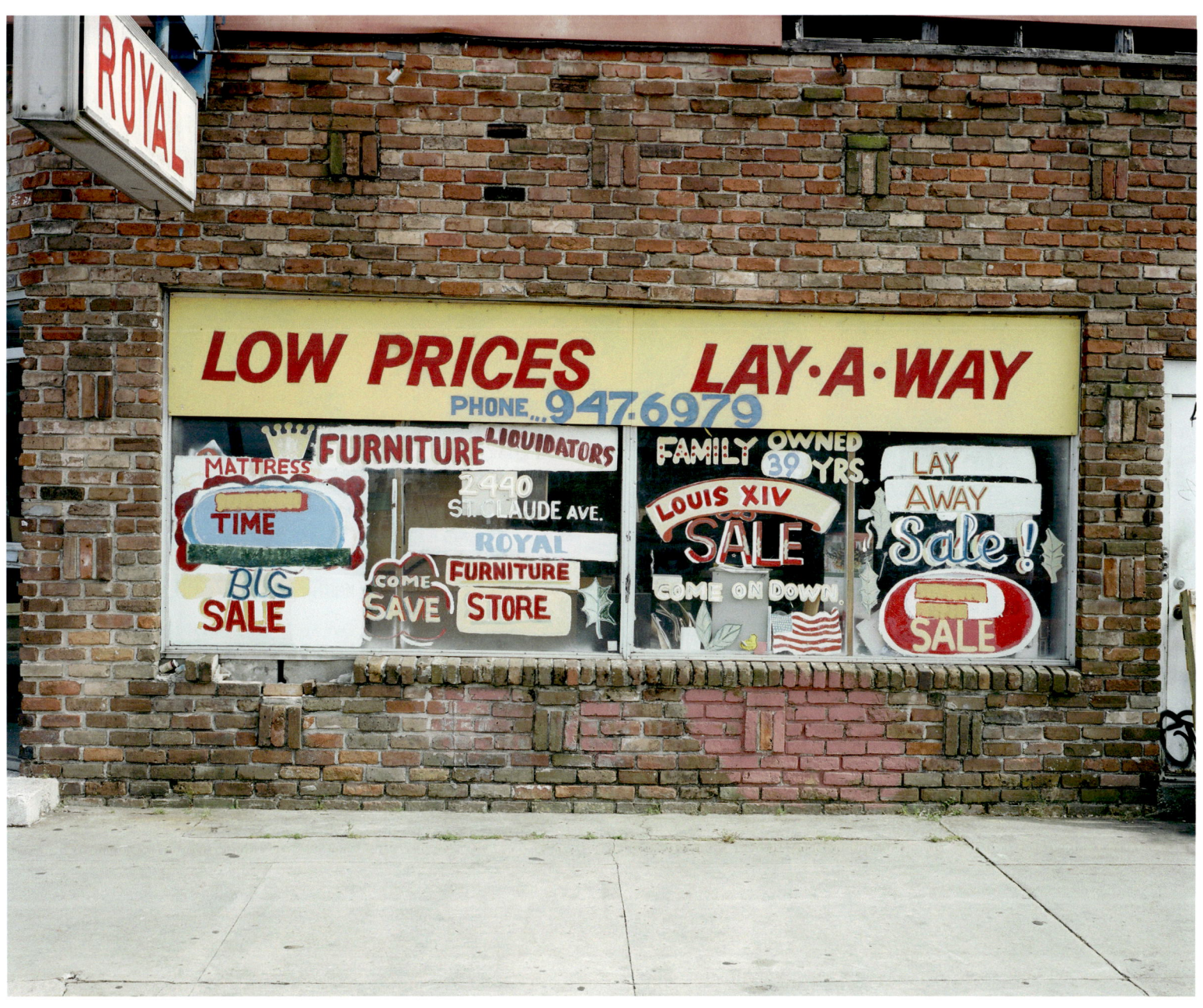

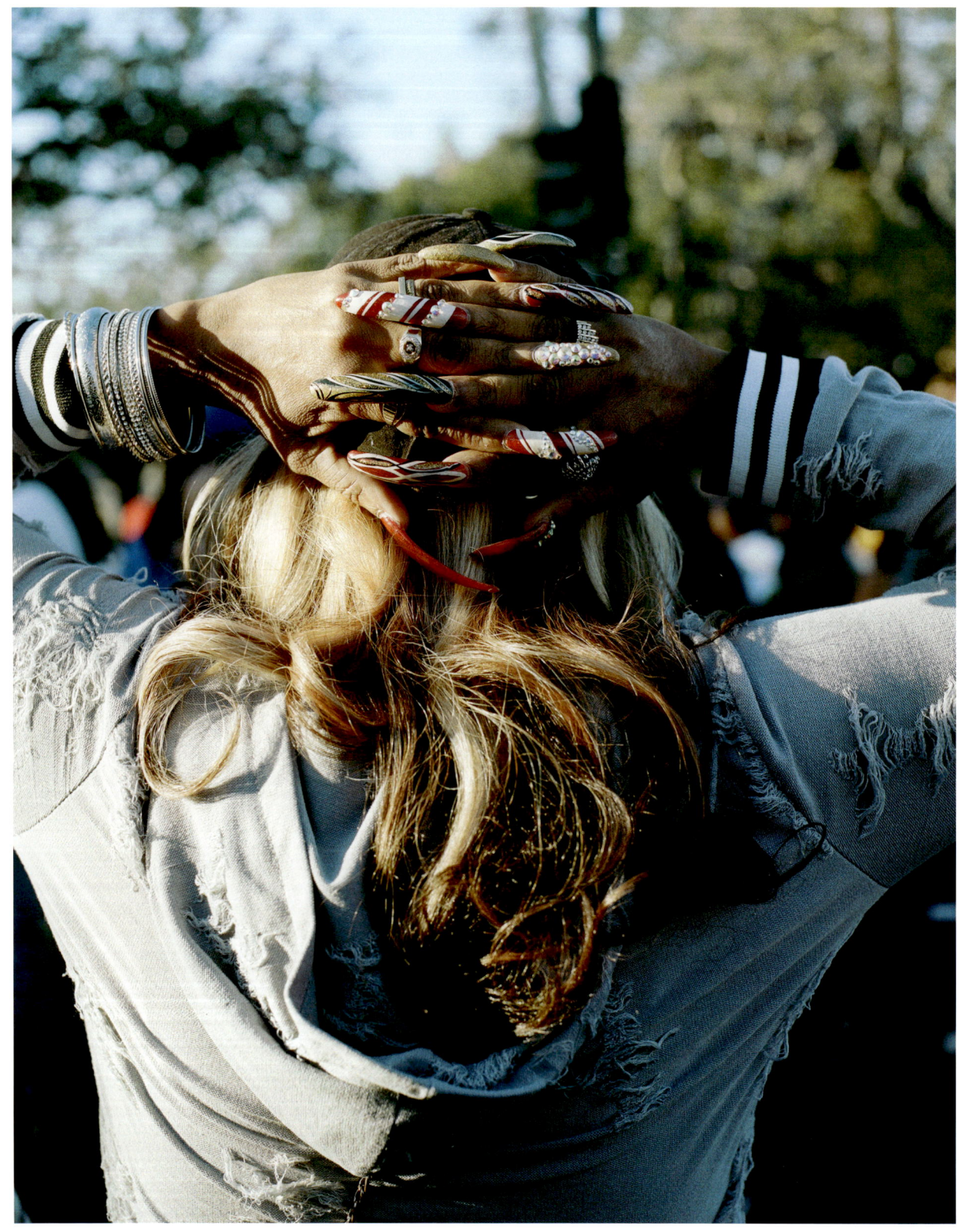

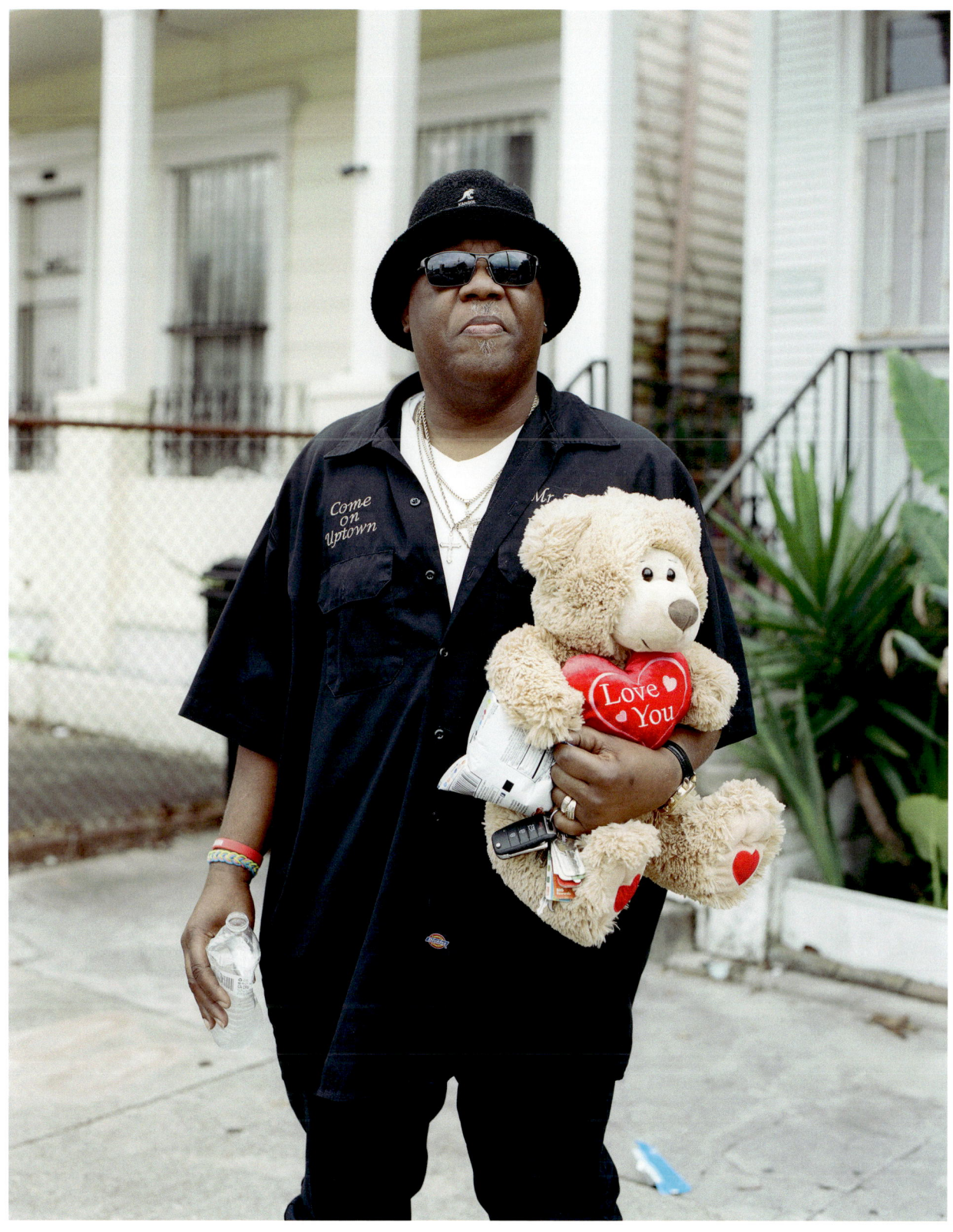

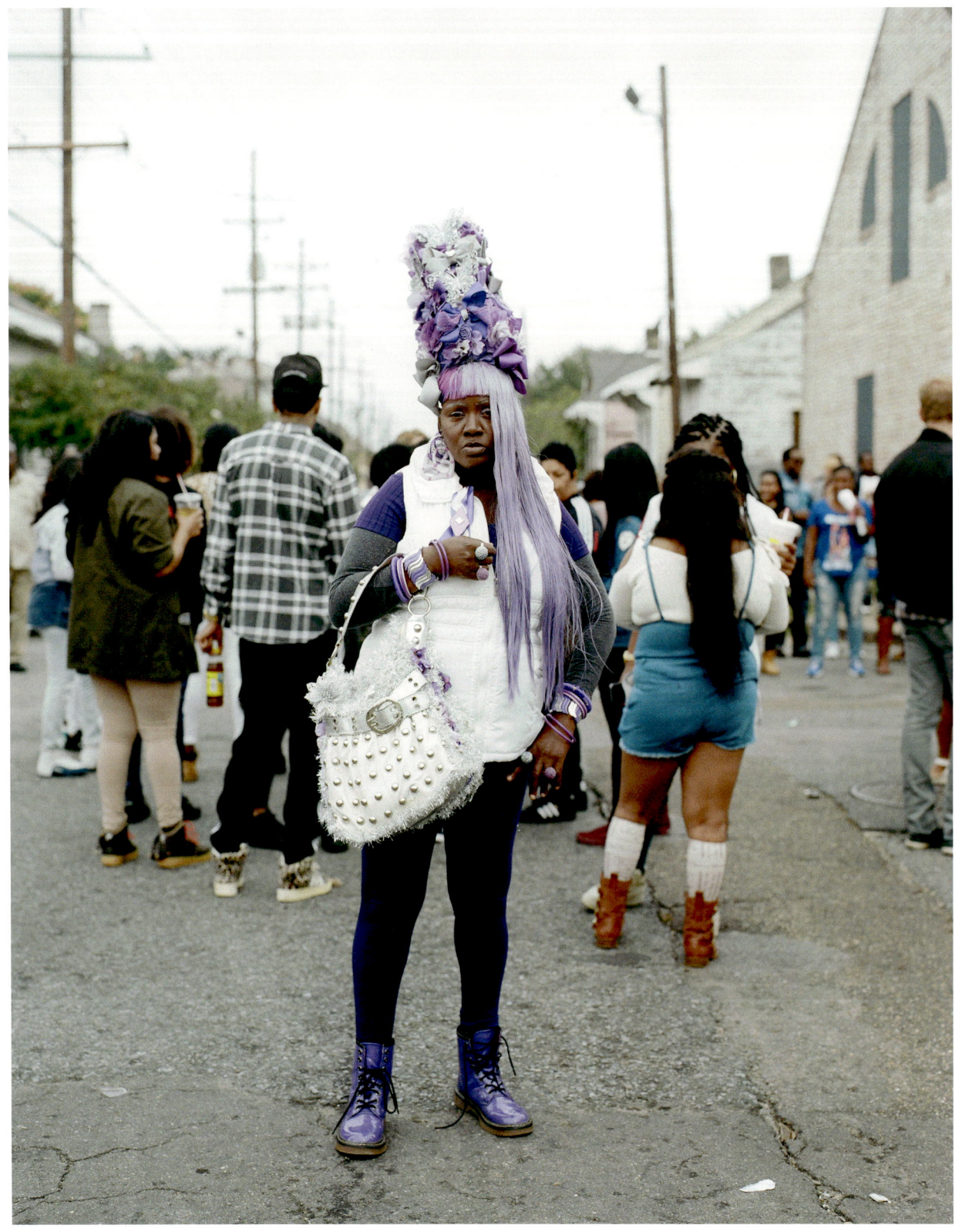

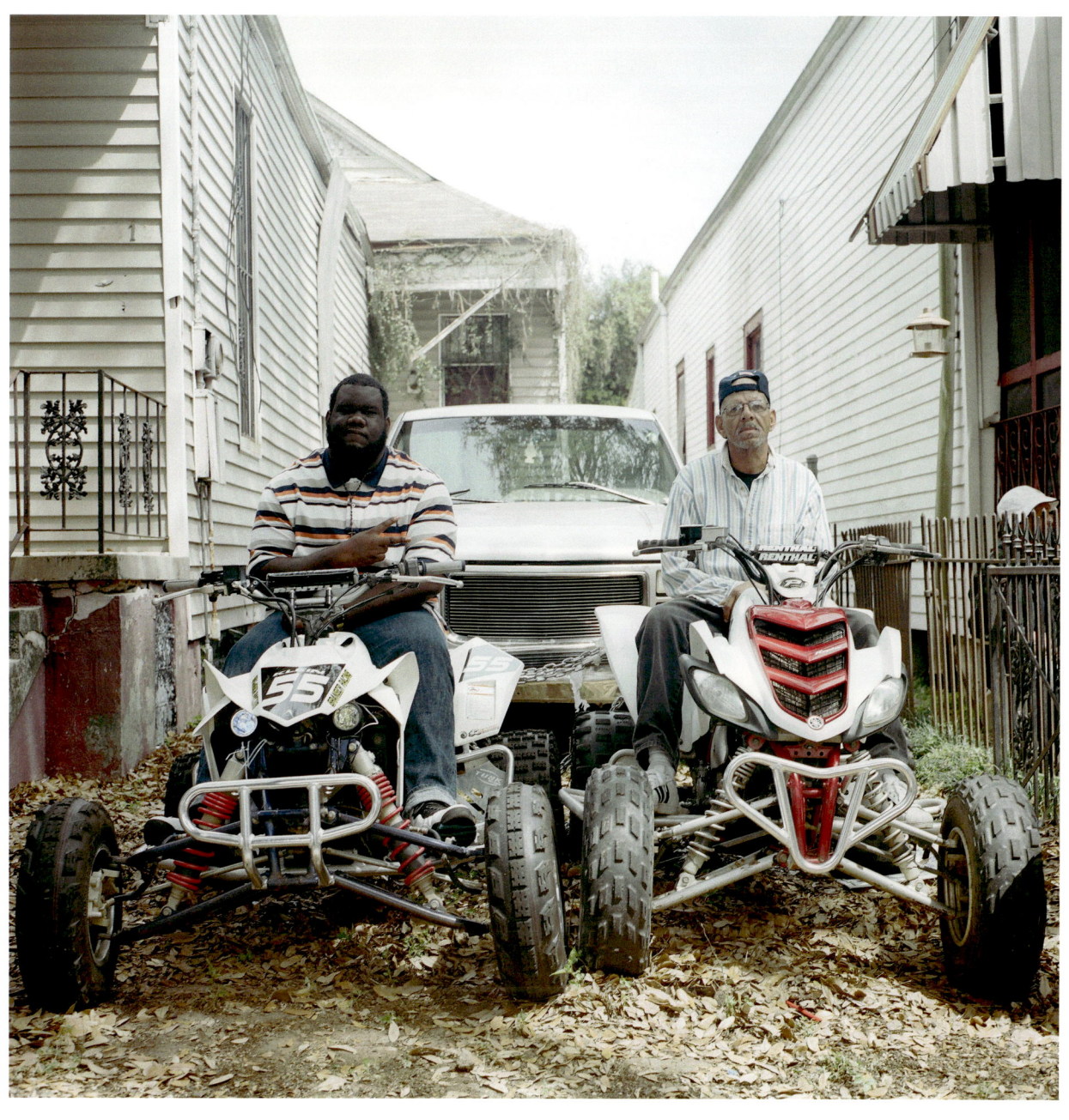

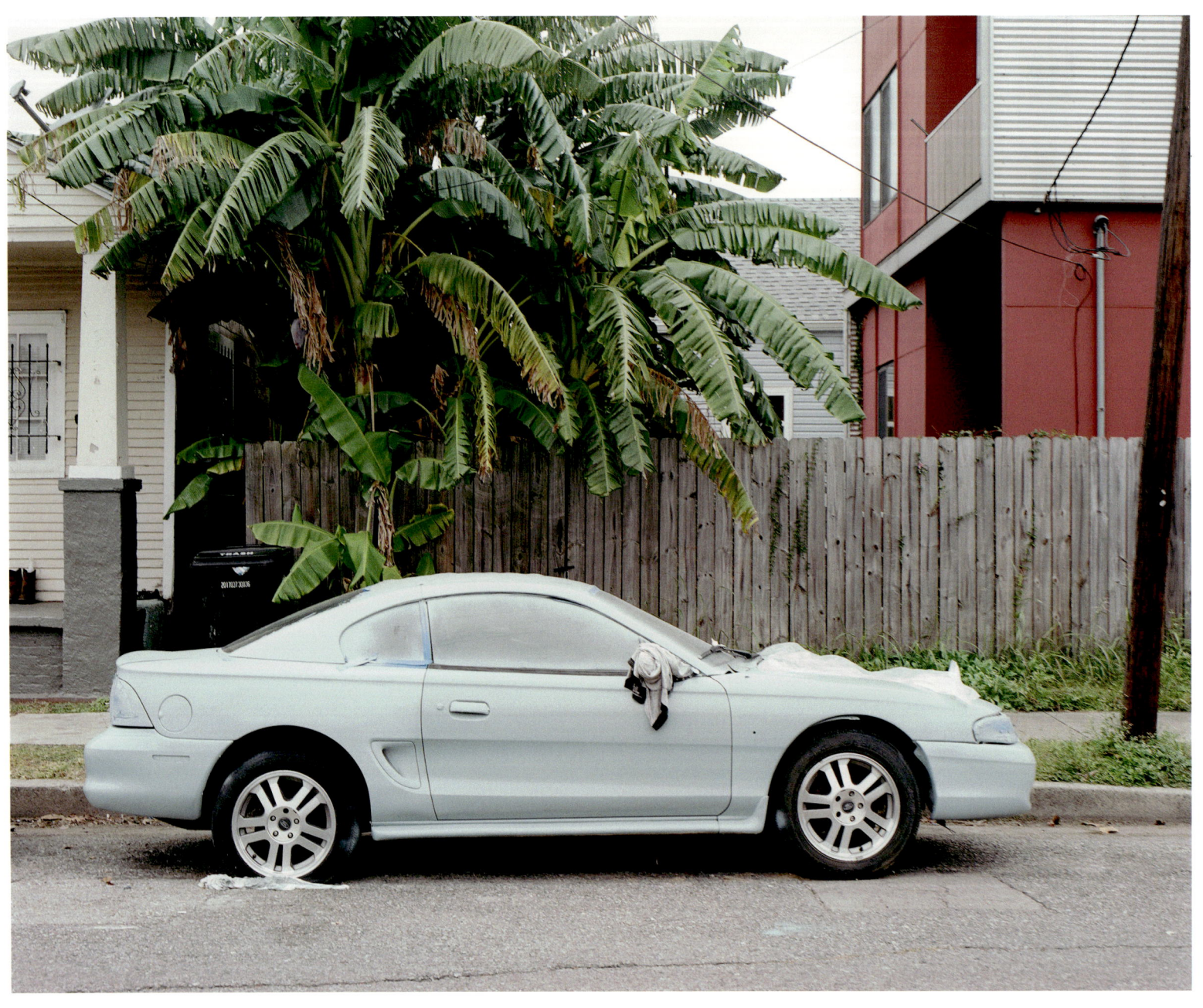

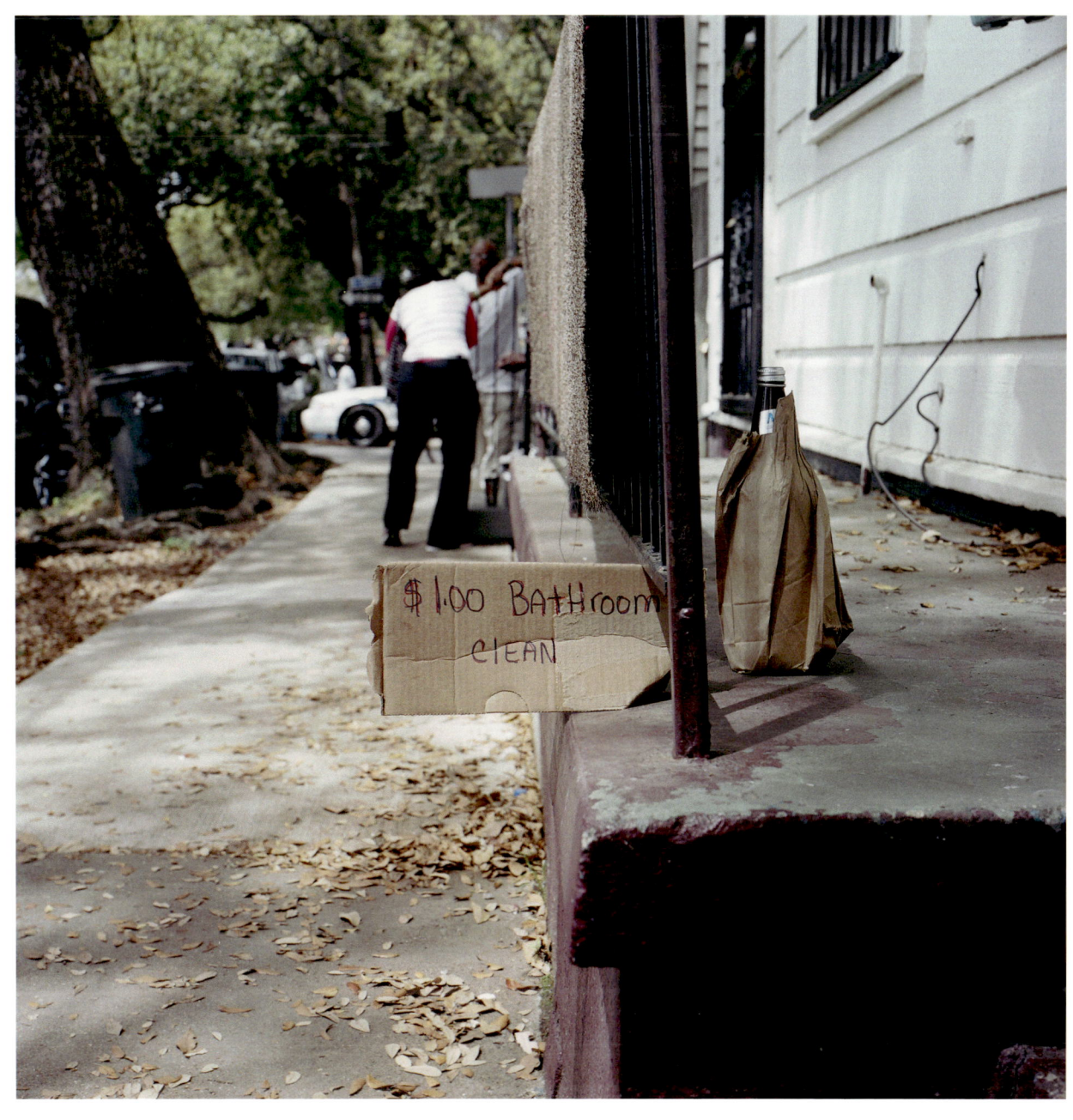

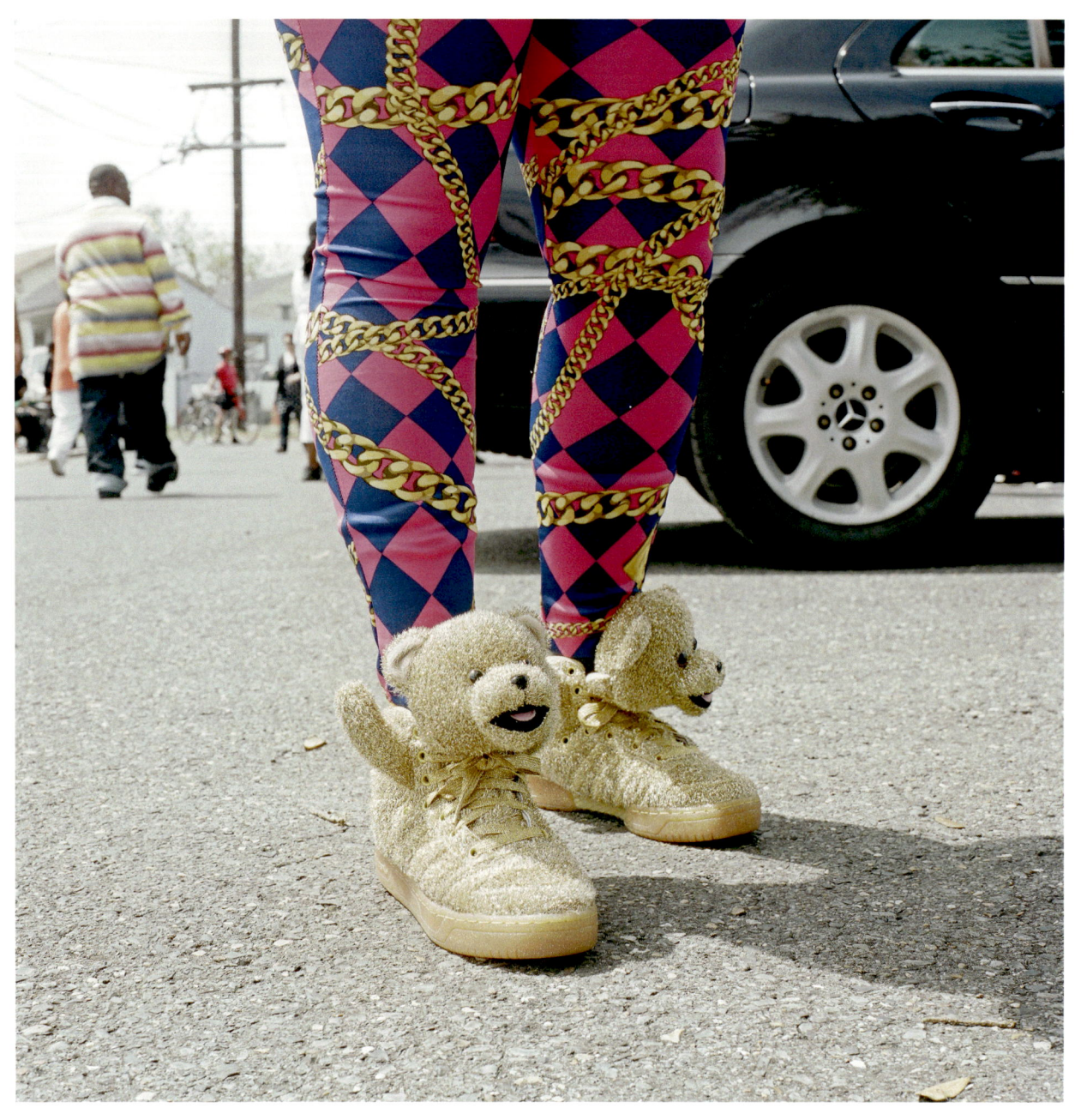

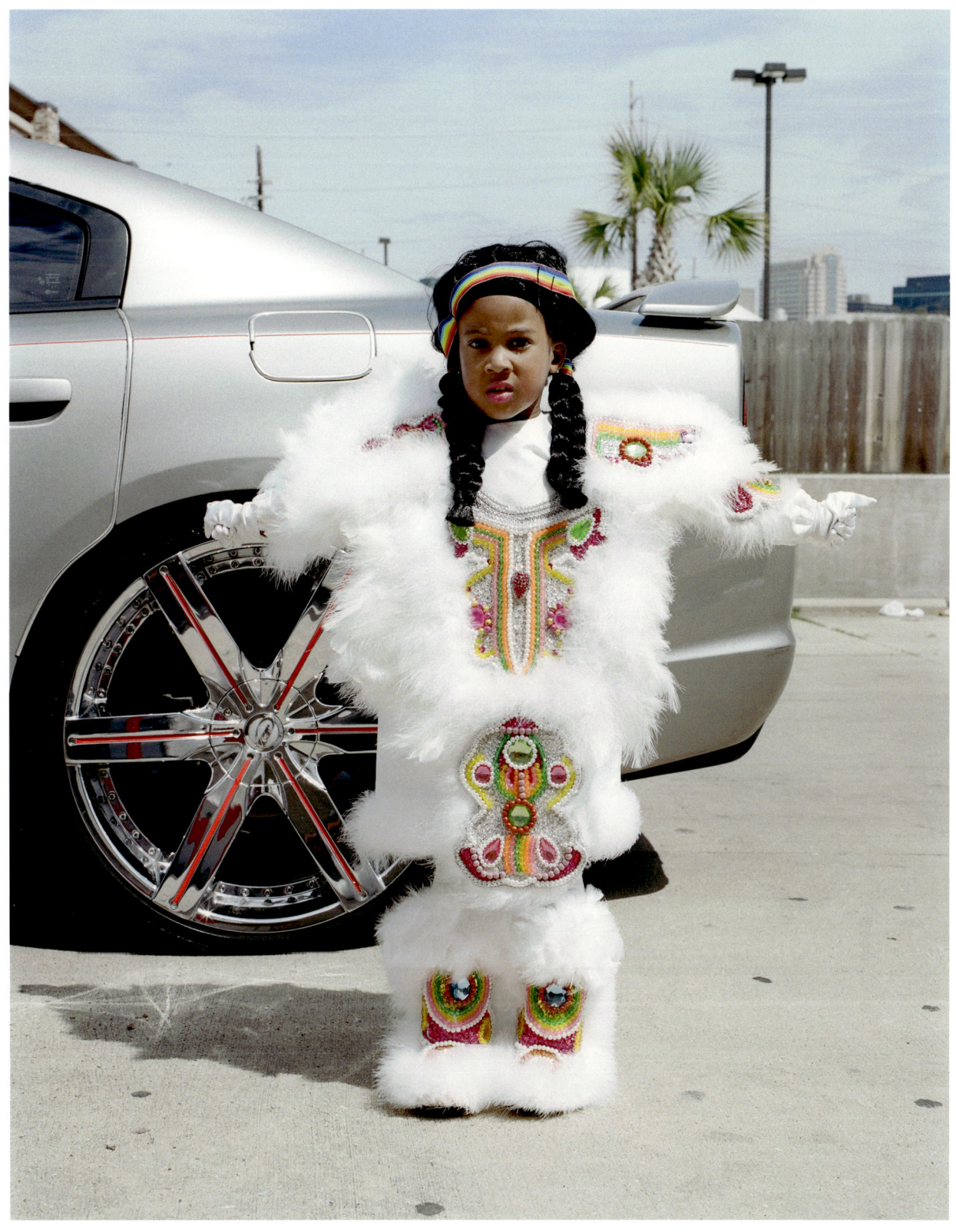

THE CARAMEL CURVES

An oral history with cofounder Shanika "Tru" McQuietor as told to the Neighborhood Story Project

TRU: Before I was born, my dad used to ride motorcycles. One of my earliest memories is of opening my mother's car door and seeing his old, dusty Honda in the garage. It was like this whole man-cave situation where he had his jackets hanging in the corner and all his toolboxes. To this day, if my mom pulls into the garage, I see the motorcycle still sitting right there. It's been sitting there for forty-five years.

I grew up in St. Louis, Missouri. I moved to New Orleans eighteen years ago by way of Xavier University. I have a doctorate in pharmacy and now I manage my real estate investments and own a vinyl supply shop for a living. I got my first bike when I was twenty years old. I took a motorcycle safety course with Dana, a friend of mine from school, and we bought our bikes within a month of one another. My dad didn't want me, his baby girl, to ride, but deep in his heart he knew I was just like him. When I got the bike, he couldn't contain his excitement: "Oh my God, let me see it! Does it have loud pipes?"

Instantly, he was one of my biggest fans. He has Alzheimer's now, but I know that if he was in his right state of mind, he would be so stoked about the Caramel Curves.

CARAMEL CURVES

TRU: I pride myself on being a skilled rider. When I was young, I would ride everywhere. And that's how I got very good at it. In the old New Orleans, before Katrina, I could be riding down the street and see a complete stranger, and they'd be like, "Where are you going?"

"Well, I'm just riding."

"Can I ride with you?"

"Come on, let's ride." We were instant friends because we rode these motorcycles. Usually what you saw were a bunch of guys. The girls were few and far between. Women, you know, we have real lives—businesses, jobs, husbands, children—so we don't always get to ride like we want to. We just have responsibilities that come first.

The whole inspiration behind the Caramel Curves was to have a set of females pull up on bikes together. Before the storm, it was more of an idea than a reality—there was no paperwork, there had been no rides or events yet. We were only a group of ladies with the same love of motorcycles.

But after the storm, one of our former members contacted me about getting together to start an all-female club. She and I spoke on several occasions about how we would get the club going, and despite my initial reluctance—because I was in my last year of pharmacy school and was about to start a residency out of state—I agreed.

We reached out to Nakosha "Coco" Smith. She was completely on board, and some of our earliest meetings were at her dad's barroom, off Tulane Avenue. We reached out to all the female bikers we knew in the area. We could tell this was destined to be epic. We based our club on women's empowerment: women knowing that they can do something that people thought they could not do. When I was growing up, and even now, the main image in this country of a woman and a motorcycle was a white woman riding on the back, hanging onto her boyfriend. It was not a woman who was handling her own bike. We are just trying to show women: "If you want to ride a bike, go ahead, get your bike and ride it!"

We know the dangers associated with riding two wheels, but the passion for the open roads is undeniable. The kind of bike depends on the ride you want. A cruiser is more for riding long distance. Personally, I have owned both a cruiser and a sports bike. They used to leave me behind on the cruiser! My club members are very competitive, so being able to keep up and take curves is very important. Many of our crotch rockets are stretched by putting an extended swingarm to make it longer, which pulls the wheel out. It's safer,

because you can't really wheelie anymore, and it looks better. Coco used to ride down the interstate and pick her bike up all the time. But it can be dangerous. Dezel "First Lady Foxy" Robinson Bell was on a wheelie when her back tire went into a hole, causing her to go down. Andrea "Hoodpriss" Shepherd rides on a trike, because her mom felt that a two-wheel bike was too dangerous; she got the three-wheel bike to appease her. My friend Dana from school died about five years ago on her motorcycle. Her passing away really touched my soul and made me focus on safety. When I pull my bike out of the garage, my number one goal is to come home the way I left.

When we started out, we just wanted to be these cool biker chicks. A couple of years in, we started doing more things with the community. We've helped prepare meals and donated supplies to Covenant House, and we support Habitat for Humanity. We've done coat drives and prom giveaways for less-fortunate families. Although we don't have a lot of cash to donate, we don't mind doing our part for the women and children of our community.

AN UNDERGROUND SOCIETY

TRU: You've got to understand—the motorcycle set is an underground society. There are motorcycle clubhouses all over the country. They can be in any shape, size, color, creed. Most are set up like a bar, and host other clubs. They display trophies and photographs and framed vests. In a lot of places, it's a tradition for people to sign the wall. At one point, we had our own clubhouse, but now we meet anywhere—my shop, Coco's nail salon. The purpose of our meet time is to plan rides to support other bikers' events, and to discuss our community outreach projects and wardrobes for upcoming appearances. The ideas put on the table in the meeting are voted on and majority rules. If you pay attention, bikers in motorcycle clubs are usually in all black. If you see a biker in another color, it's kind of odd. The part that represents them is their motorcycle vests. Those are called "colors" or "rags." Their colors usually have their name on the top back, the middle has their logo, which is the picture that represents their organization, and at the bottom it has what city they are from. We are a motorcycle club and we wear the same type of vest. The only difference is we don't want to be put in a box. We want to be cute on our bikes. We wear heels and makeup, lashes and nails, and changed the perception of what a biker girl is supposed to look like. The "MC" on vests originally meant "men's club." Over time, it's evolved into meaning "motorcycle club."

The way bikers do second lines in New Orleans is we go from stop to stop. We get the route sheet and we'll ride to a location and hang out to wait for the parade to arrive, watch it, and go to the next stop. Just picture this: a group of girls in badass outfits and dope shoes. The gloves match. Our nails are done, our makeup, our hair. We are on these machines. We control them. I remember at the Lady Buckjumpers' second line, twenty of us pulled up with pink-and-white outfits on. There were so many people on all sides, and it was just us in the center of everything.

SMOKE SIGNALS

TRU: Motorcyclists base their clubs on territory. New Orleans is where the Caramel Curves are from—this is where our domain is— and each of us have areas that are important. When we did a photo shoot with Akasha for *Bust* magazine, in the Calliope Projects in Central City, Andrea told us she'd spent a lot of her childhood there. She said it was magical to be in that space because it was right before the New Orleans Housing Authority tore it down. All these memories came back, of people playing cards and dominoes in the courtyards. But we are not defined by one place. People ask us where we go. We tell them, "We're real bikers. We're nomadic." That's the cool thing about it—you can't just find me.

On the road, you might hear us first. We definitely rev our engines. Remember my dad asked me, "Do you have loud pipes?" You want to be heard. When someone's in a car, talking on their phone, or listening to their stereo, sometimes they're not paying that much attention to

a little bike that may have just rolled past their blind spot. I want you to hear me, to know that I'm here, so you don't pull out and hurt me.

When we're at a parade at a stop, we don't necessarily rev our engines that much. But we do burn out. The loud noise is more the mechanism of the motorcycle. When we hold the front brake and give it gas, the back wheel keeps moving, and the tire spinning in place against the asphalt creates the smoke. I was the first one to burn pink smoke. Most tires are black, but Shinko makes one that has a red film mixed into the tire. The tire burns pink. They're very pretty. We used to call it our "smoke signal." If you want to know where the Curves are, look in the sky for the pink smoke!

We don't have to be loud to get attention. We draw people. We could be sitting there quietly, but there's something about a girl sitting on that bike that just makes you want to go over and be like, "Yeah girl, you're doing that." We pride ourselves on being friendly, open, nice people. Other bikers still tend to gravitate to us and want to ride. We pick up our own crew as we go. I'm not going to lie, I'm usually the person who's sighing, like, "Oh, we got all these people riding with us! Come on, can we look cute by ourselves sometimes? Like, we're in the matching outfits, you're messing up our whole swag right now!" But hey, it's all in the love of the vibe.

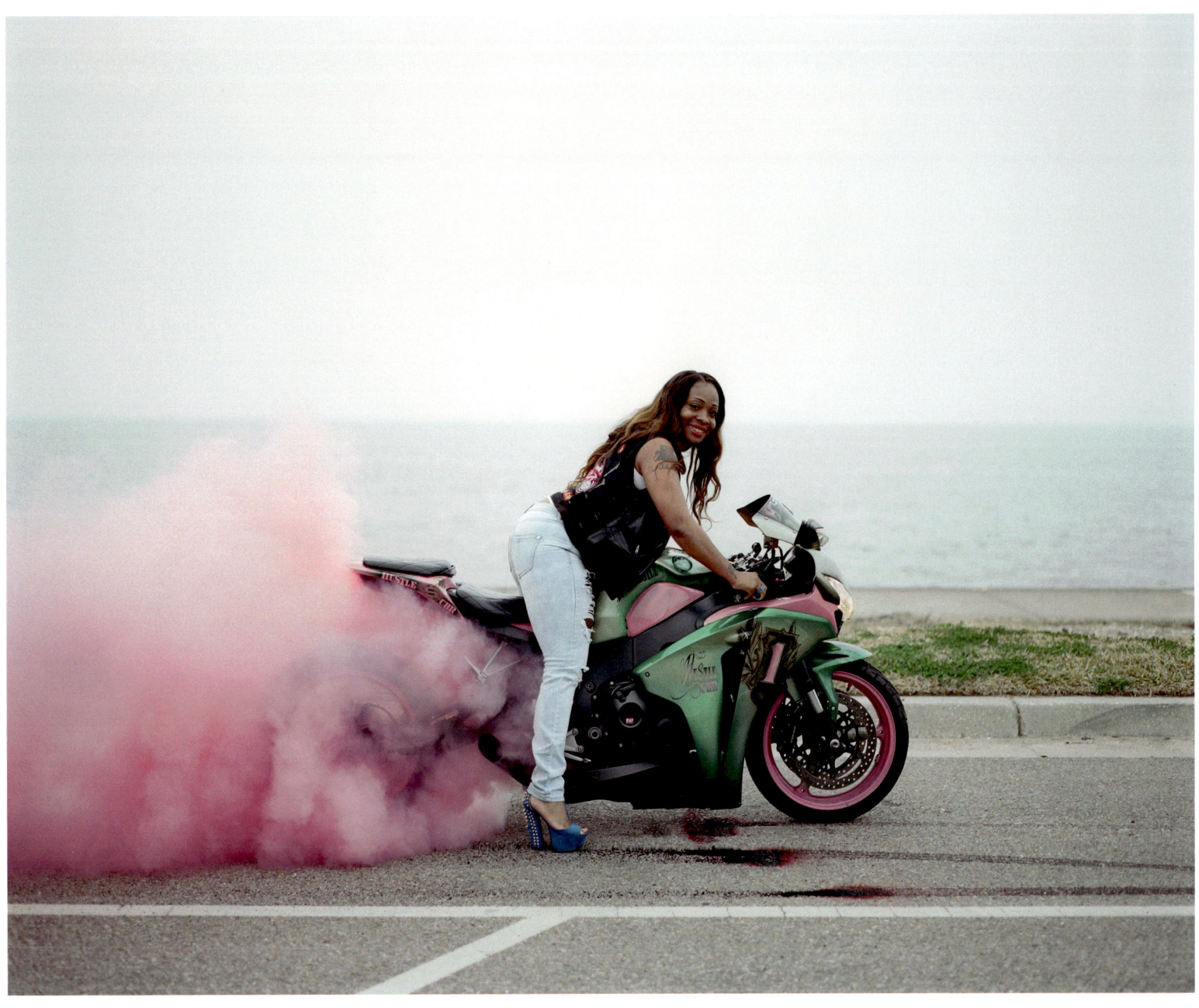

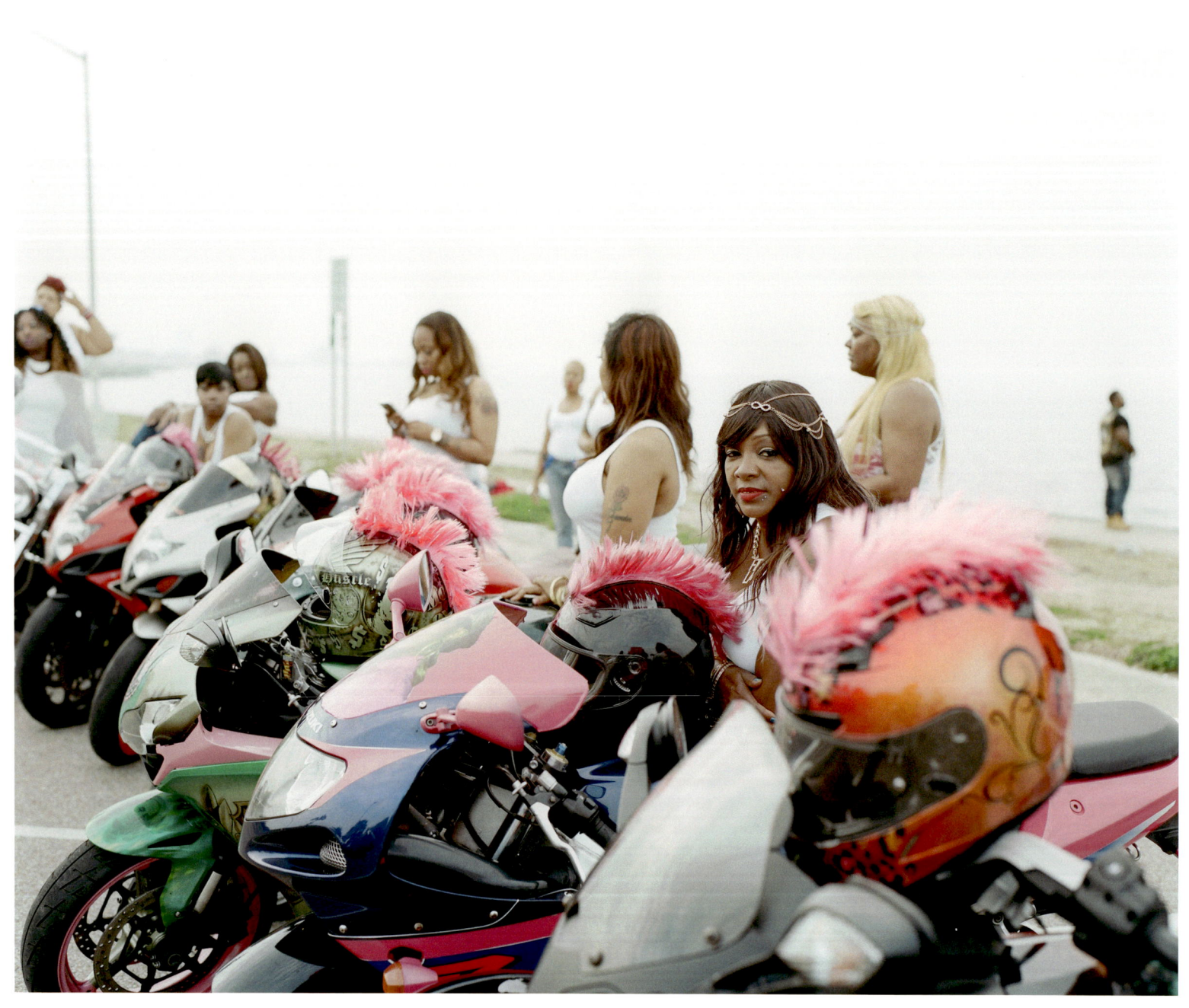

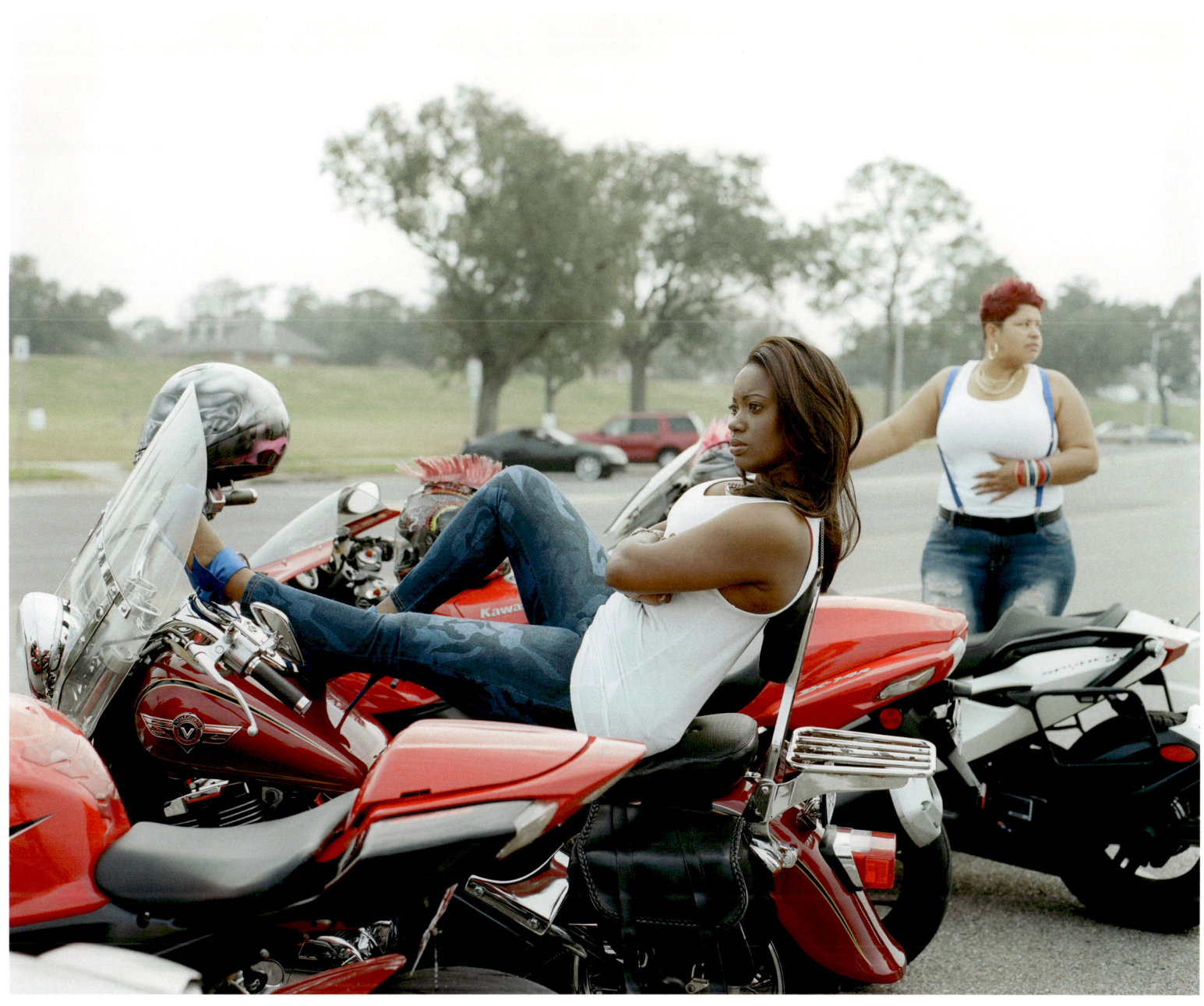

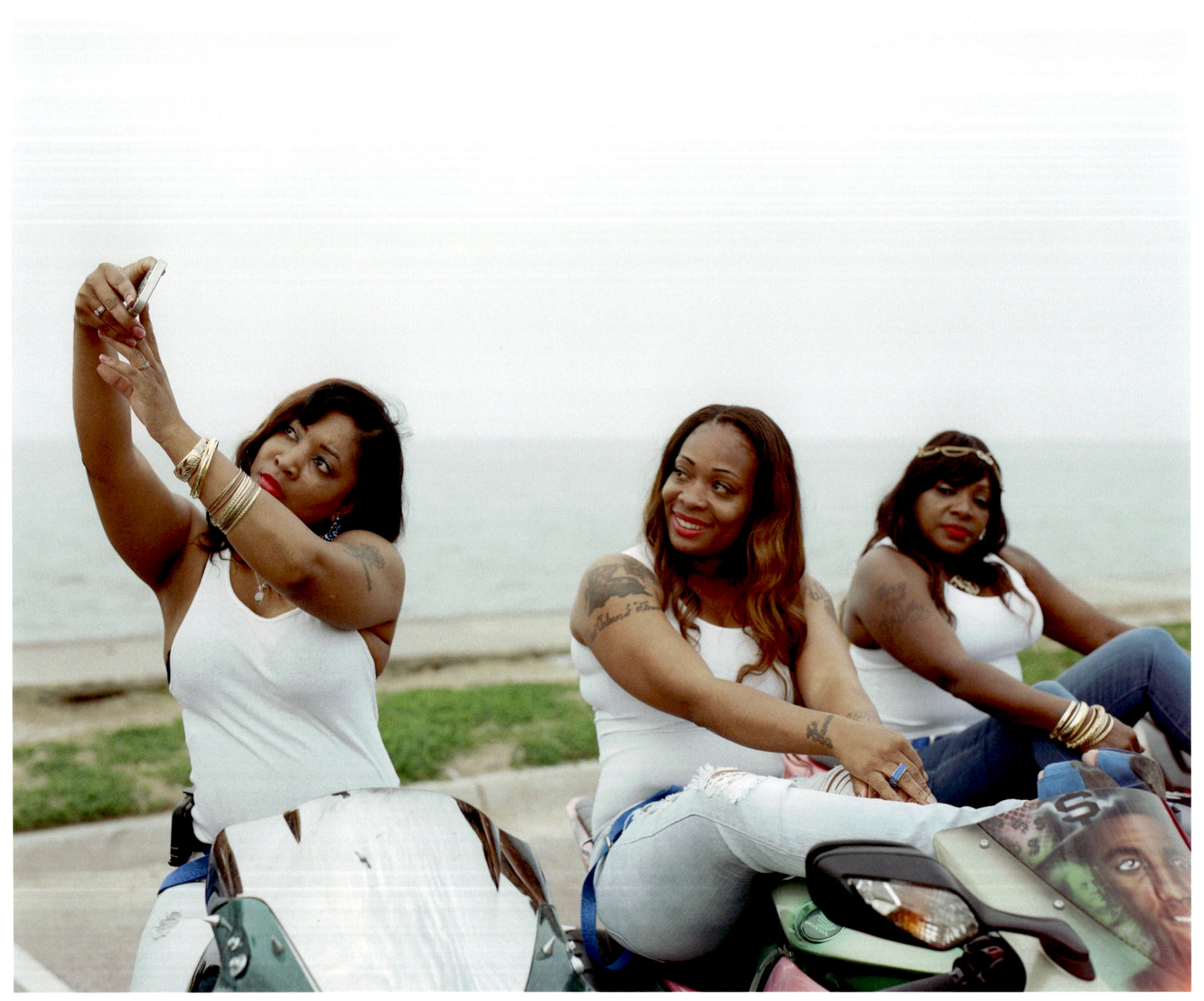

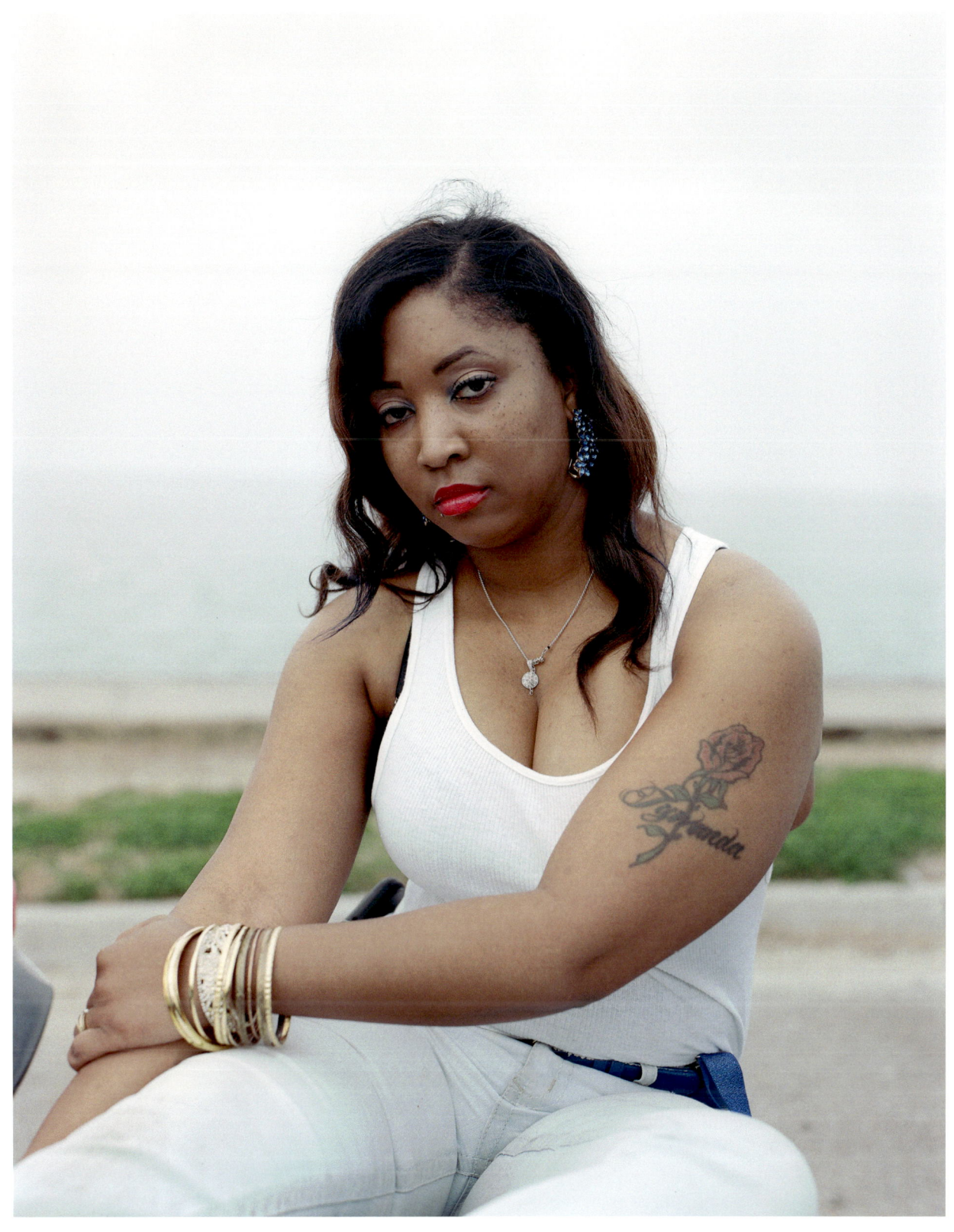

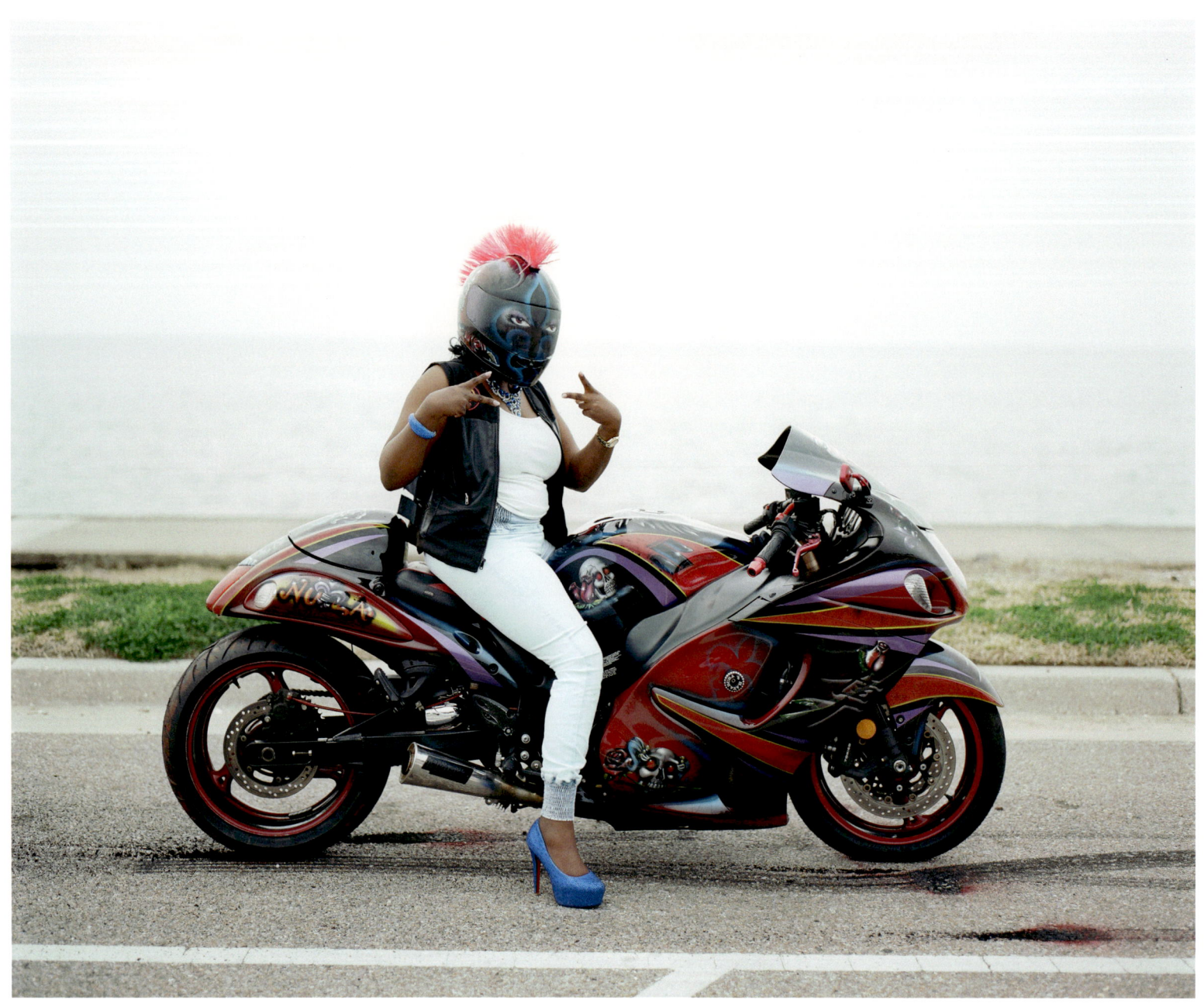

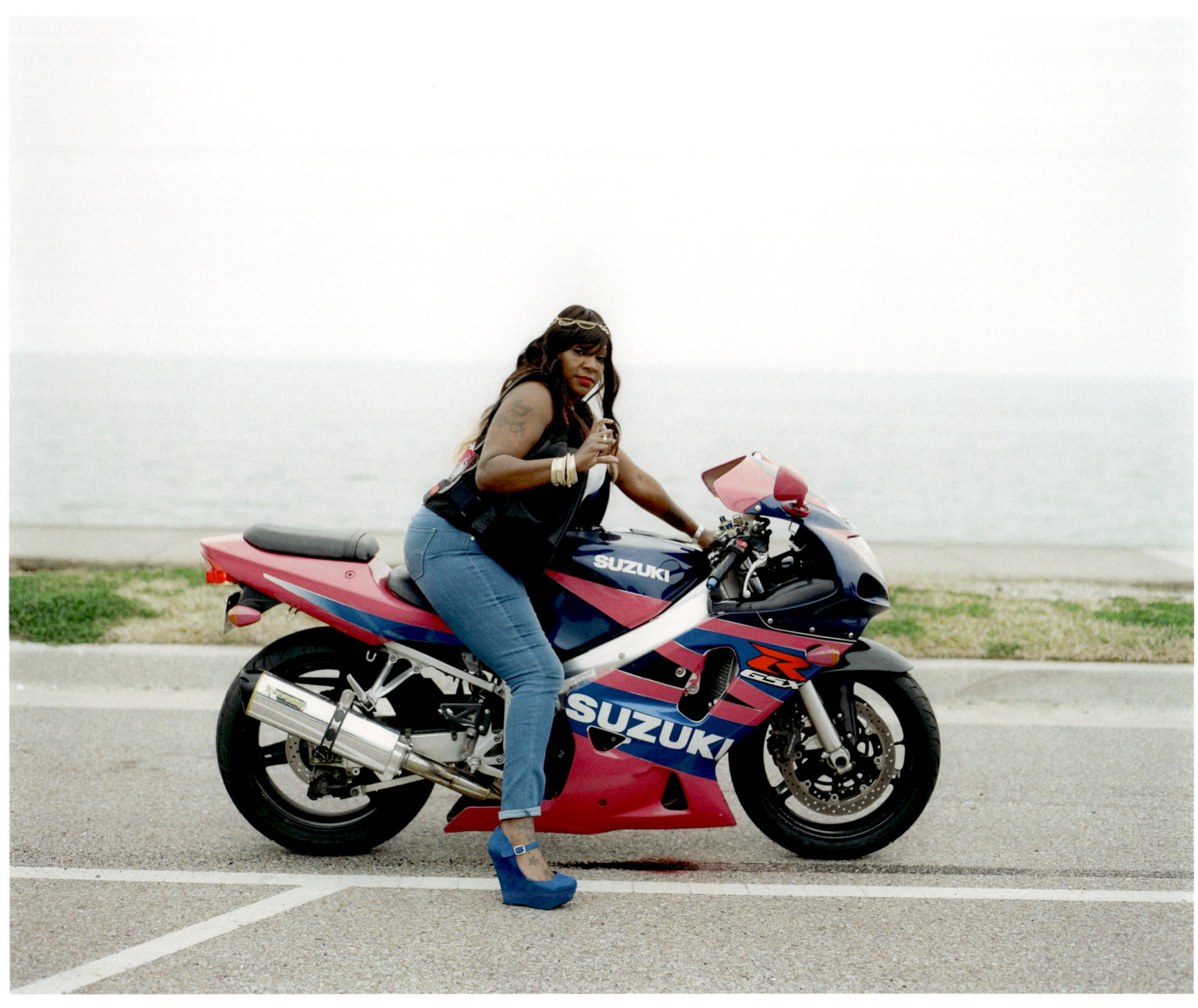

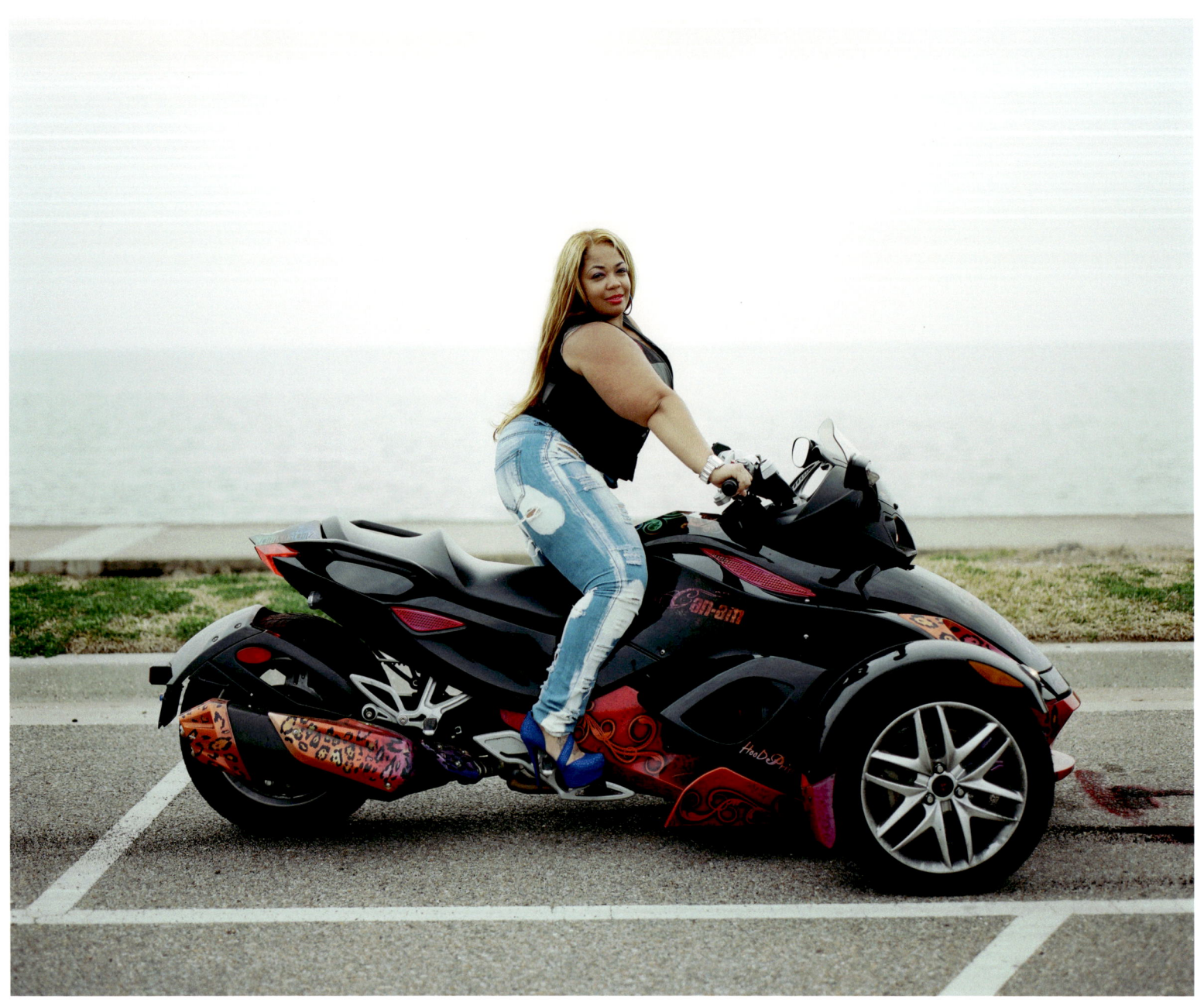

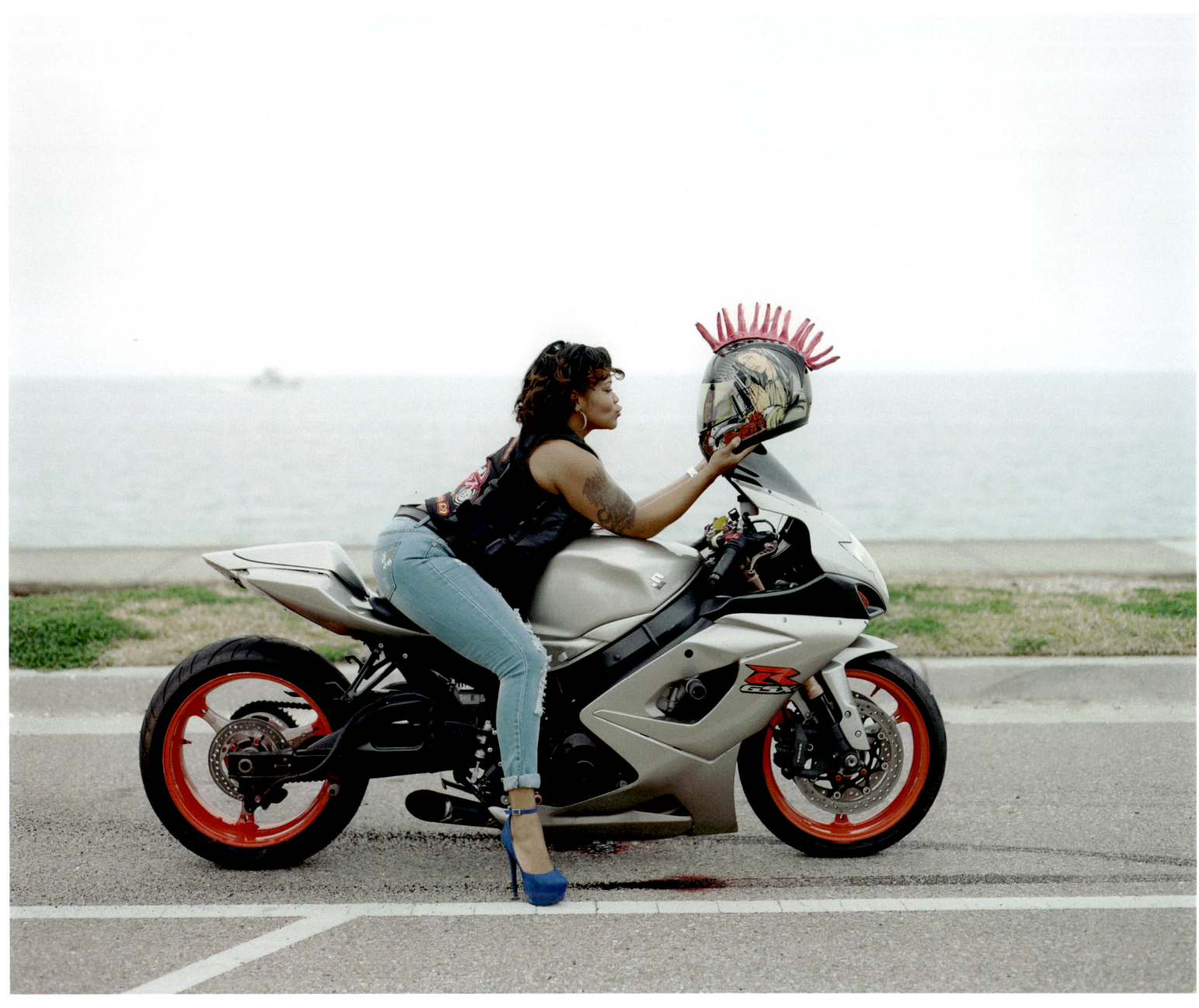

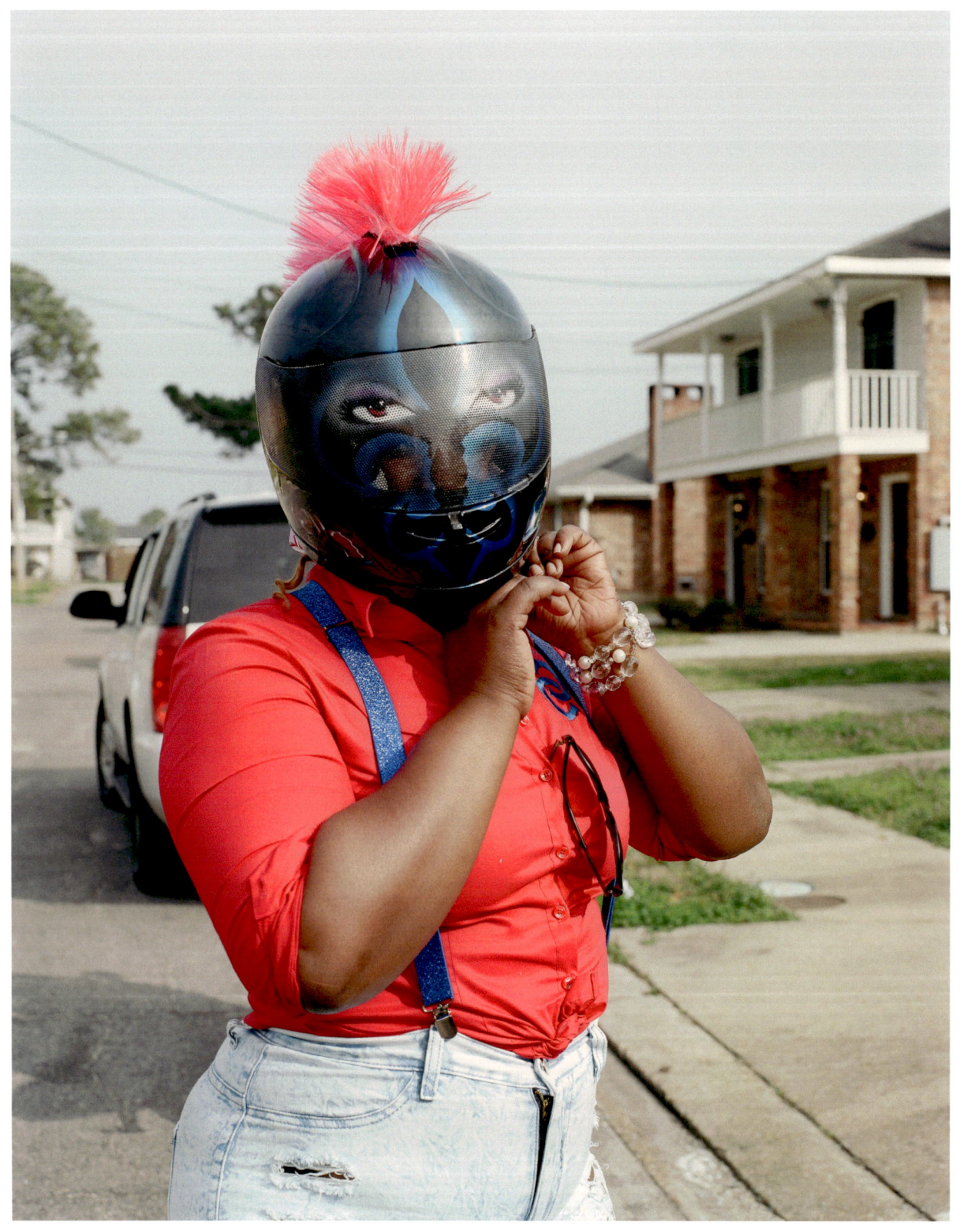

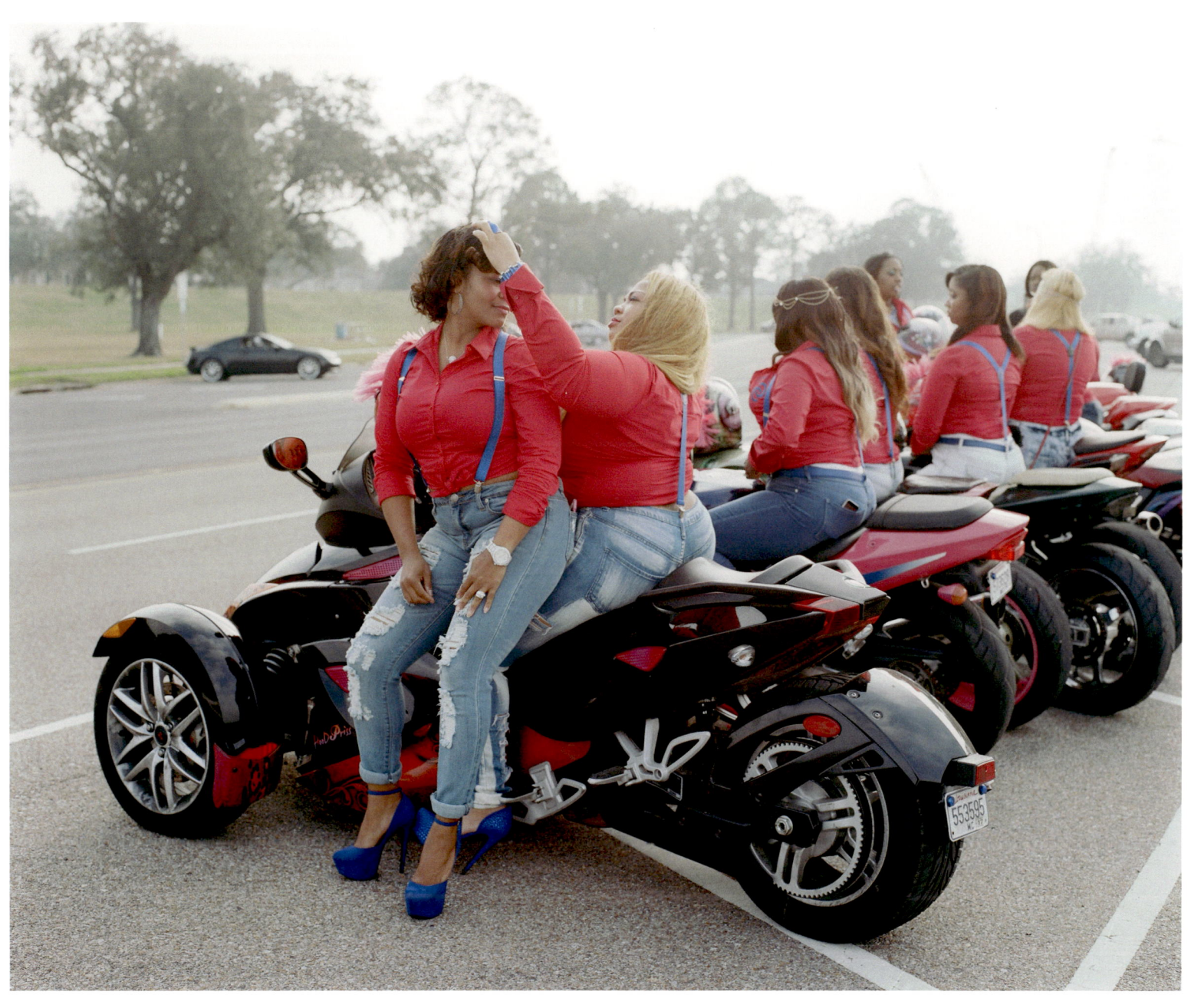

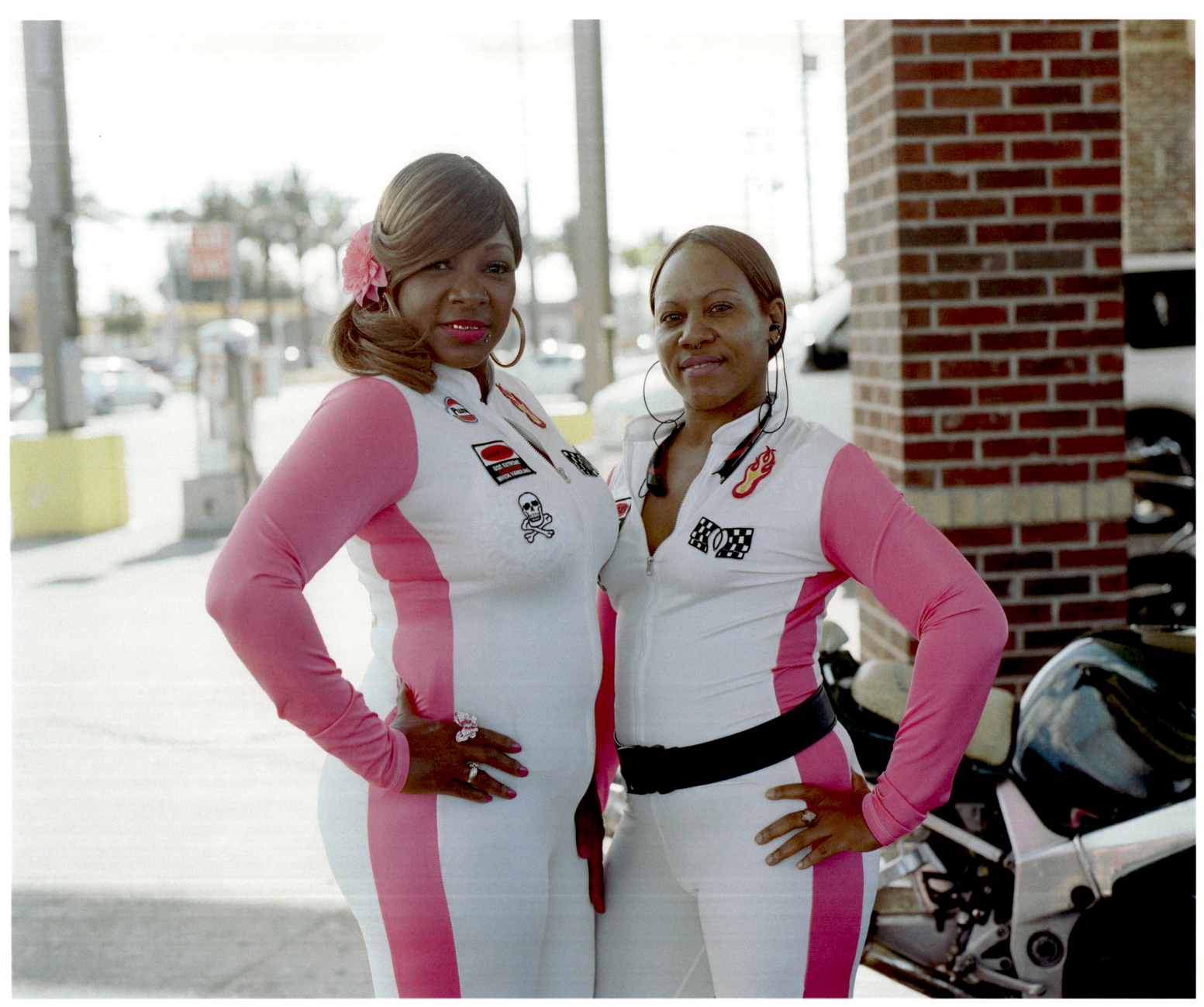

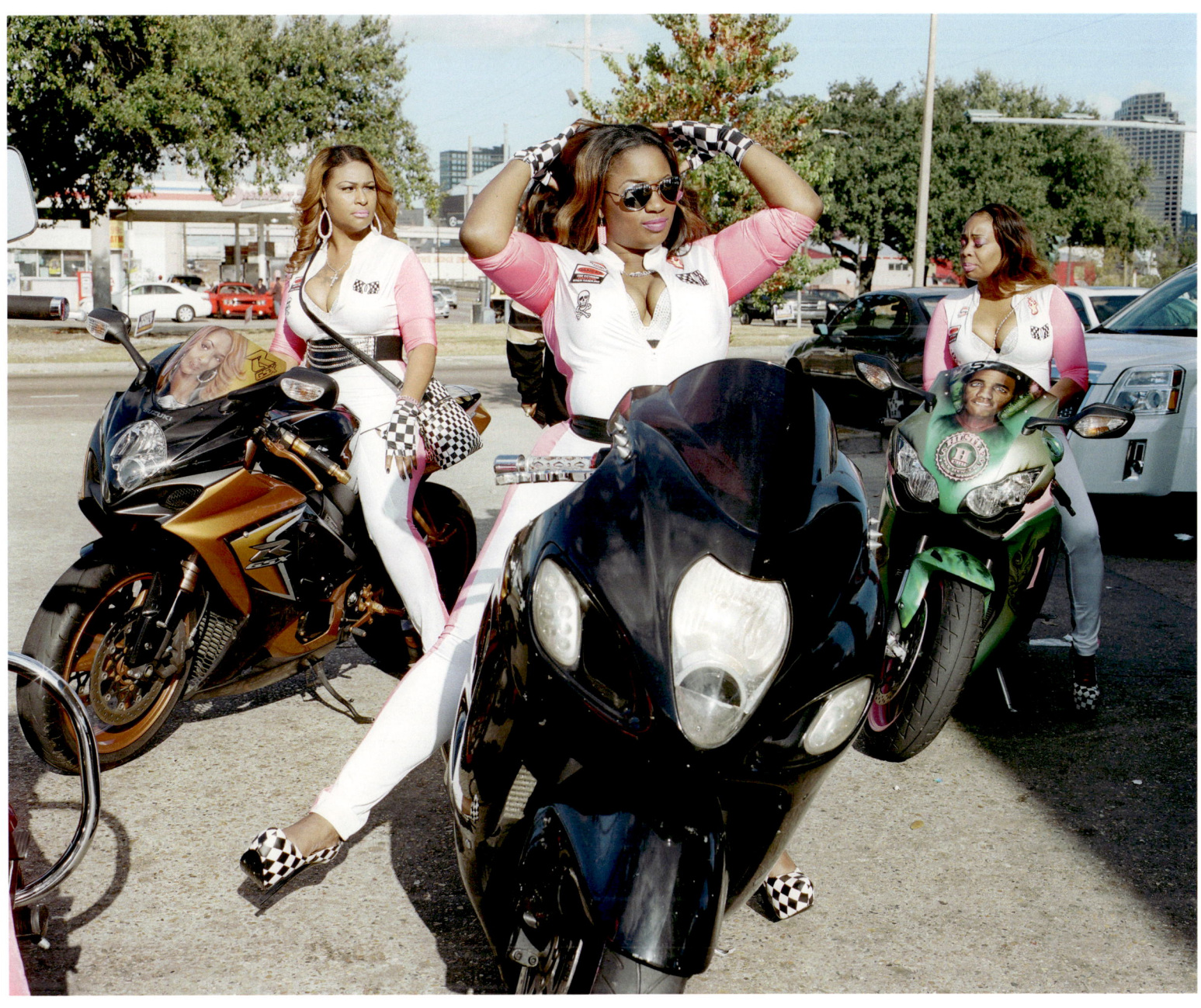

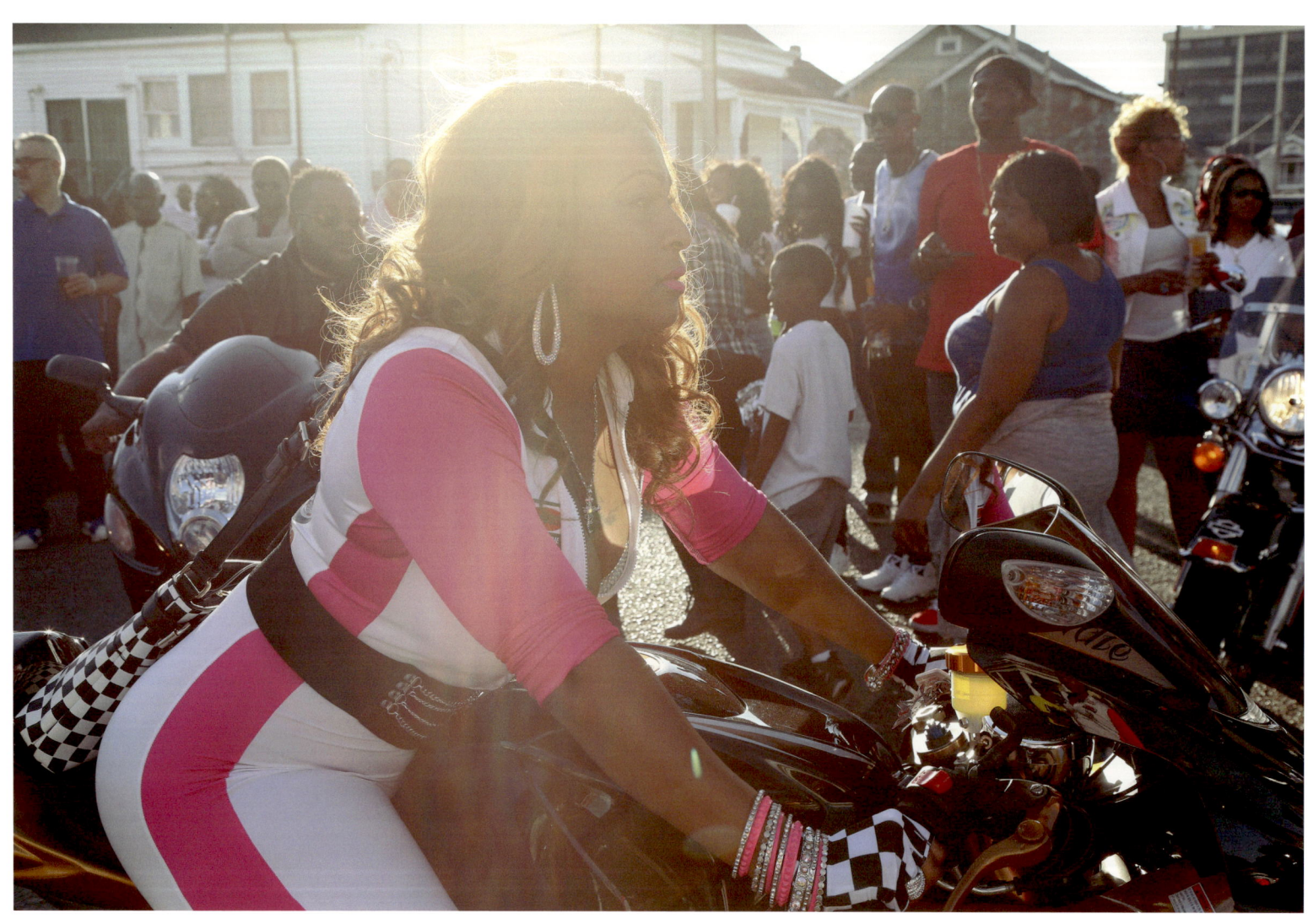

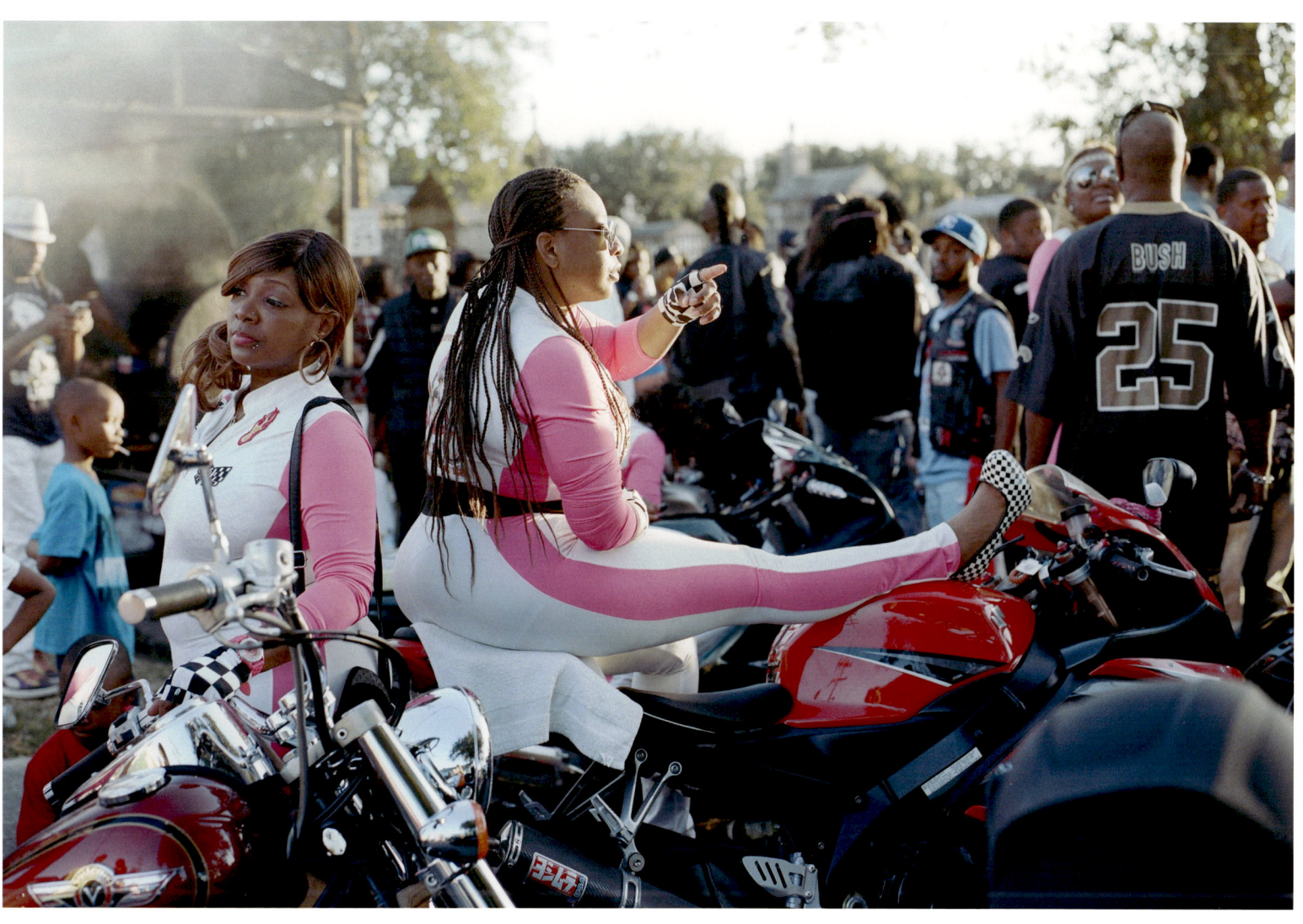

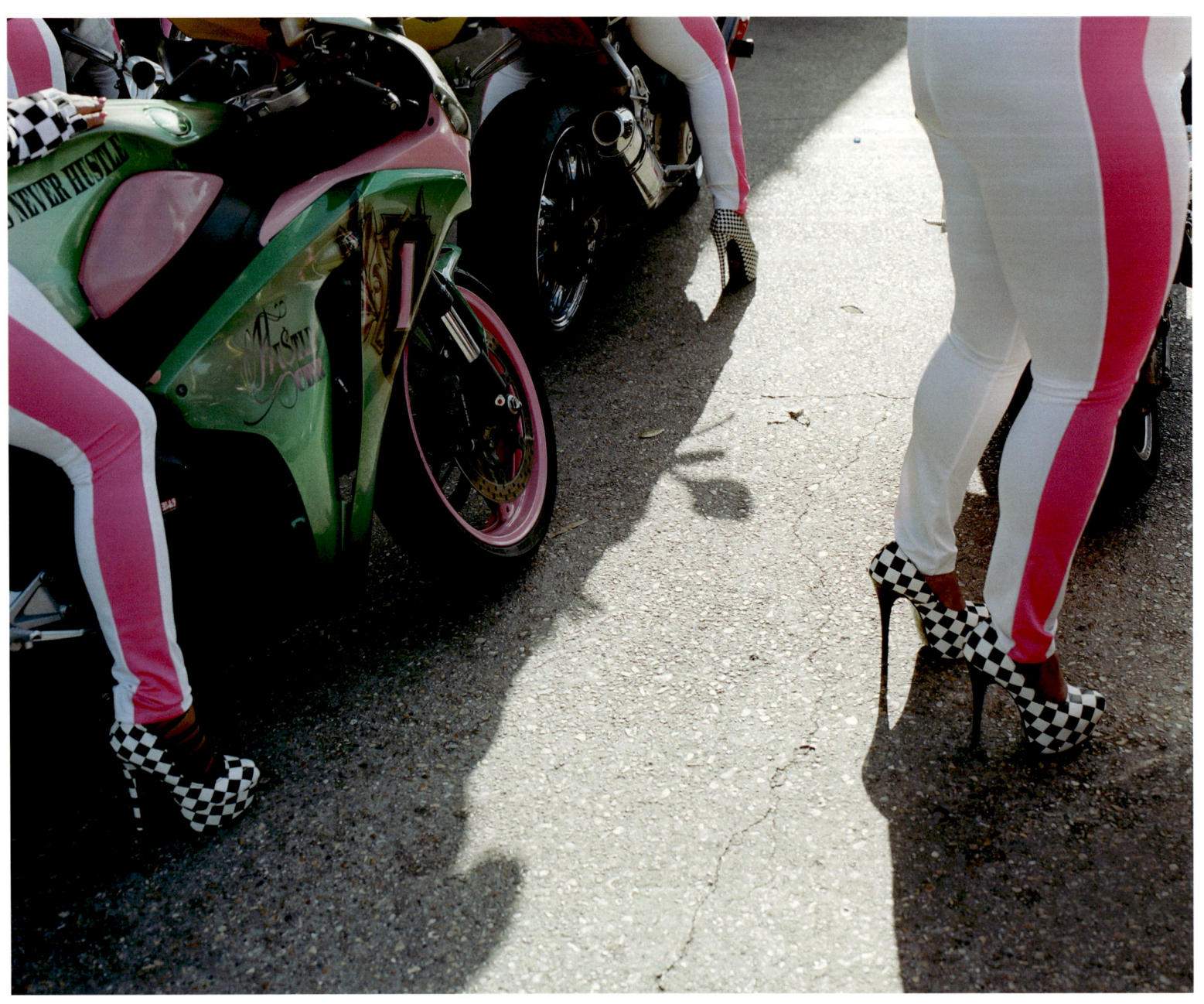

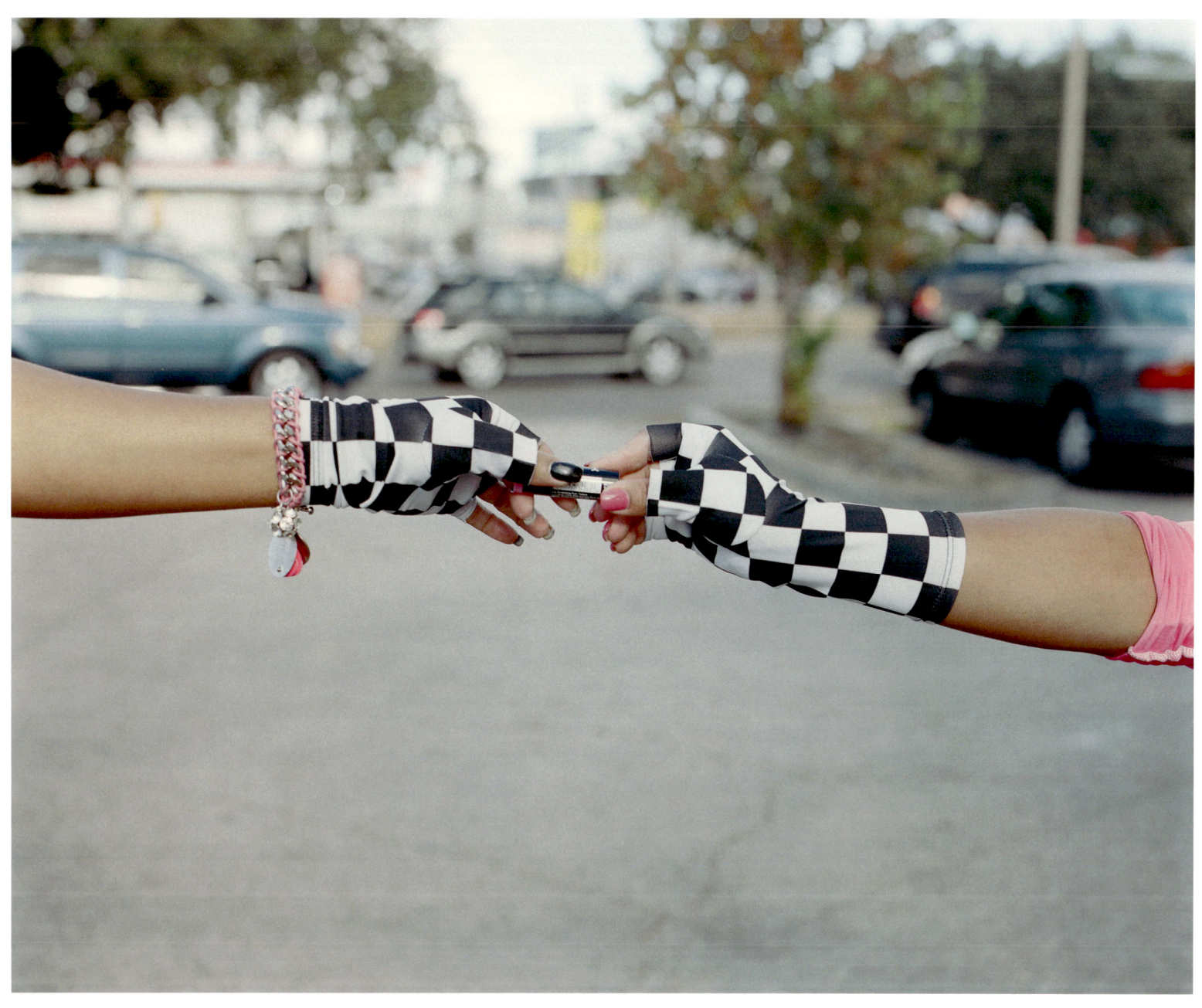

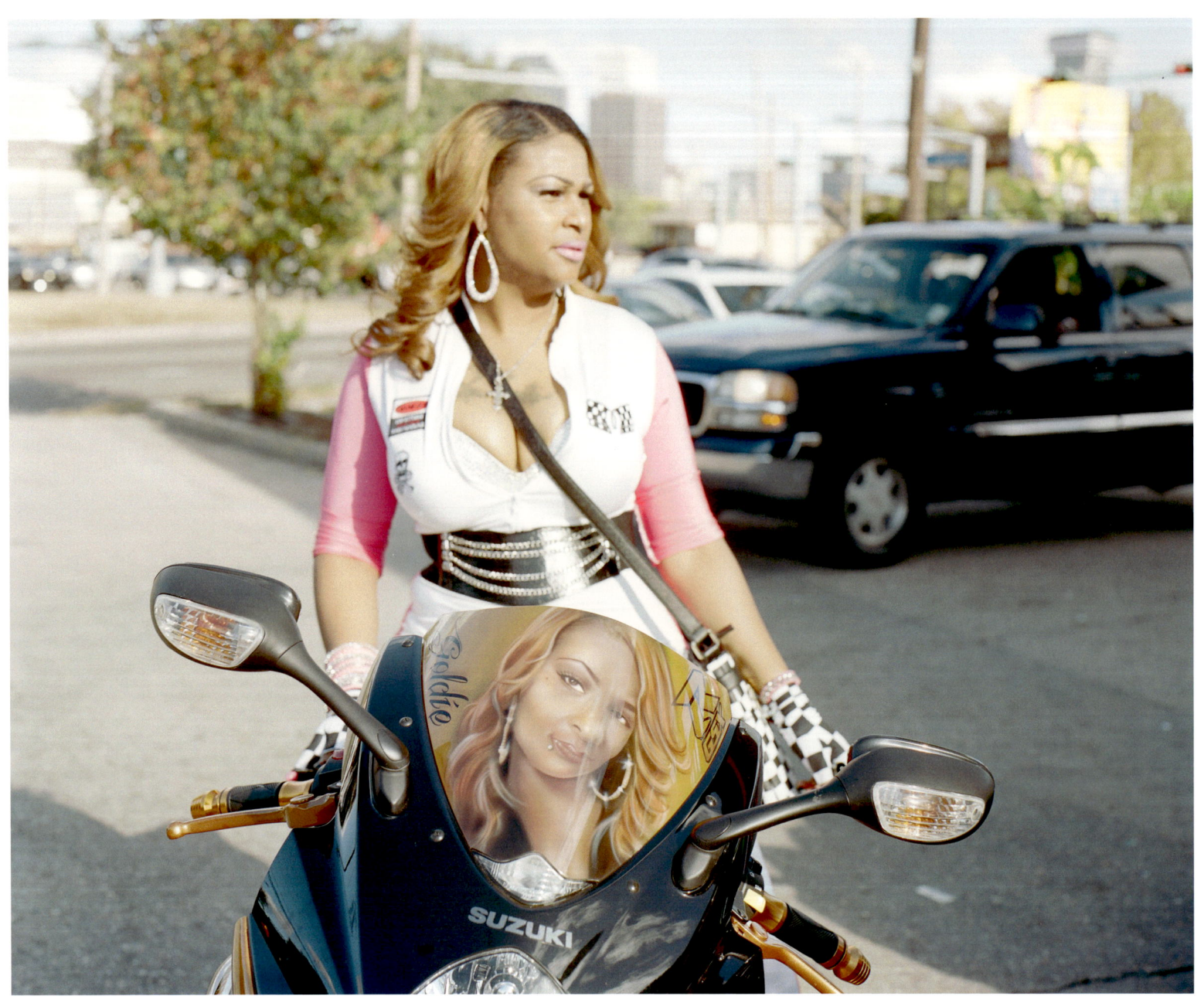

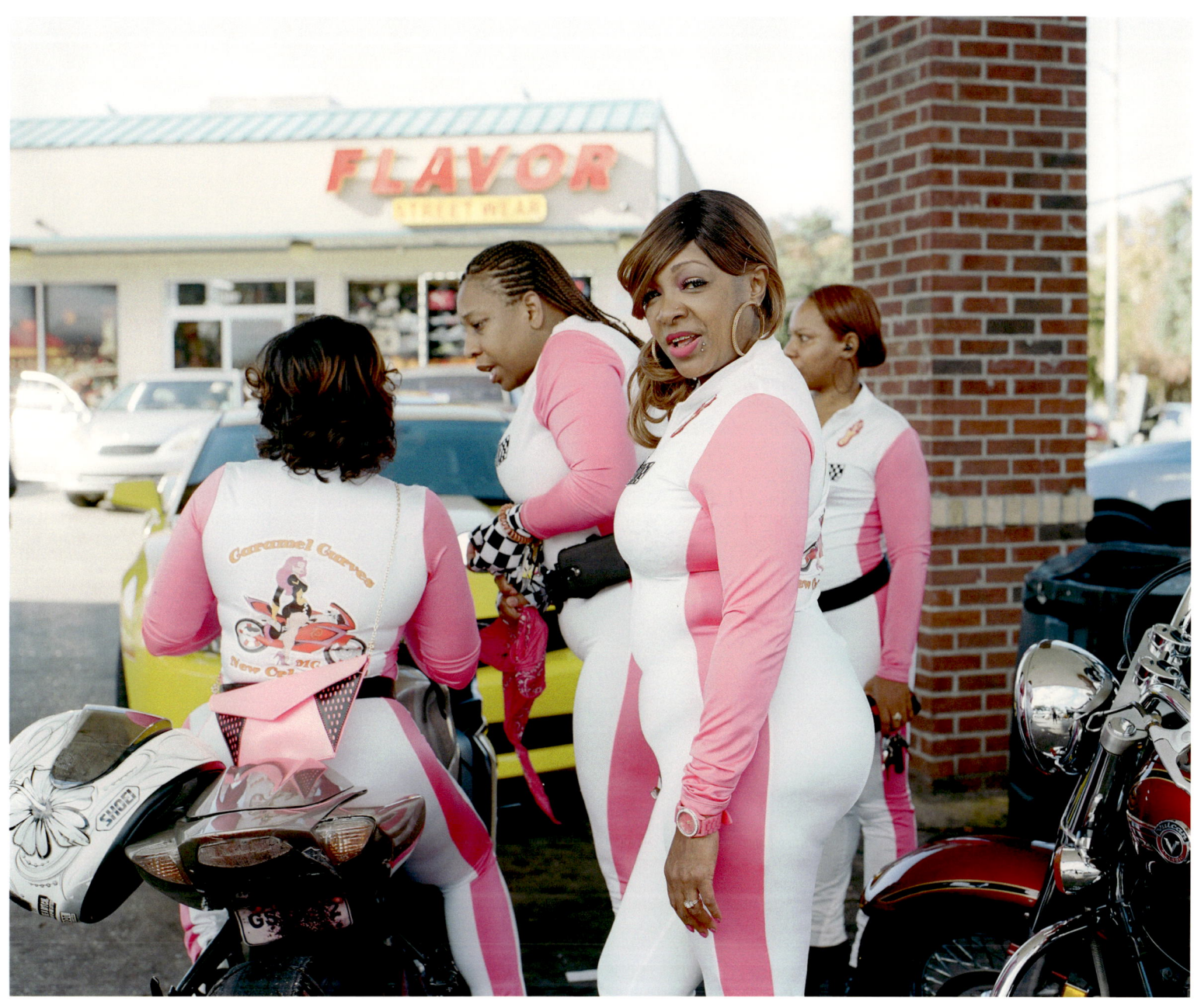

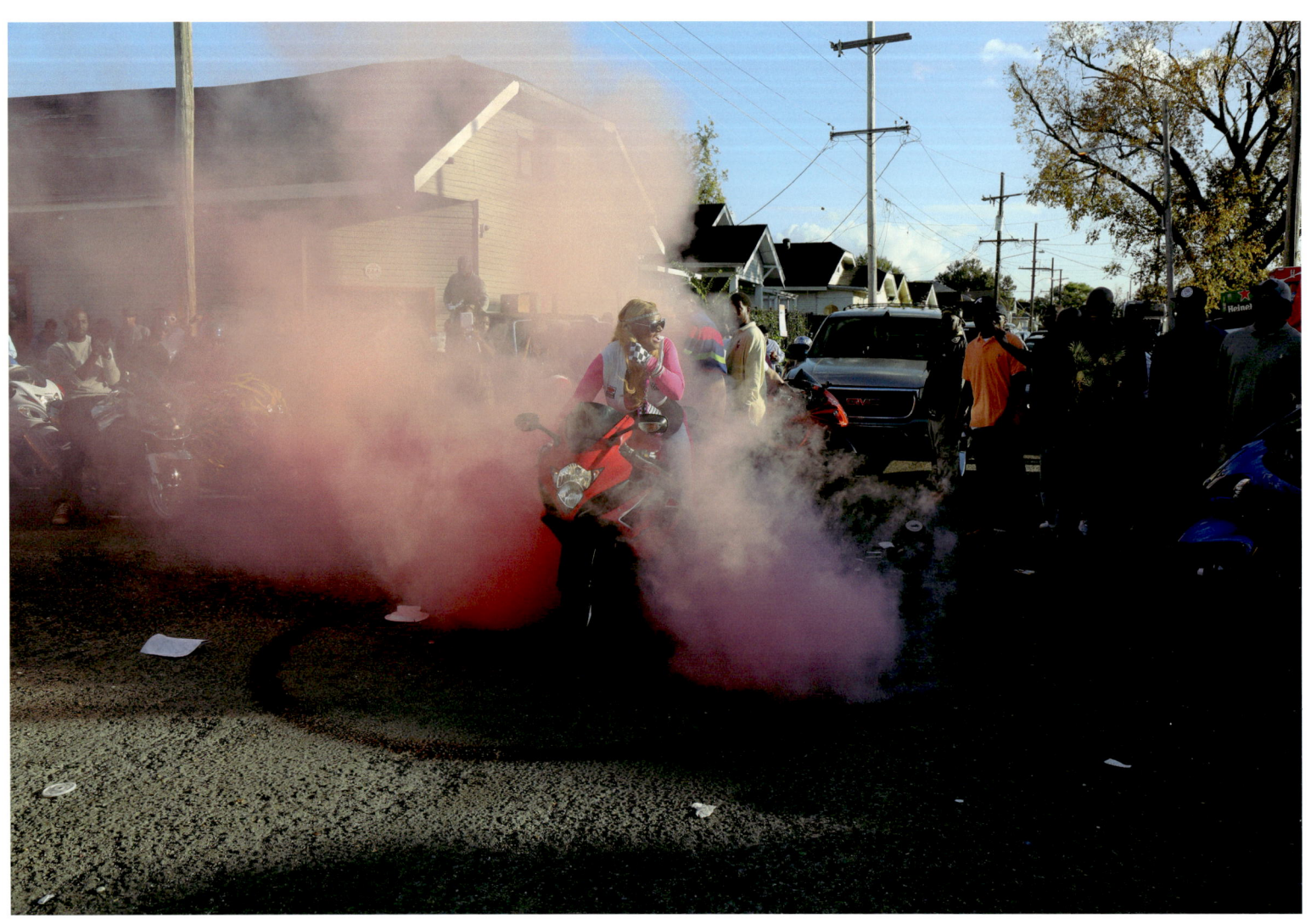

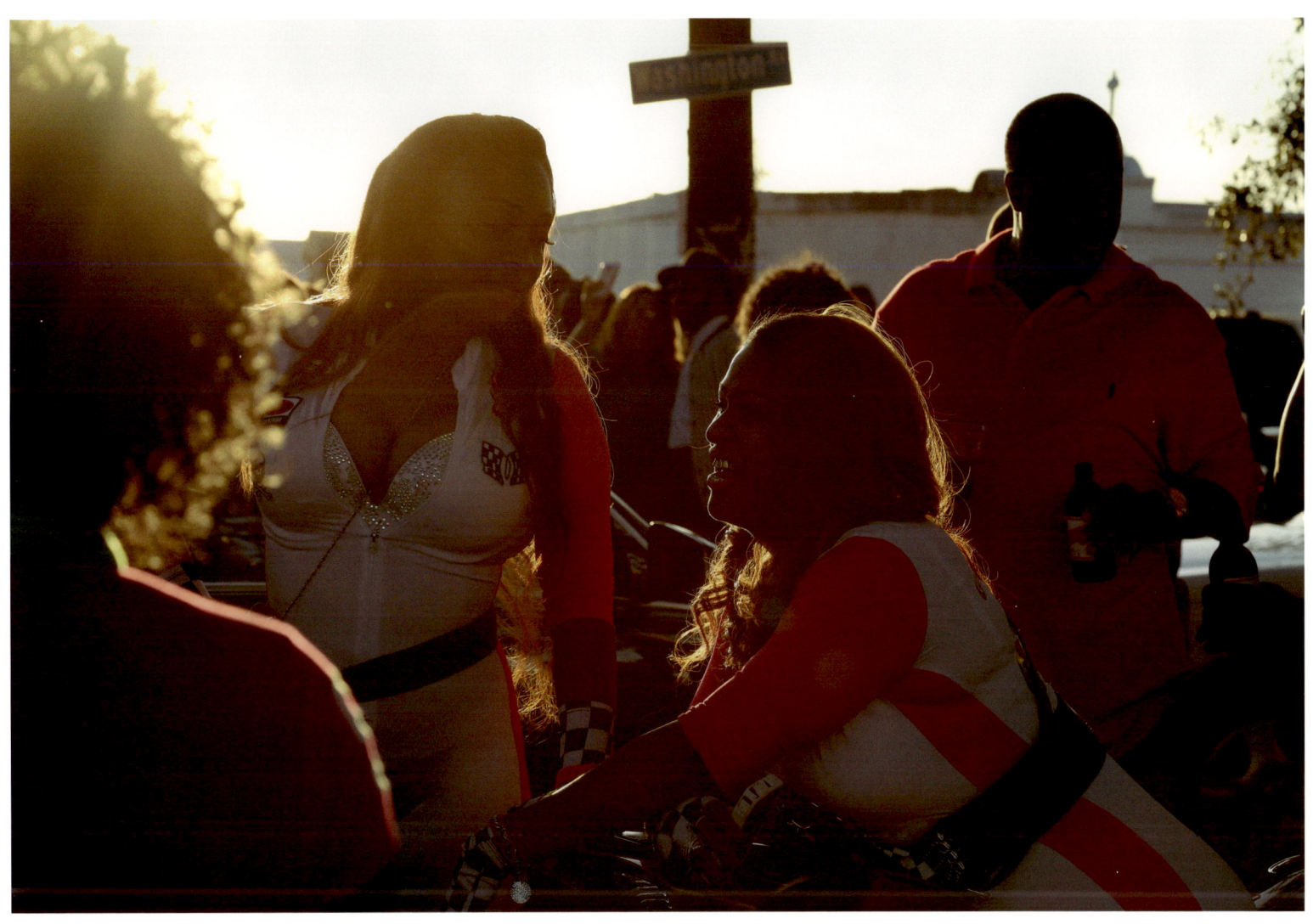

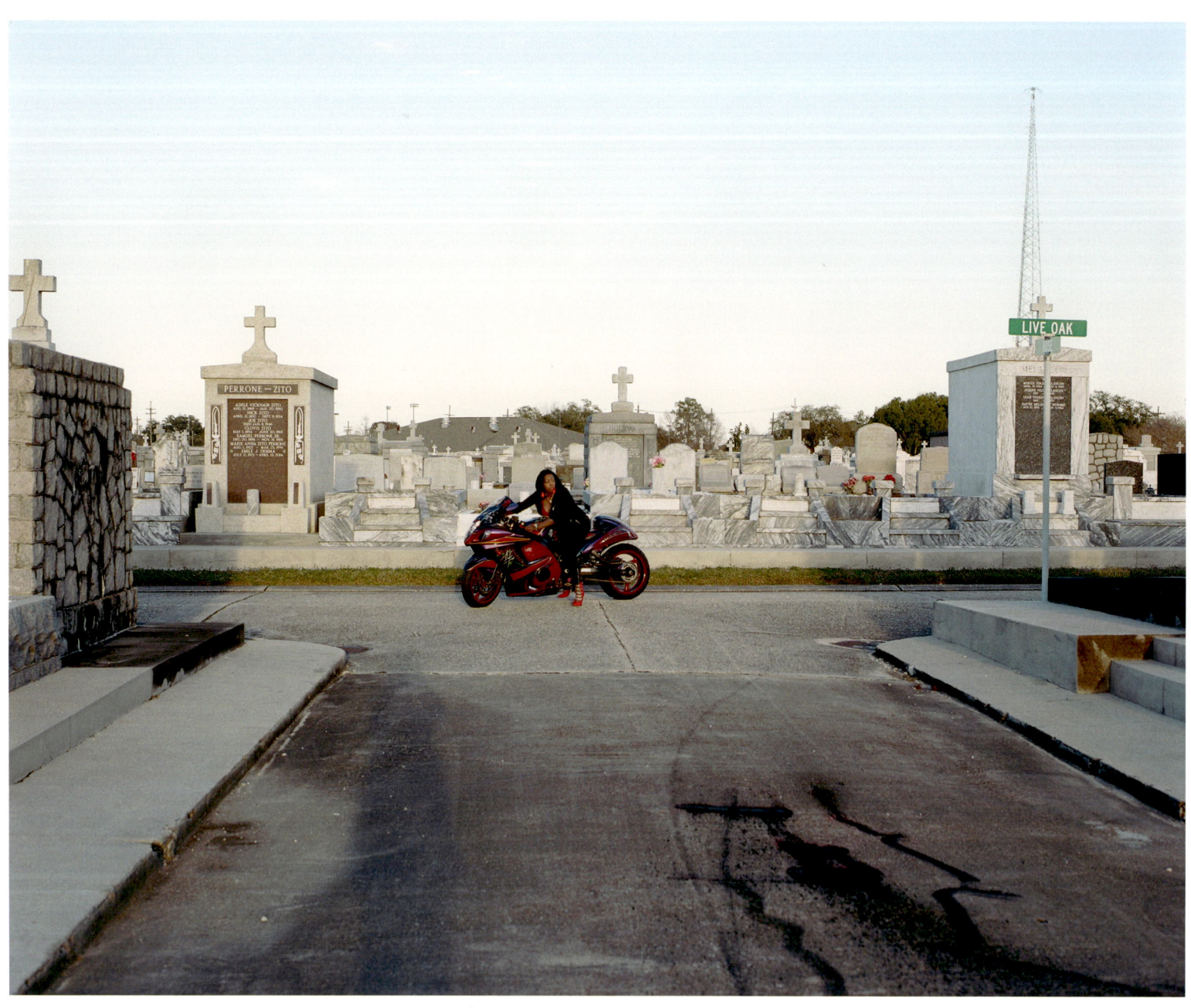

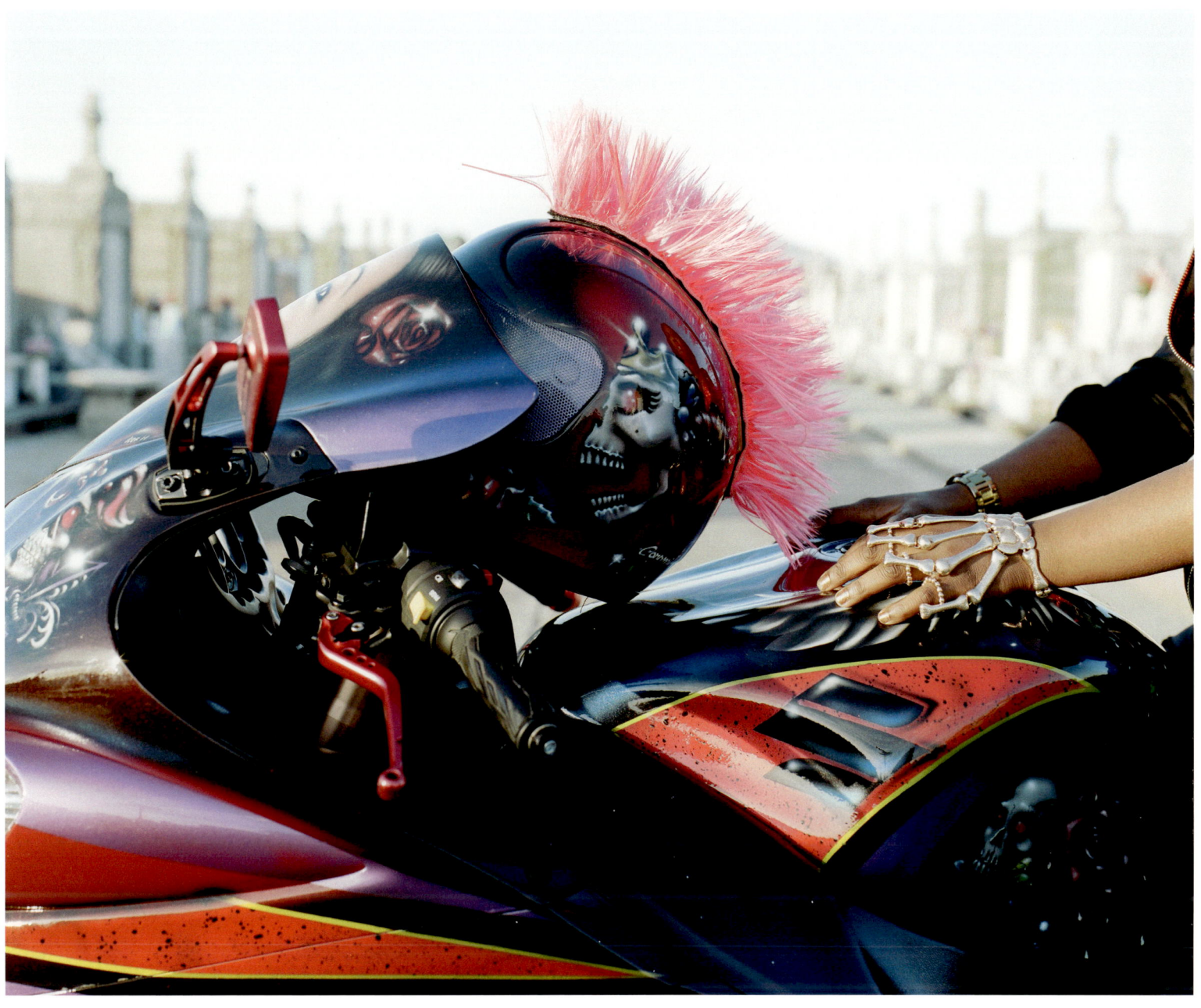

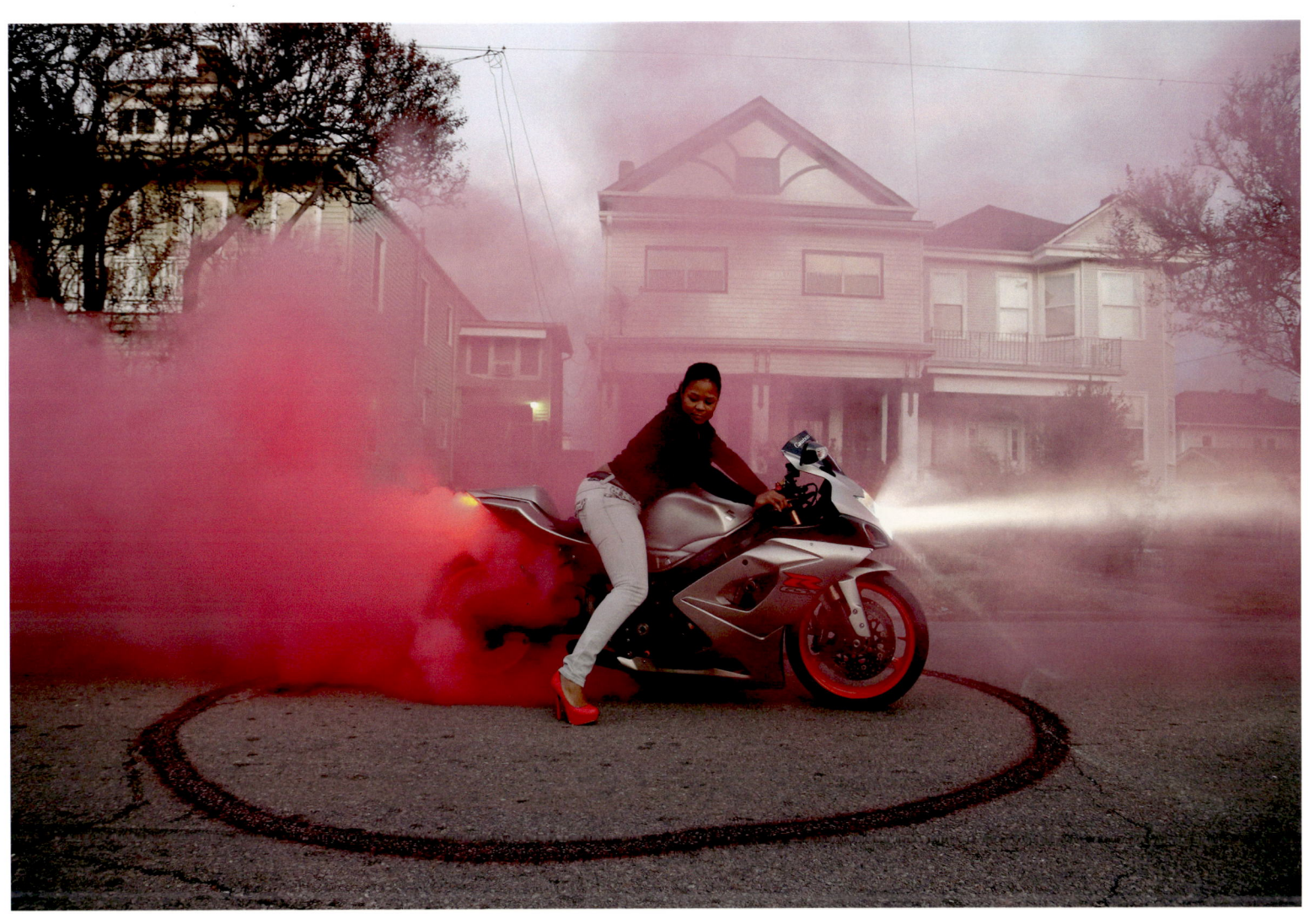

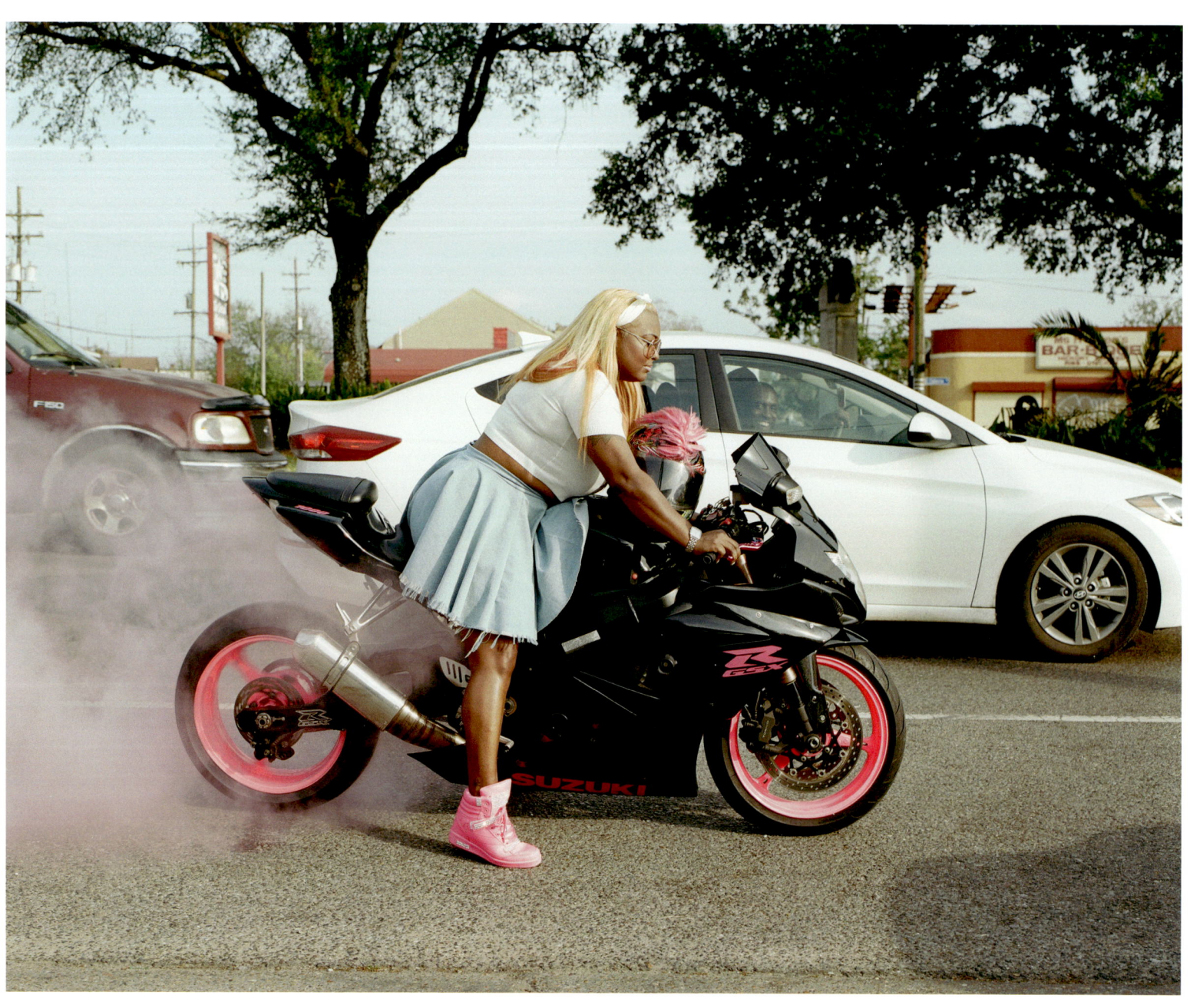

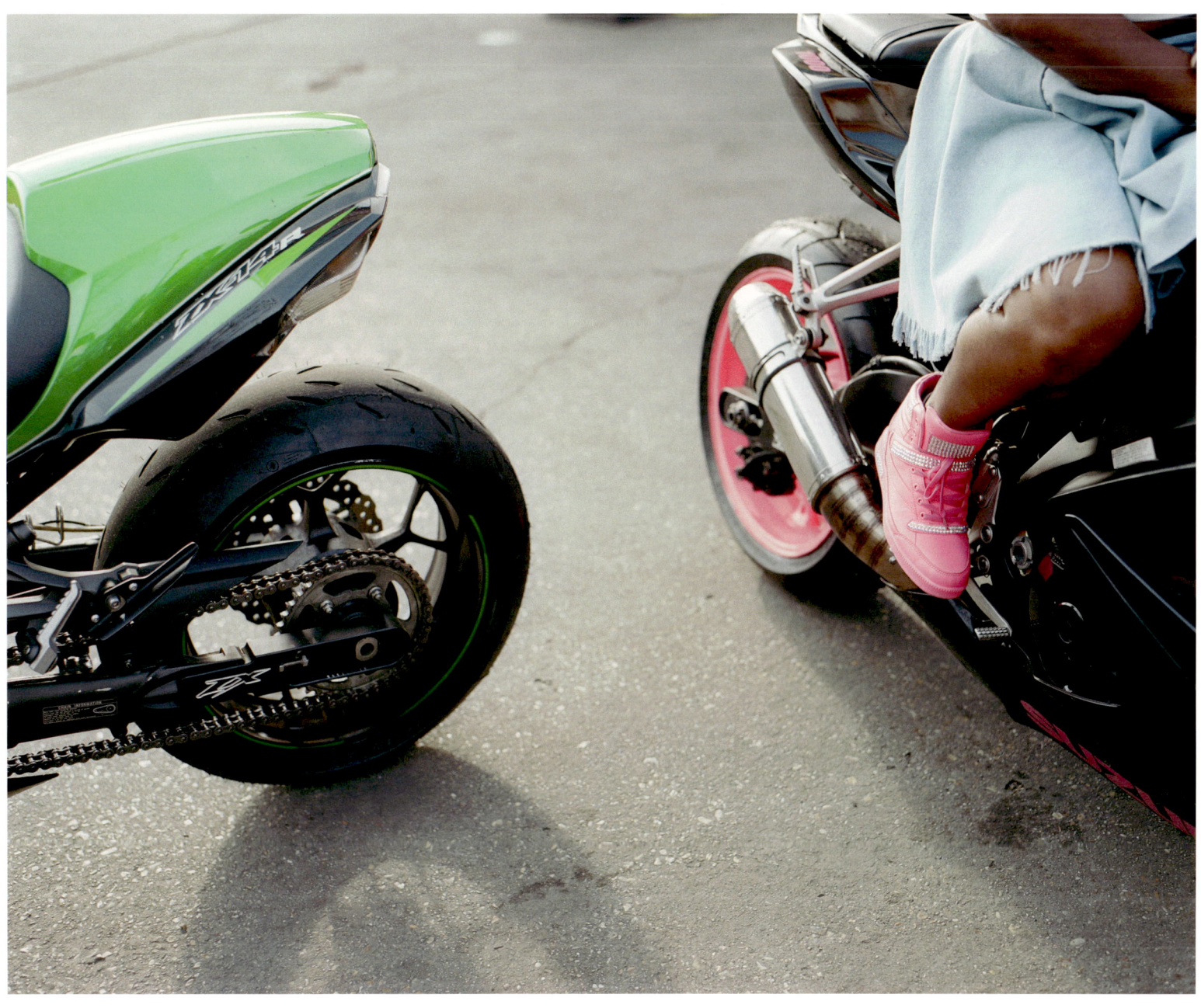

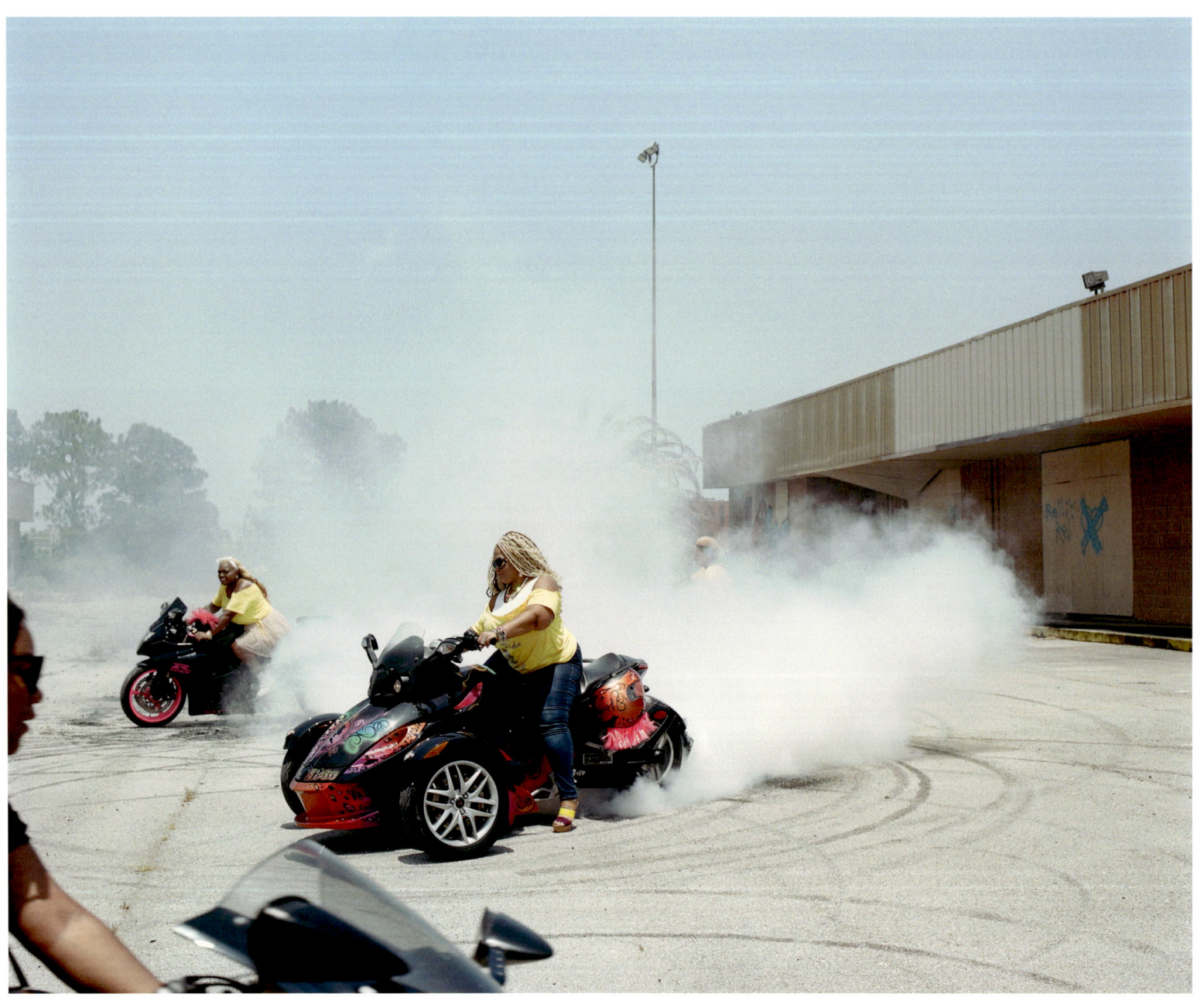

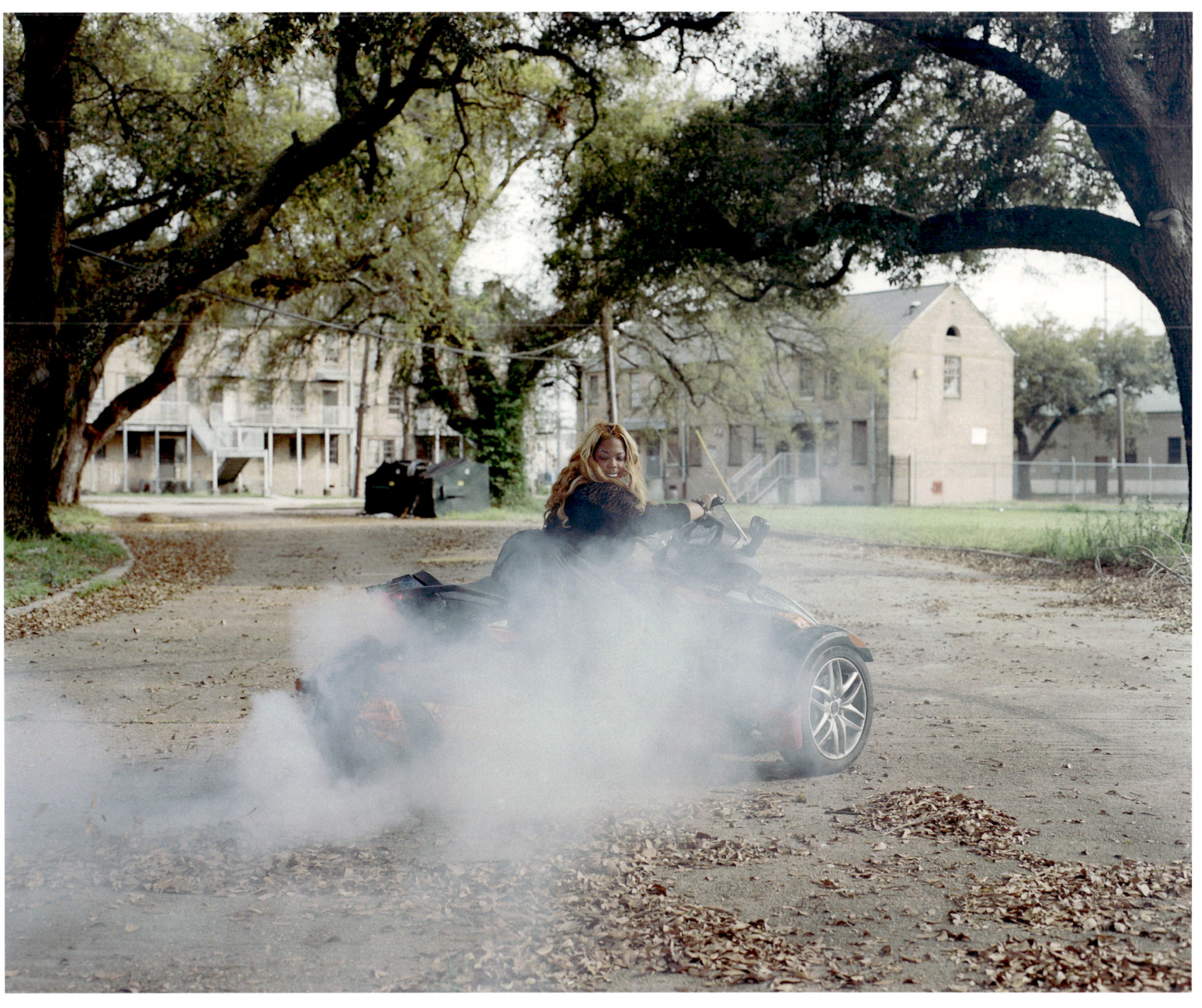

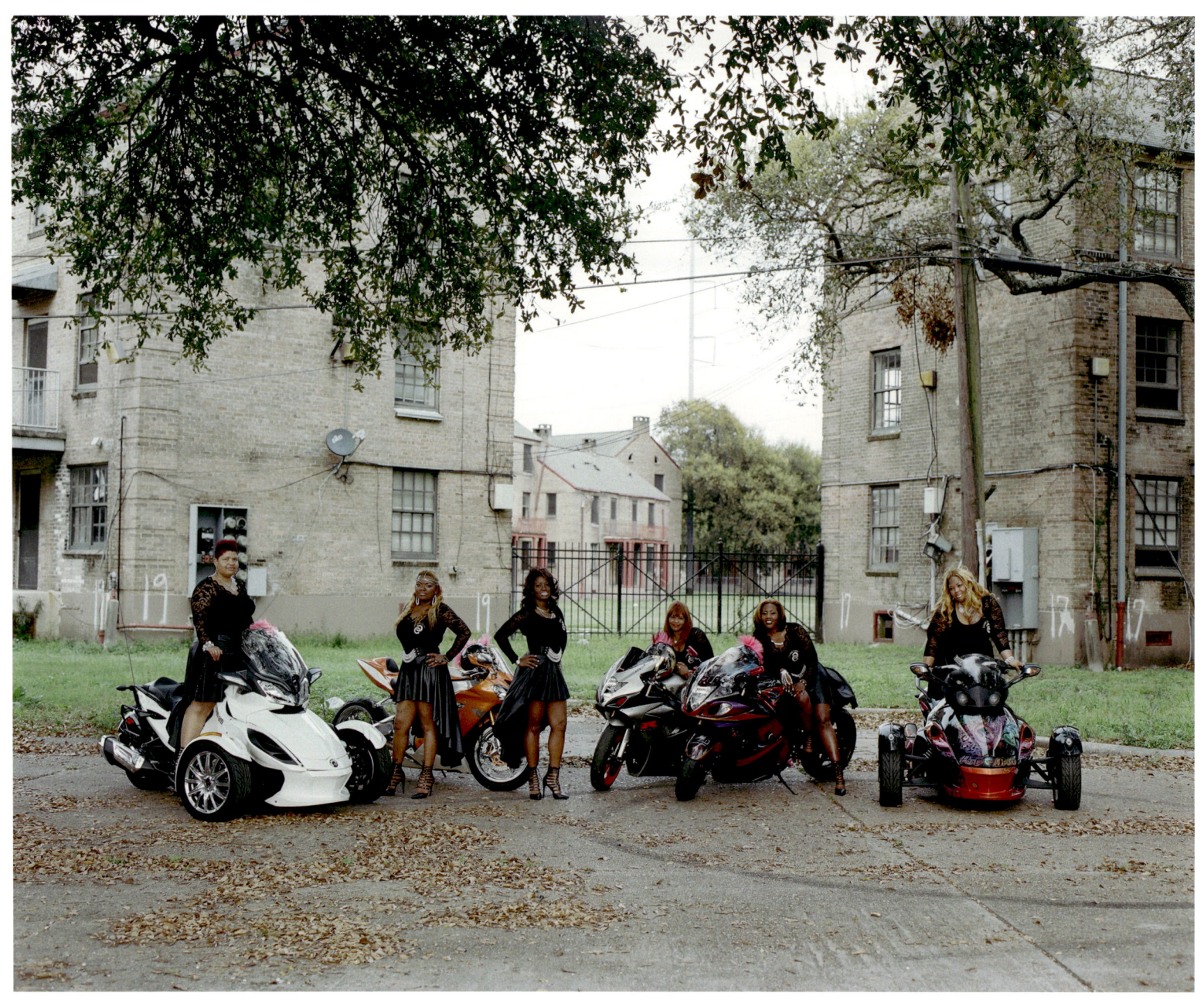

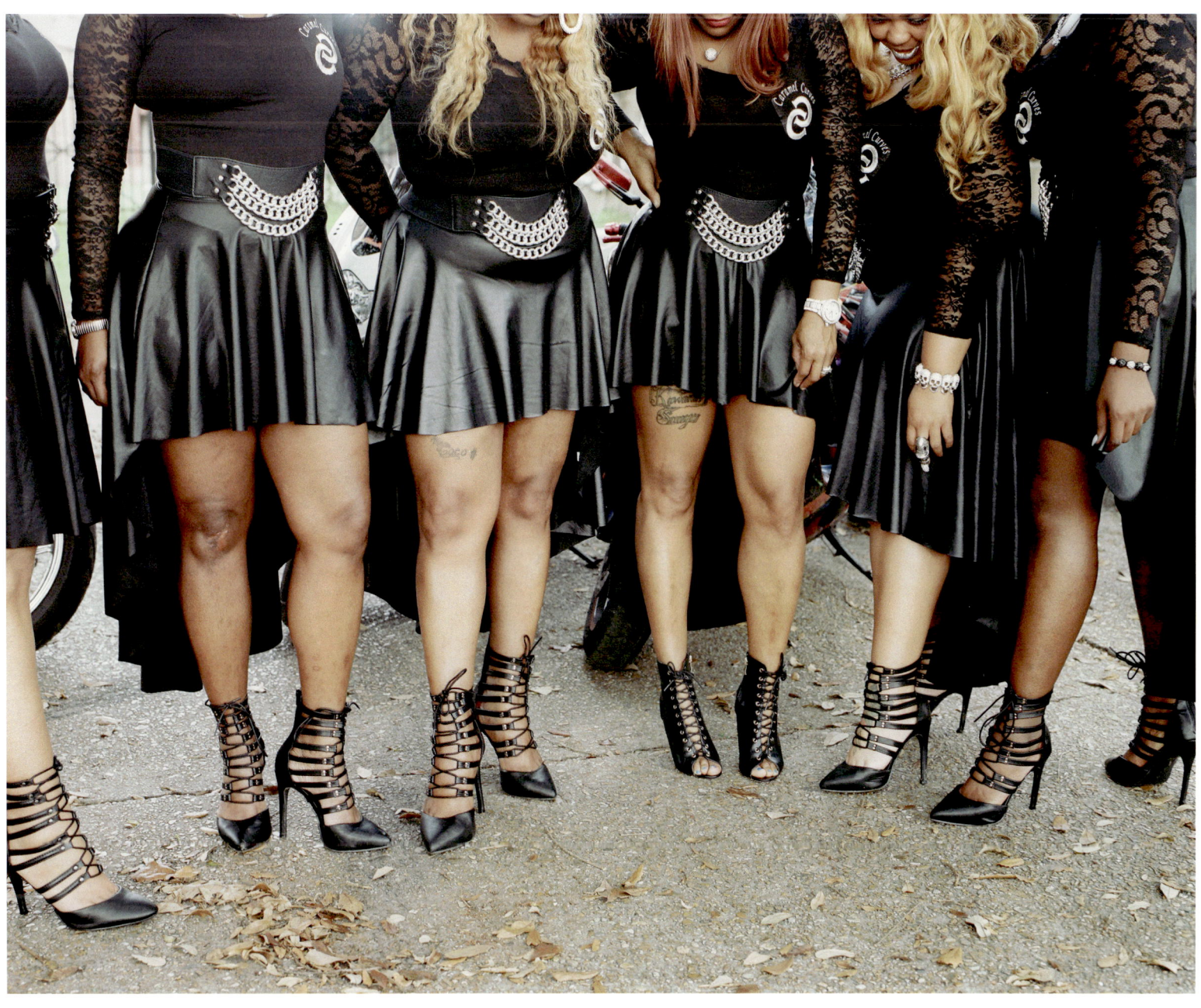

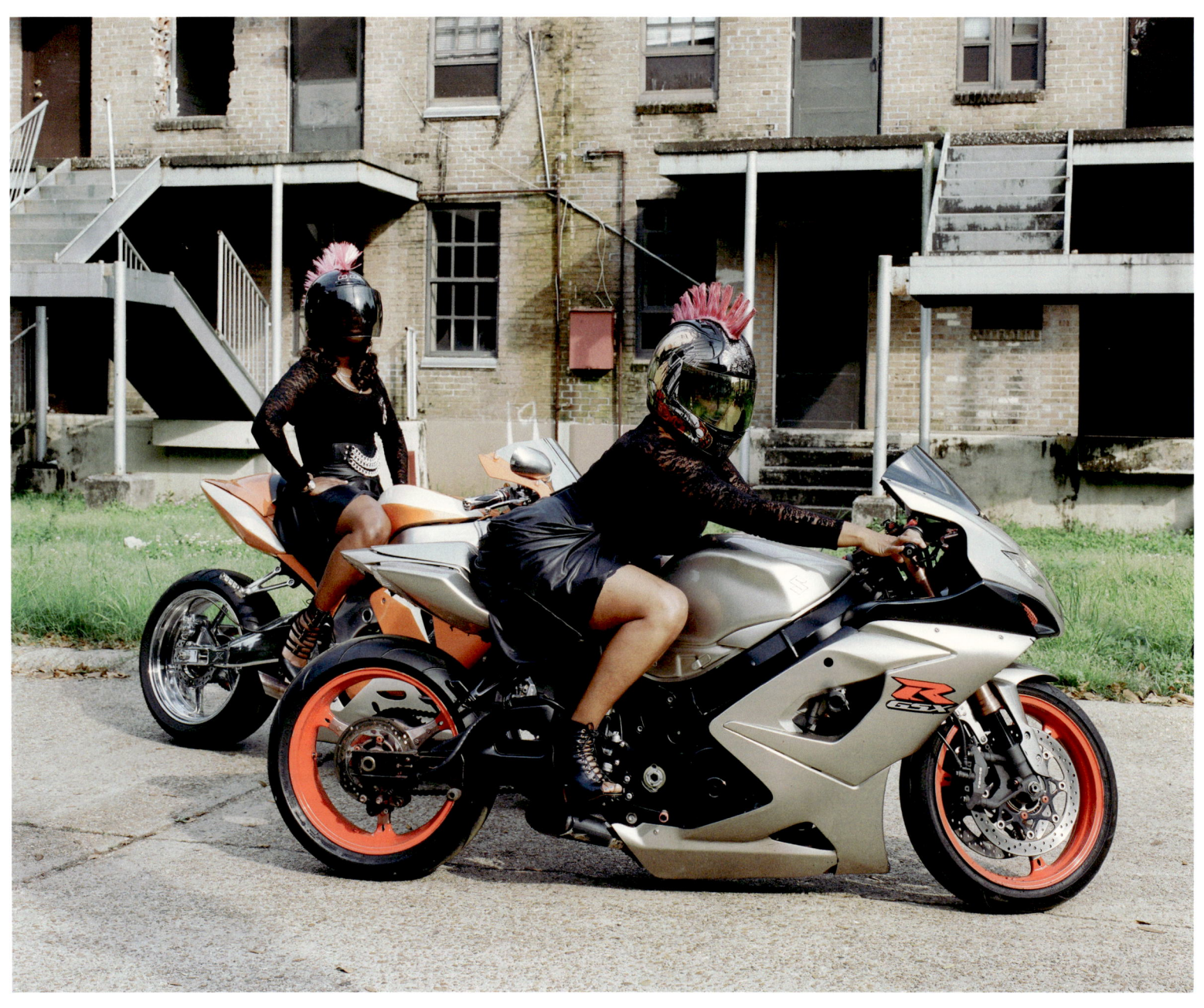

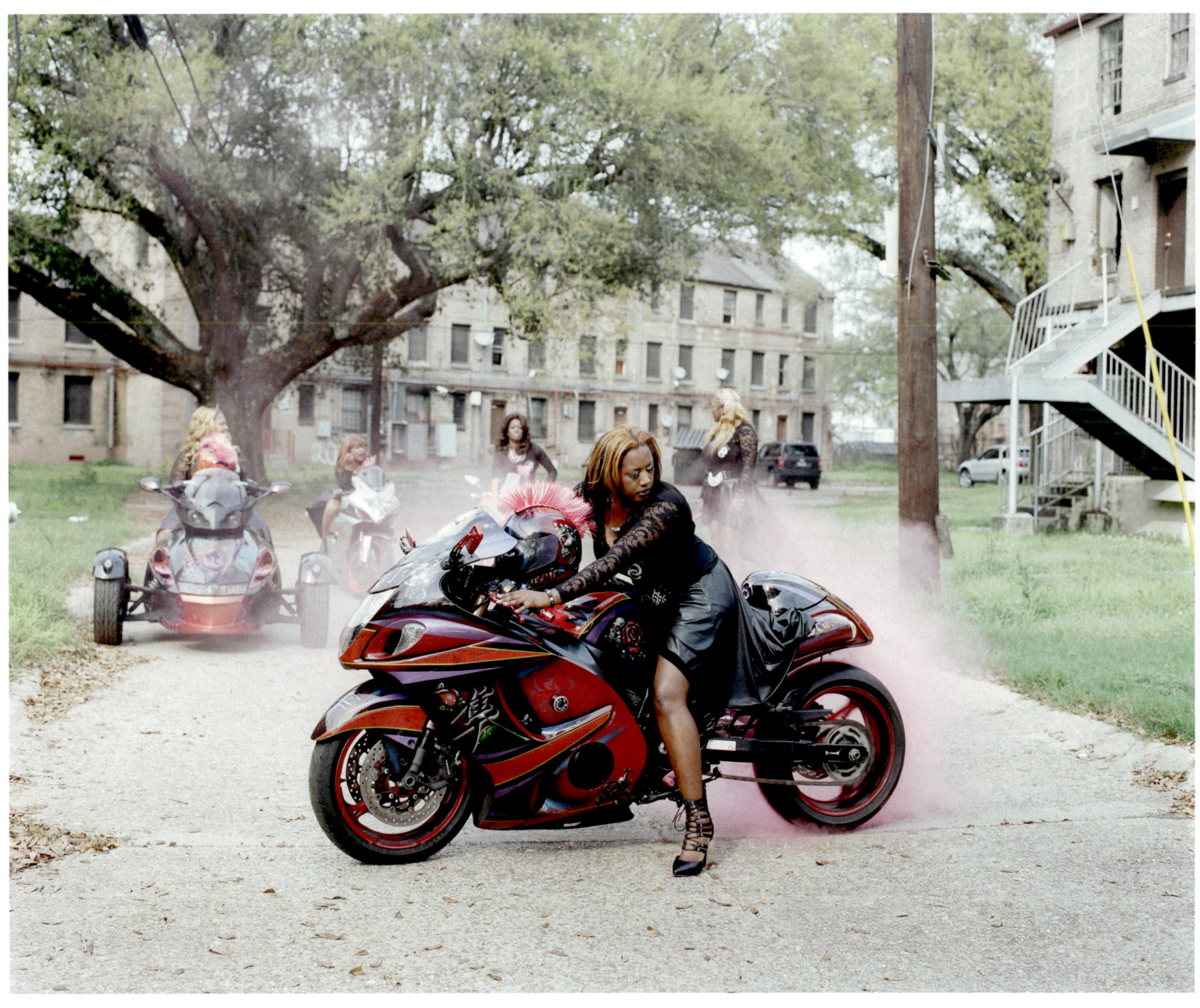

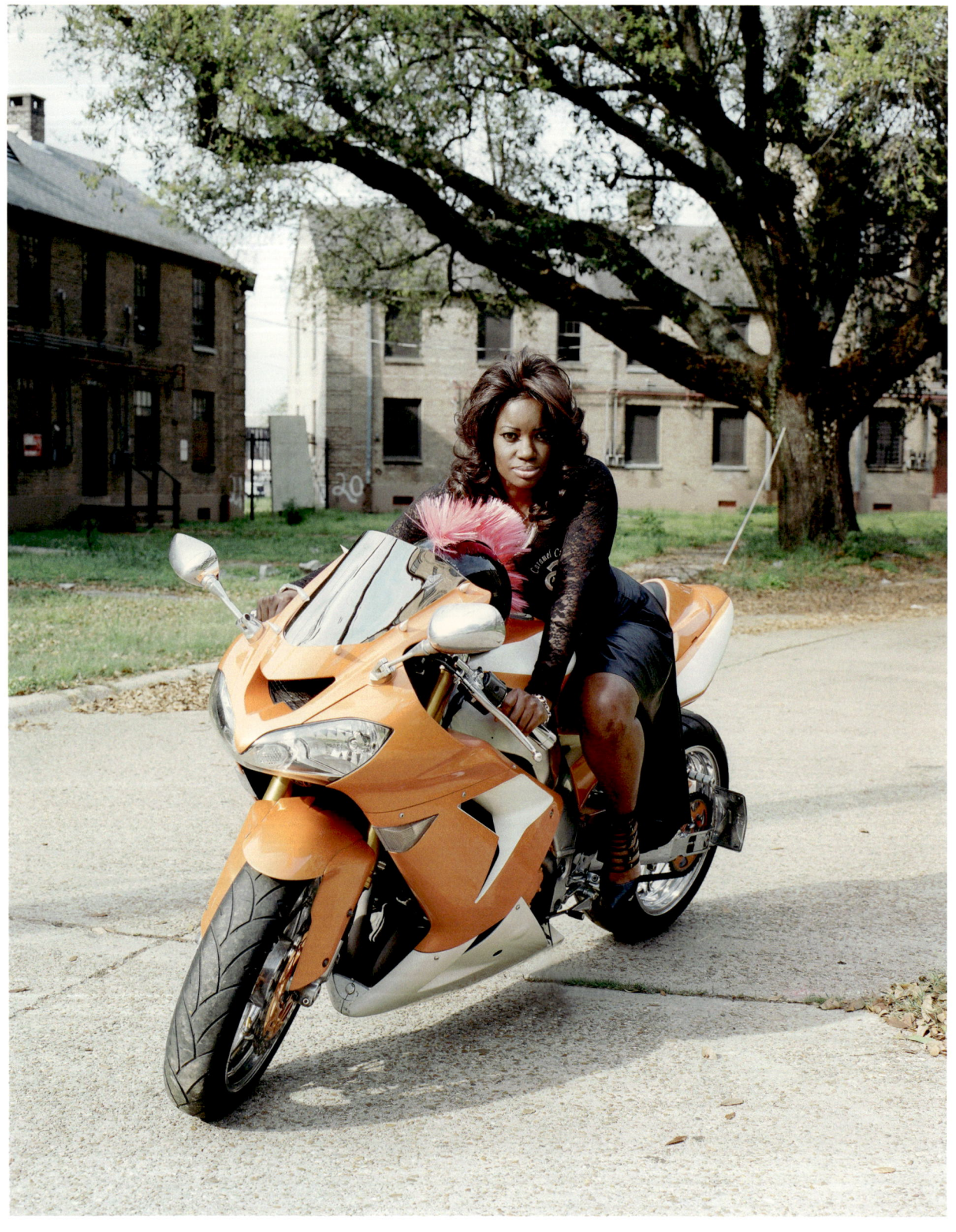

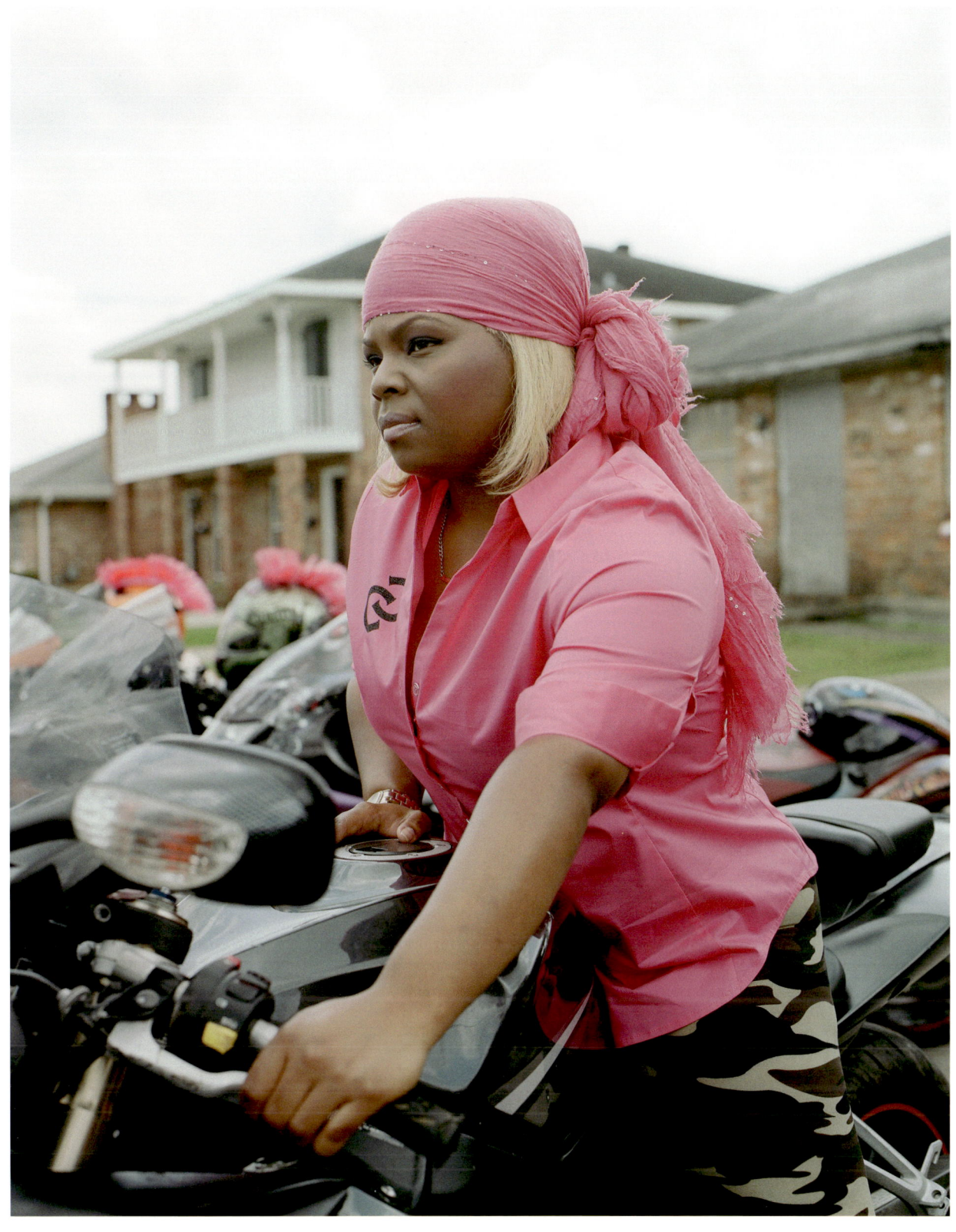

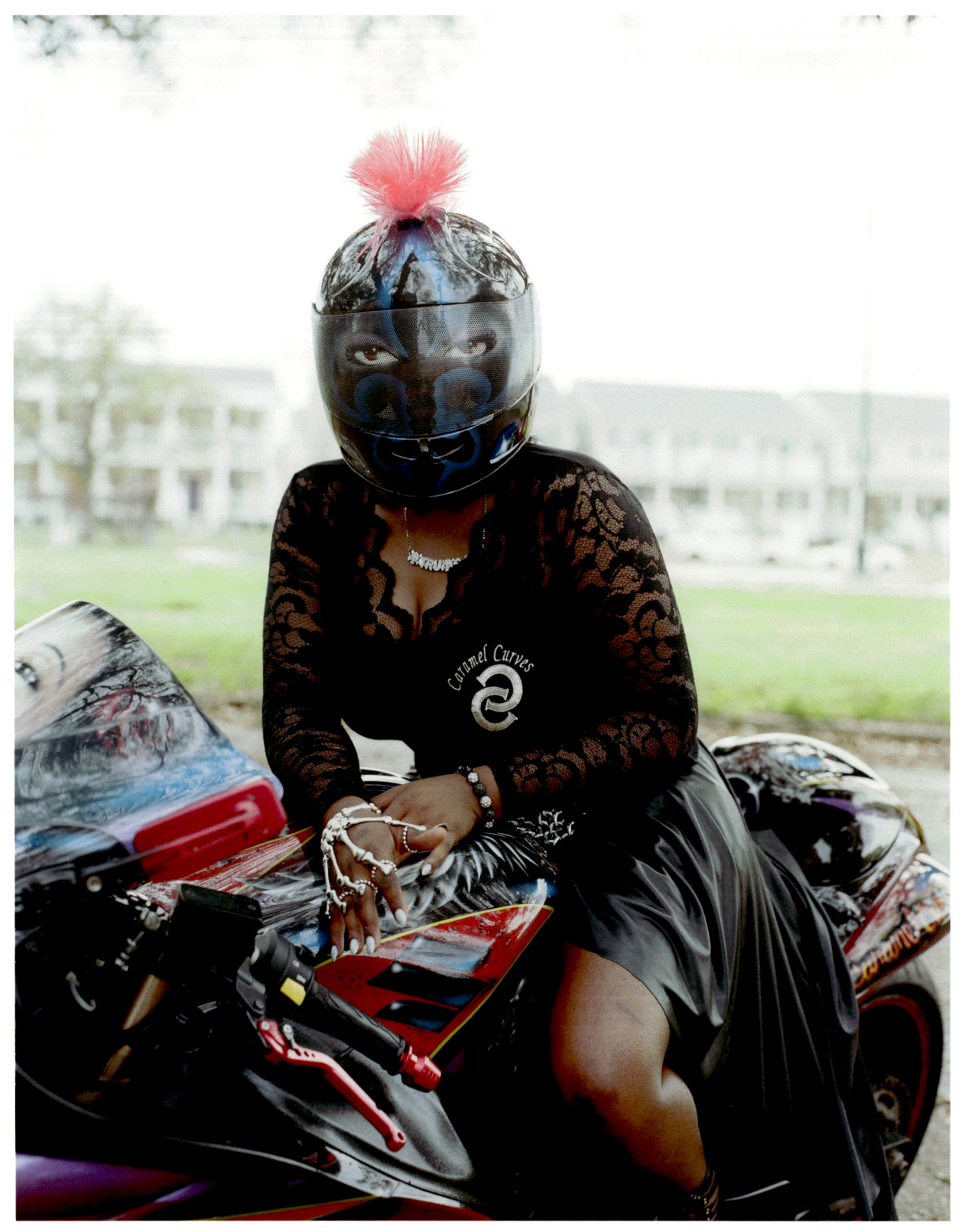

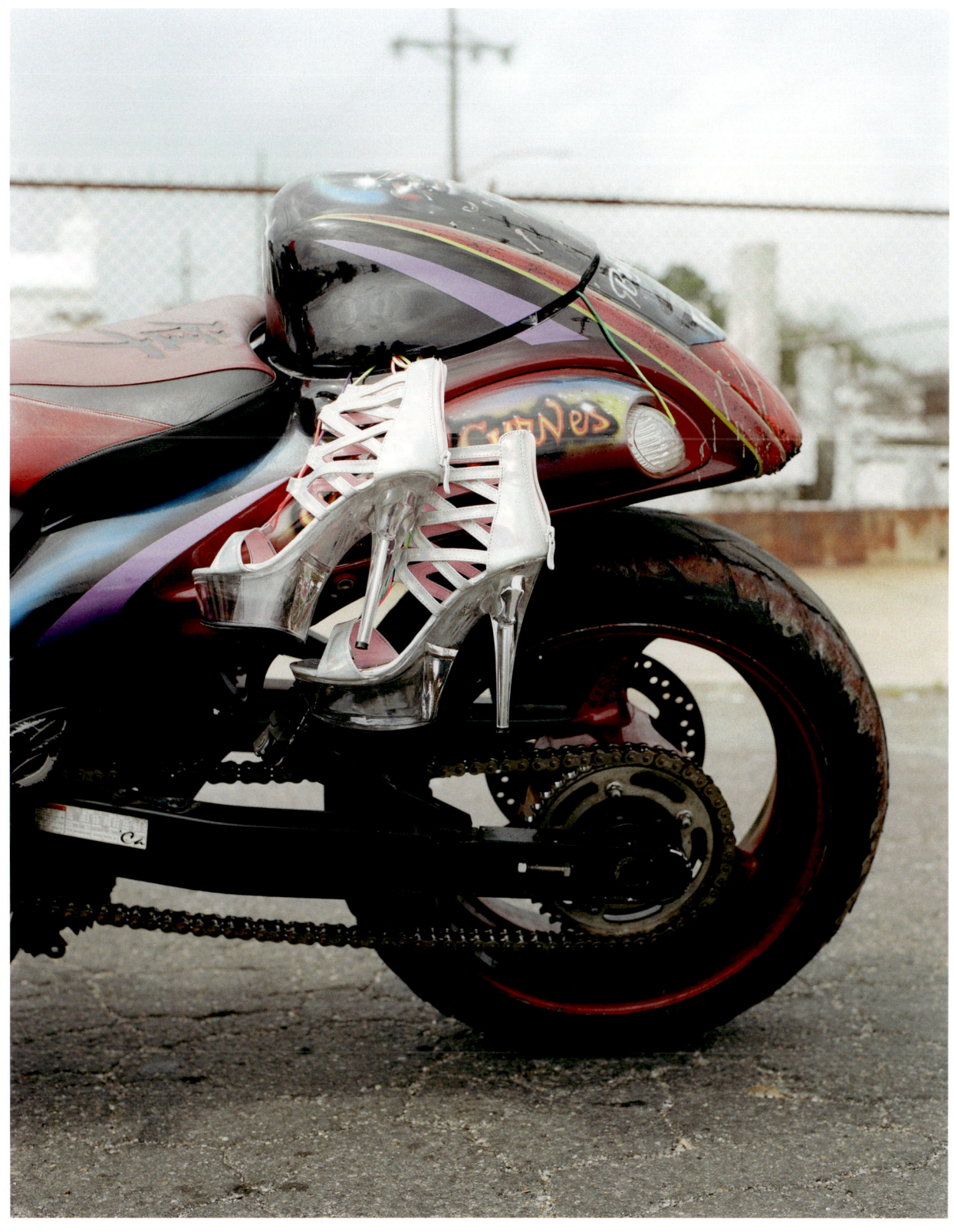

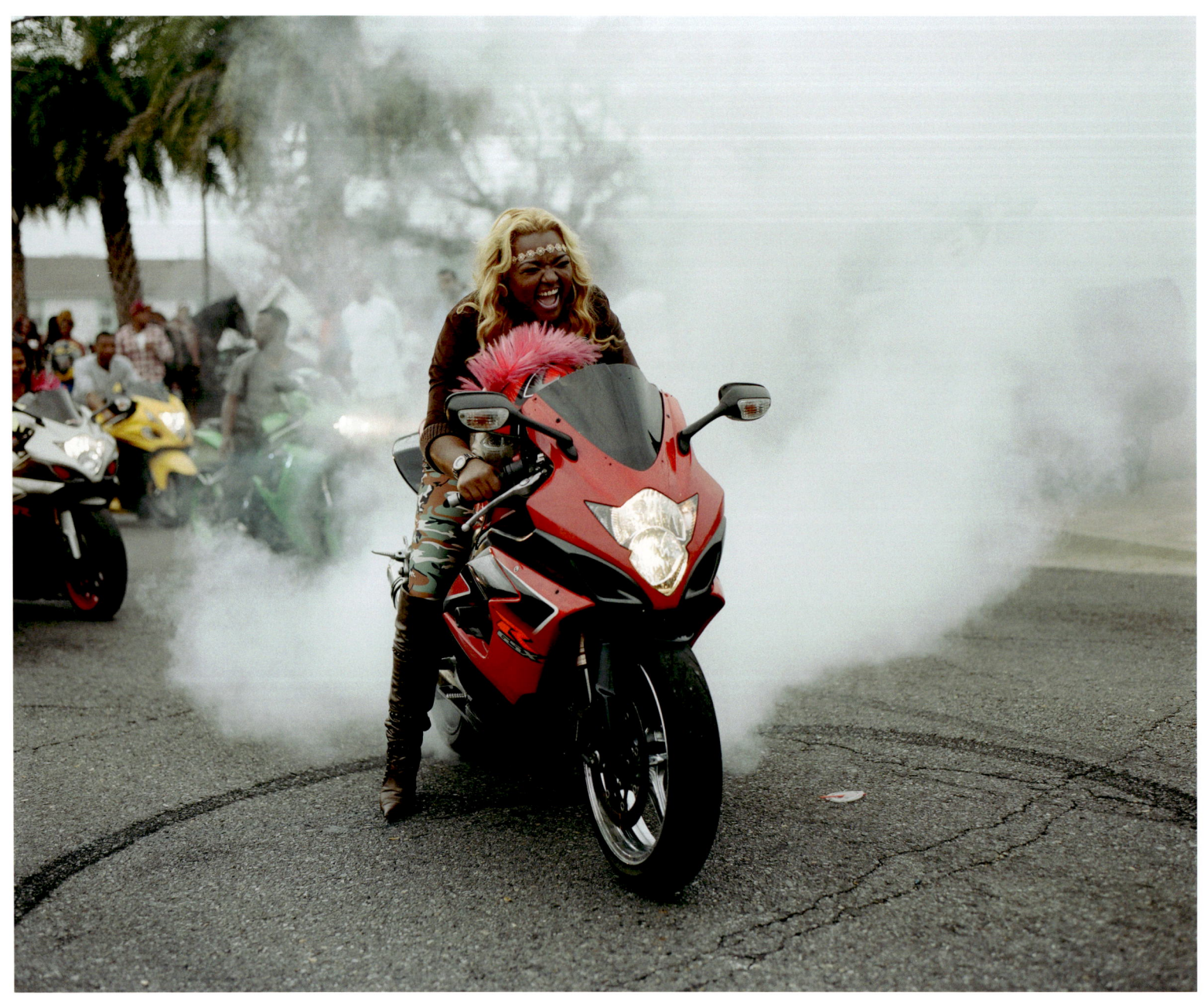

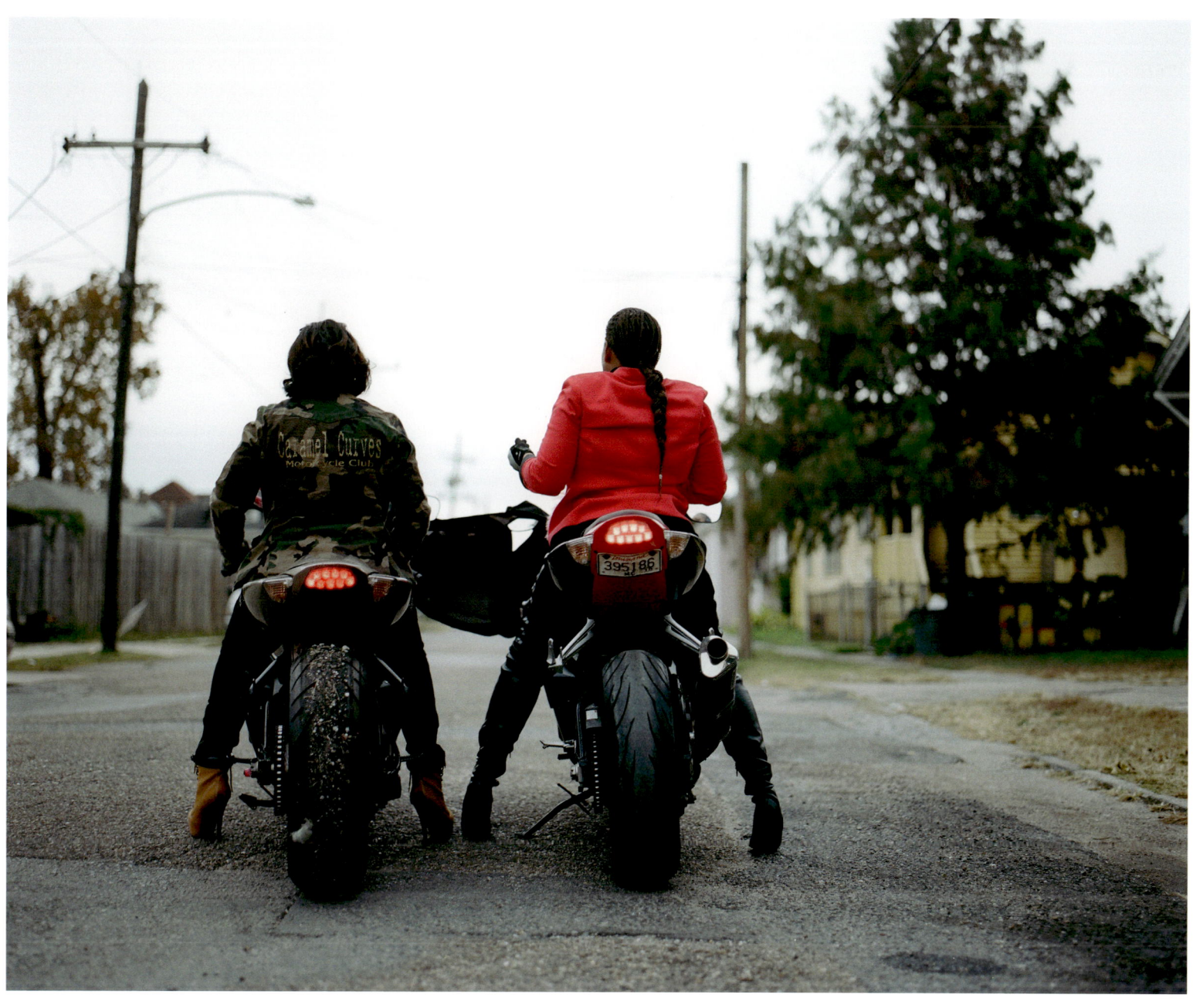

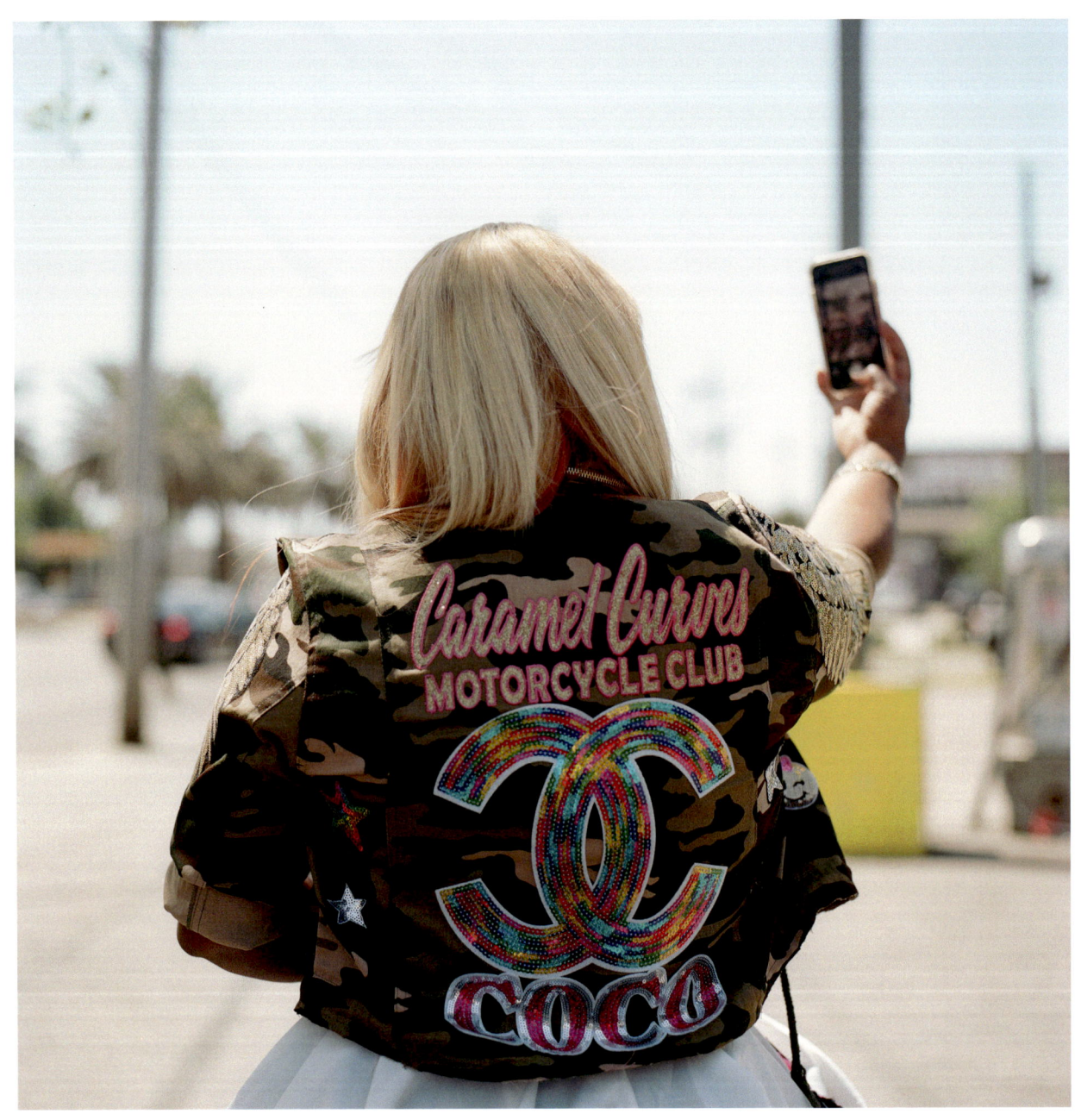

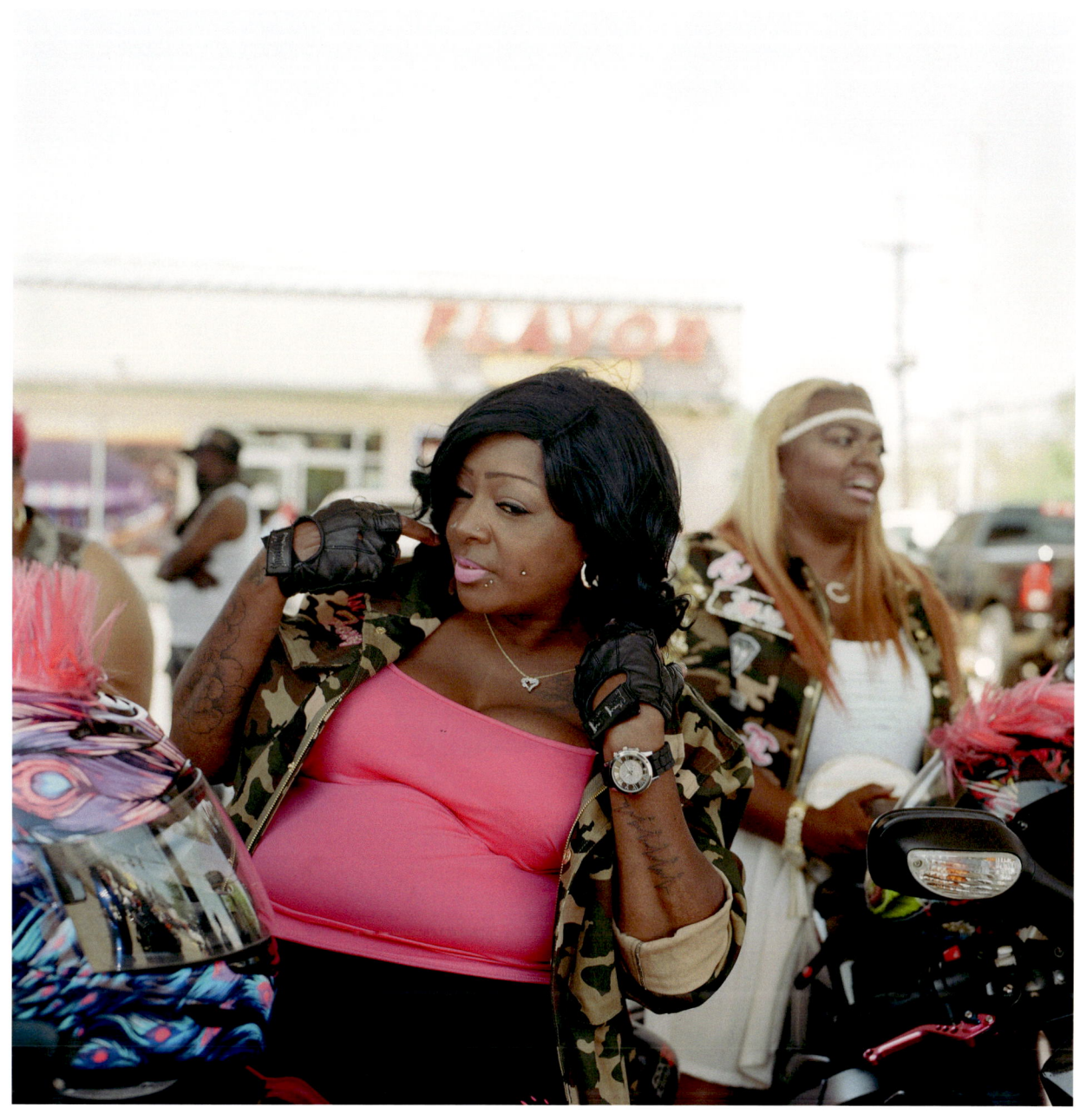

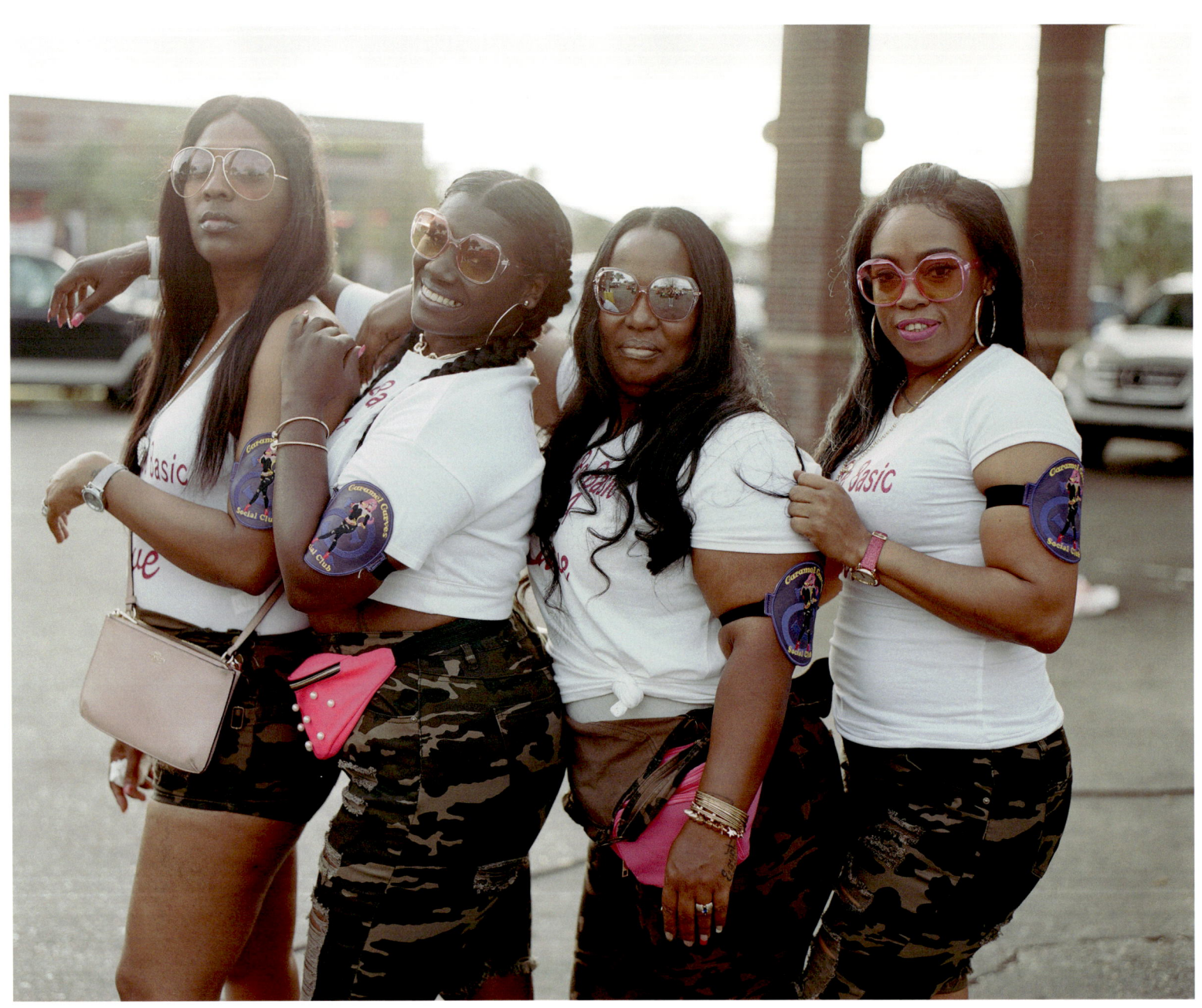

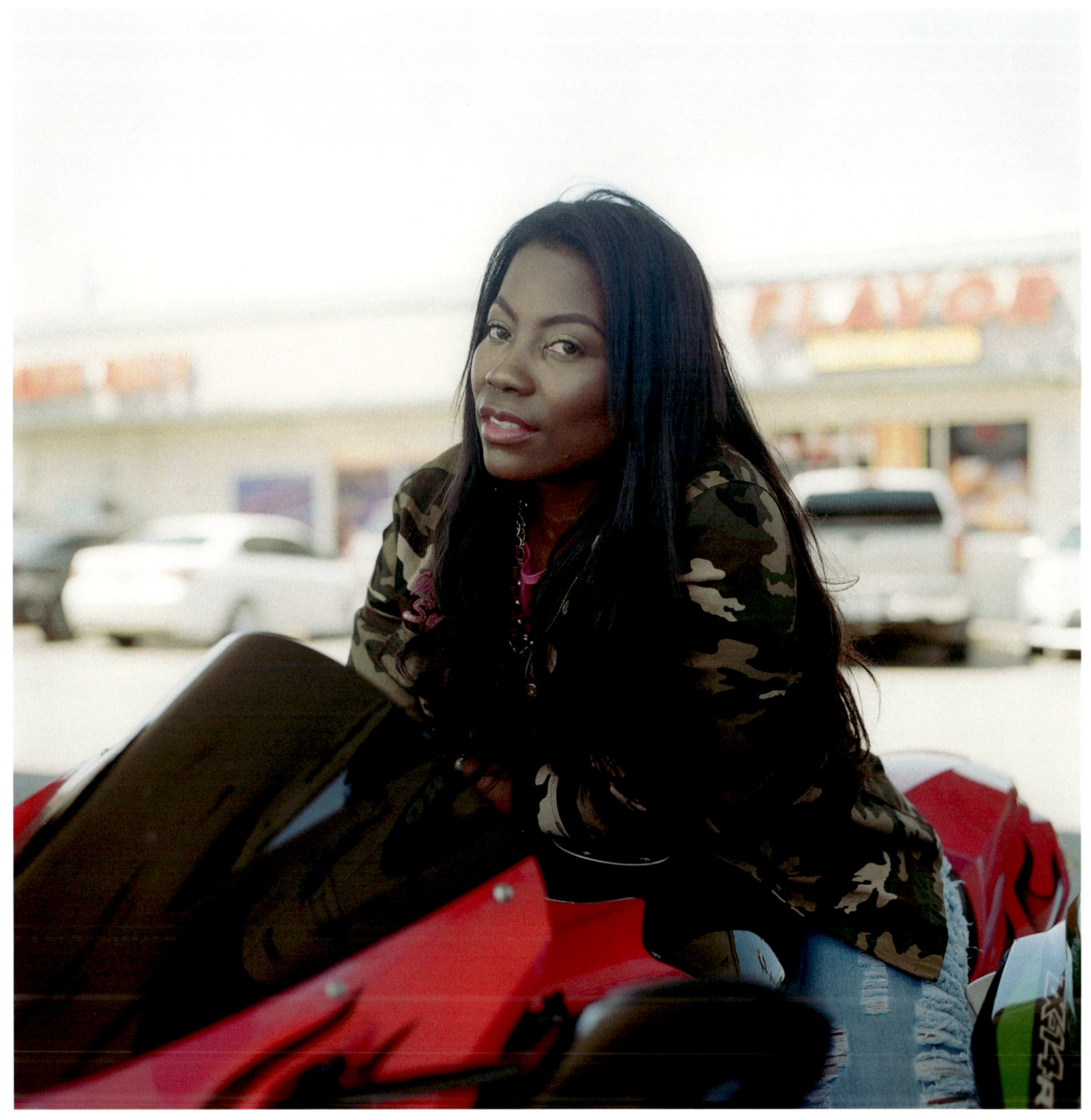

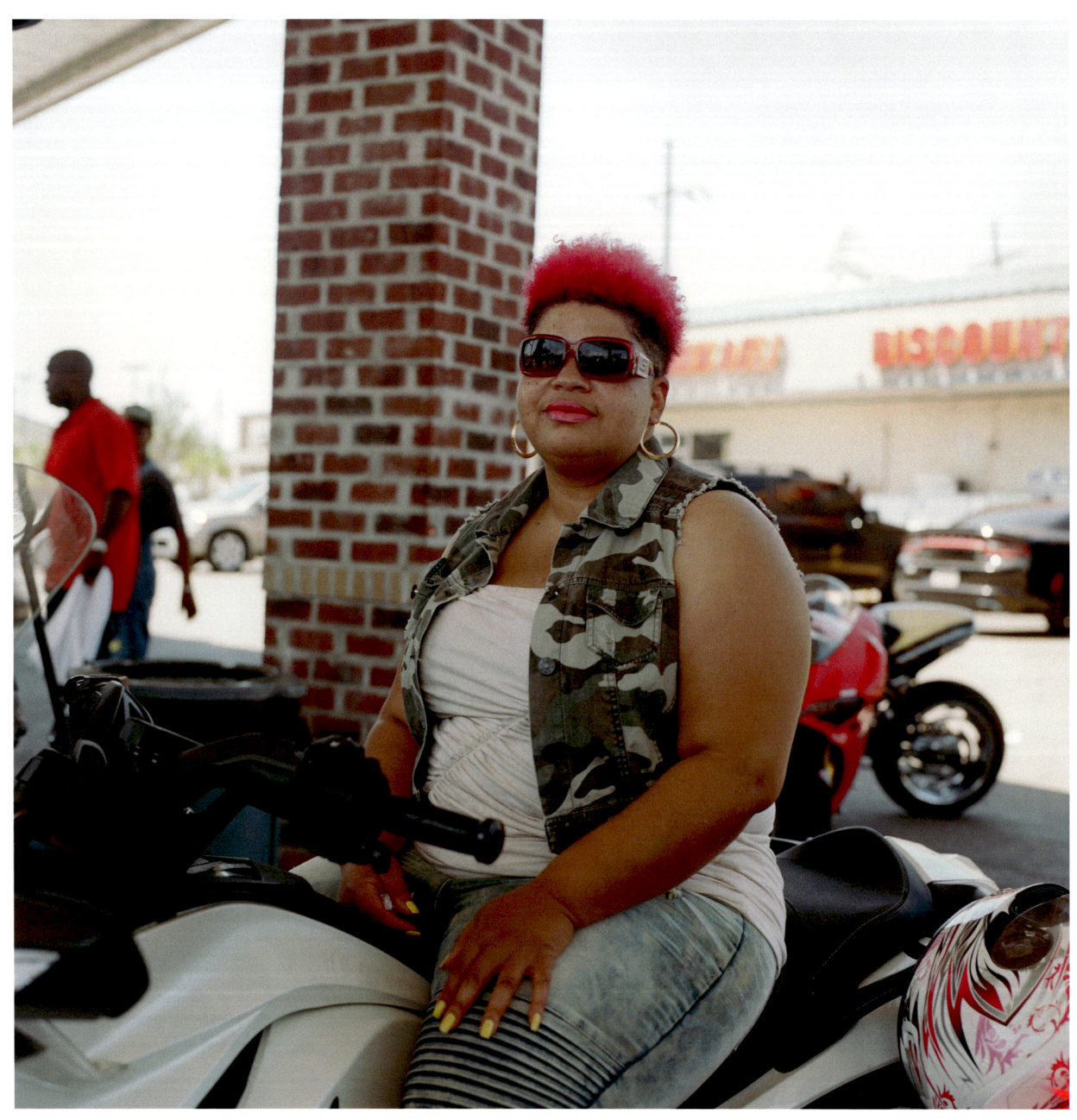

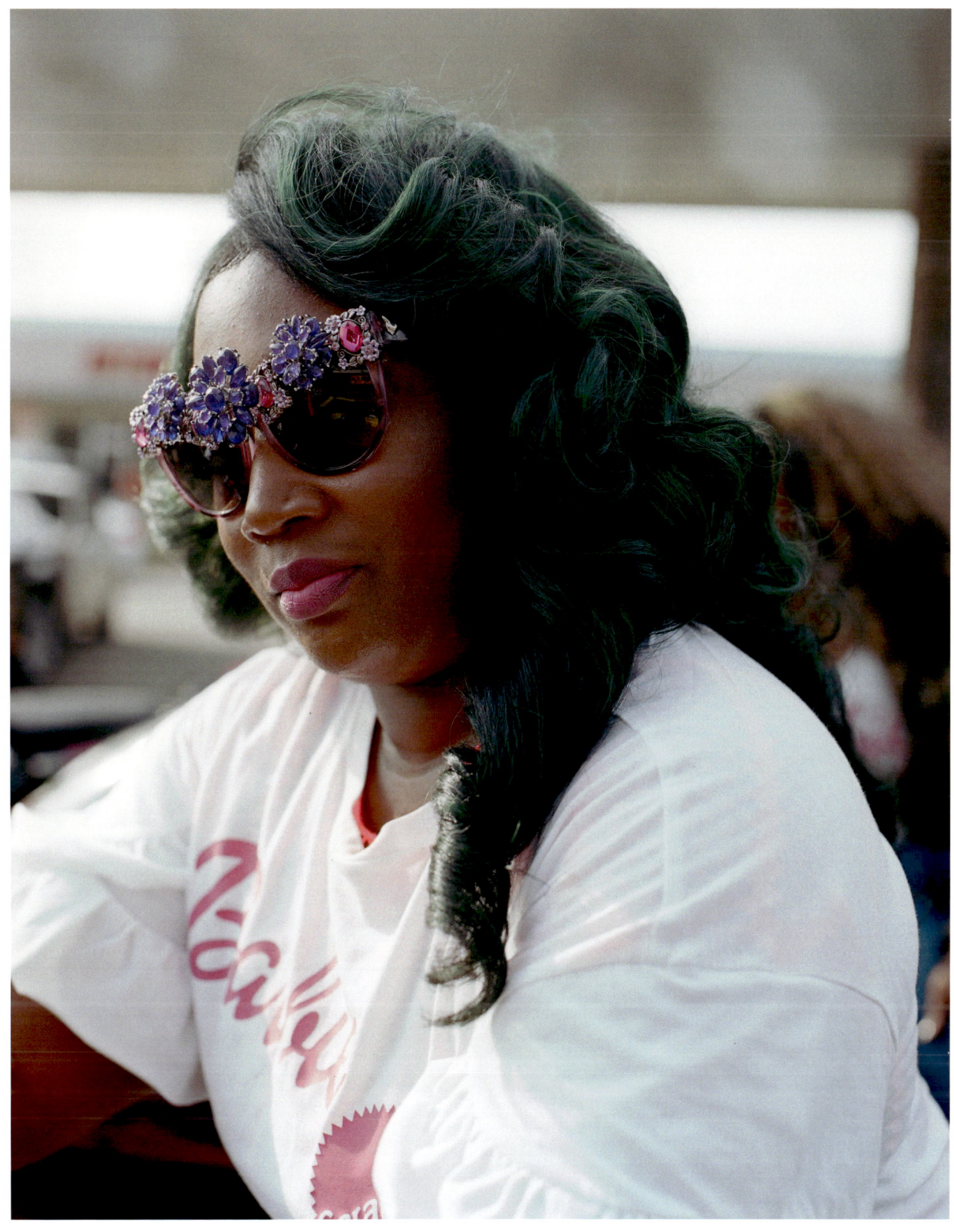

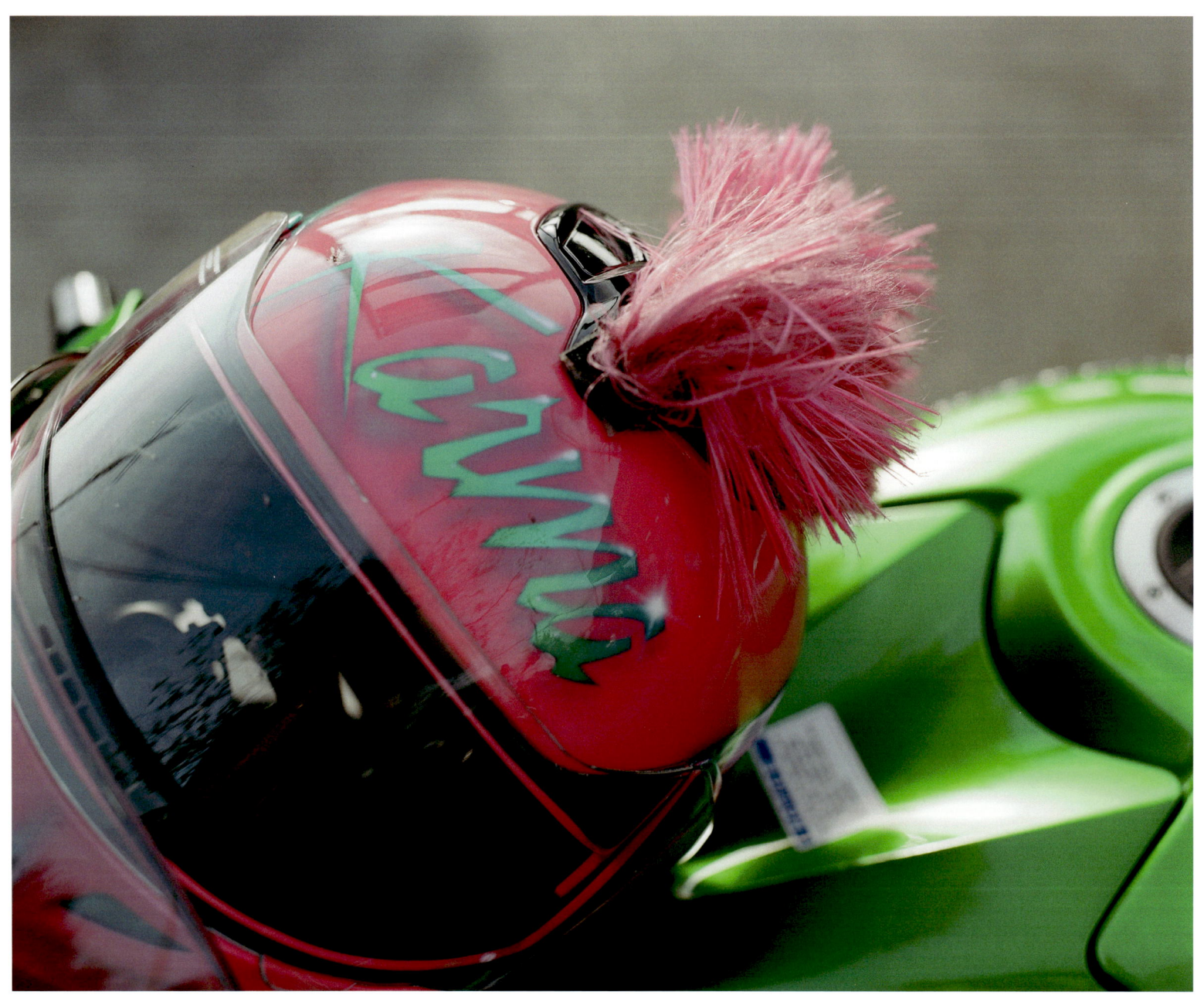

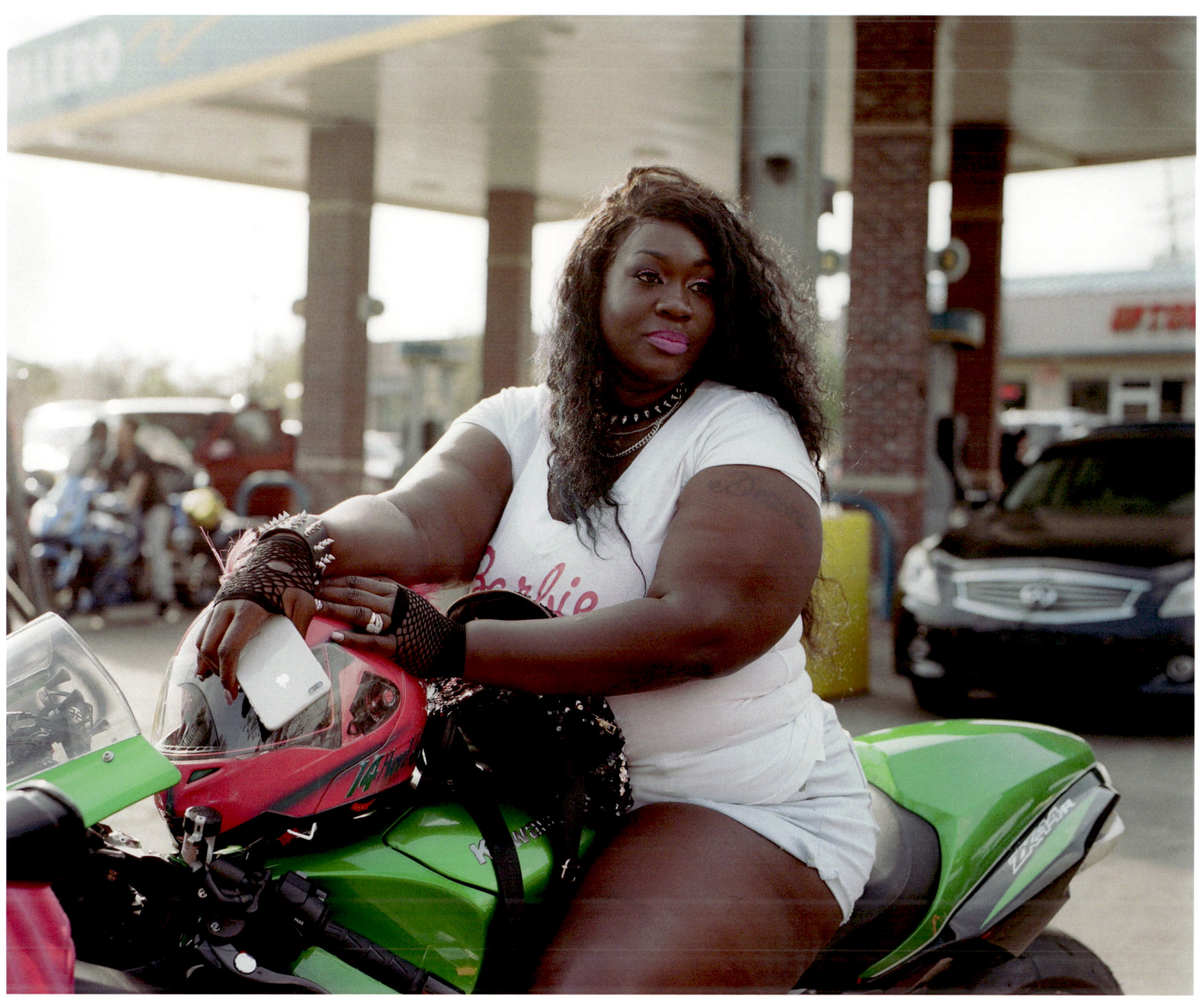

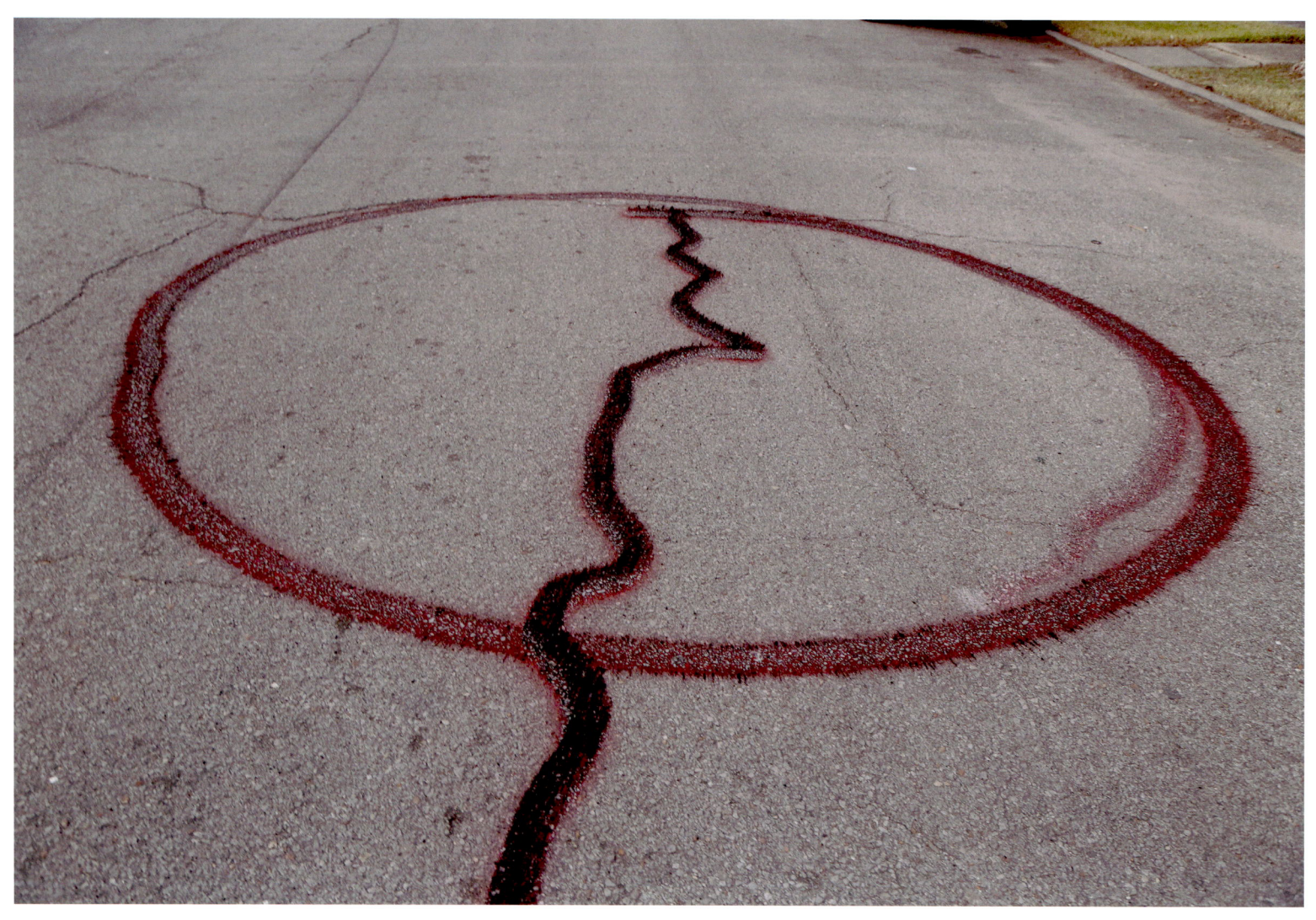

SOUTHERN RIDERZ

An oral history with Chris Carr, Louis Chancellor, Devence Hampton,
Kris Lewis Hampton, and Dwayne Monette as told to the Neighborhood Story Project

DEVENCE: The first time I saw a black man on a horse, it was my uncle. When I was small, he had a horse named Alexis, and they were with a club called the Midnight Riders. They rode in Mardi Gras parades. When he let me ride Alexis, I felt like I was on top of the world. I would ask him, "Hey, man, you going back by the horses today? I'm coming!" He got rid of her when I was about ten, but I still followed people with horses. Them boys used to come through my neighborhood in Marrero with fifteen to twenty horses. I followed them on my bike. When they stopped at the store to get them a beer or whatever, I'm going to touch the horse. I can't ride anywhere, but I'm going to sit on this one. Get off that one, get on another one. When they got ready to ride again, I got back on my bike. When I got home, I caught a whupping. "It's ten o'clock at night!" My only explanation was, "I was just following the horses!" That was my thing.

CHRIS: When I was growing up, my uncle had horses in New Orleans East. He was a part of the Buffalo Soldiers. One Thanksgiving, he brought me to the barn, and said, "Hey man, come feed the horse." I was like,

"Cool." Ever since then, I was excited. "When you taking me again?" Sometimes I'd just pop up there after school and be waiting on him.

LOUIS: When I was about twelve, I used to ride my bike to Pontchartrain Horse Stables to help out. I came up under a man named Harry Hill. He used to take it serious. Horses used to eat before he ate! Every morning, he was up at six o'clock. If he wasn't there by six, you knew something was wrong. I started out cleaning the hallways and other people's stalls, washing and feeding horses. I wanted to jump on everybody's, but they were telling me no. My daddy said, "Don't worry about it, I'm going to go buy you a horse." The next week, I had a horse. It teaches responsibility—to become a man in life.

CHRIS: It kept me out of trouble. It just clears your mind.

LOUIS: Just you and your horse. Every other thing is blocked out.

CHRIS: Later on, I became a Junior Buffalo Soldier. Louis was, too.

LOUIS: The Buffalo Soldiers go deep in history. Many people take it really seriously, but growing up, I considered it a horse riding club we did for pleasure.

DEVENCE: They stayed on my mind. One day, in college, I woke up and decided, "I'm going to buy a horse." I called my mom, my girl, and Dwayne, and told them what I did.

DWAYNE: I was just in shock. We grew up together in Marrero—childhood friends. We stayed right down the street from each other. I didn't believe Devence until one day he told me to take a ride with him. It felt like I blinked my eyes, and we were in some woods. We pulled up, and I saw two horses standing out there. Devence said, "Yeah, that one right there mine." "What?! You serious?" Her name was Dream. It was on from there. I never thought I'd be riding a horse, getting up close and personal, looking this sucker in the eyes.

DEVENCE: I was studying criminal justice and living in New Orleans East. I had to go back and forth across the river to feed her. I asked Dwayne, "Hey, man, I need you to do me a favor. I need you to take care of this horse." Dream developed a stronger bond with him than with me, and then someone gave me another horse.

DWAYNE: When Devence told me he was about to get rid of her, I said, "Hold up, man, you can't let her go like that."

DEVENCE: I gave her to Dwayne, and he still got that horse to this day.

DWAYNE: Dream ain't going nowhere. She's going to stick around. She's the veteran. She trains everybody who comes in. If they can't handle her, they can't handle nothing, baby.

SOUTHERN RIDERZ

CHRIS: When you say you own a horse, people's eyes get big. They ask, "Where you staying? In the country?"

LOUIS: Right up the street!

CHRIS: They never think to have horses in the city. We call ourselves the city cowboys.

LOUIS: In Mardi Gras parades, the Dirty South Ryderz [formerly Southern Riderz] are known for the biggest, prettiest, baddest horses.

DEVENCE: The club's been running about twenty years now. We're horse advocates. If it's not a culture, make it a culture. And if it is a culture, make it stronger. We have thirty-one members, who are in their twenties through their fifties.

CHRIS: Some of the older cats might not ride like they used to, but they still own horses, and come to the stables to feed them.

DEVENCE: I catch them riding in the dark around their barn—nobody around.

LOUIS: There's no drama. We get together to ride, barbecue, do backpack giveaways and food drives.

CHRIS: It's a brotherhood. They have other riding groups as well. Besides the Buffalo Soldiers, they have the 504 Boyz…

DEVENCE: New Generation…

CHRIS: The Iron Shoe Steppers. Even though we're all a part of different groups, we are still considered all as one.

DEVENCE: I don't do this for competition, I don't do it for money, I don't do it for no other reason beside I like horses.

CHRIS: It's a lifestyle.

DWAYNE: While you're out there working on your car, I'm in the stall cleaning up, doing the hard stuff.

LOUIS: Most people look at it from just the riding point of view.

CHRIS: Like I tell anybody, horses are ninety percent work and ten percent fun.

LOUIS: Every day.

CHRIS: If it's storming outside, you got to come feed the horse. I had many days when I walked to the barn in a flood just to make sure every-body's horses ate.

DEVENCE: It's crazy, but that's part of my pleasure. I look forward to cleaning the stalls, feeding the horse. I ain't going to lie, if something's going on, I'll say, "Hold up, I got to go feed my horses!" And I don't mind. The day we go riding—my wife, Kris, will tell you—I get up at six in the morning. I've got to make sure all my stuff is laid out. I got to make sure my wraps are clean, and everything is perfect, because somebody's going to be out there taking pictures, and I want to look good for the camera.

KRIS: Not *he* look good, just the horse!

LOUIS: Your horse look good, you going to look good, regardless. Any horse you get on, you want them to be clean, fed, pretty, dressed— an eye-catcher.

DEVELOPING TRUST

DEVENCE: We are known for bringing our horses to parades, but you can't just put on a saddle, hop on a horse, and go take a chance on him running over thousands of people. There's got to be a trust. If he gets antsy and you get nervous, too, you're going to lose him. That's how you going to end up in a crowd with your horse kicking. You have

to start off by letting them get accustomed to people. Through those experiences, he's going to trust you. You've got to take your time with it. There are levels. The horse is going to tell you if he's ready. When you're approaching the crowd of a parade, you're going to feel the horse. If you feel his body tensing up, you've got to back him out of there, and bring some other horses with him. He'll feel a little more comfortable following.

CHRIS: They're group animals, so when they see another horse acting calm, they calm down with them.

DEVENCE: Eventually, you can progress to him going in by himself.

CHRIS: To get them ready for a second line, or Mardi Gras parades, you can take them to watch the high school bands practicing. You sit there, keep them still, and let them hear all the music playing while the flags are waving and the batons are twirling. Sometimes when we are by my mama's house in the Ninth Ward, we'll go by Carver High School because they have a big band. We won't even ride—just sit on their backs and let them chill to develop that trust.

LOUIS: We also have police officers who come to the barn, pull up in their unit cars, and put on the sirens. Horns. Right down the street from one of the barns is Interstate 10. We go underneath the bridge and let them get used to the cars overhead. Some of the horses freak out; they want to rear.

DEVENCE: That's a tough one.

LOUIS: Let them get used to the echo underneath the bridge. This is where, in a second line, people run up to you. Kids try to pet your horse. People don't watch their kids that closely at parades. There's a chance they're going to run underneath the horses; you've got to be aware of all that.

DEVENCE: The kids ain't scared. We're all out here on these horses, and they look pretty calm, but those are our relationships; bonds.

CHRIS: People don't understand—if I put you on a horse and you don't know how to ride, and you go out there and hurt somebody, or hurt the horse, then I'm responsible for it. Now I'm looking at lawyer fees and vet bills for the horses…

DEVENCE: Every now and then, I'll put a kid on the saddle. I was at a second line and one little boy must have followed me for fifteen blocks. I'm looking at him and I see me! I'm like, "Alright, let me let him ride," because I know the feeling.

PARADING

LOUIS: At this point, we do ten Mardi Gras parades a year. That's the whole two weeks. Every day we ride. One day, we ride two times. People of all races and ages be clapping for you, saying, "Ooh, I like that horse there! That horse pretty." You catch the crowd.

DEVENCE: They always going to have that older man going, "Make them step, nephew!"

LOUIS: "Make them dance!"

DEVENCE: Some horses do dance.

CHRIS: Some horses like to hear the band. I had a horse that liked to hear Mardi Gras Indian music. When he heard the Indians chanting, he'd start dancing on his own. I didn't tell him to do nothing, and he started stepping.

DEVENCE: If I could tell the crowd anything, I need them to do me a favor and don't ask me where I rent this horse from.

CHRIS: "Who own the horse?"

DEVENCE: They say, "That's your horse, for real?" When I say yes, they say, "Oh, he lying." And we kind of understand, because, for one, we're in New Orleans. For two, many of us are not over thirty years old. None of this stuff makes sense to them.

MENTORSHIP

CHRIS: Knowing that we all are young and have pretty horses feeds my fire. We can be hard on each other sometimes. If I see someone in the club slacking, I'll be like, "Hey, man, your horse looking raggedy, let's get it together."

LOUIS: Criticism.

CHRIS: Criticism among ourselves keeps us going. The older cowboys raised us; they used to stay on us. One day, I pulled up, my horse was dirty; my tag was pink, purple, yellow, and blue. And they looked at me and said, "You not riding with us." I had to take my horse and go back to the stall. I couldn't ride that day. Now I see why. When you pull out, you want to set an example. Like right now, if I'm riding on all blue, everything I have on the horse will be blue. I might even be dressed in blue.

LOUIS: Everything that happened, that he thought was cruel and mean, paid off.

CHRIS: It made us better horsemen.

DEVENCE: They used to call me Party Boy. In parades, I liked to make my horse dance, and an older cat named Rob would fuss at me, saying, "Dev, you always doing that!" I told him, "You're just mad because you're old, and your horse don't do all that." After ten parades, he told me, "My horse do anything your horse do." He had it walking sideways, and I was outdone. At horse club functions, I'd be standing on top of tables, partying. He'd be, "Hey man. Not in here. Get on down." He was just always the disciplinarian. I remember standing on top the horses and riding down the street. I still do it from time to time, but it can be reckless.

LOUIS: The horse might start taking off.

DEVENCE: Now I'm making the transition to where I'm a mentor. I hear myself saying, "Hey, man, people watching us, you can't do that."

KRIS: I'm a high school teacher, and I tell my students, "My husband rides horses, and if y'all want to ride, he's not opposed to you coming over." I have a student who is in the club with them, because he was serious about it.

DEVENCE: This is a lot of love. There are a lot of life lessons being learned out here, man.

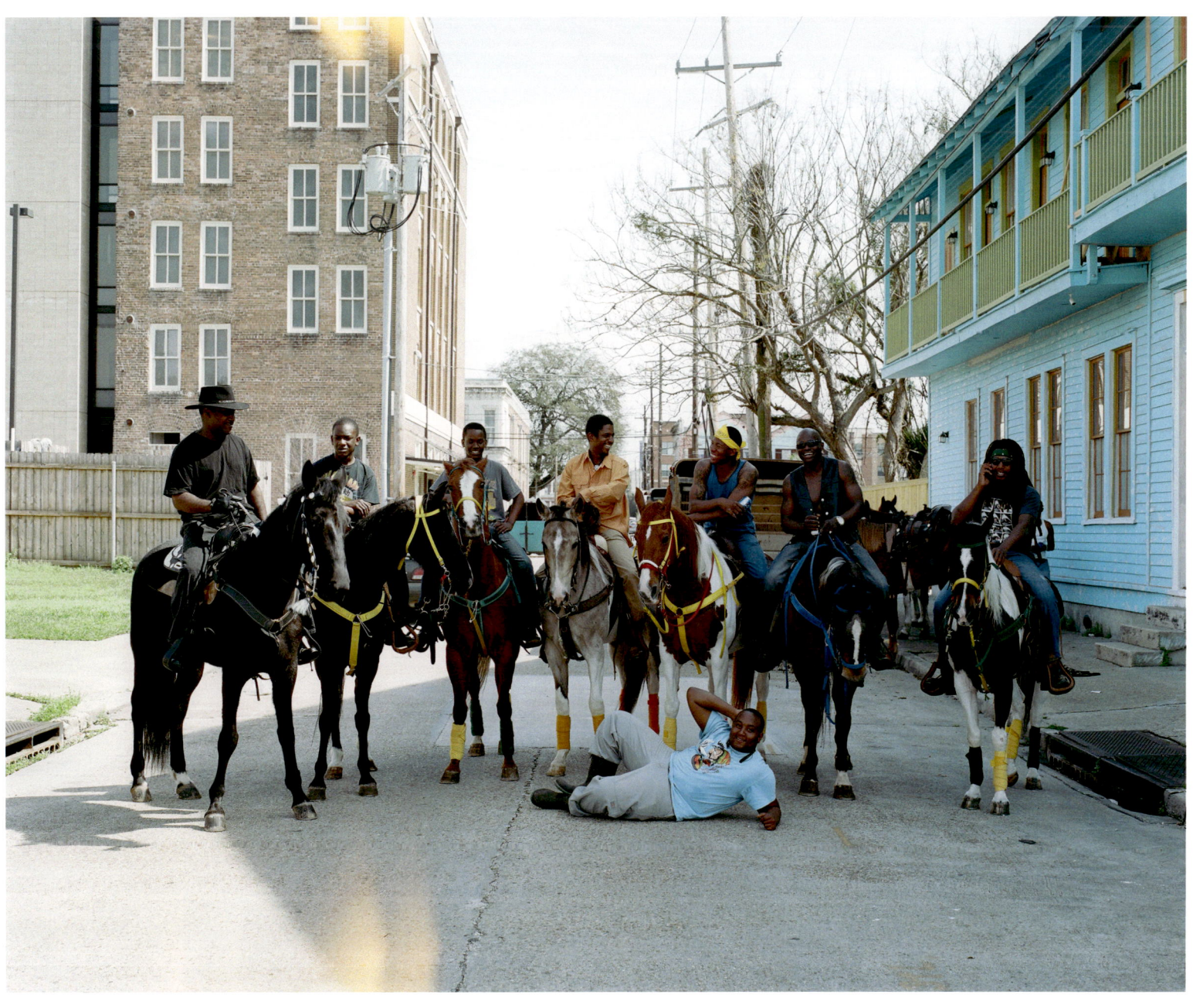

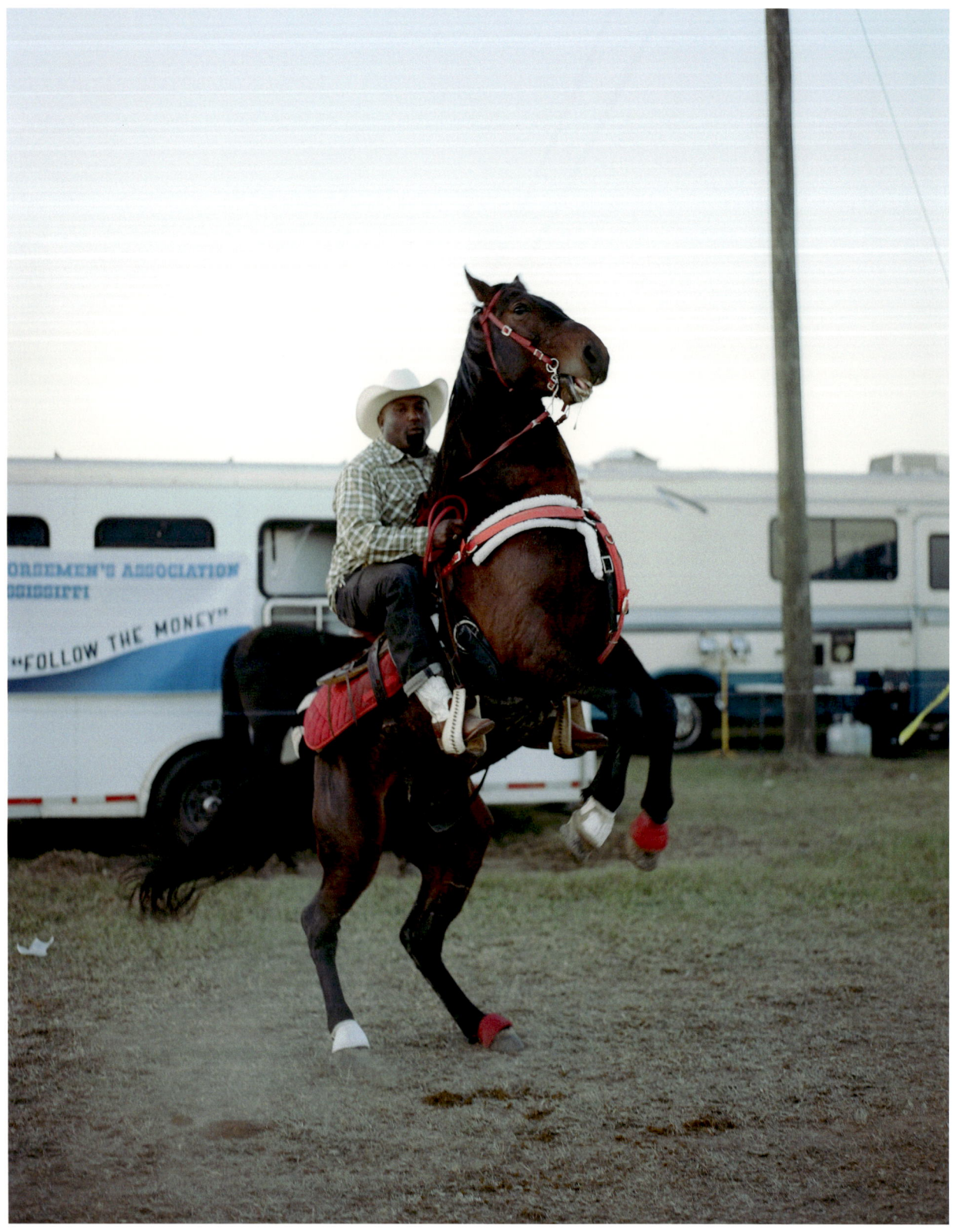

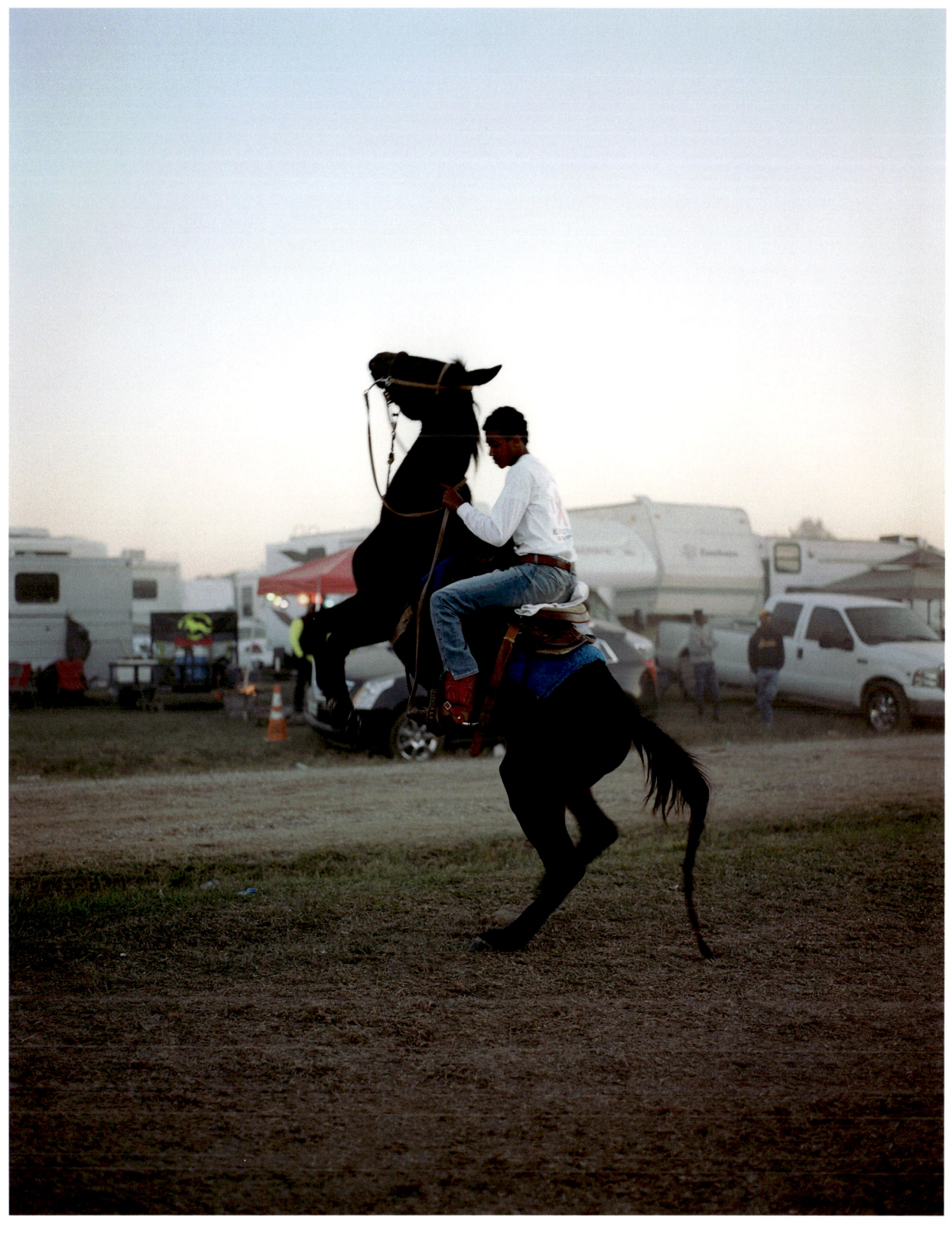

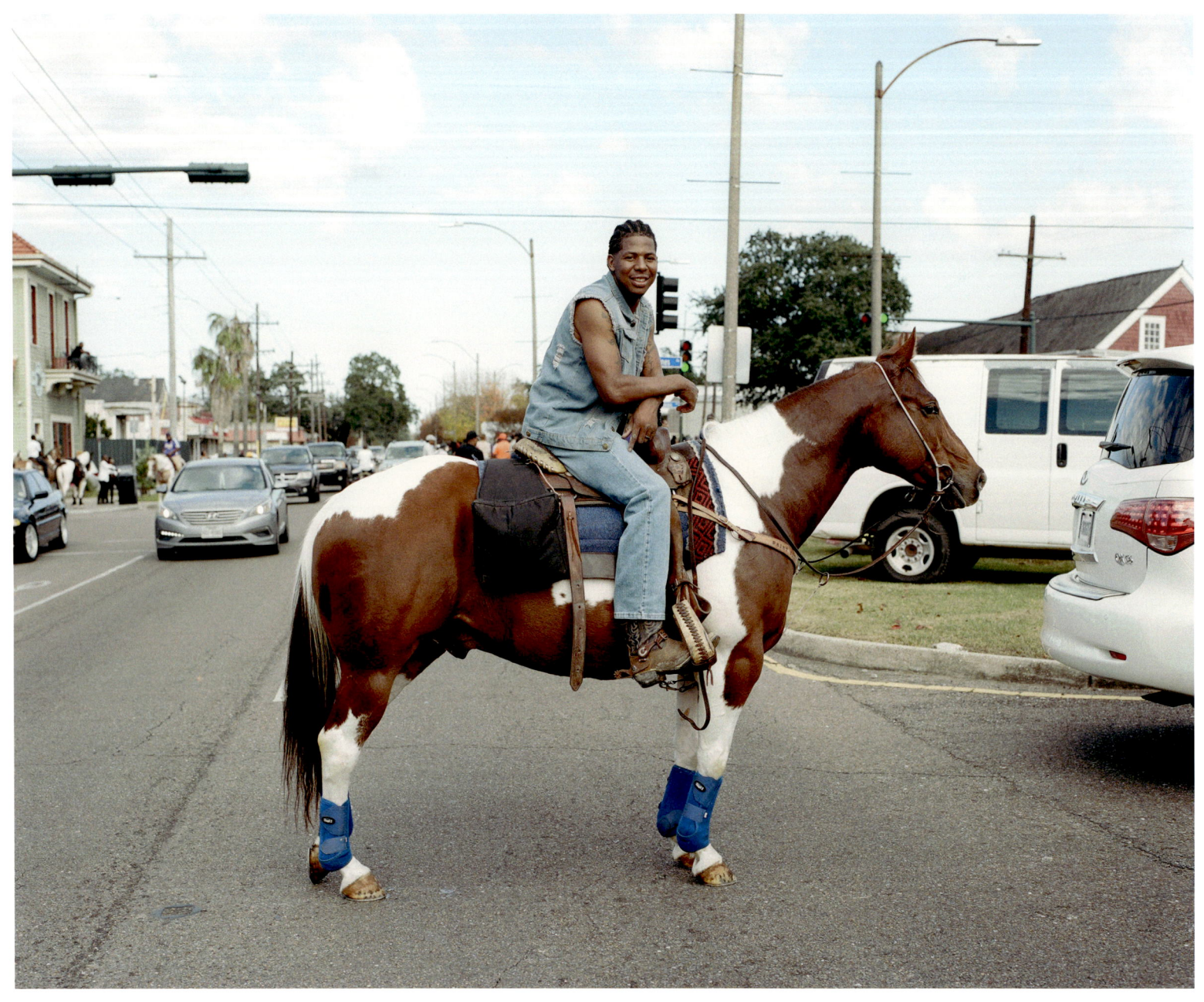

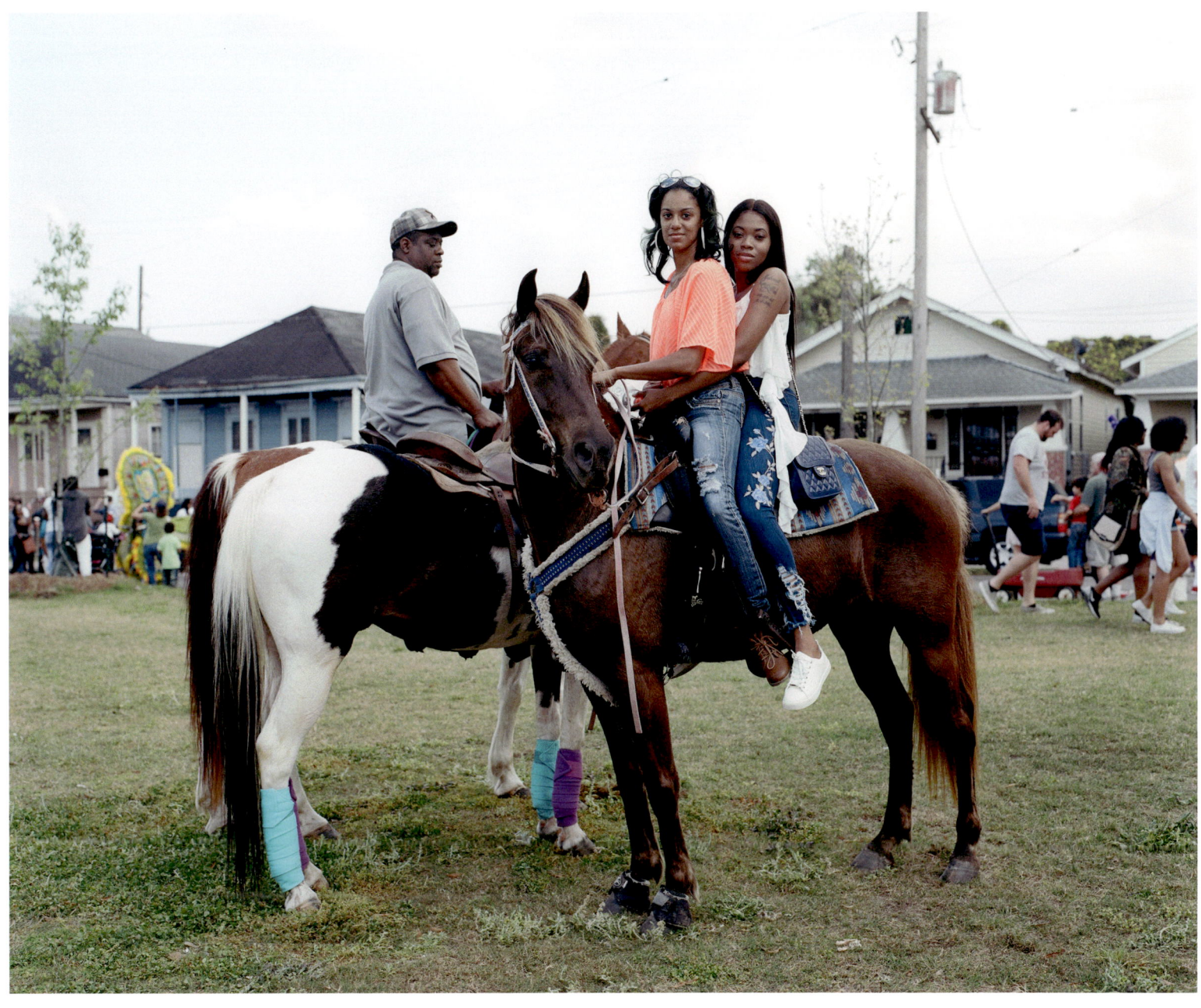

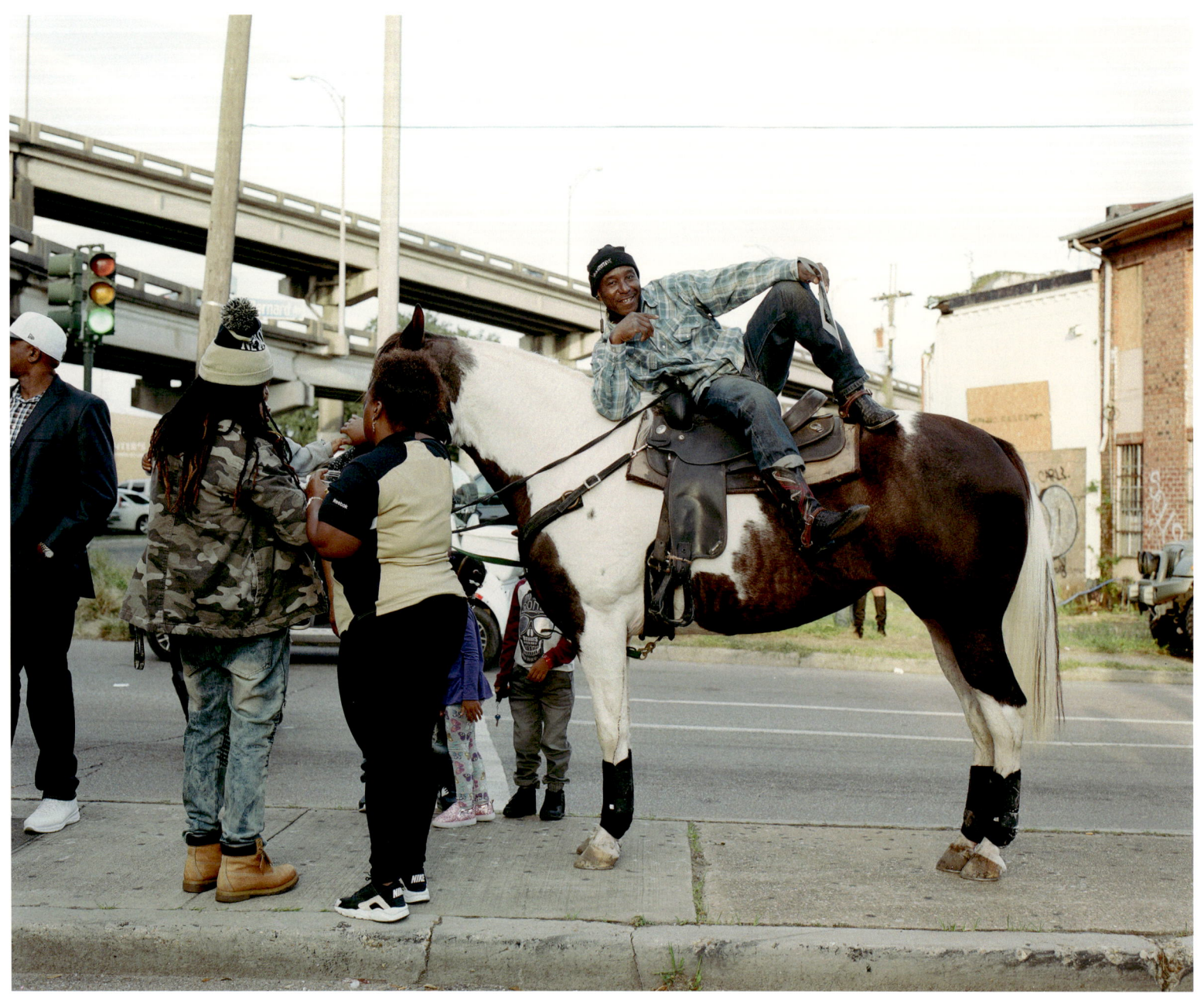

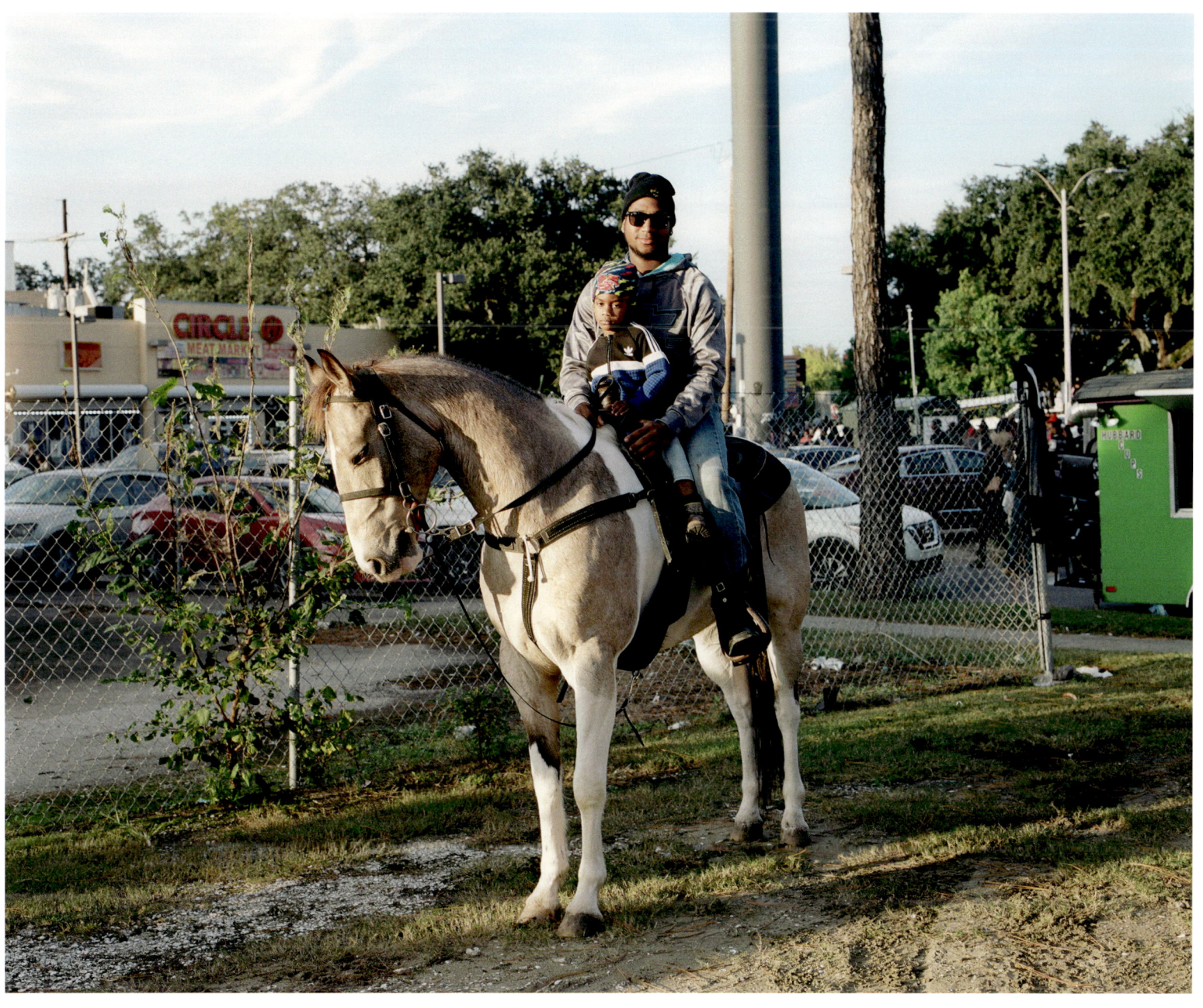

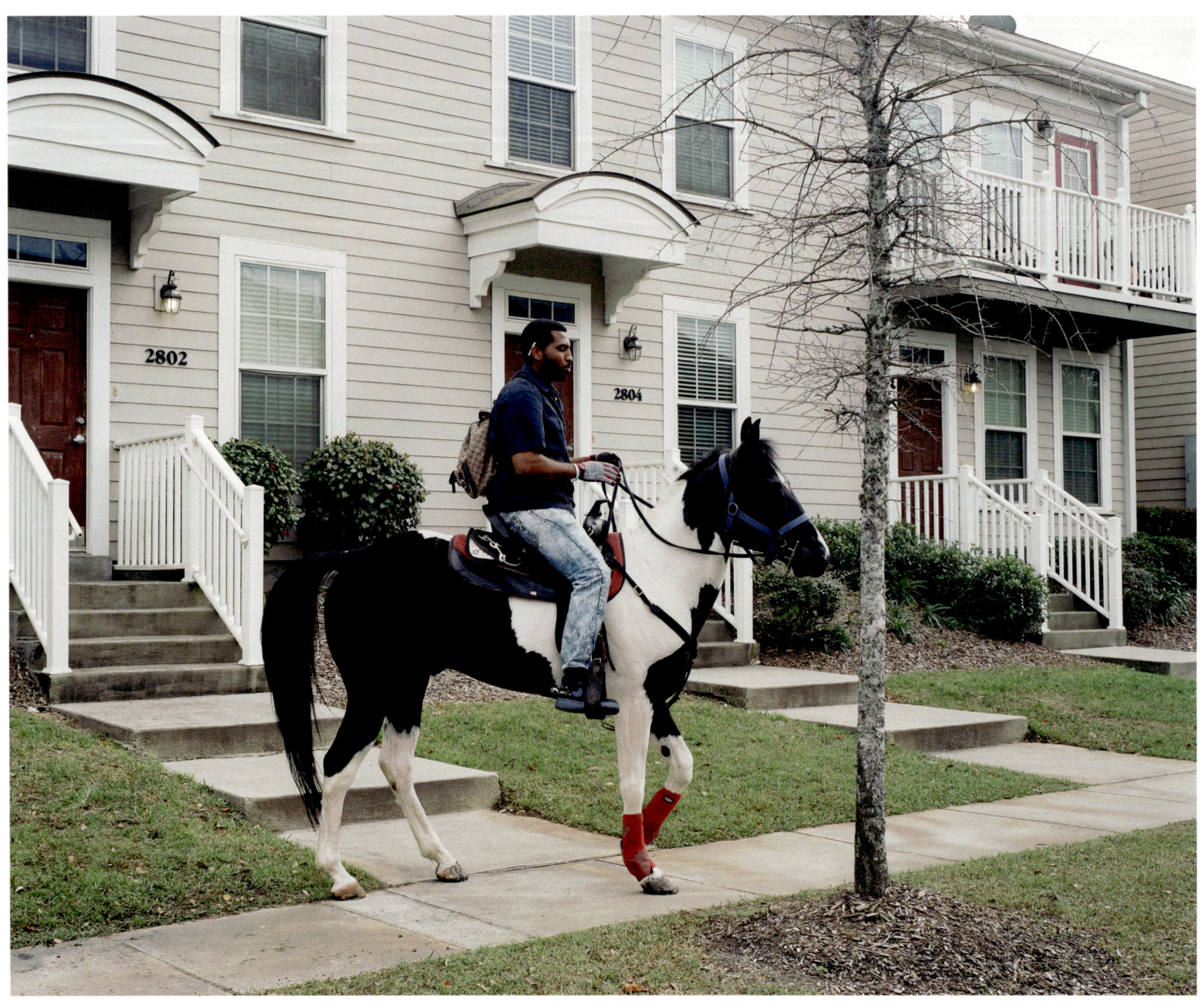

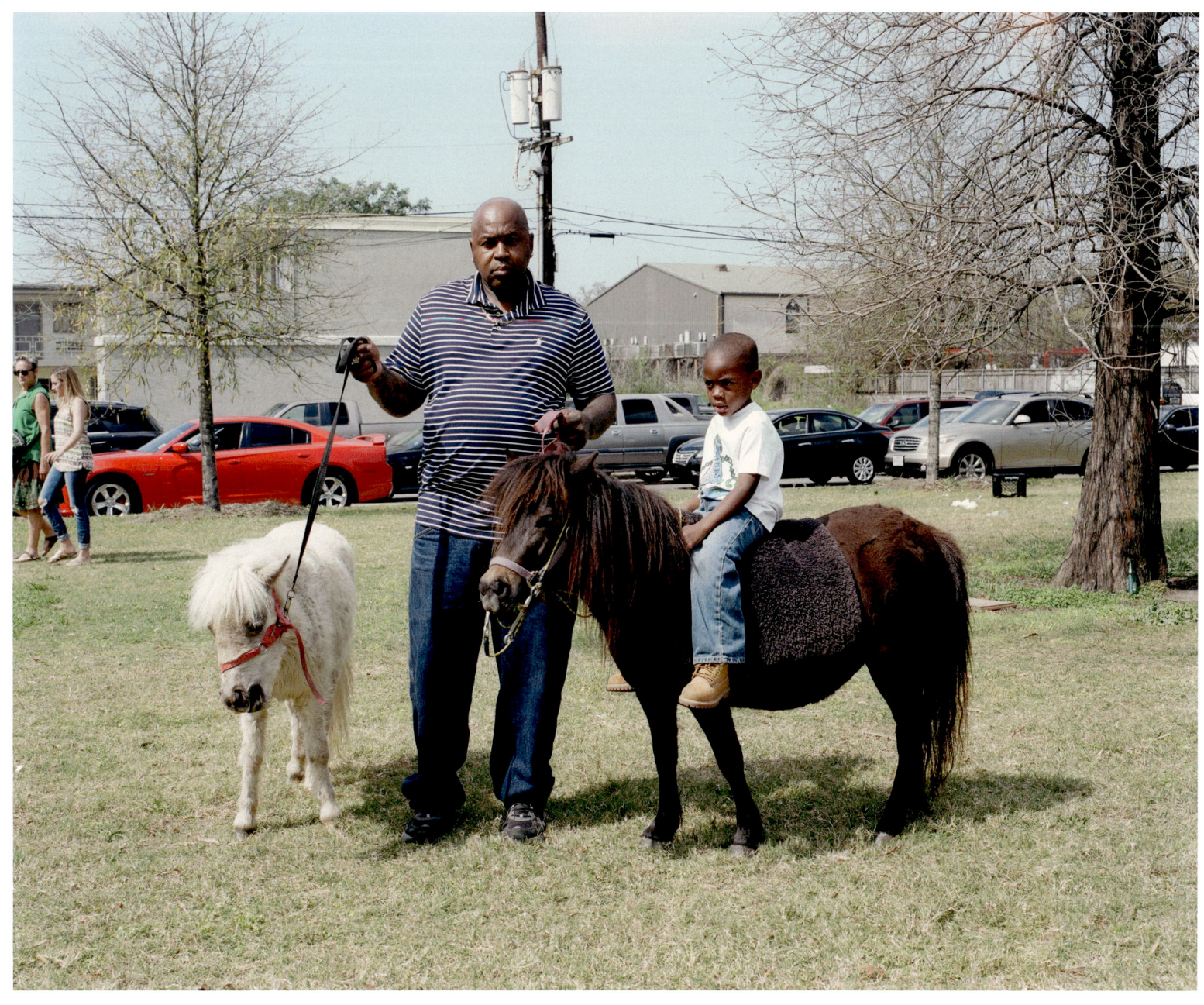

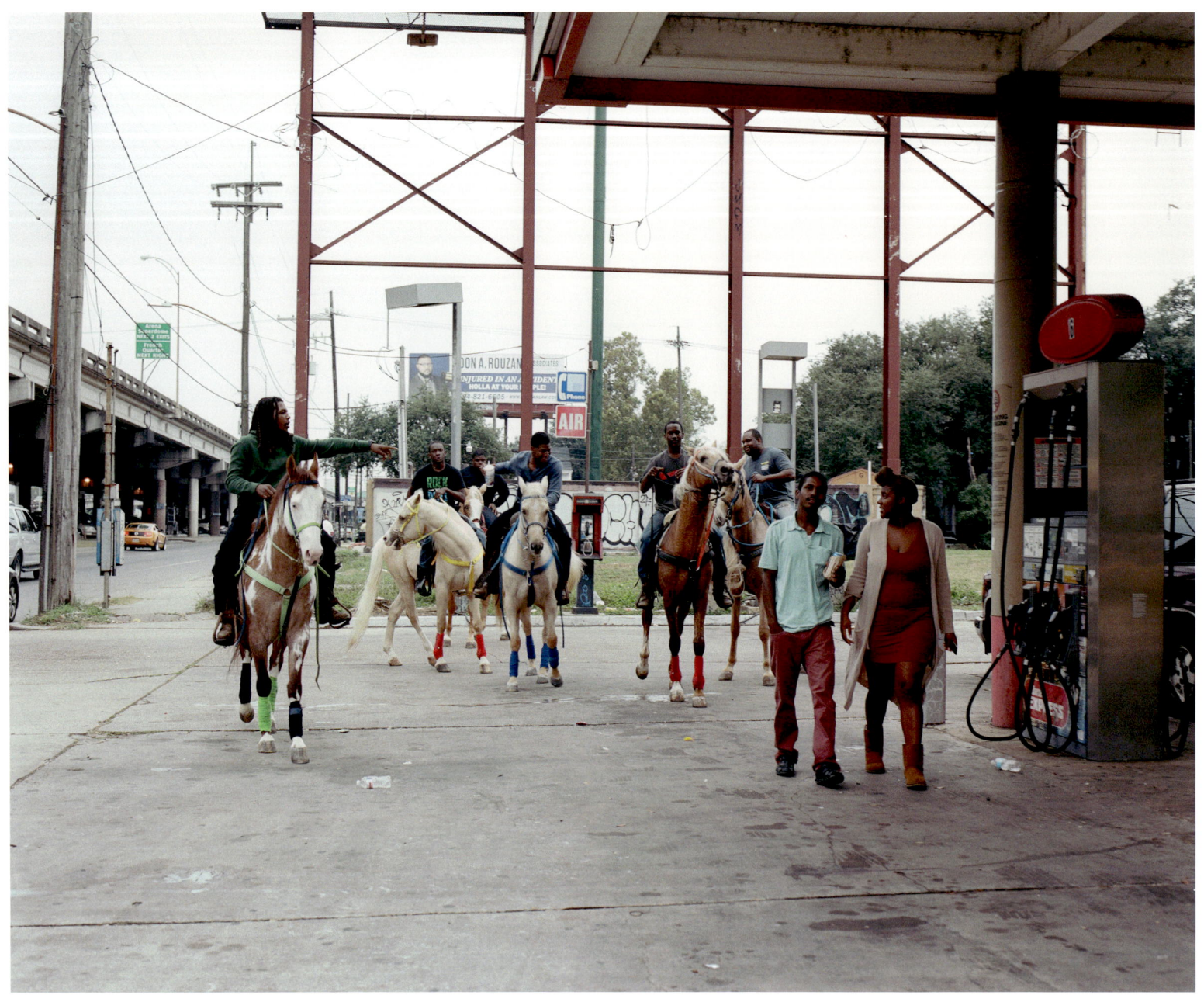

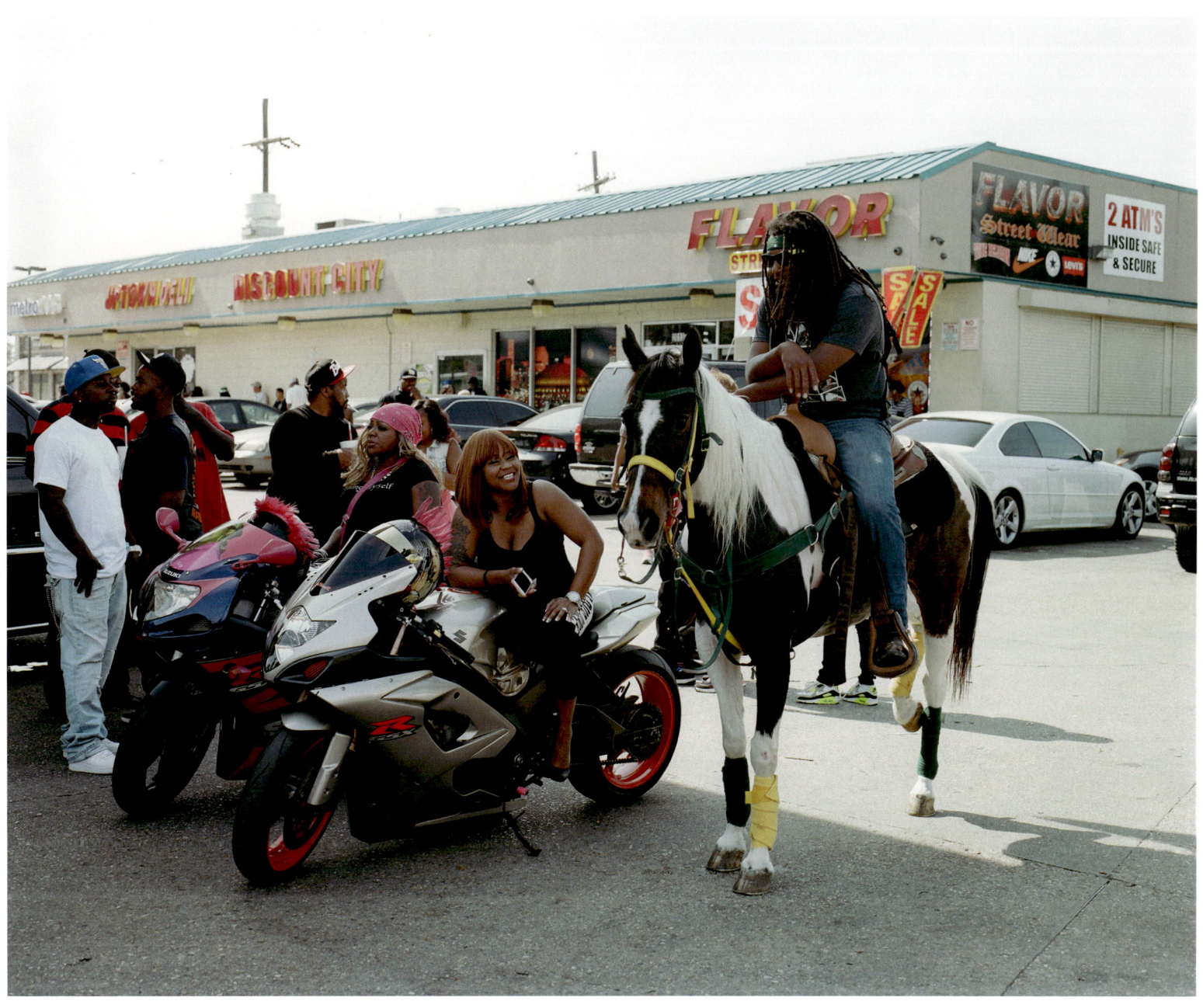

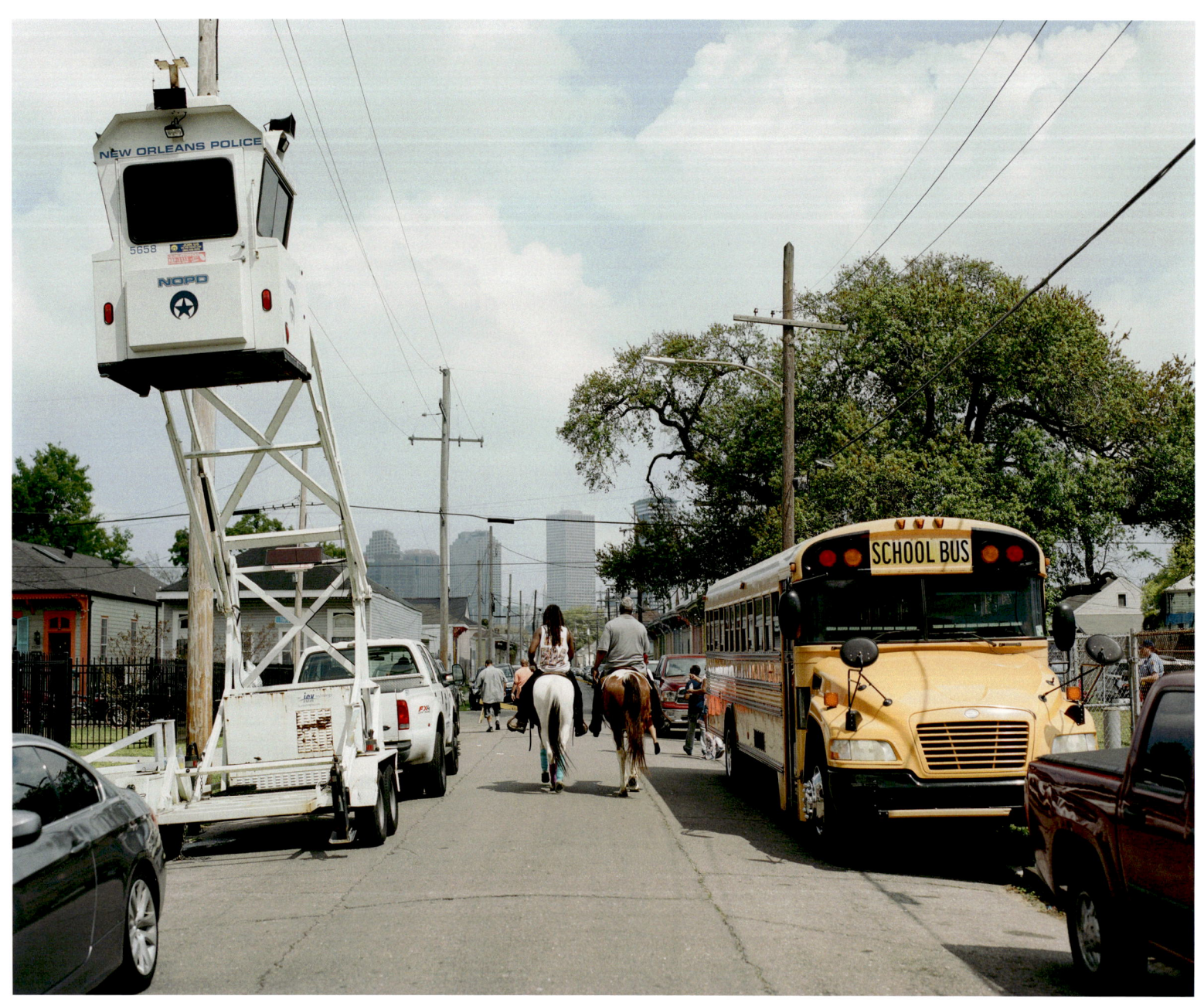

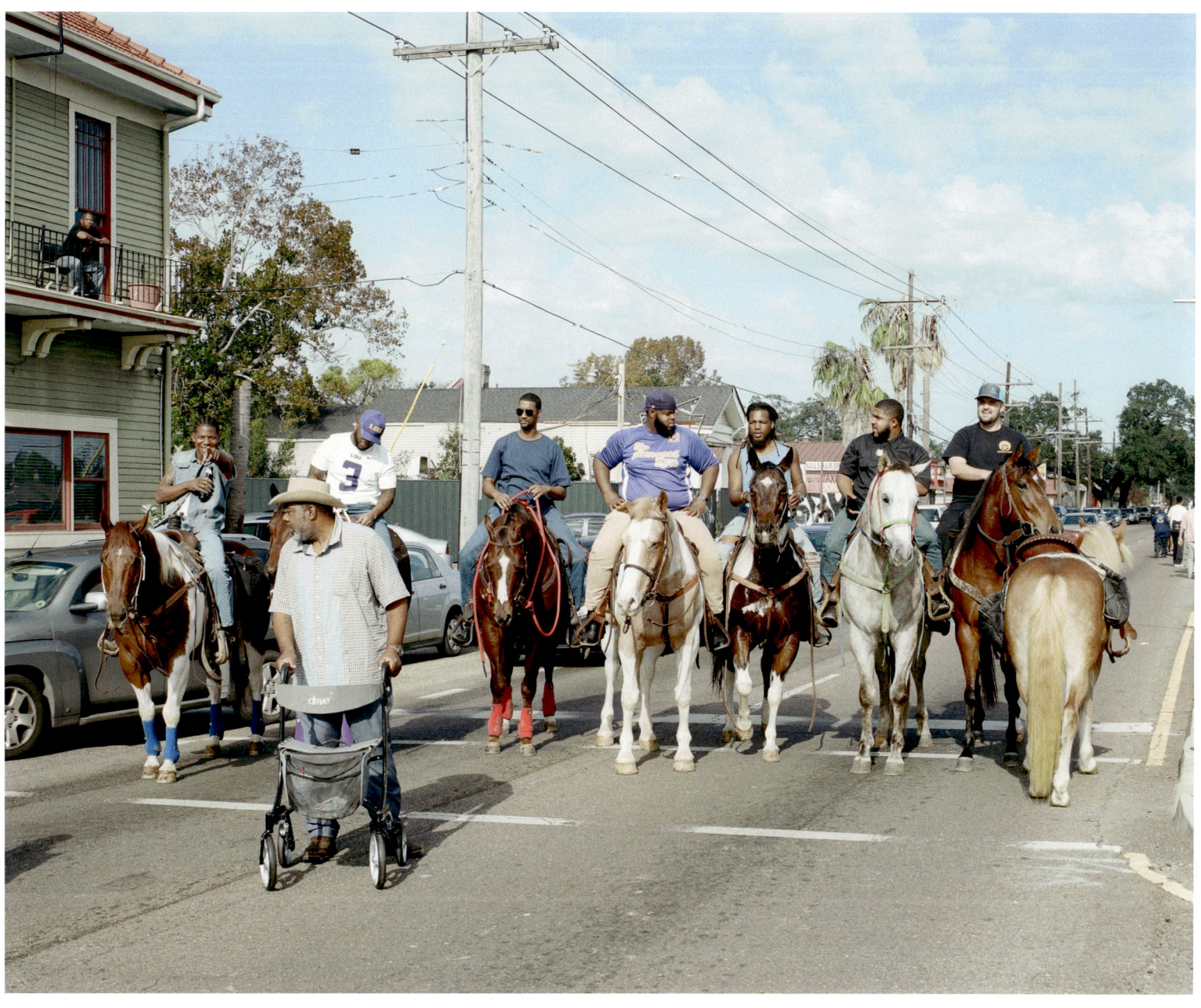

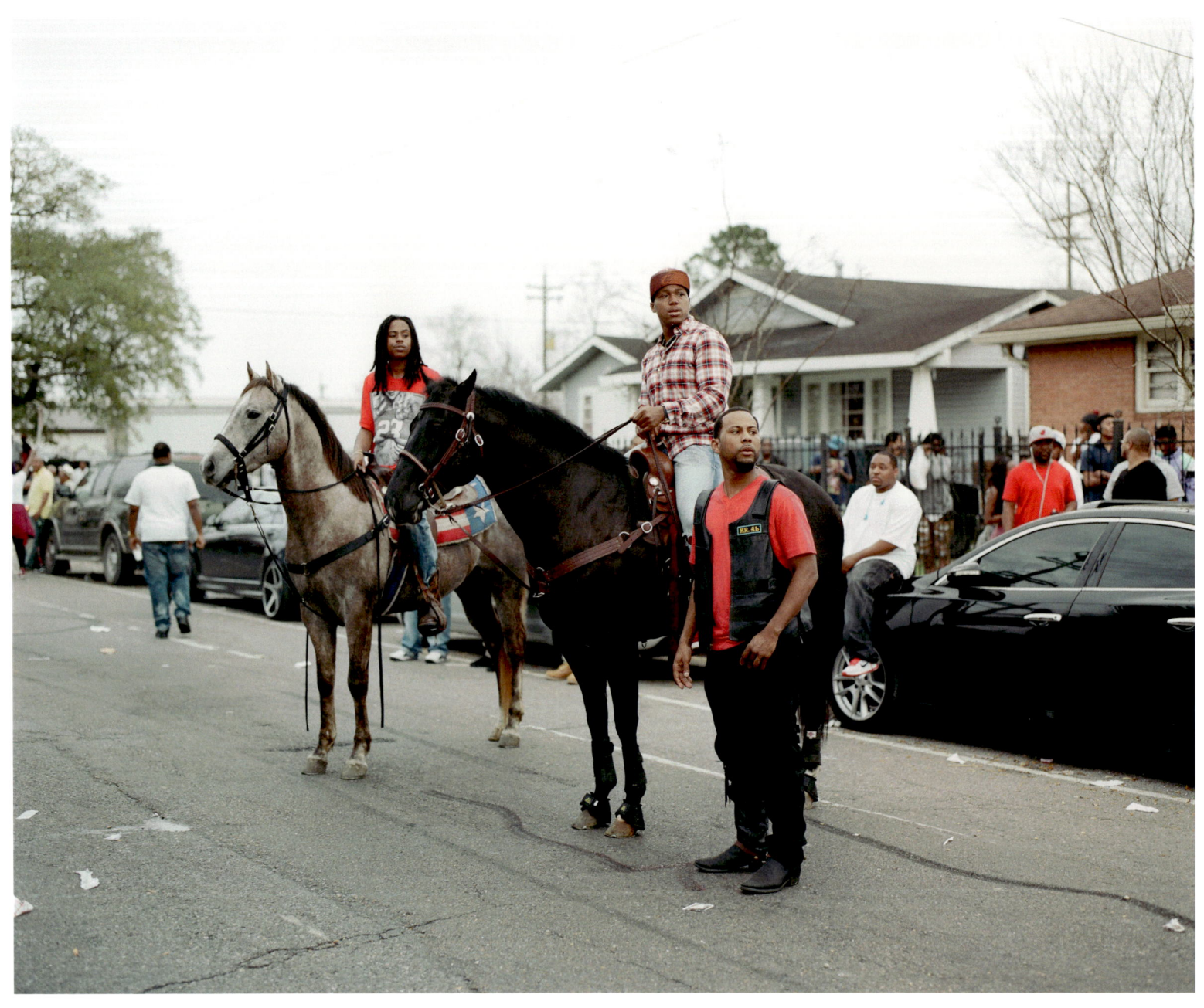

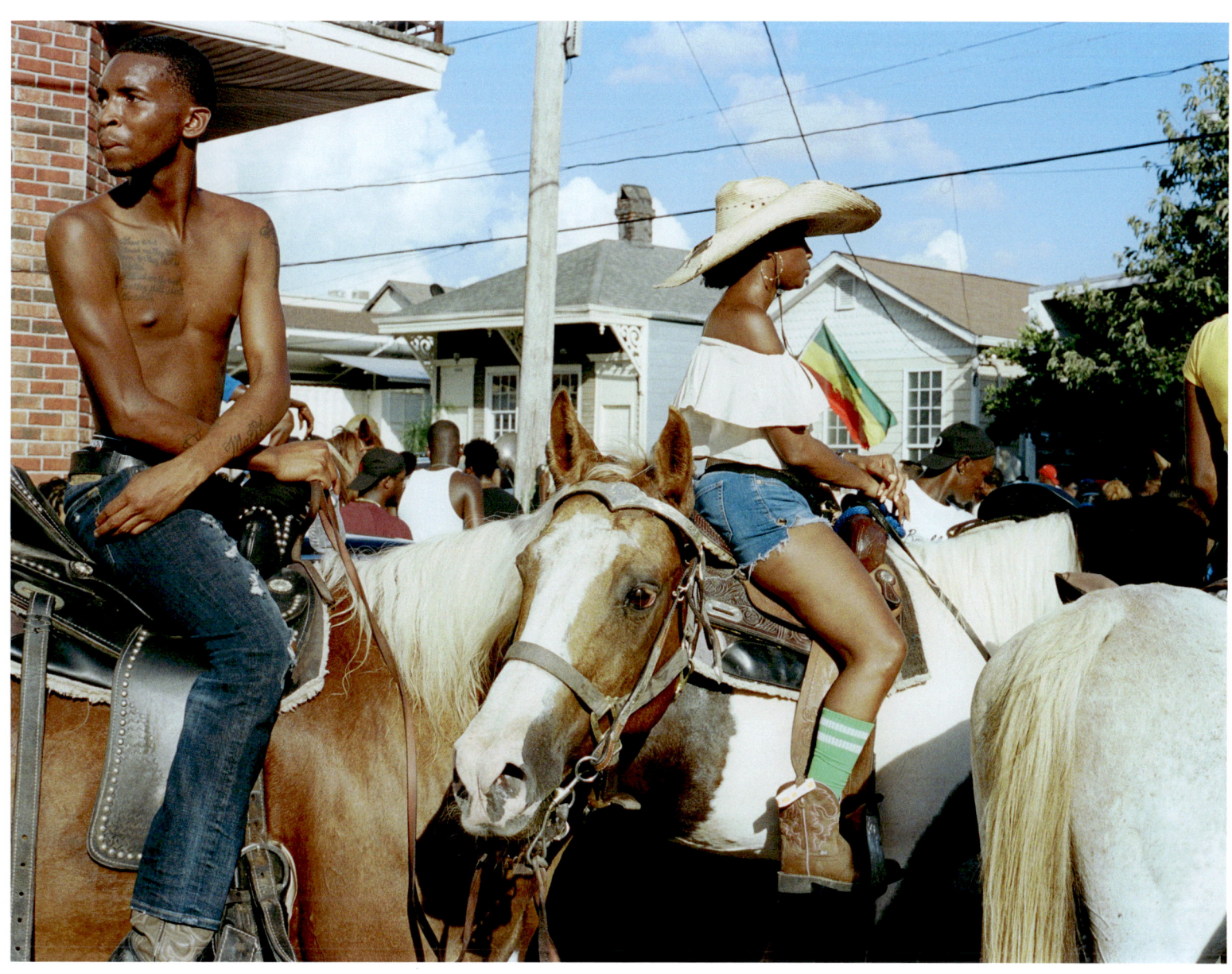

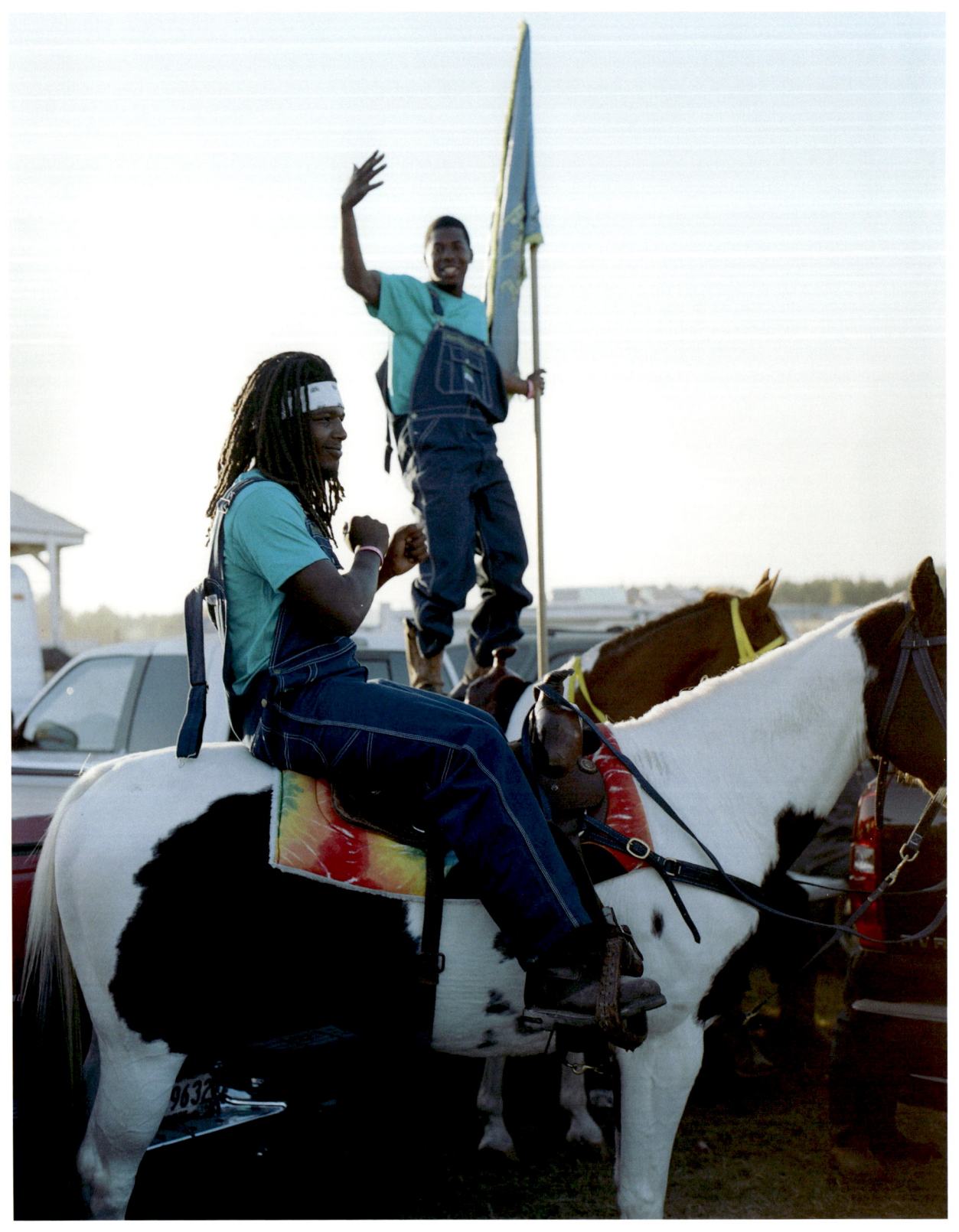

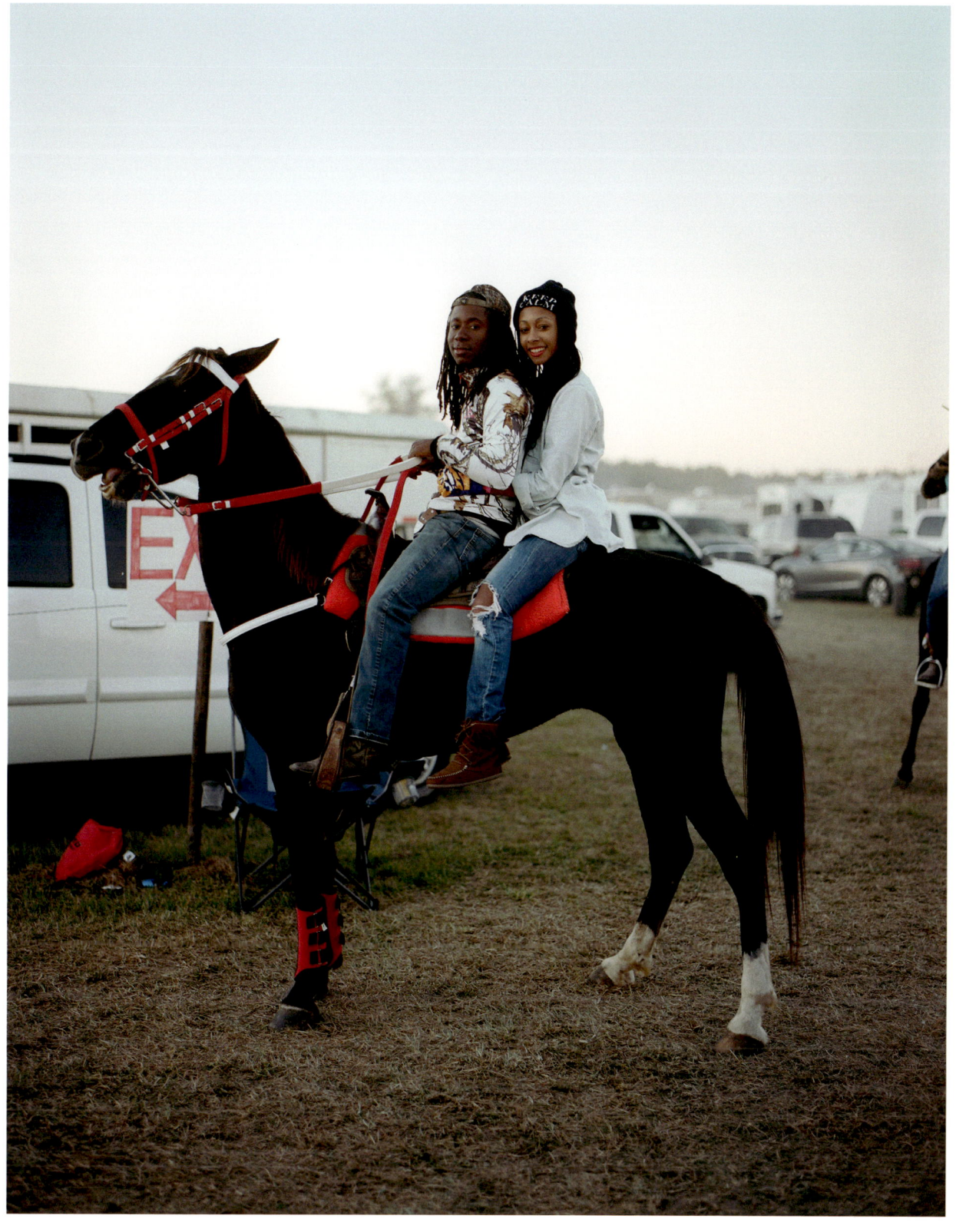

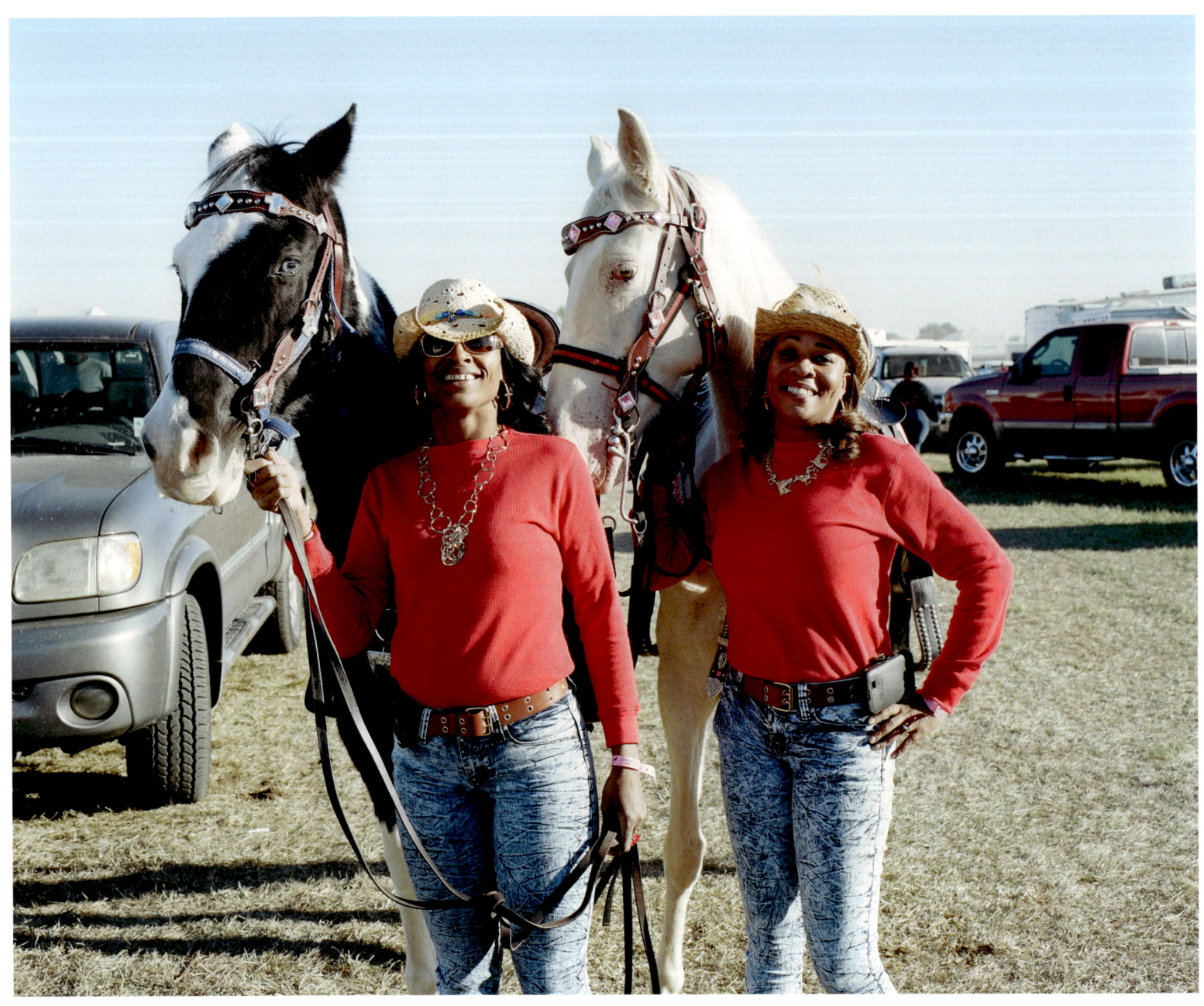

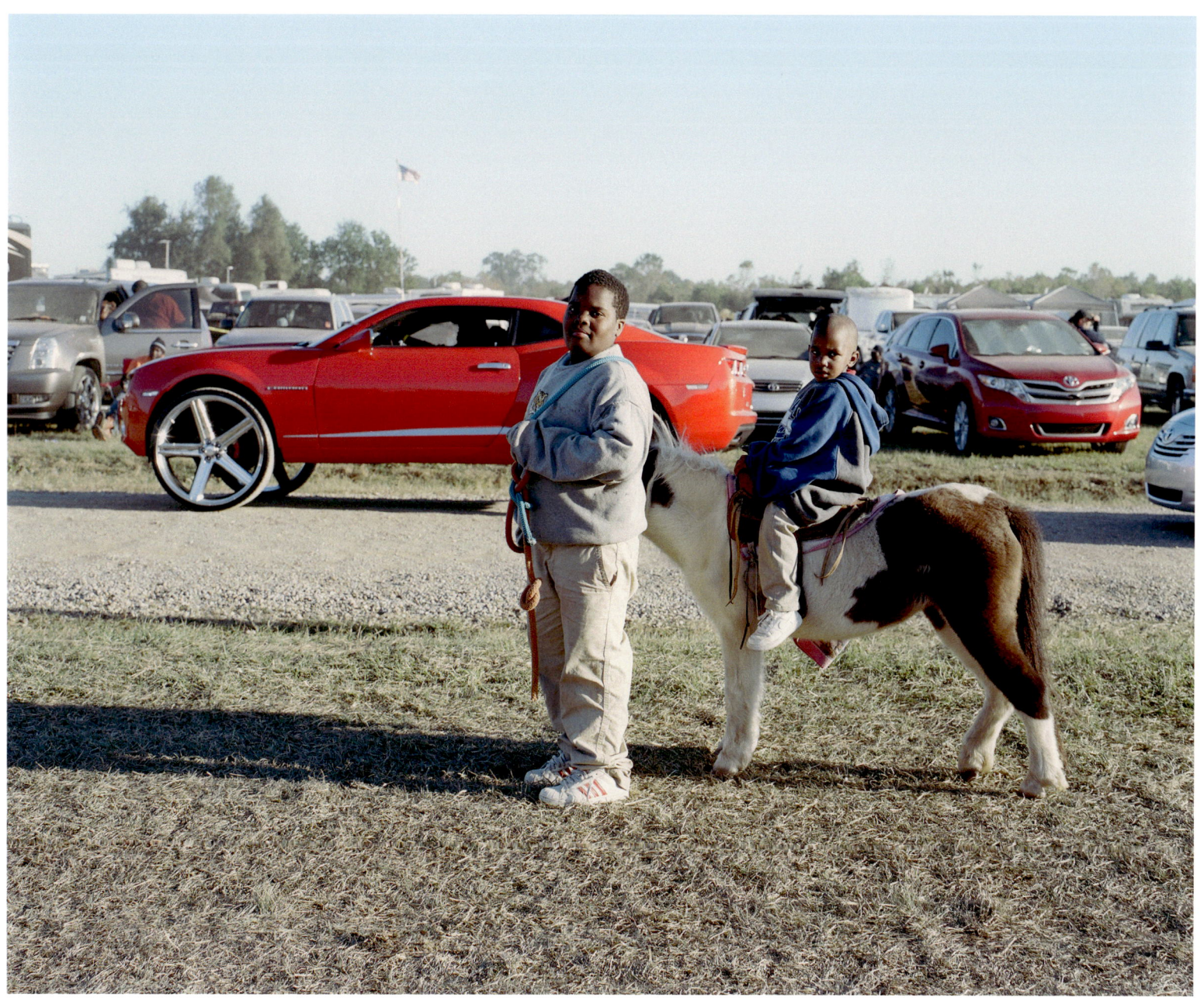

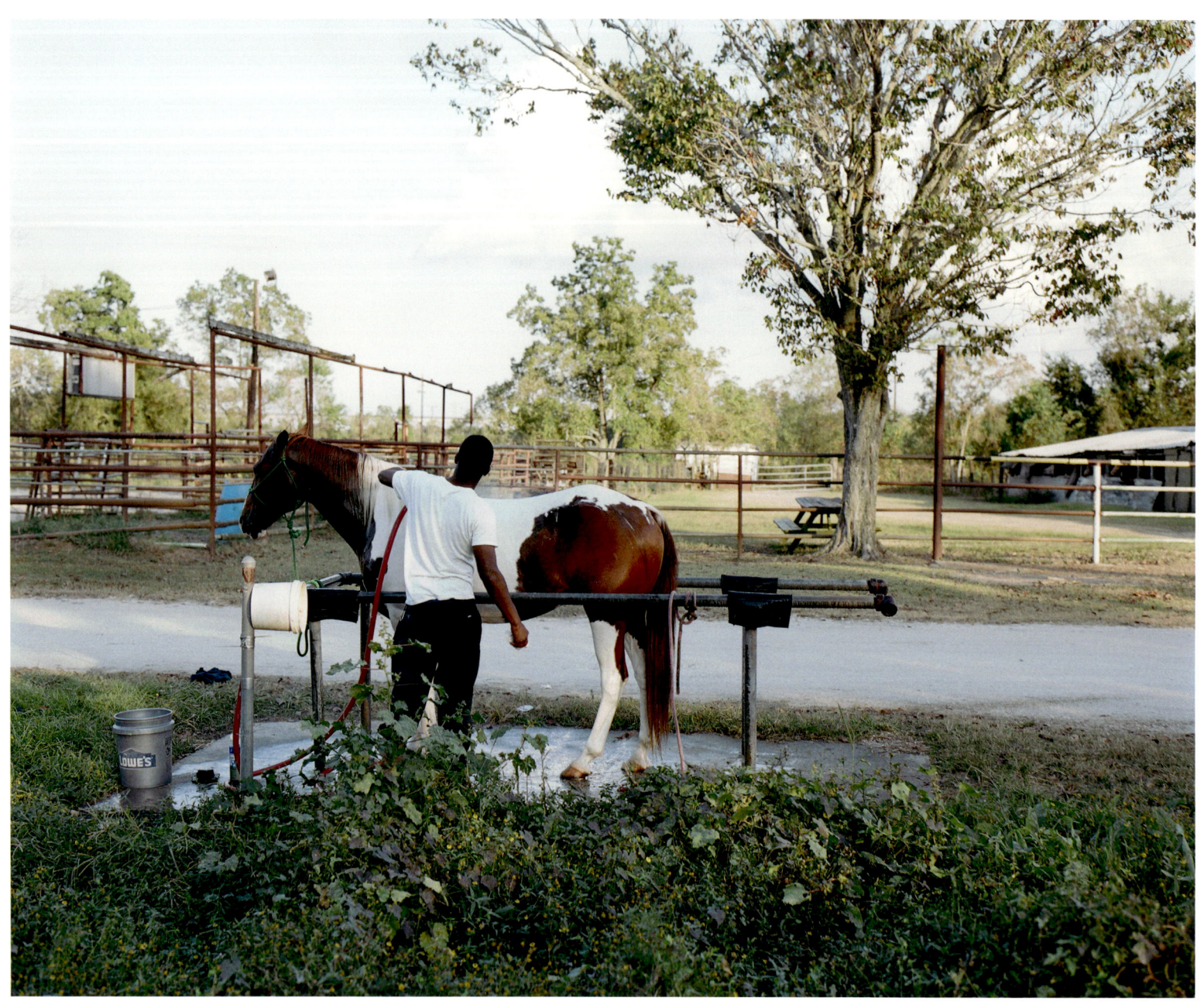

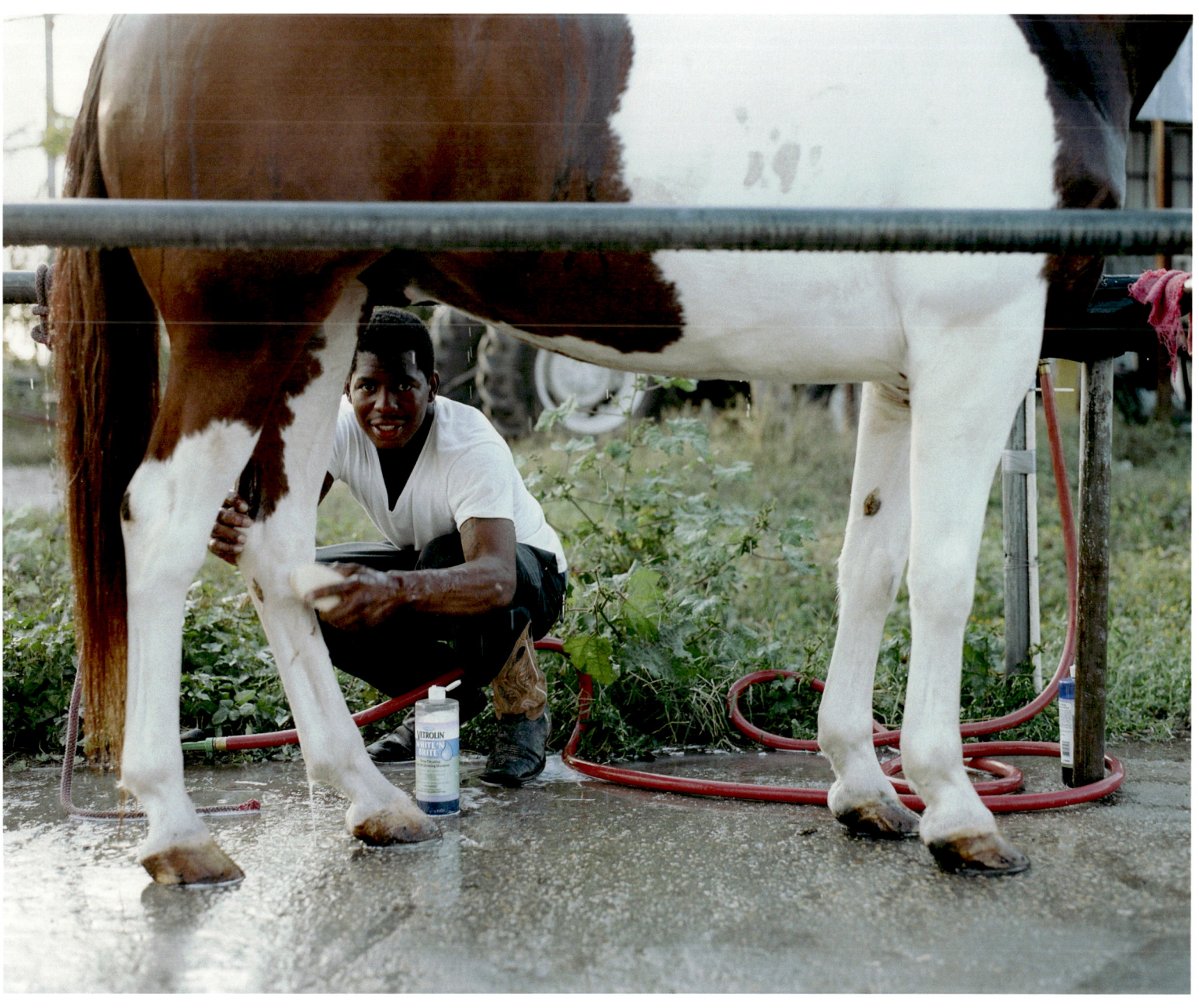

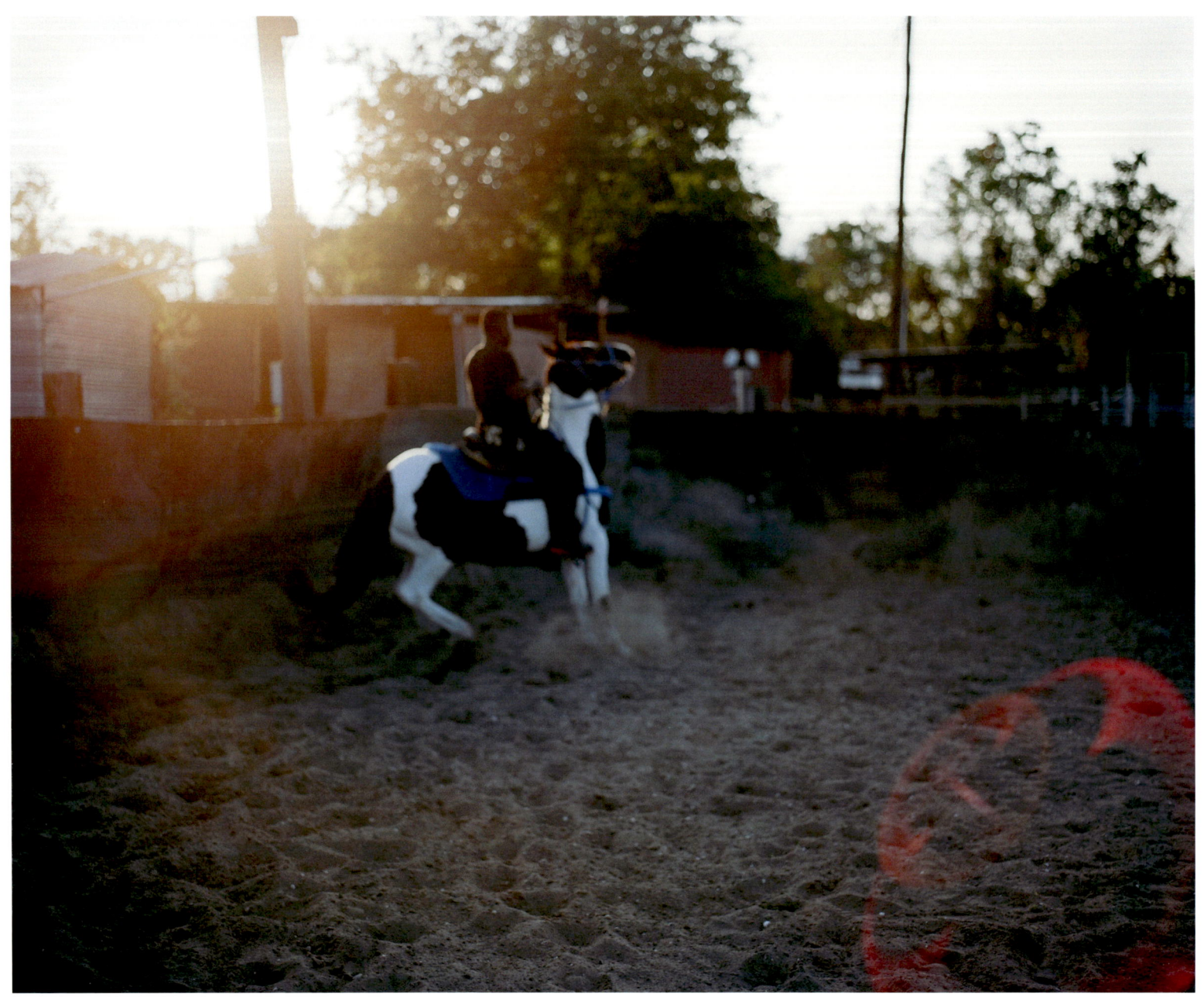

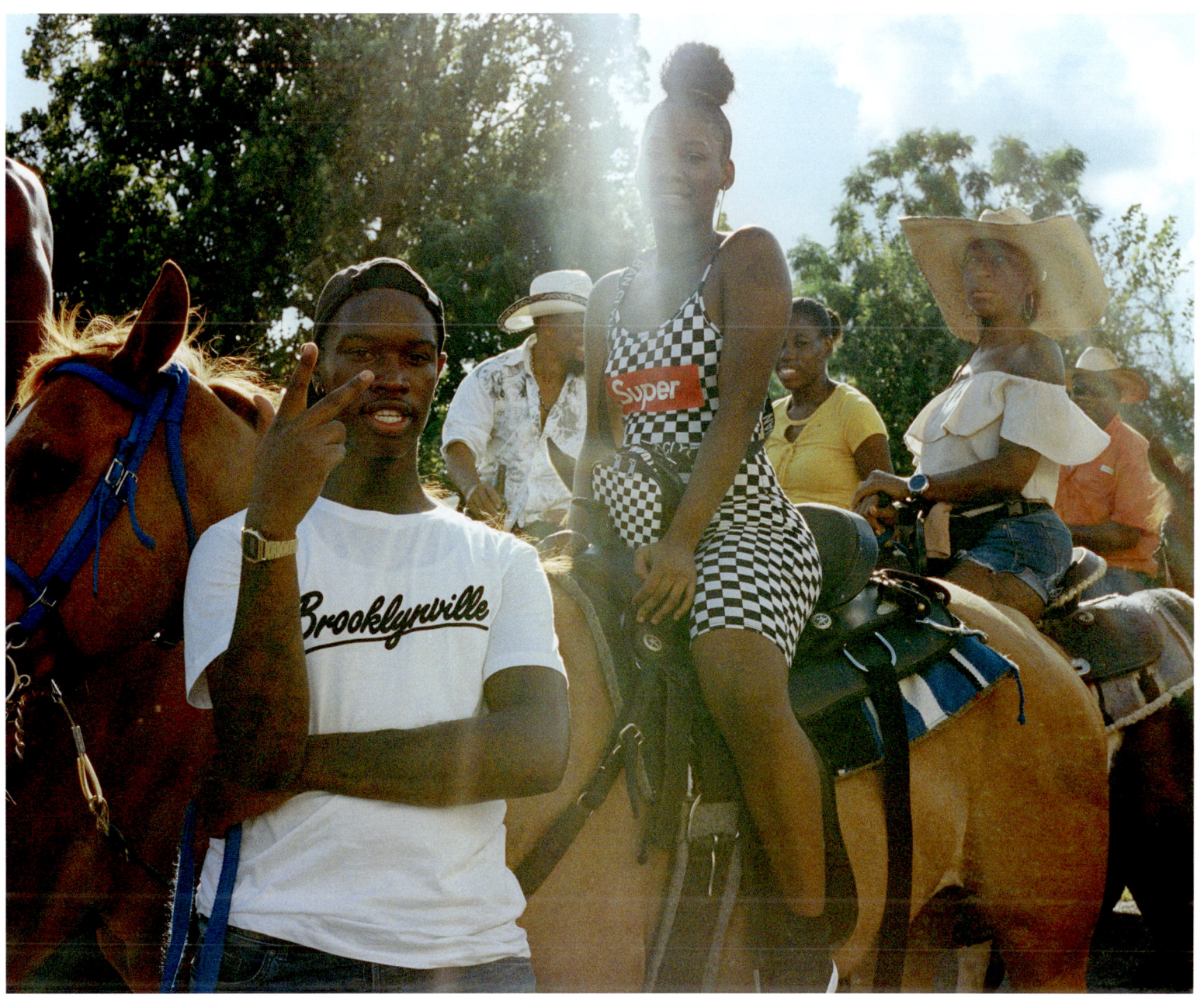

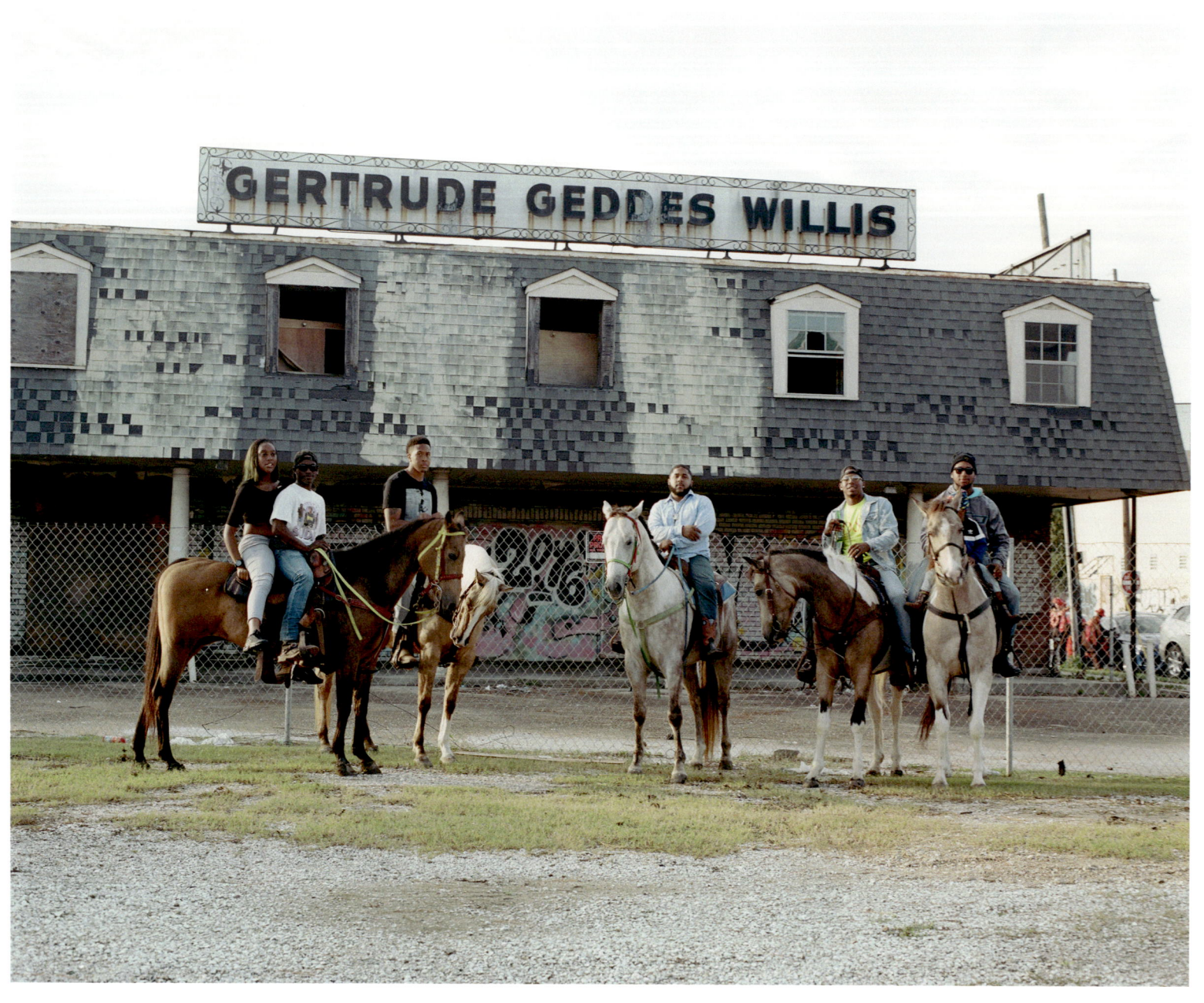

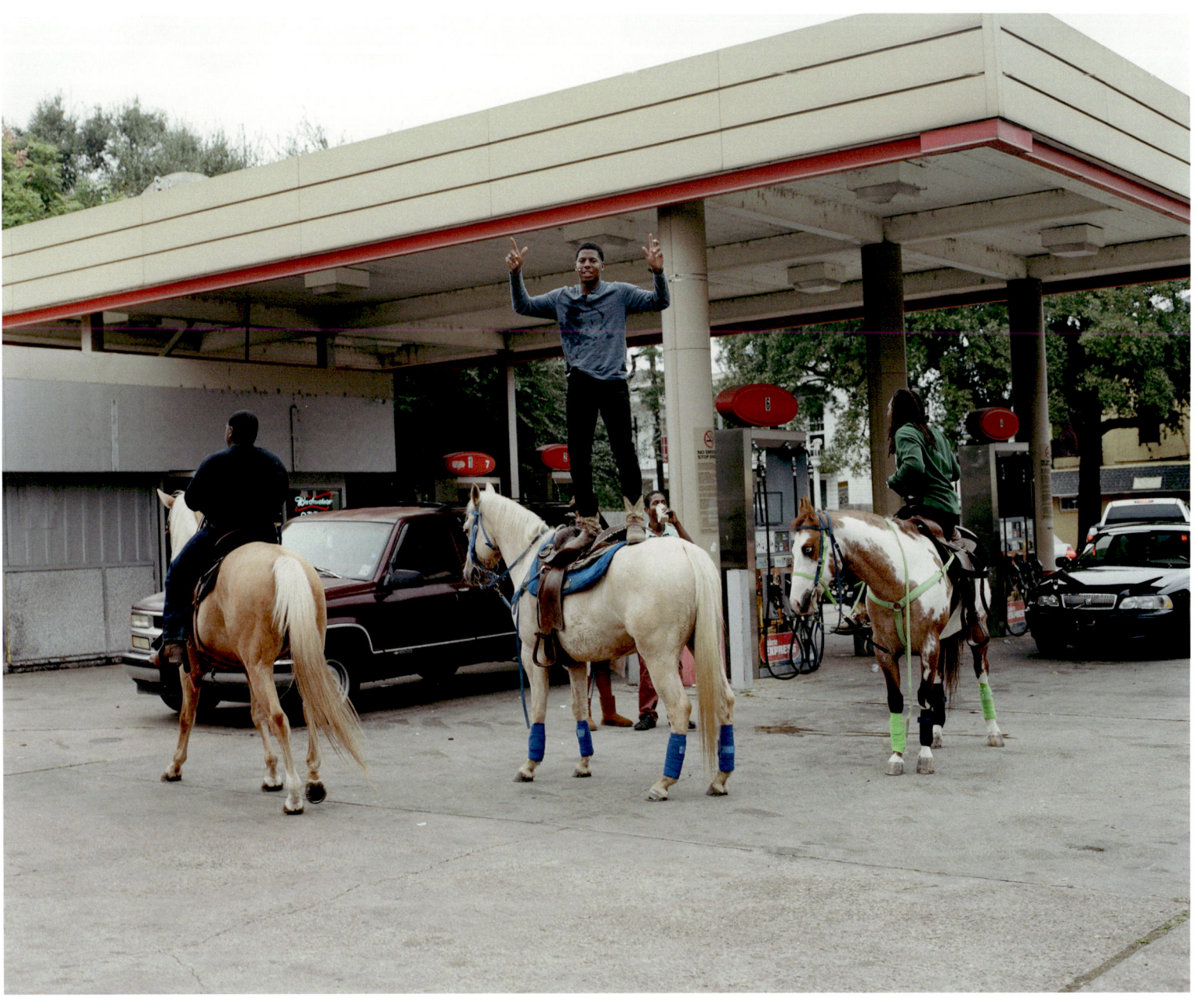

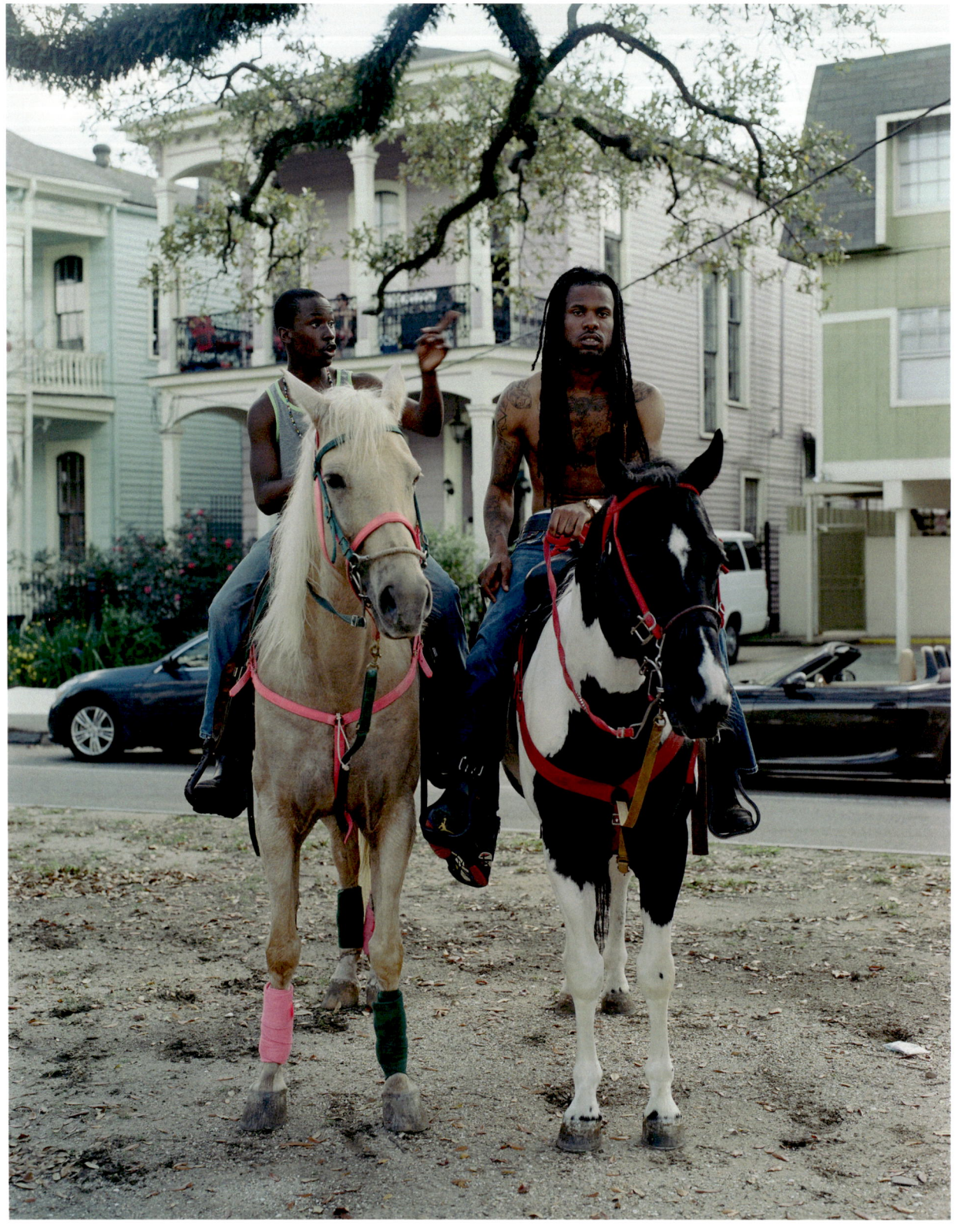

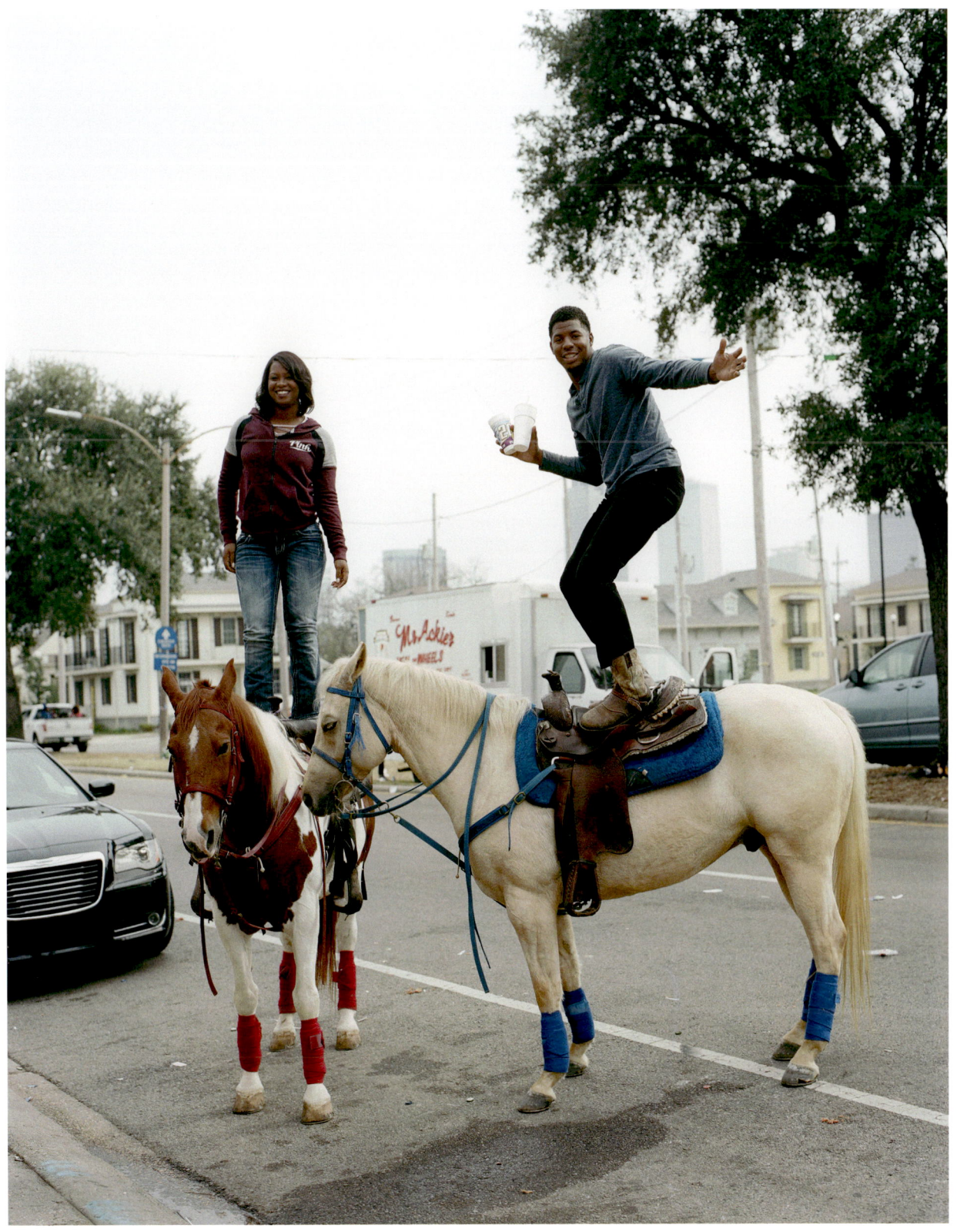

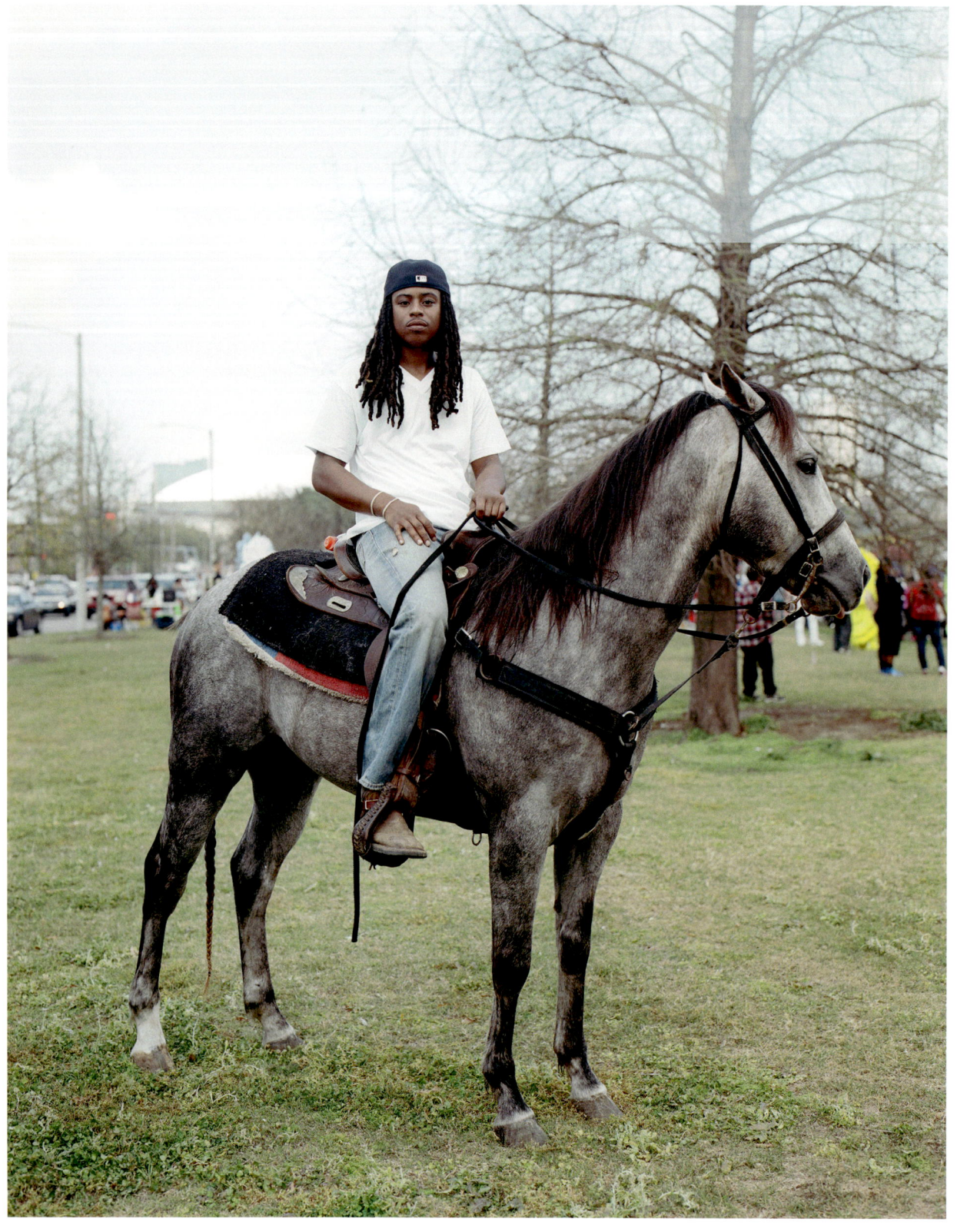

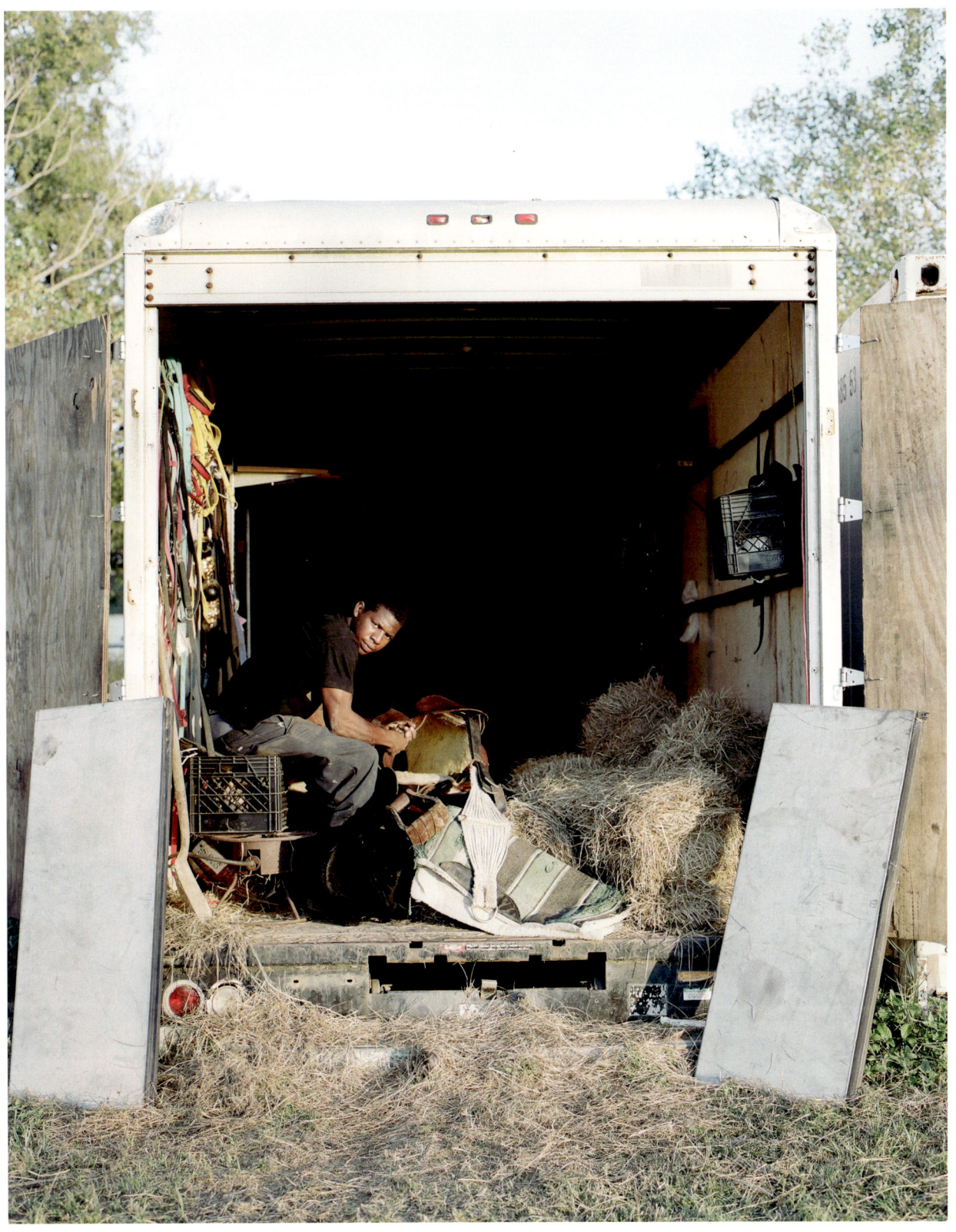

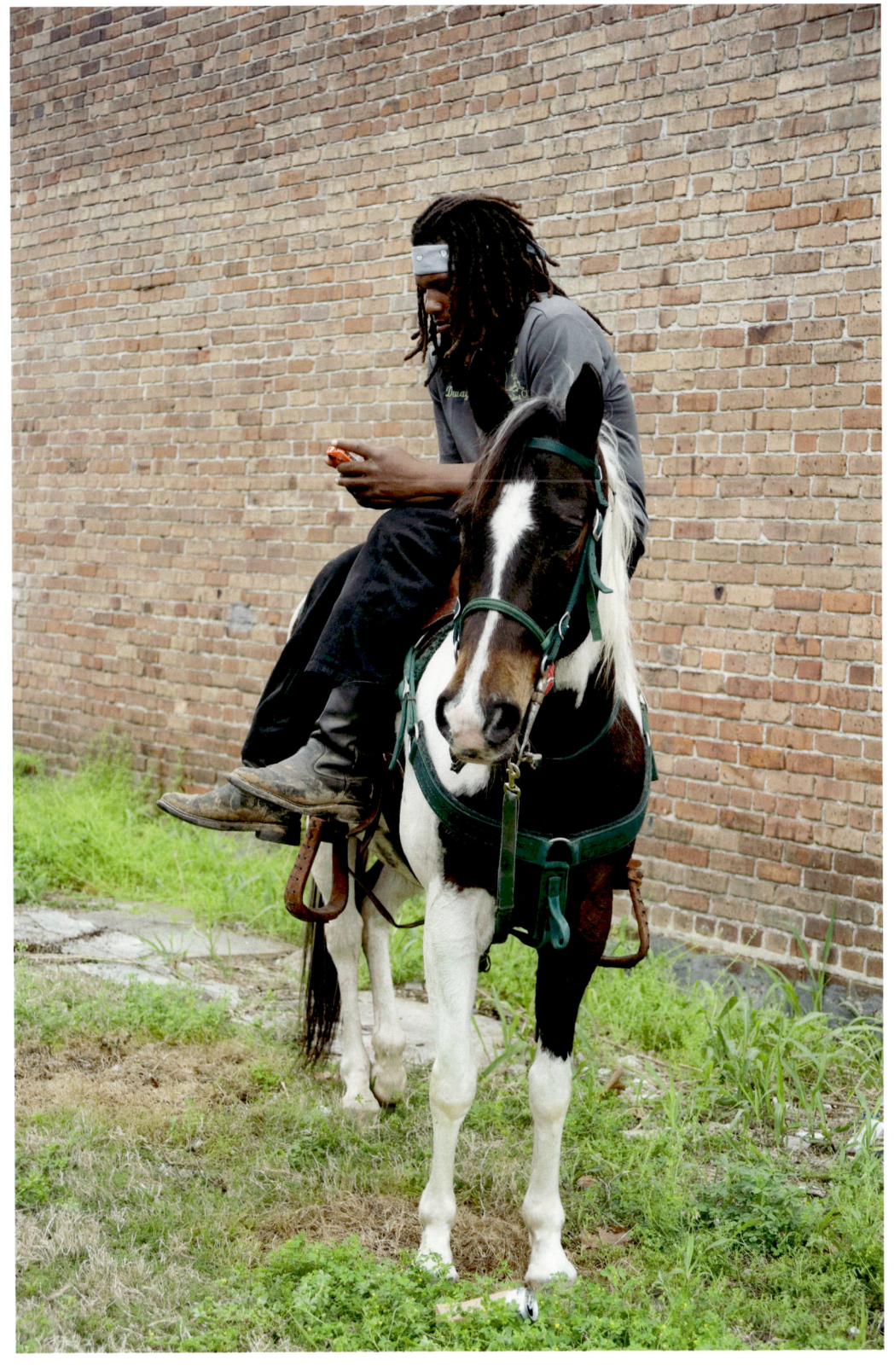

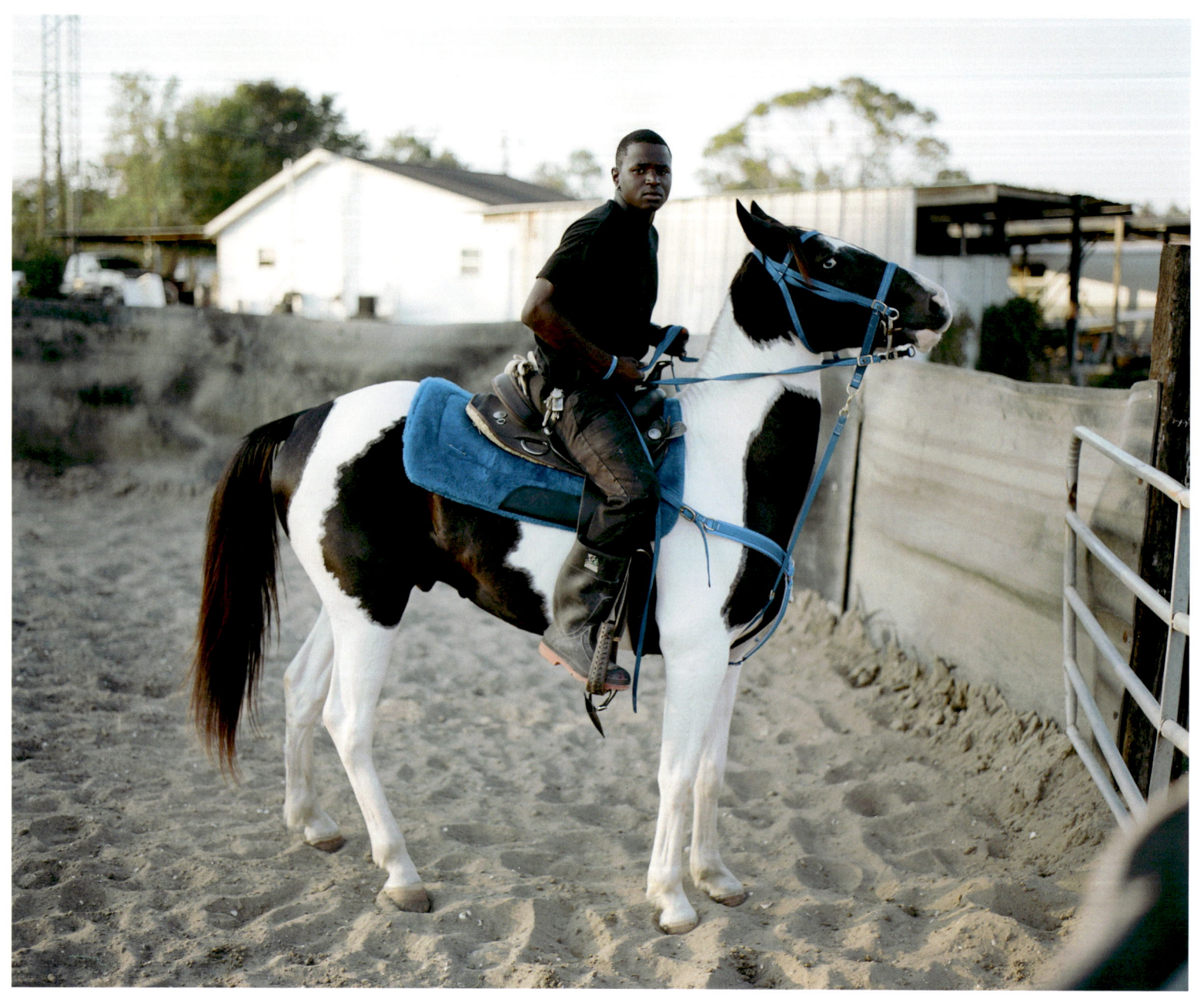

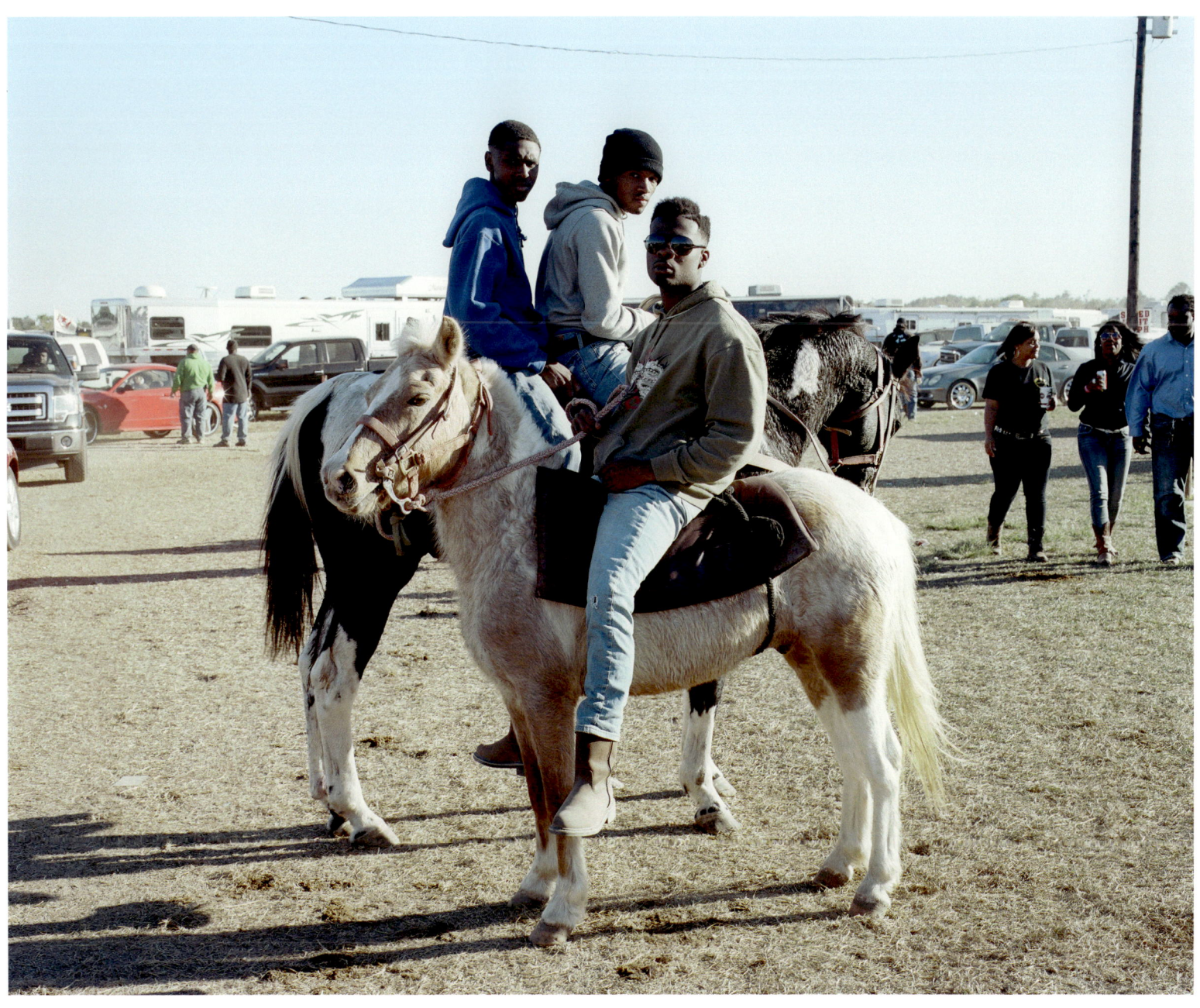

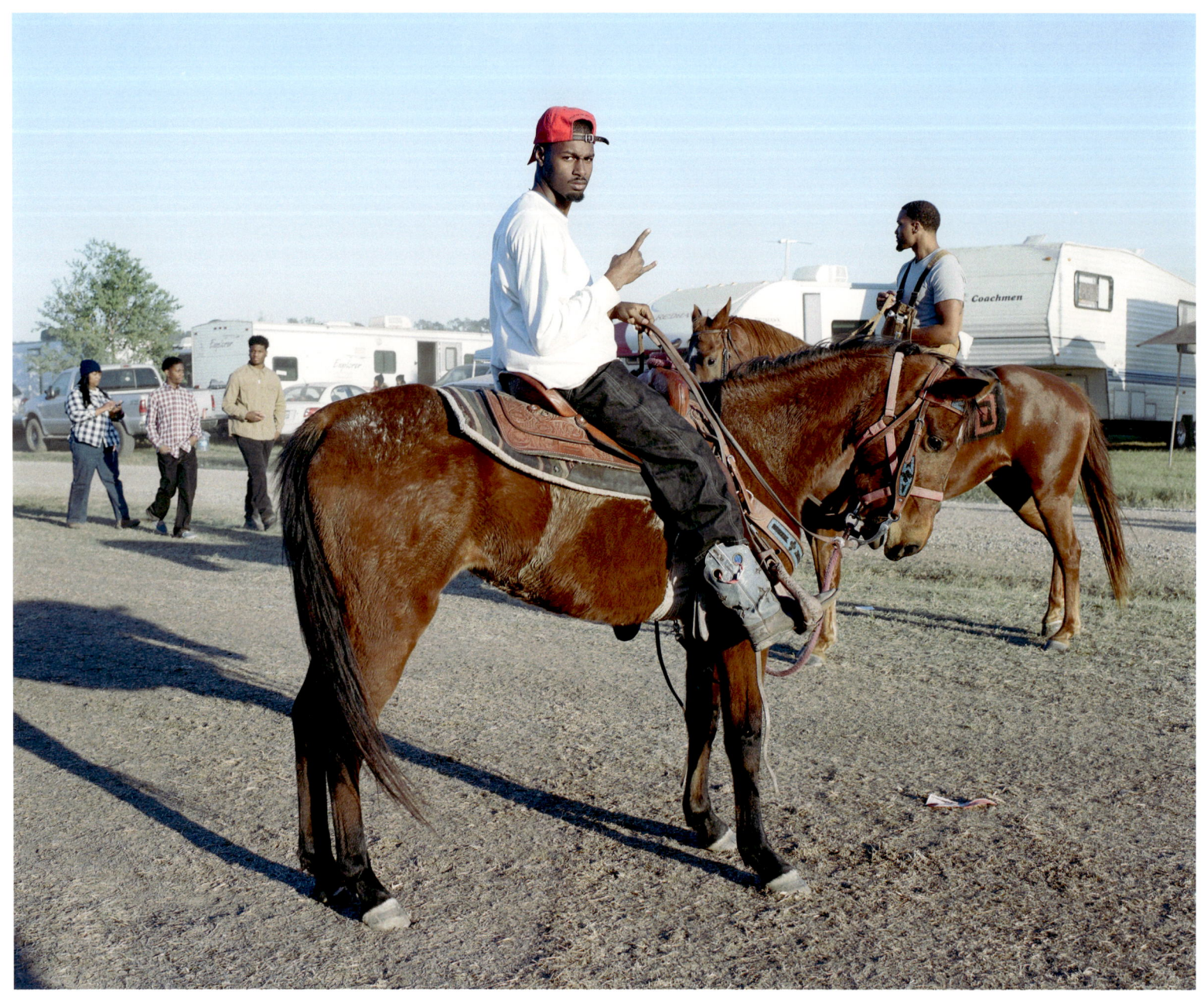

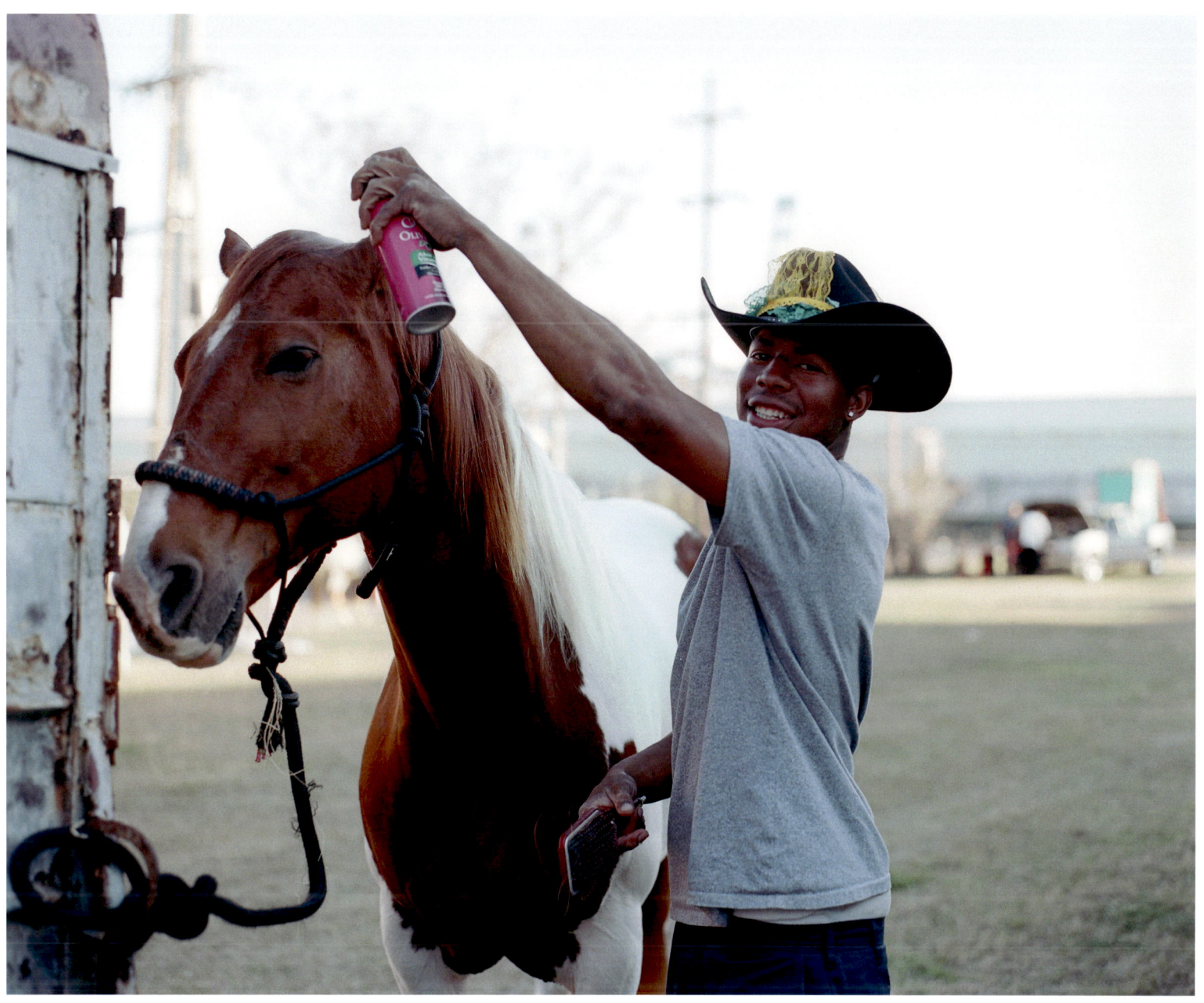

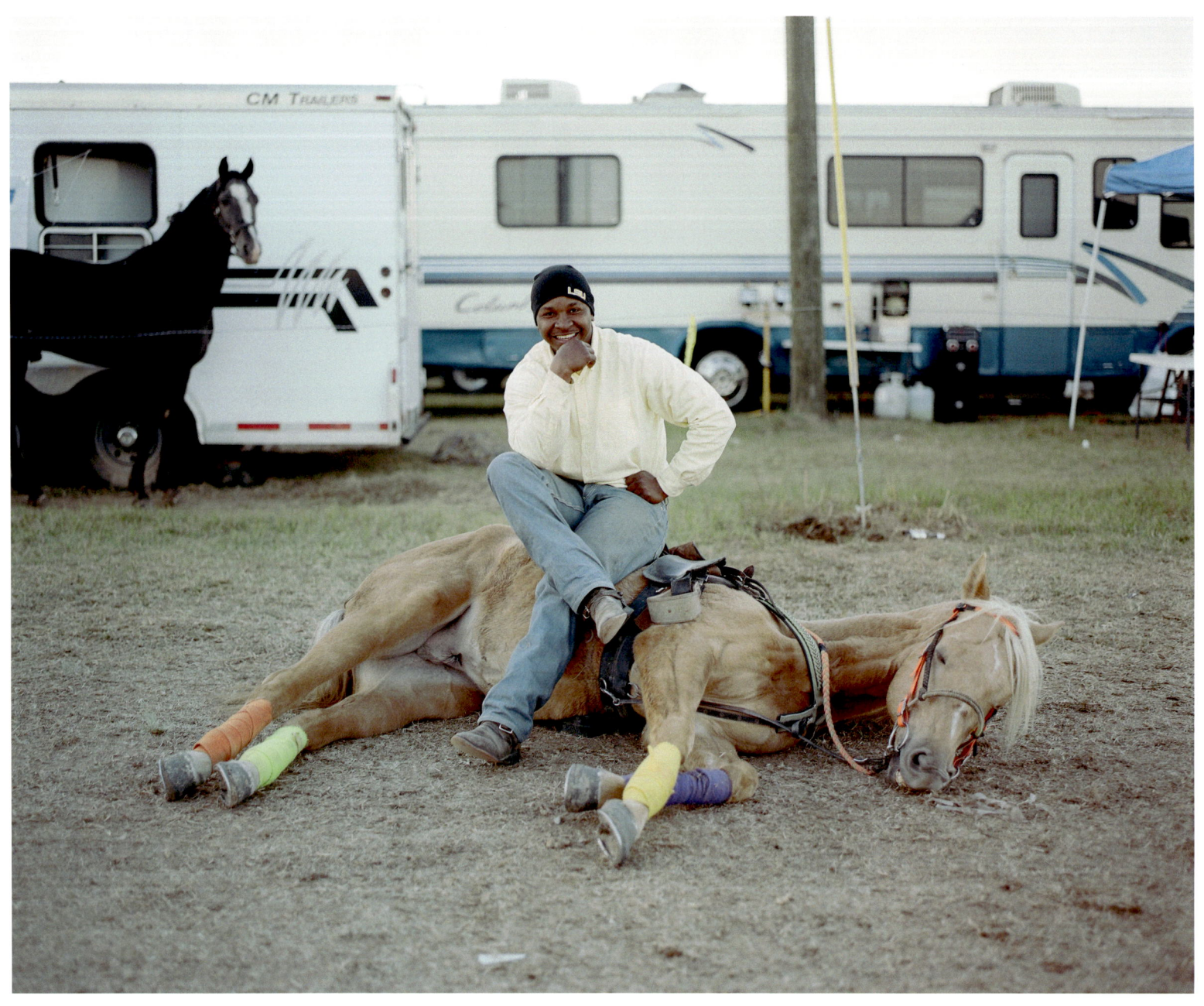

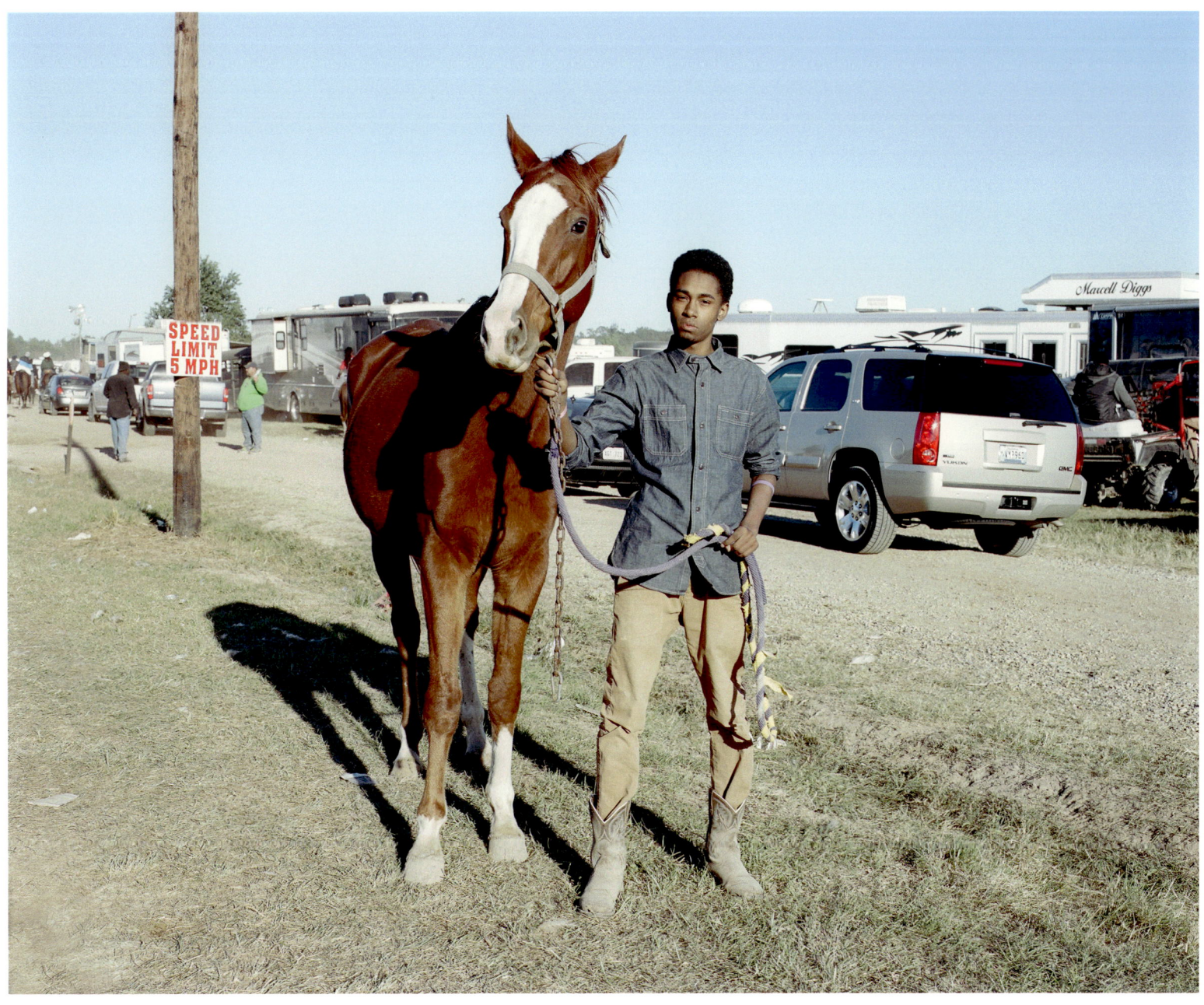

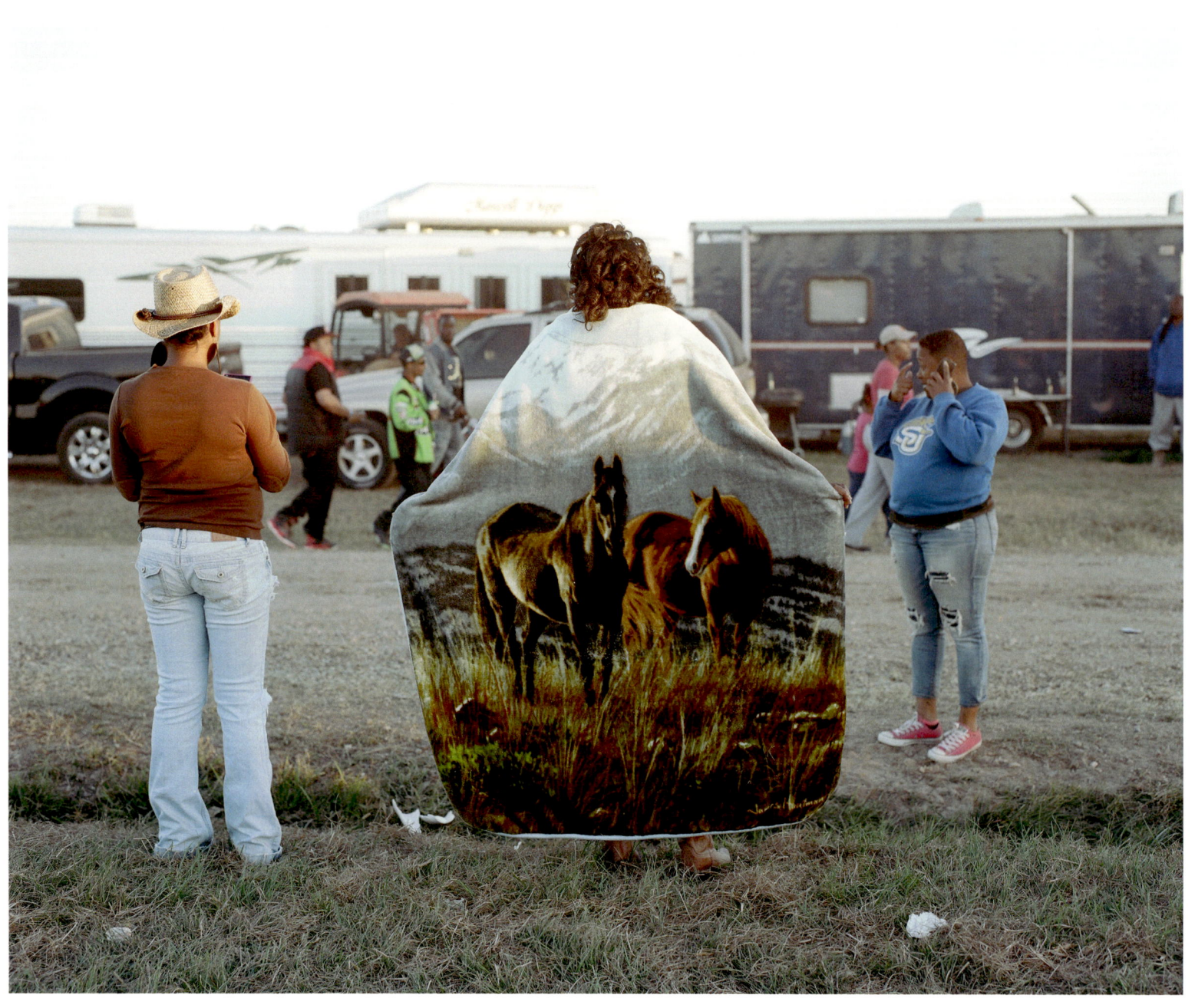

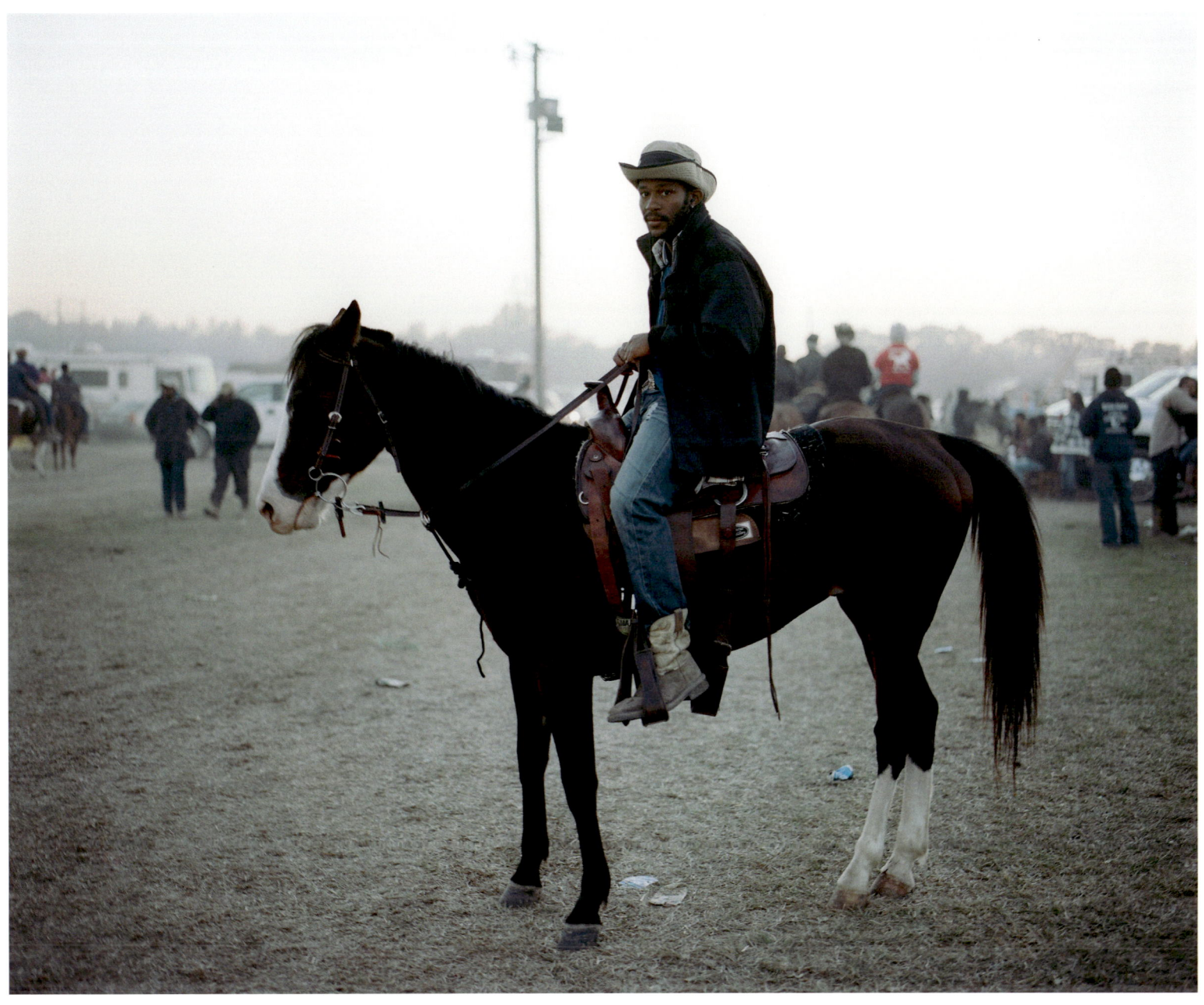

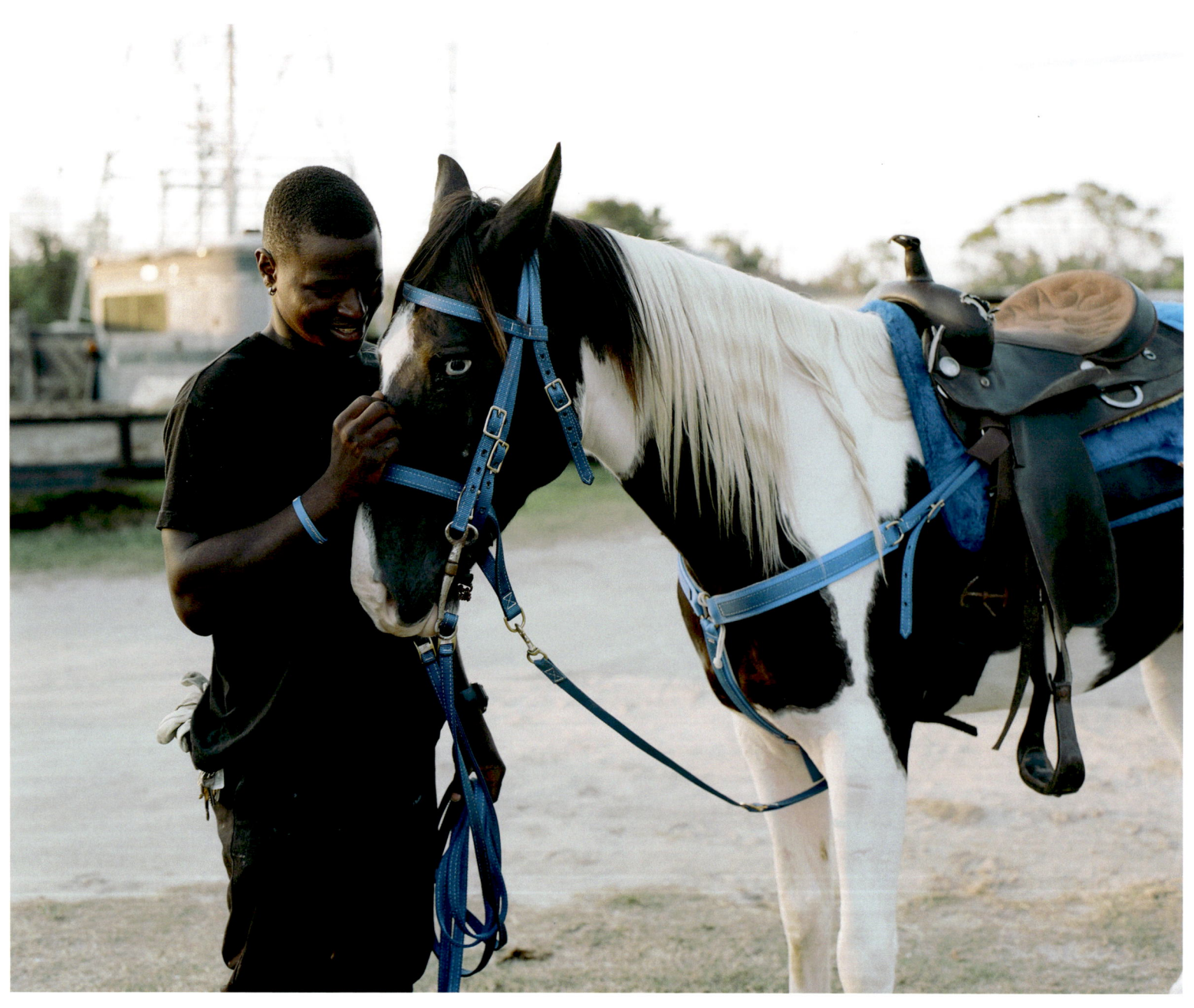

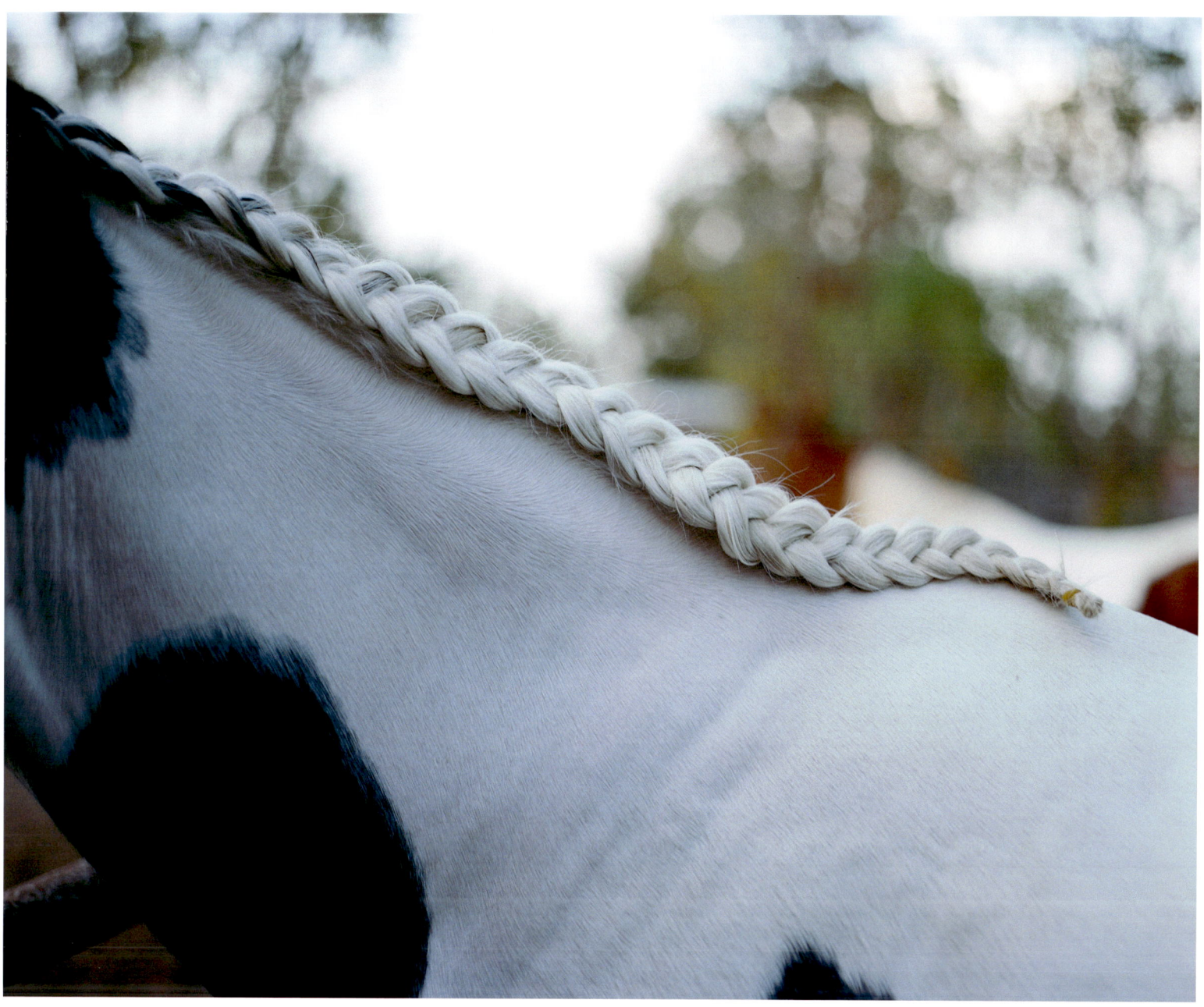

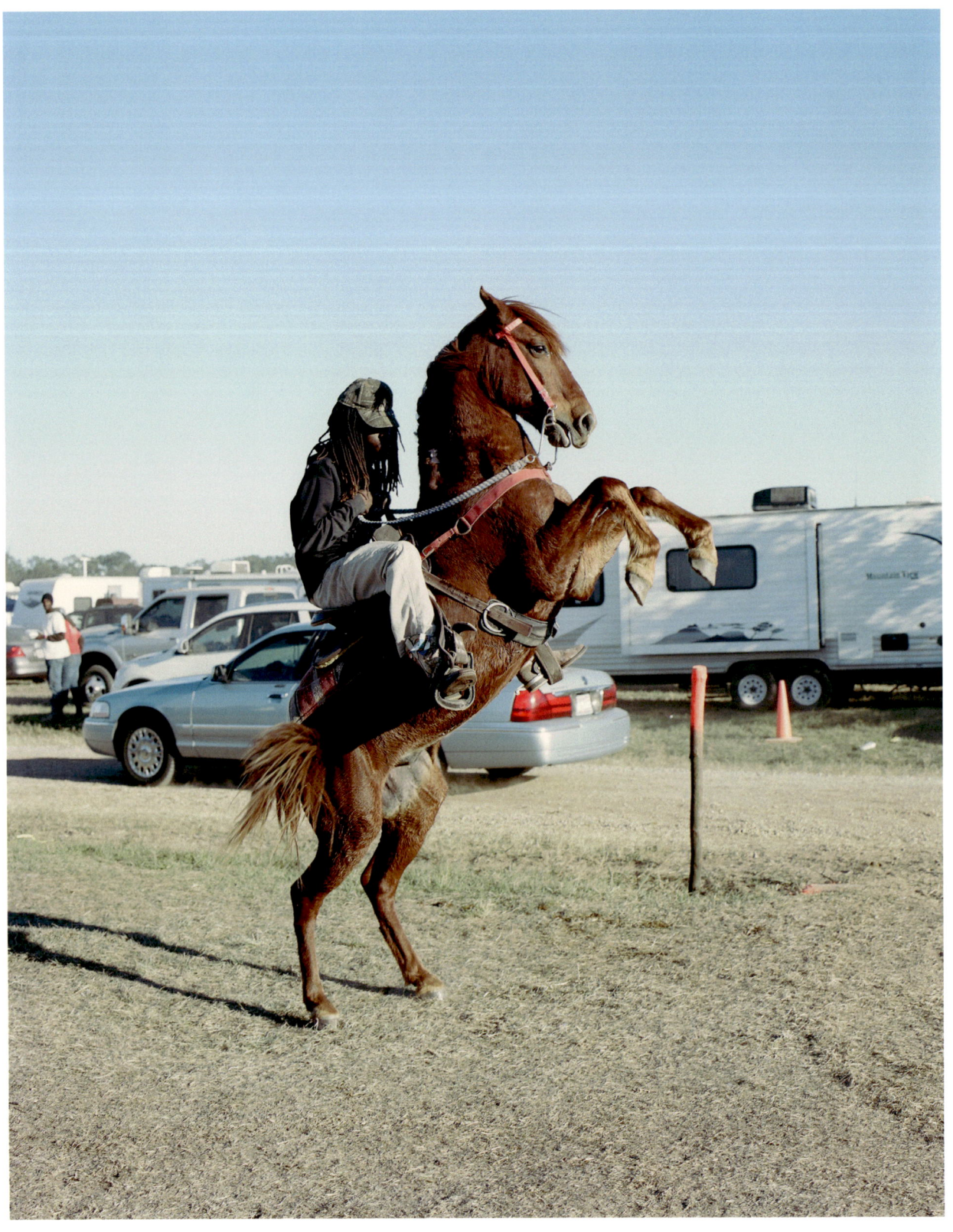

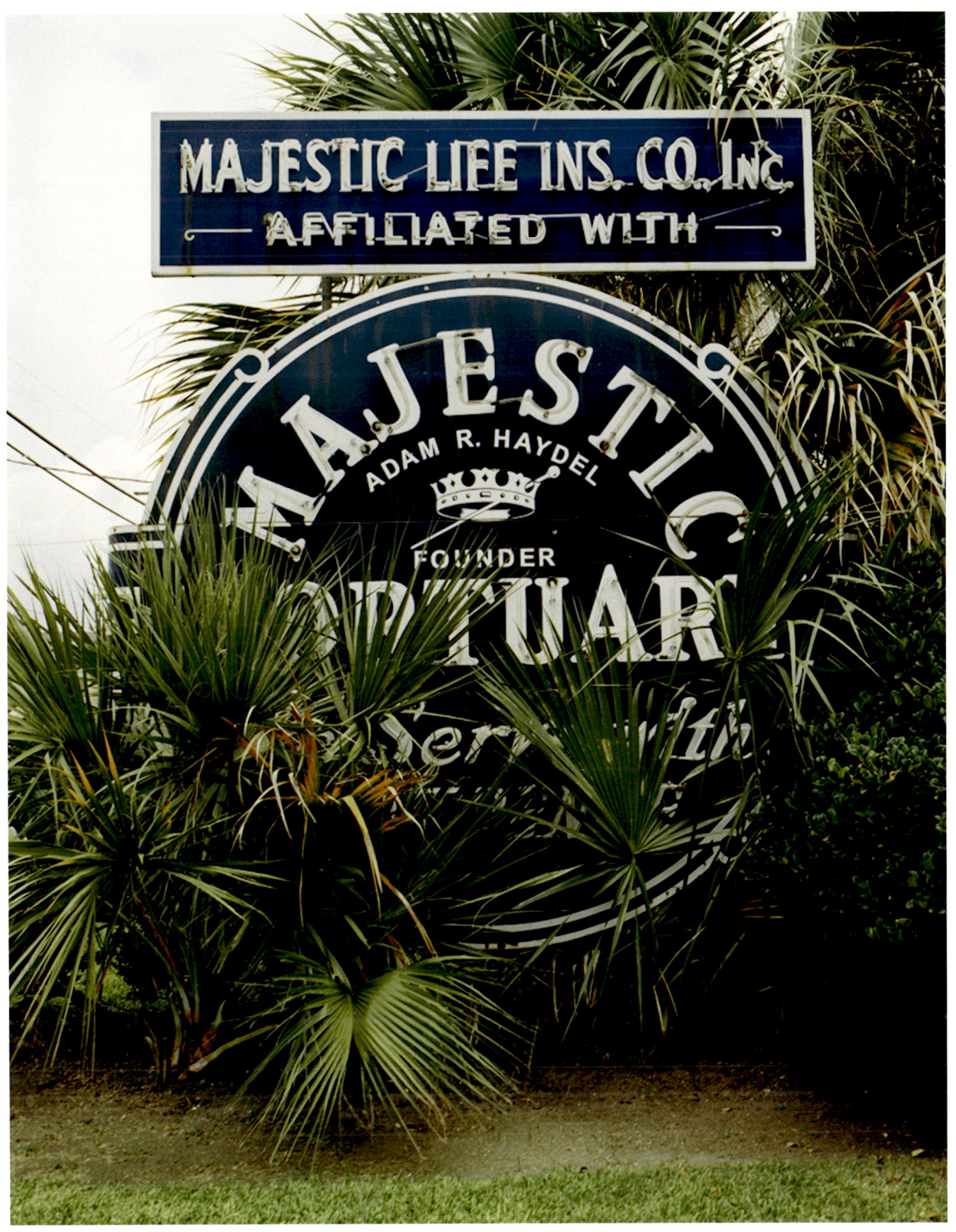

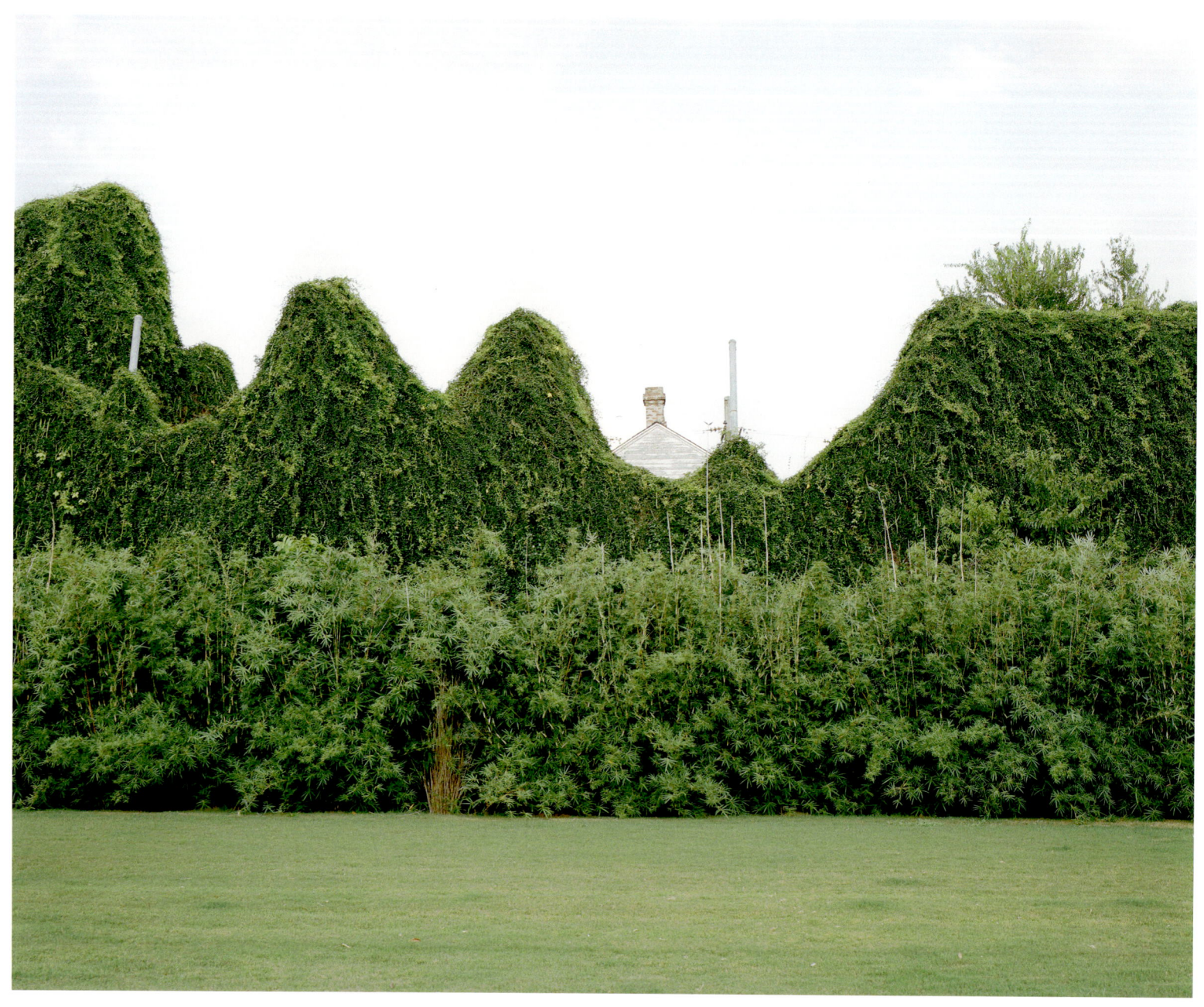

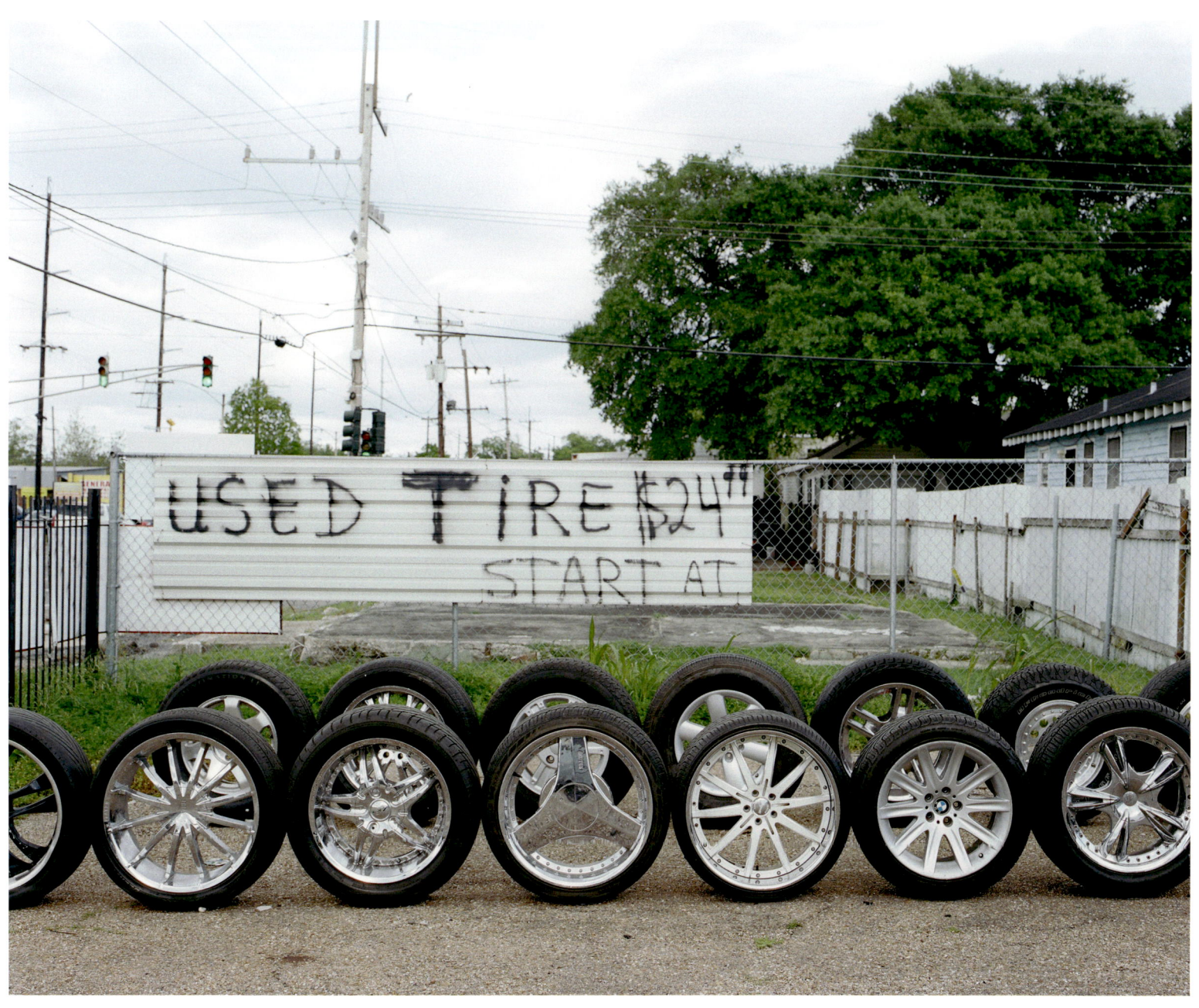

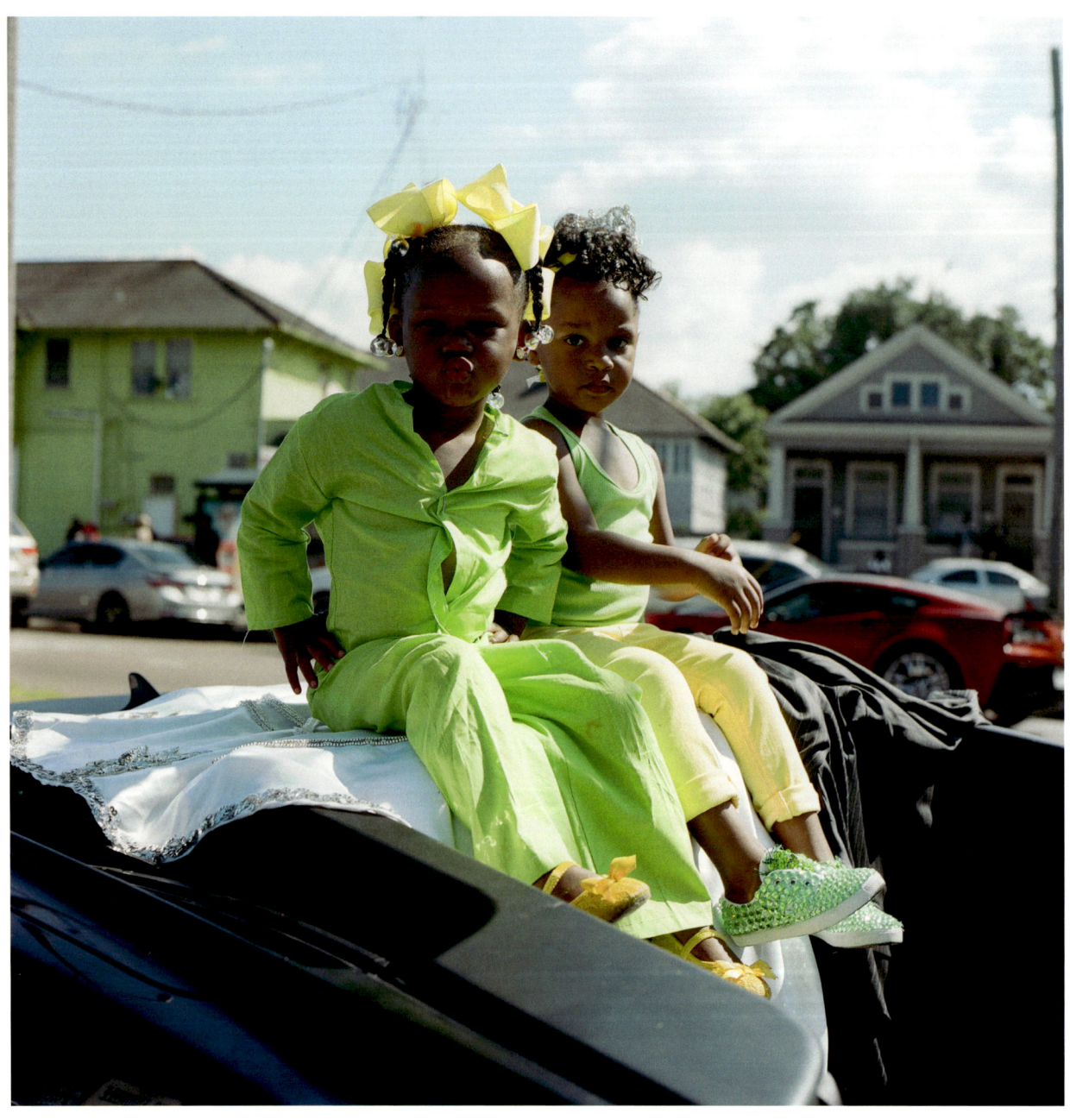

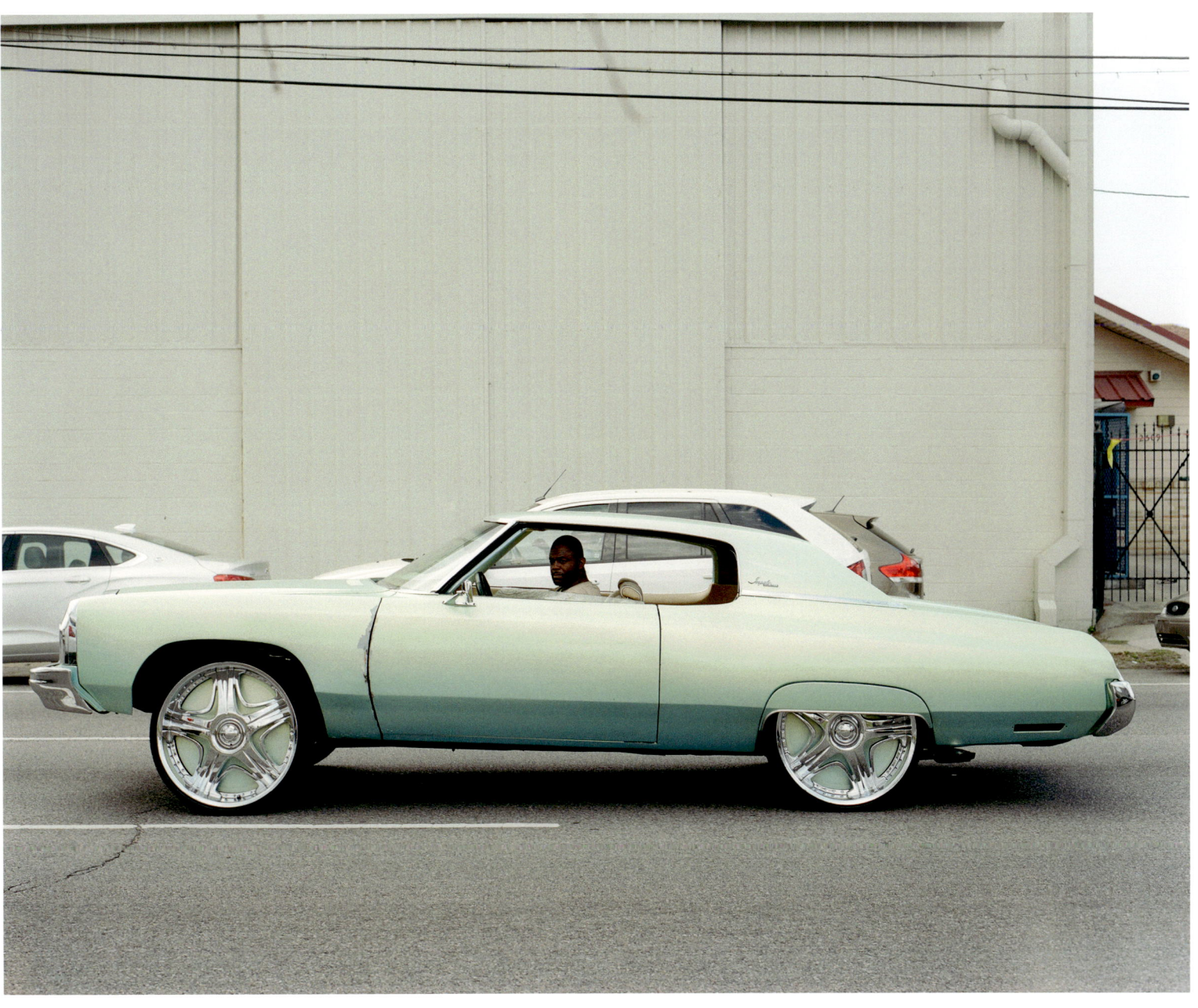

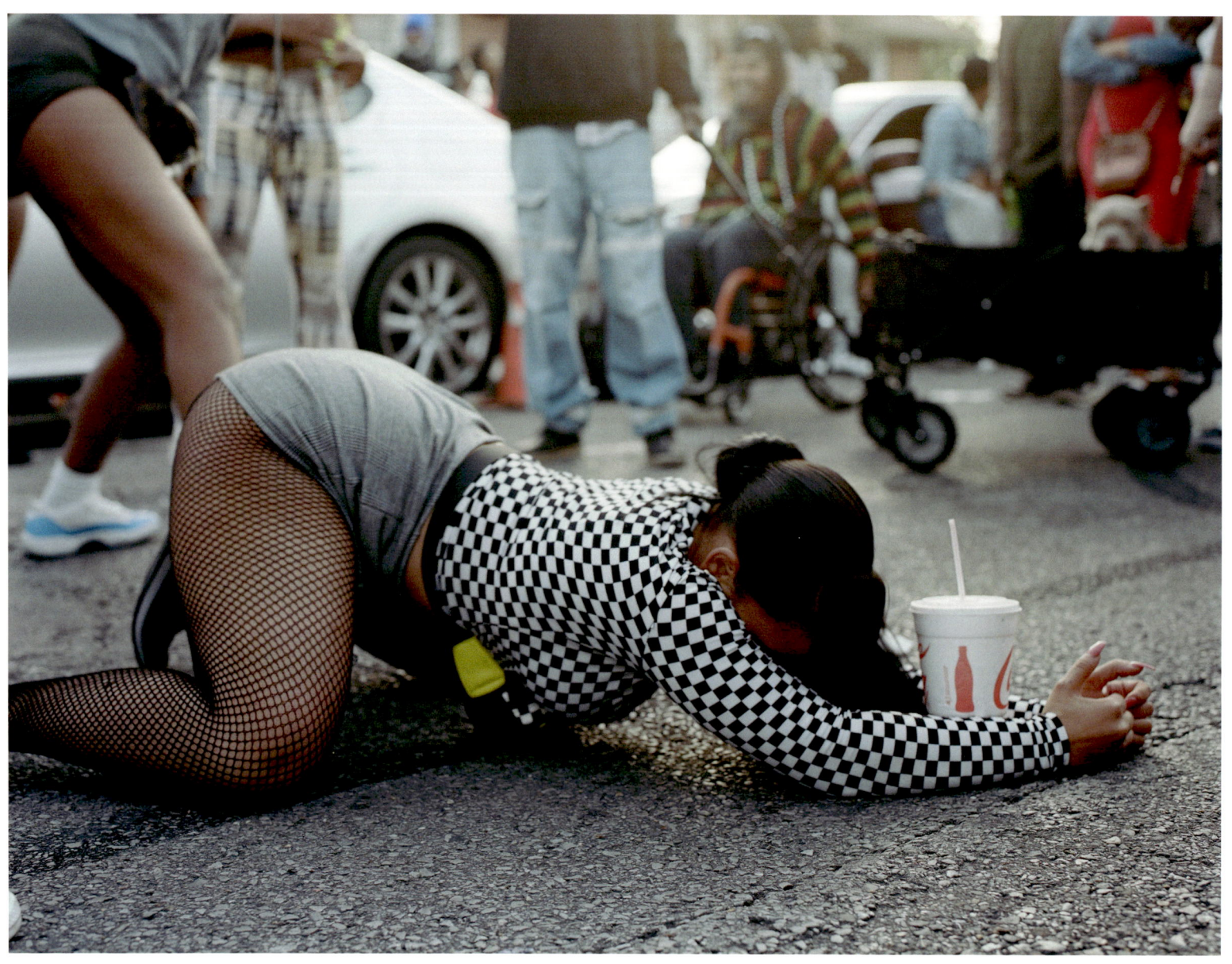

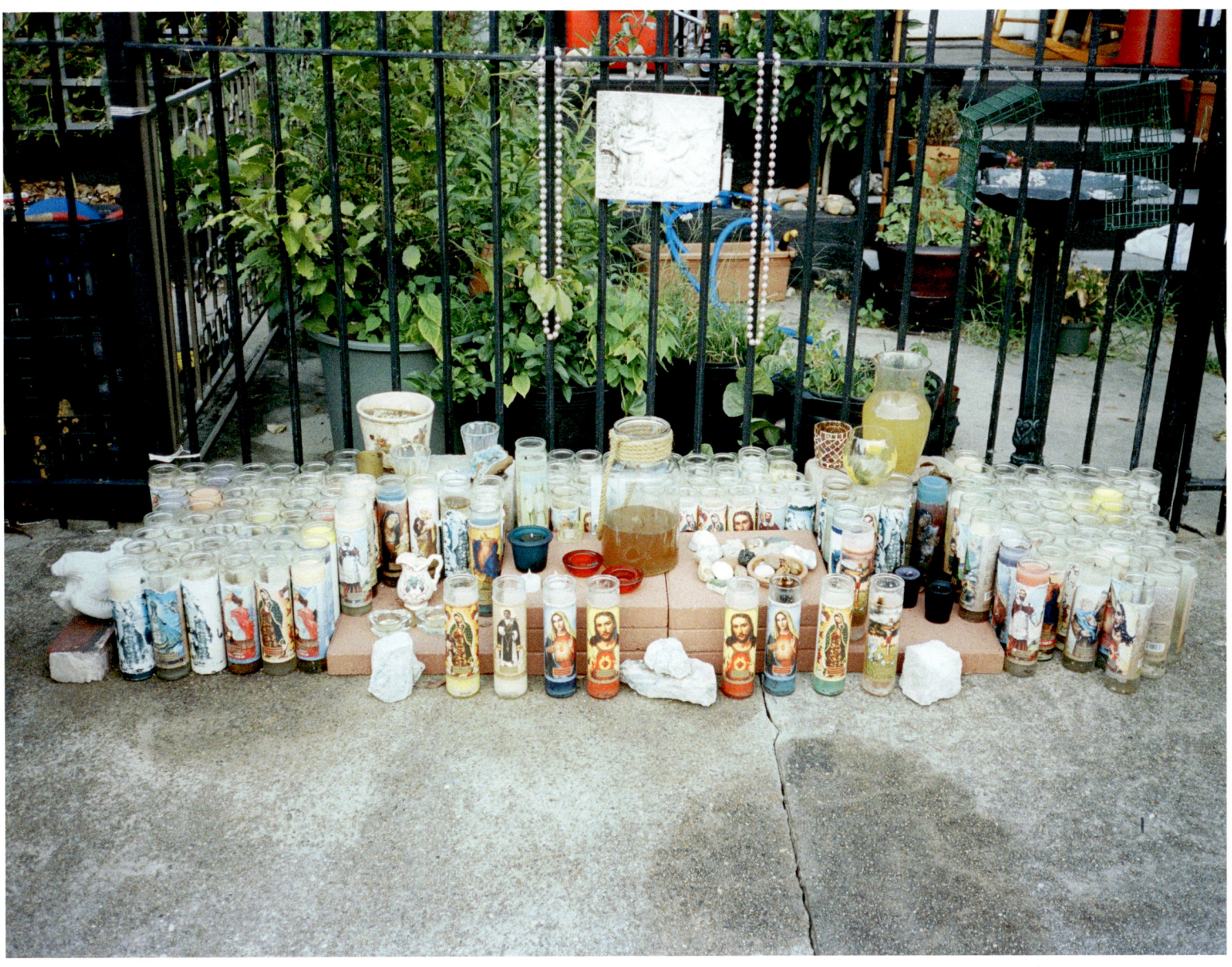

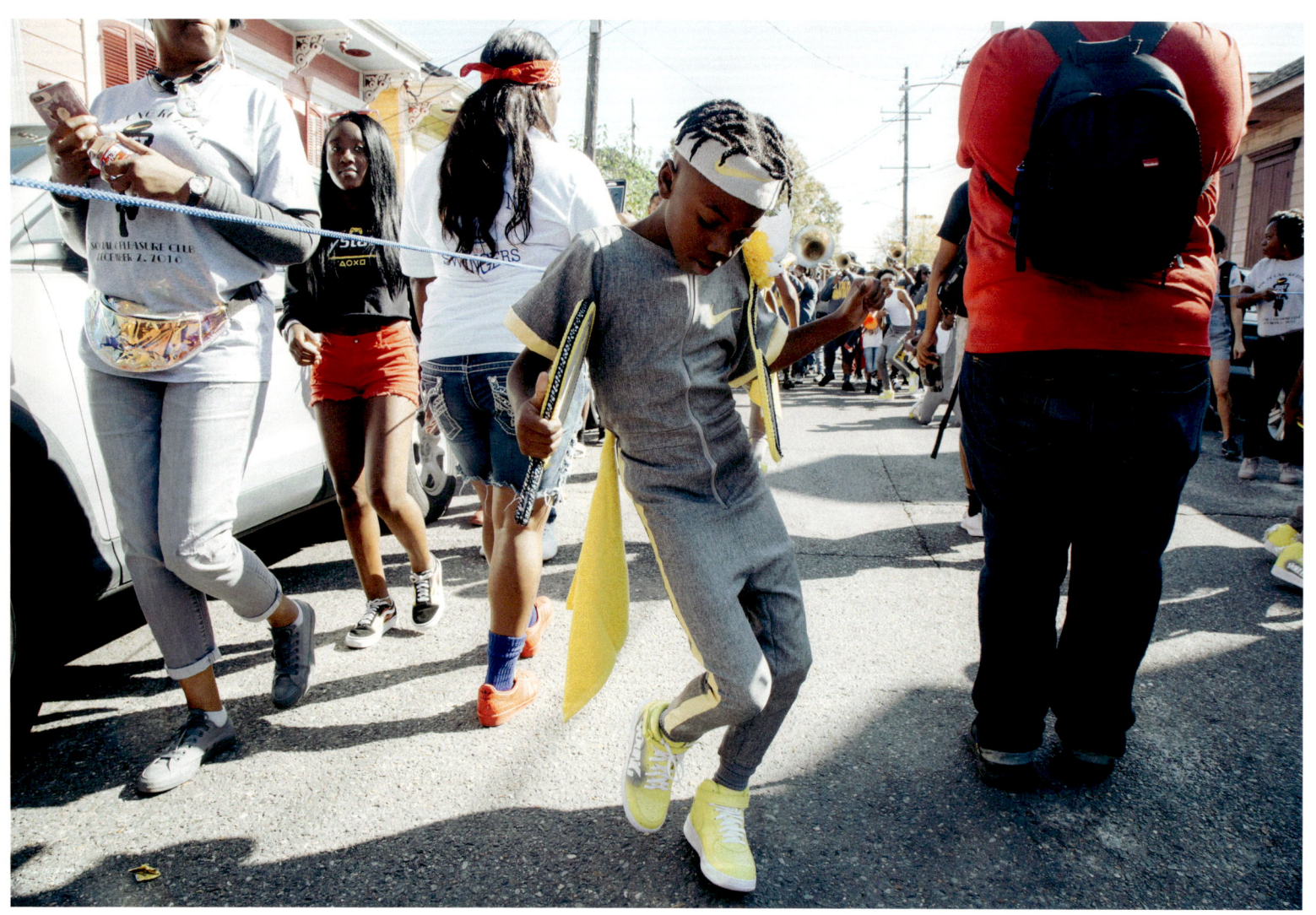

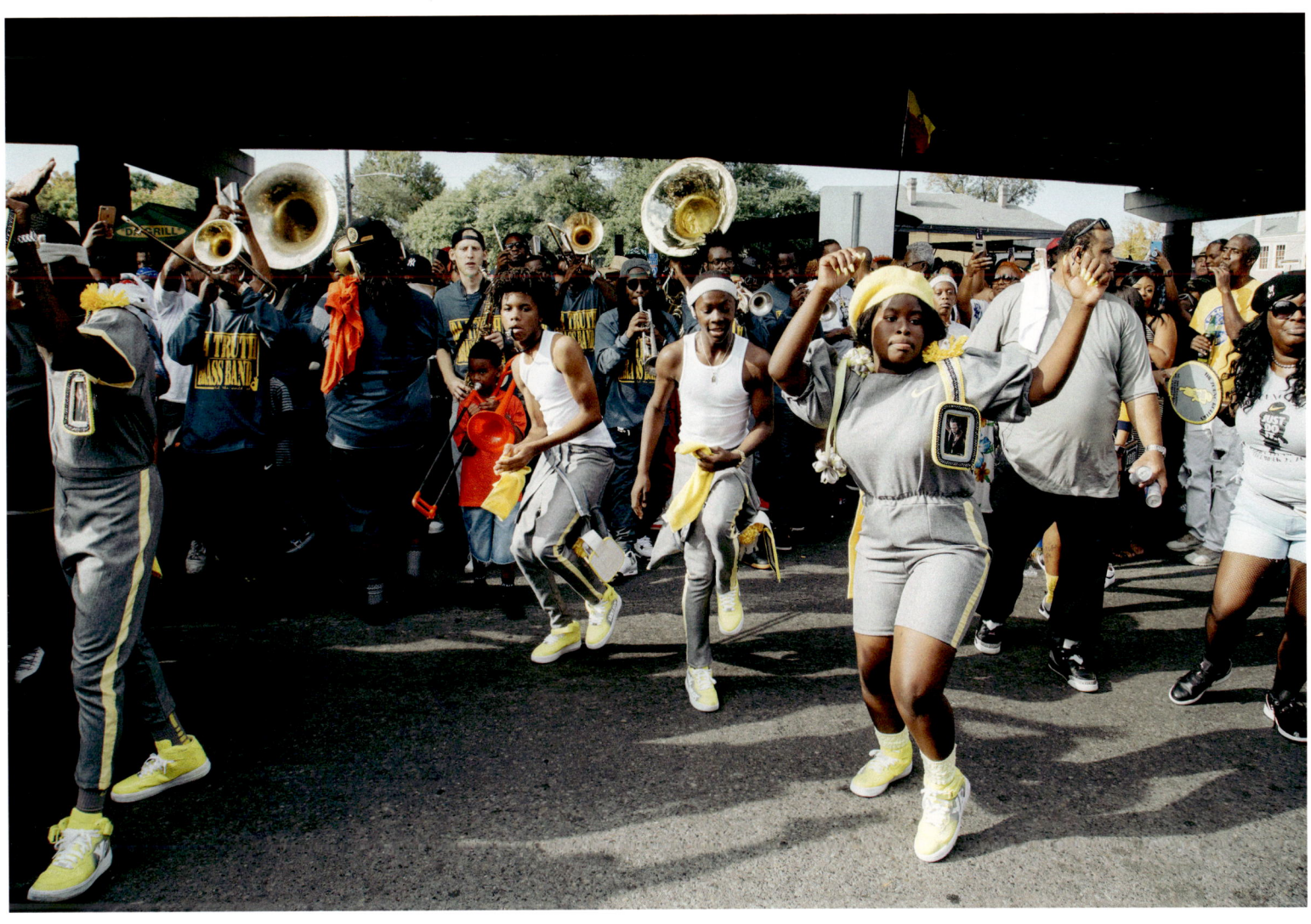

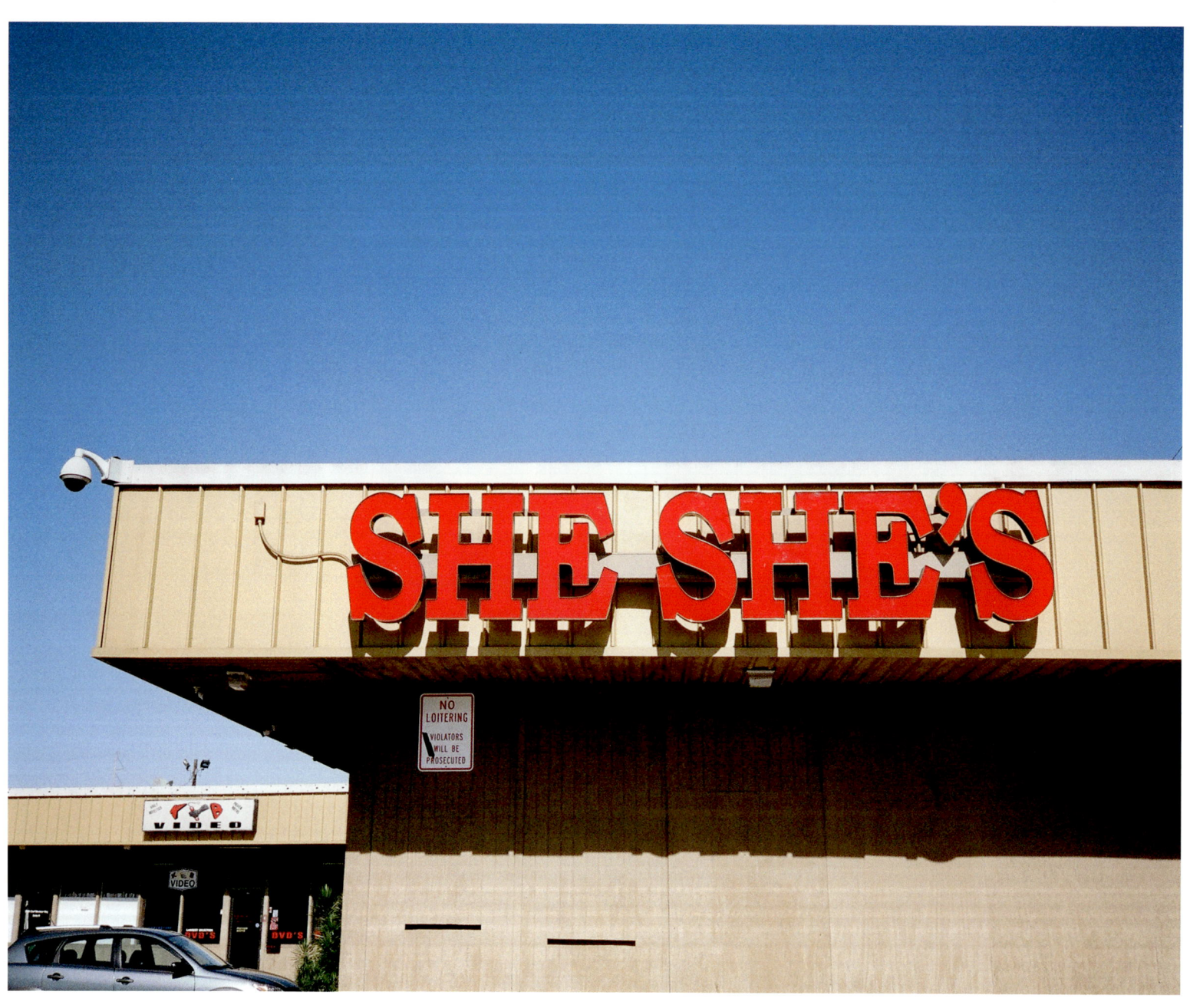

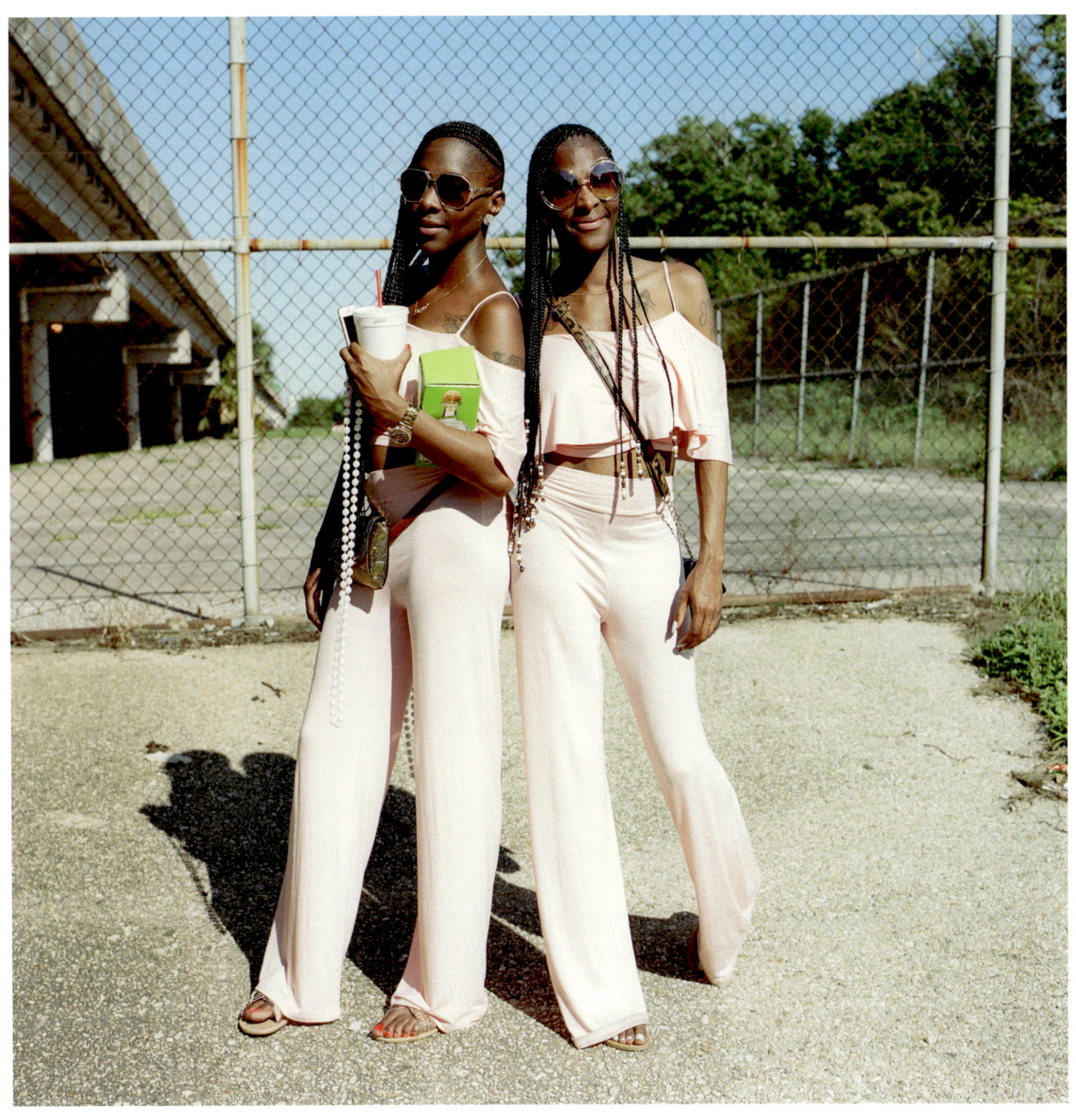

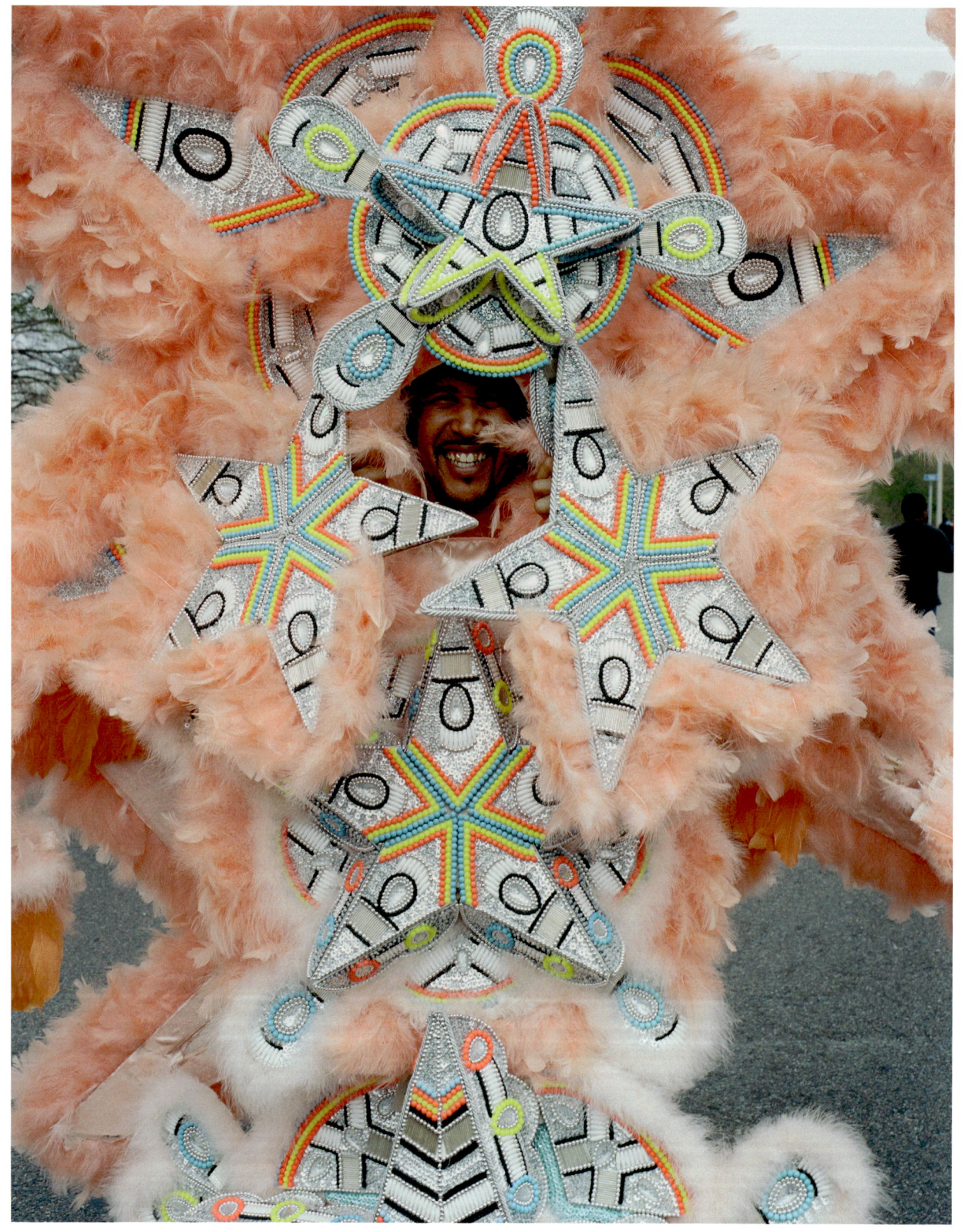

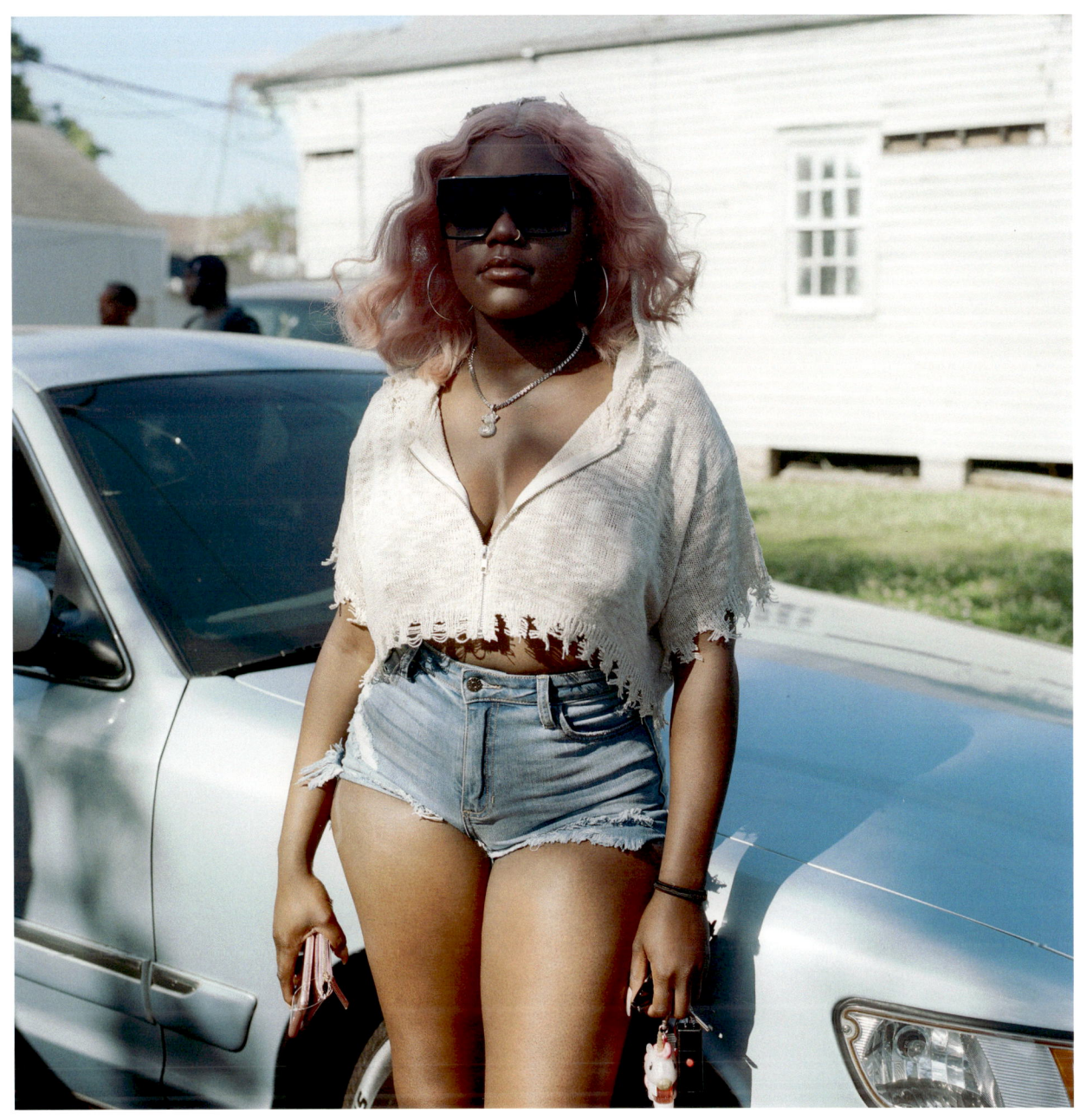

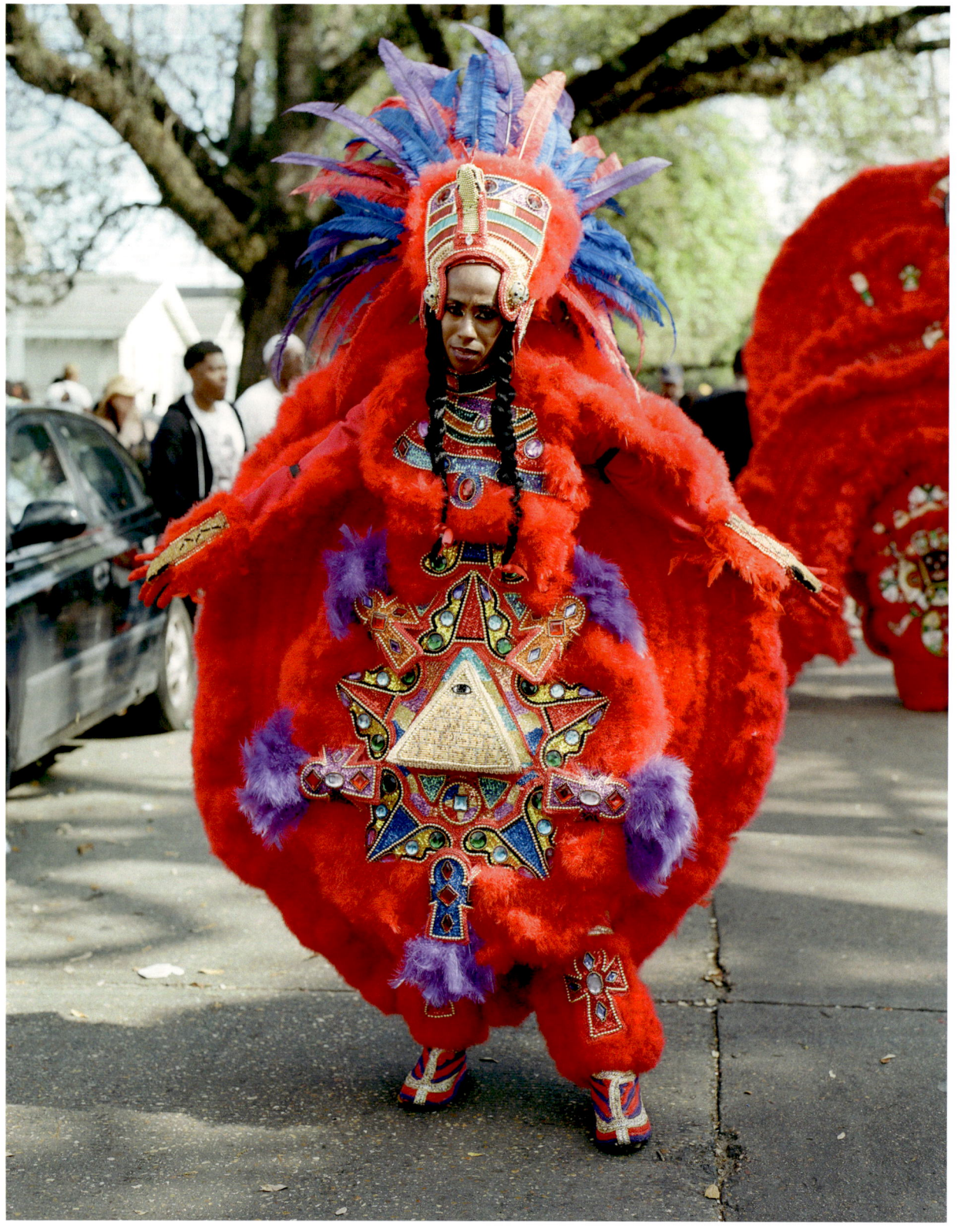

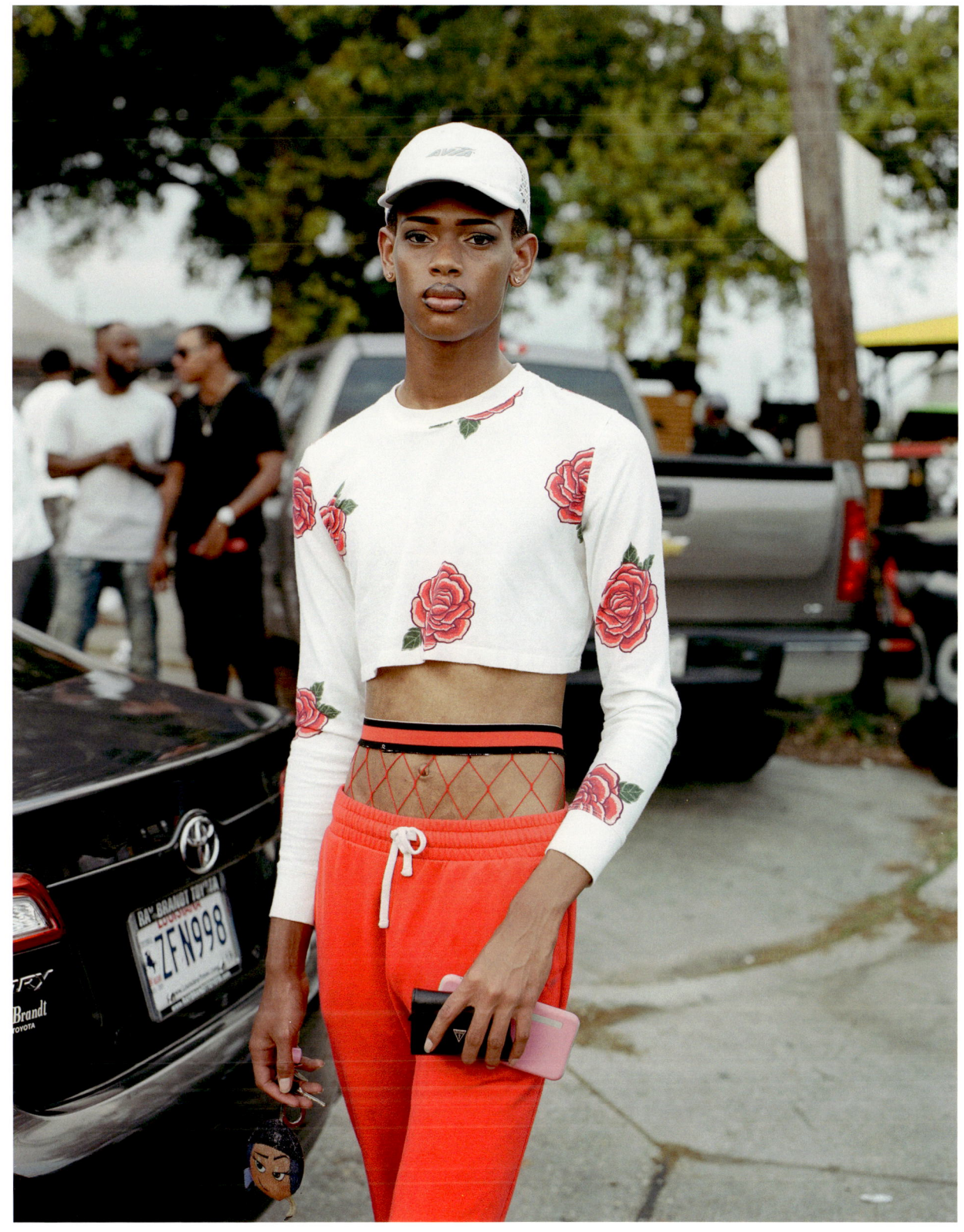

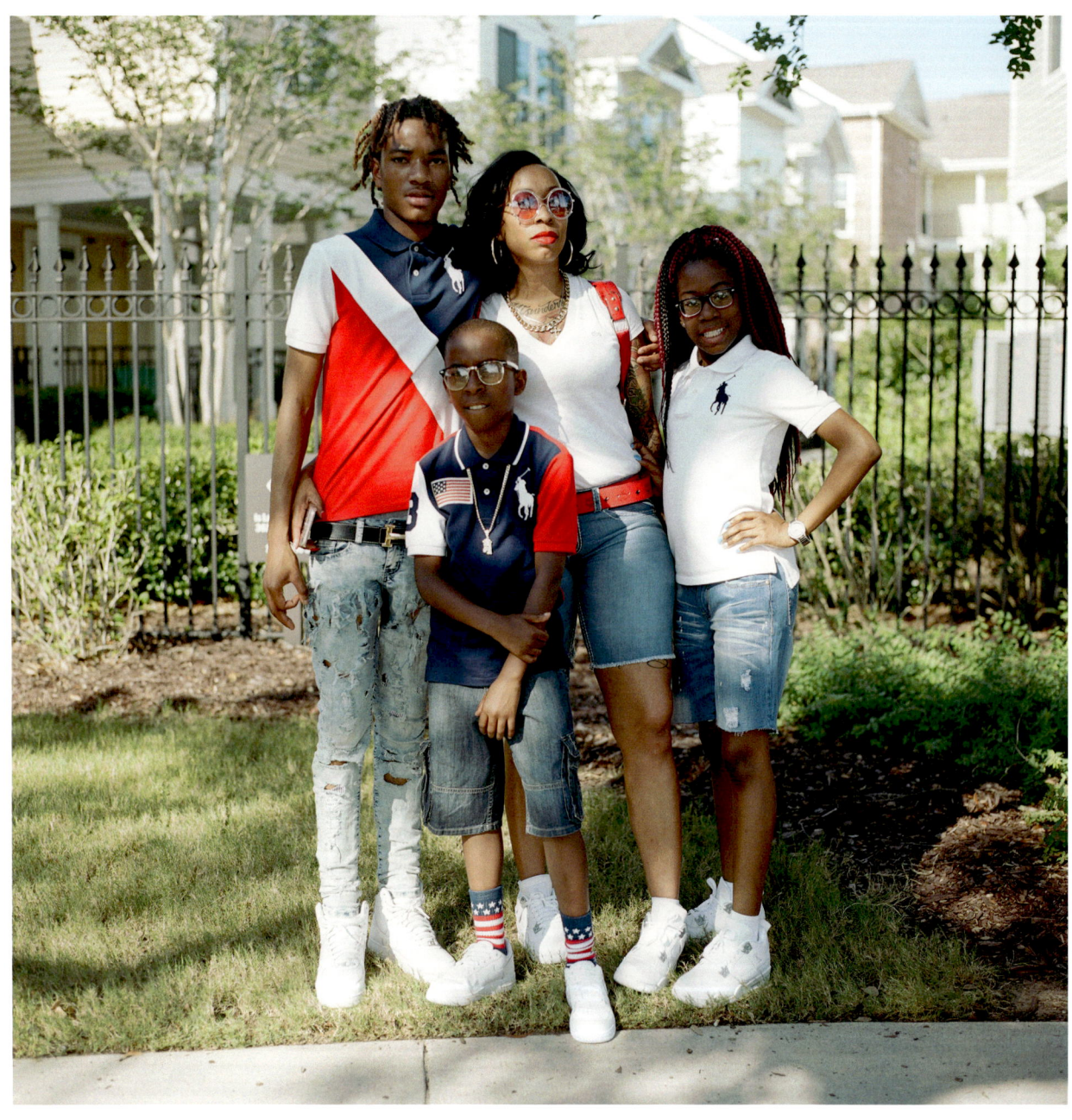

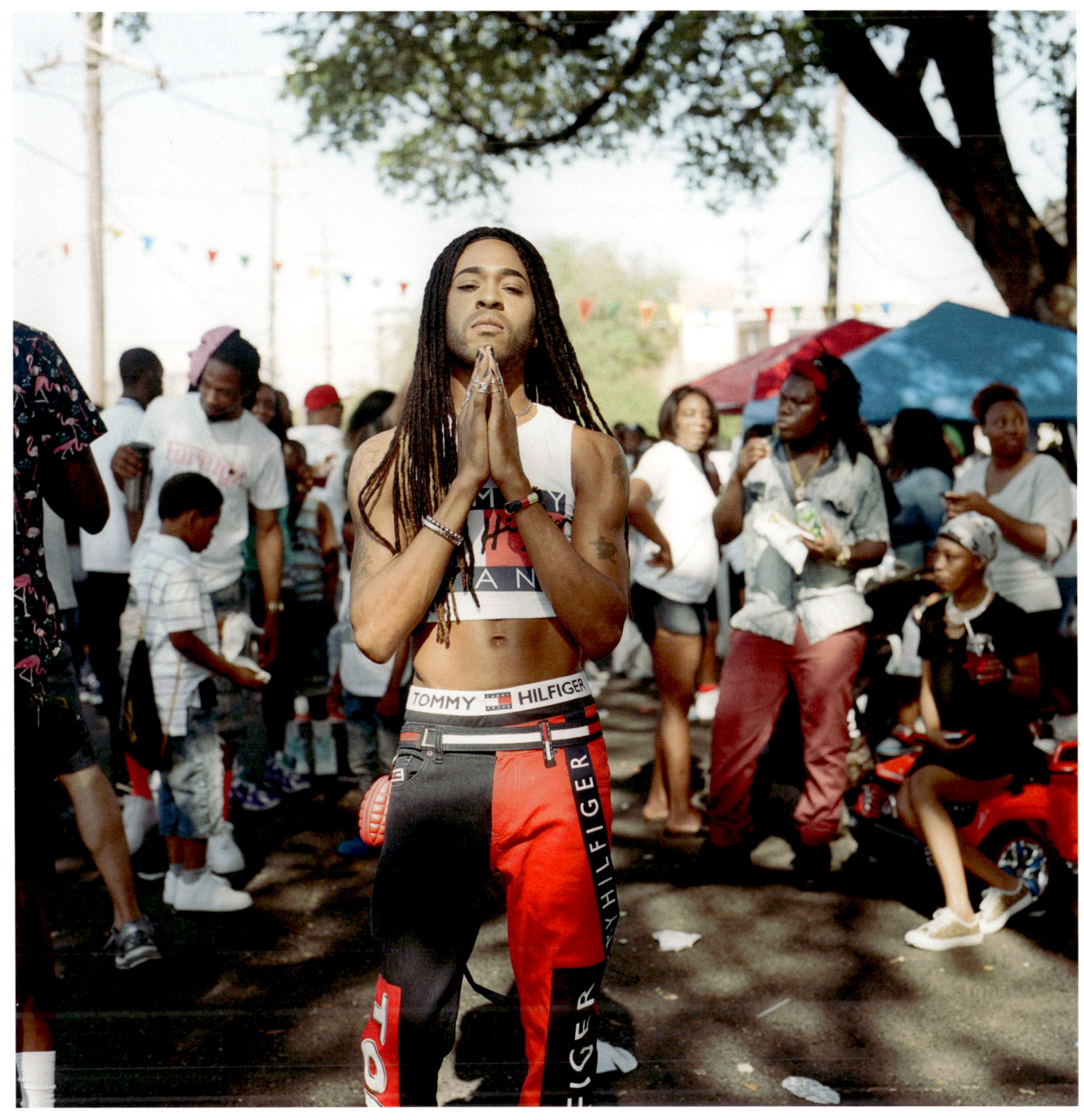

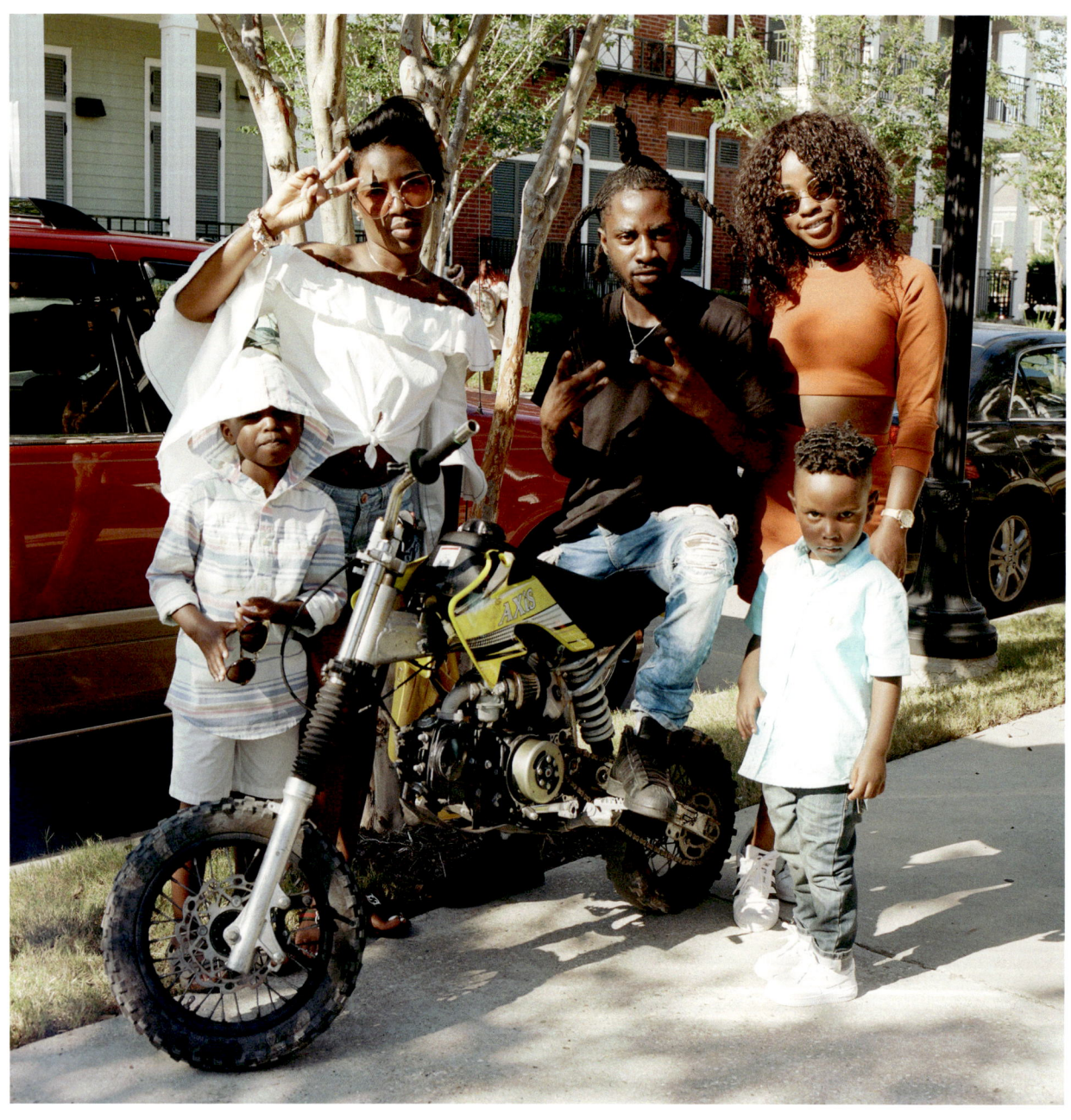

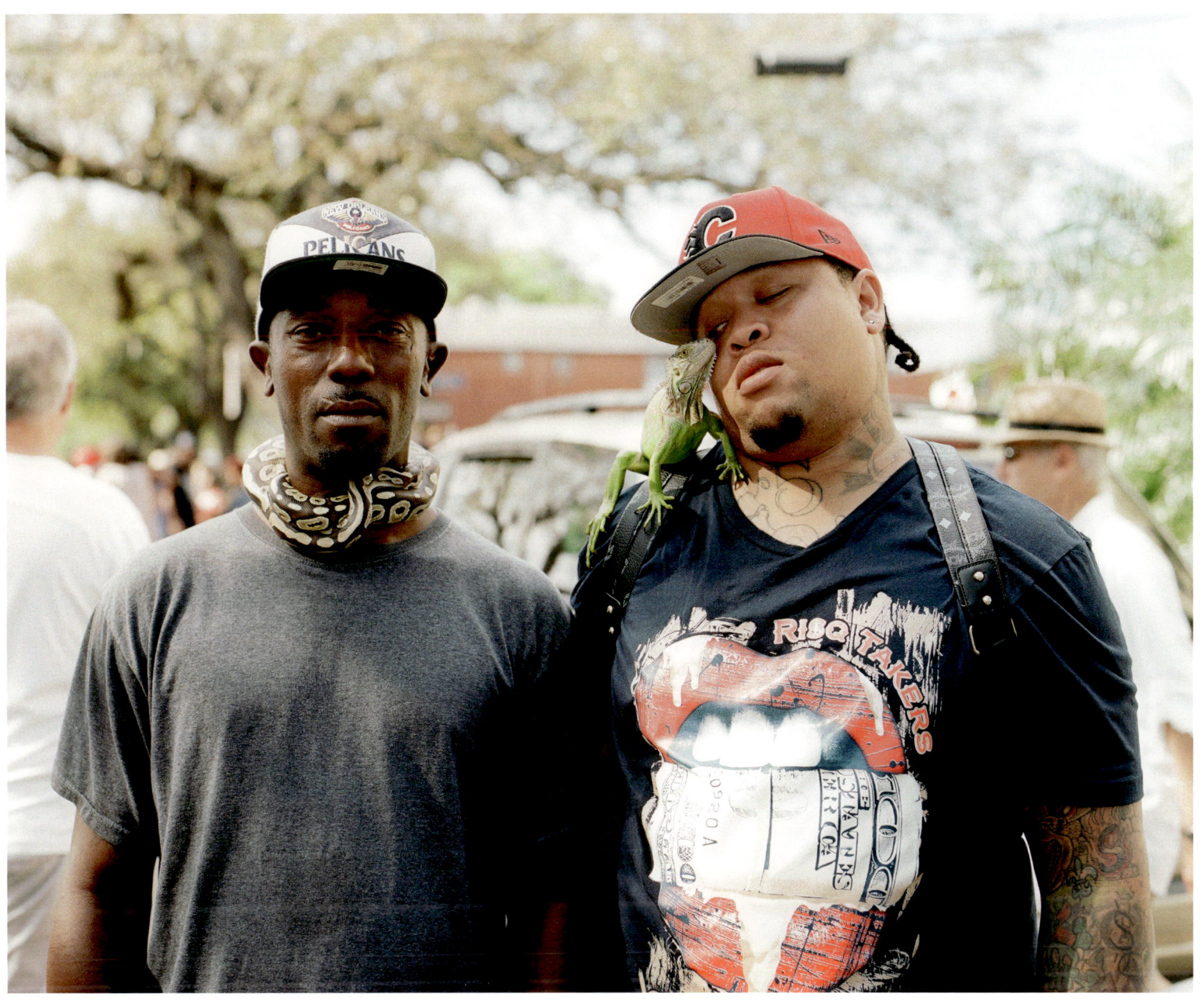

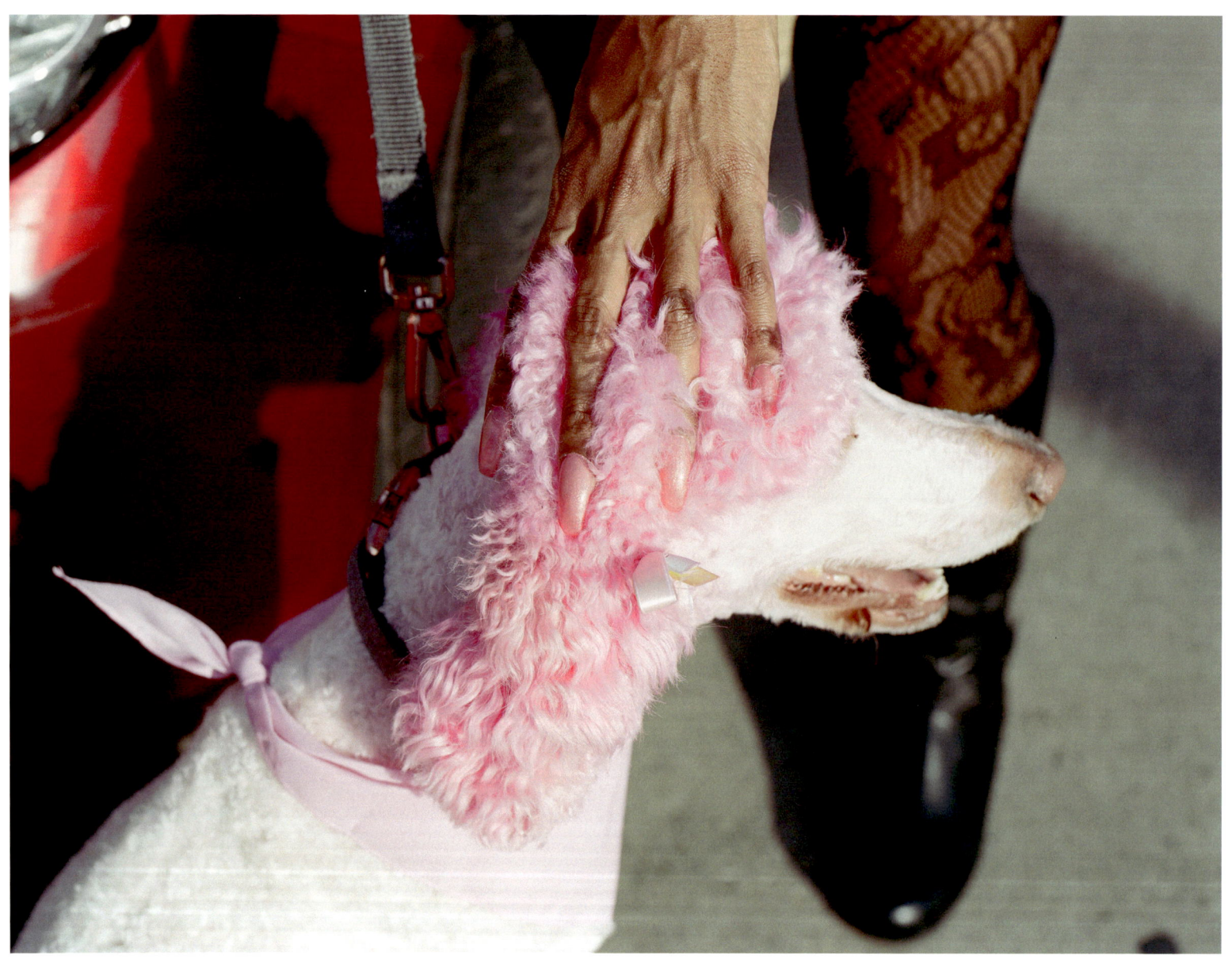

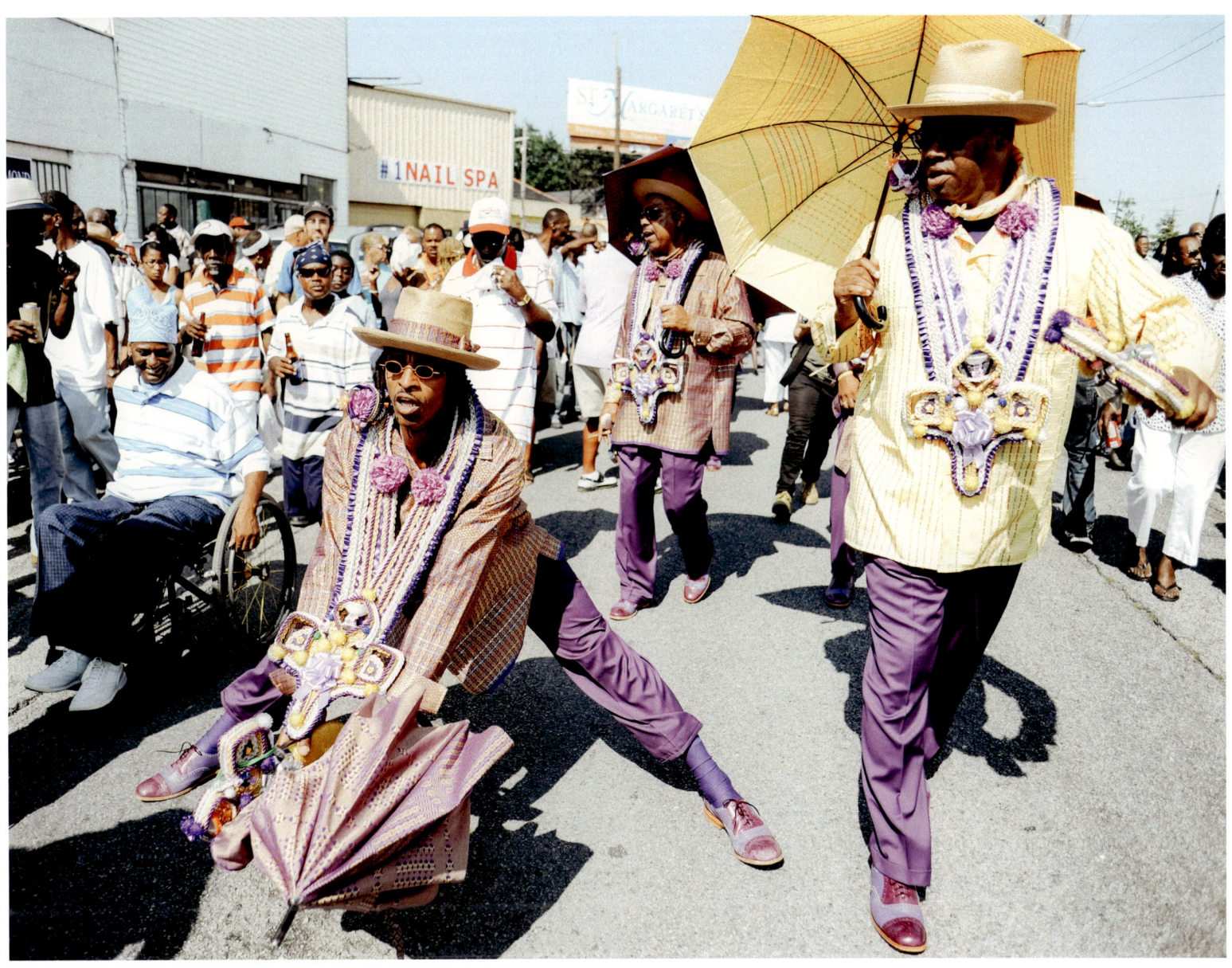

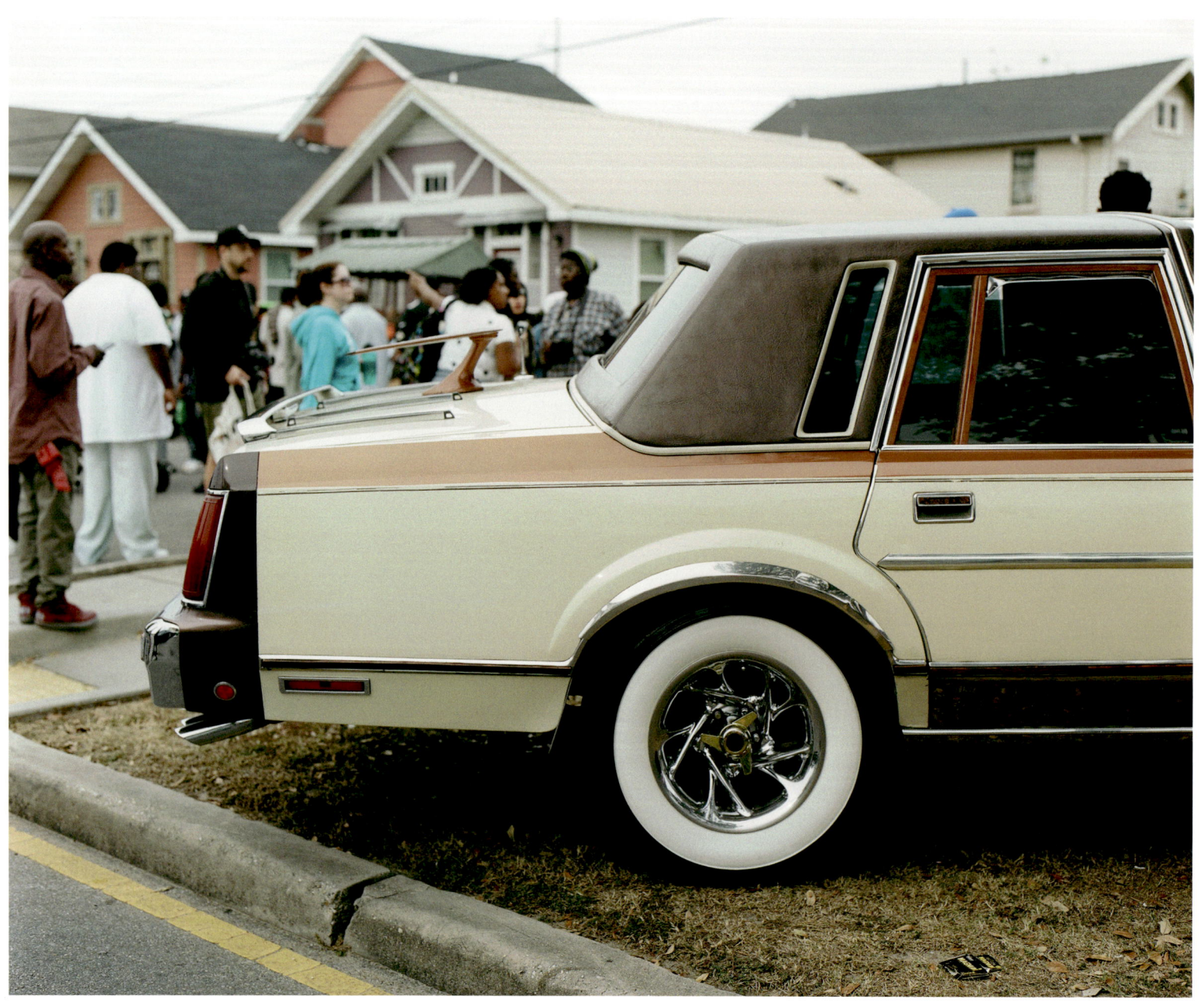

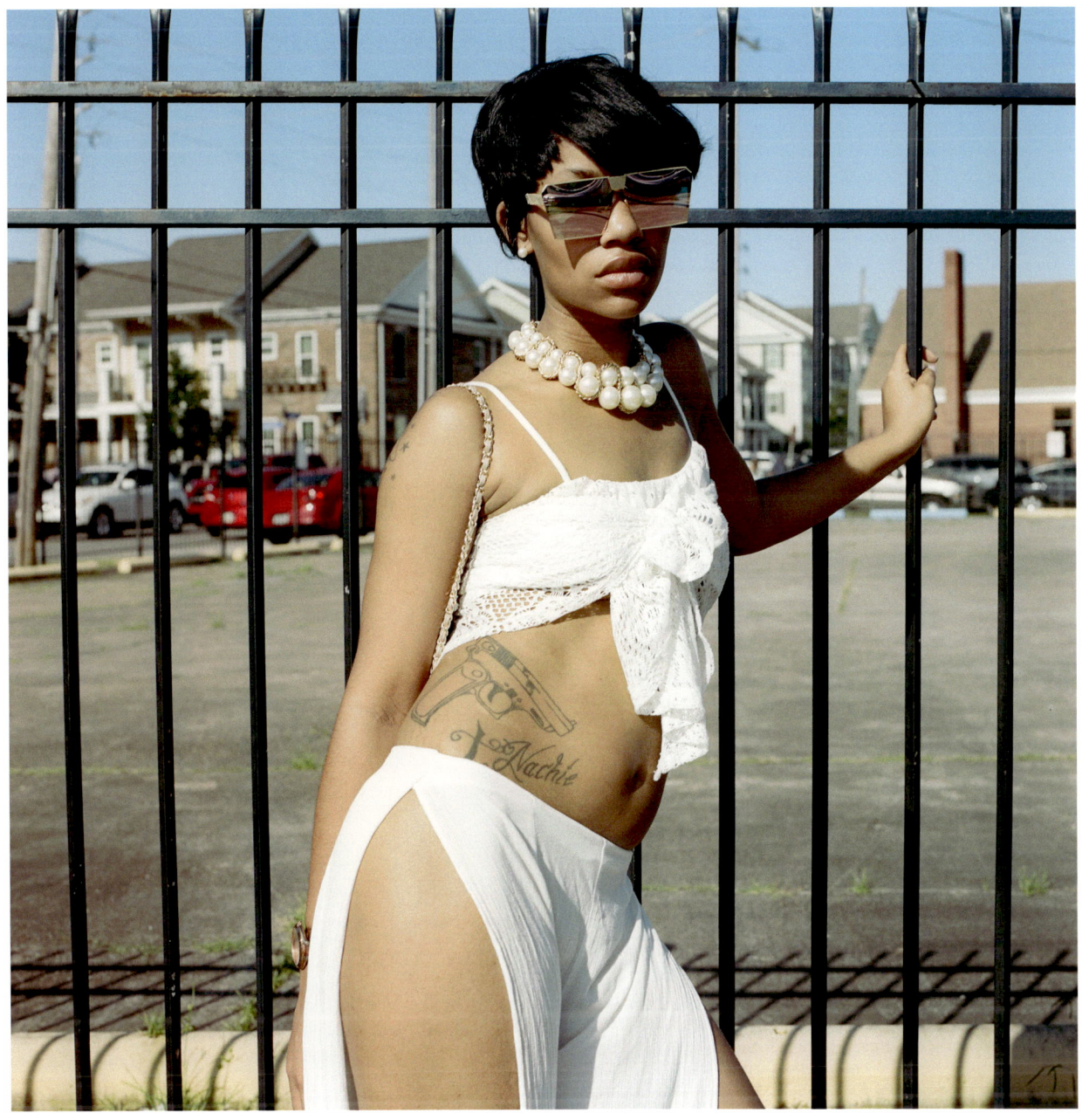

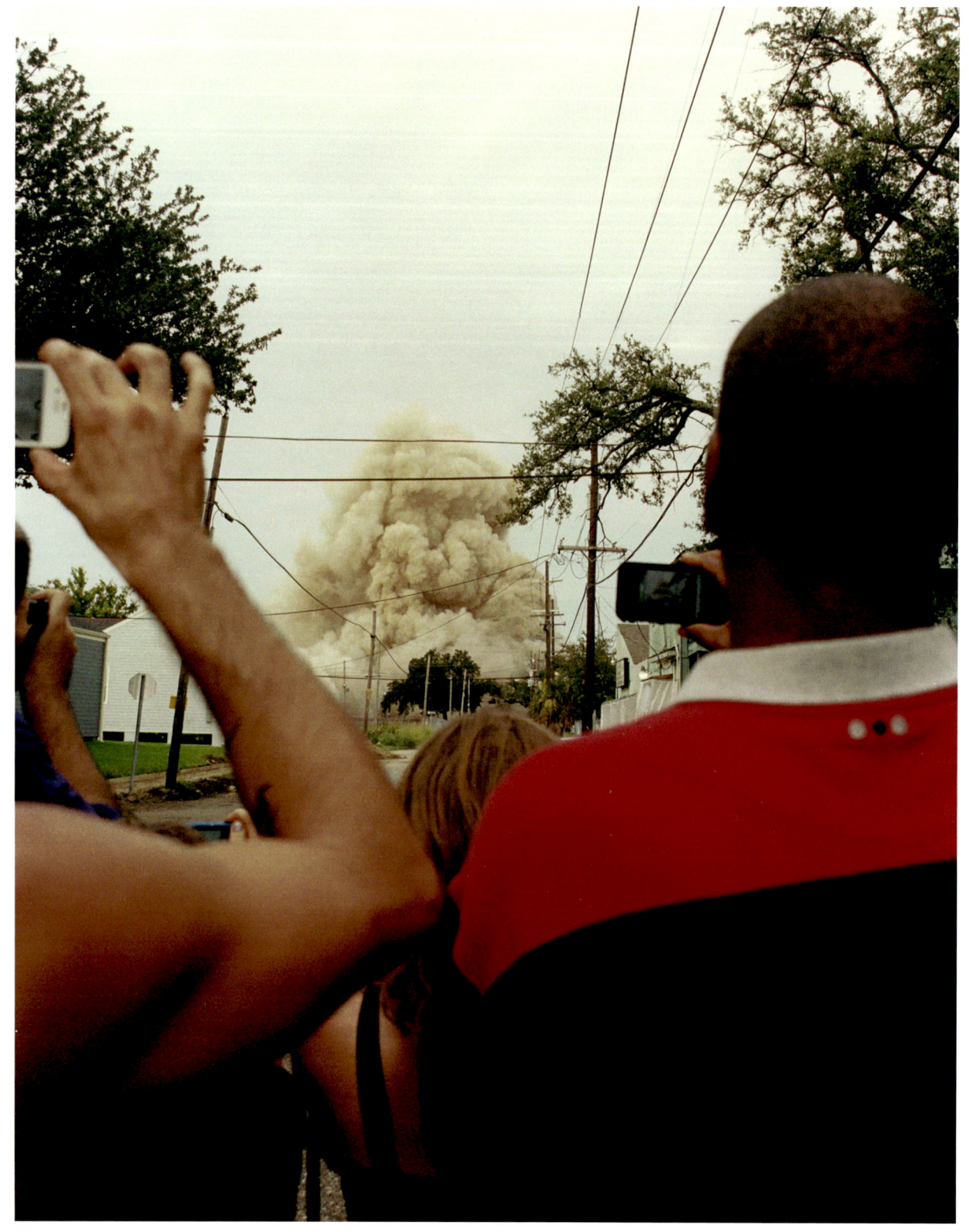

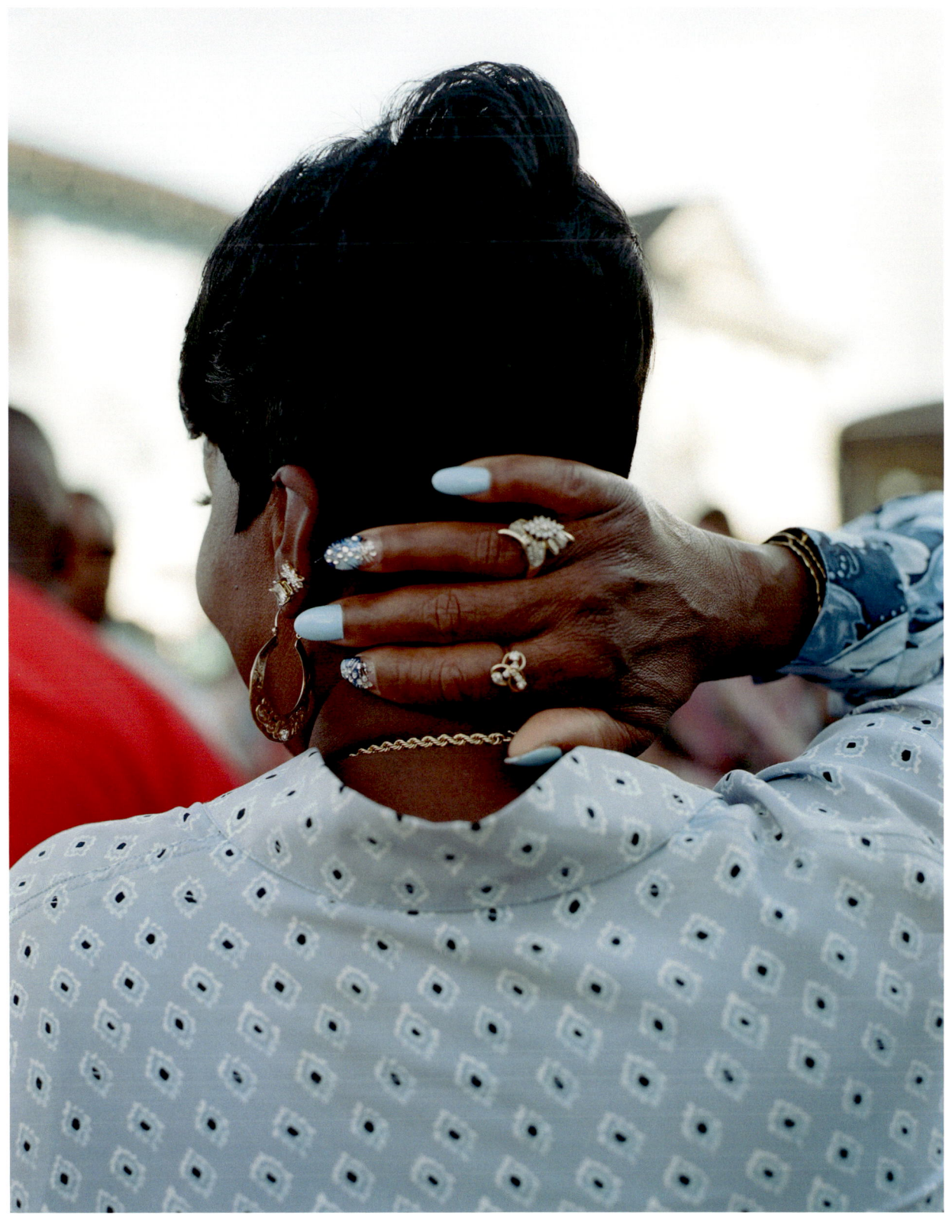

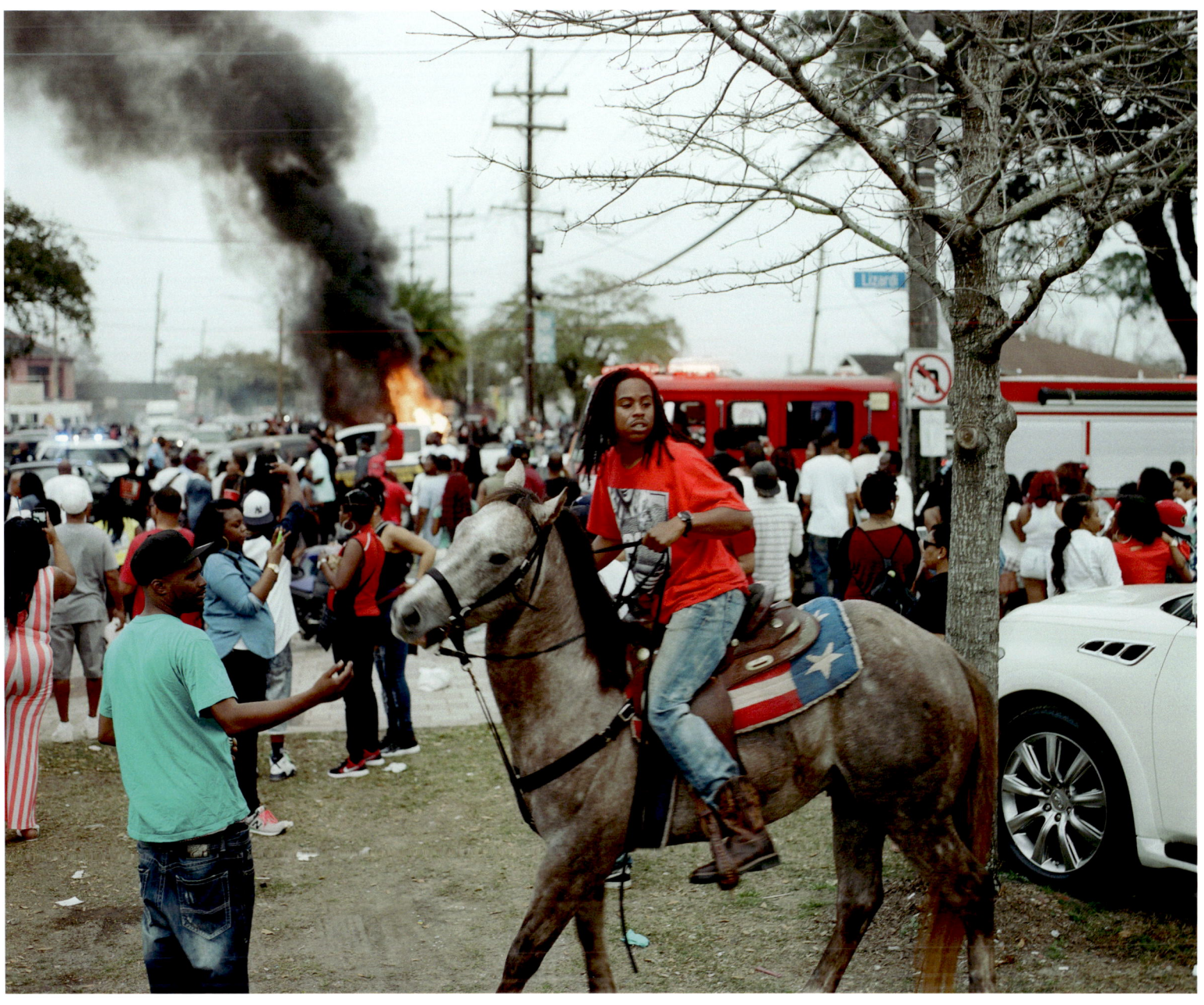

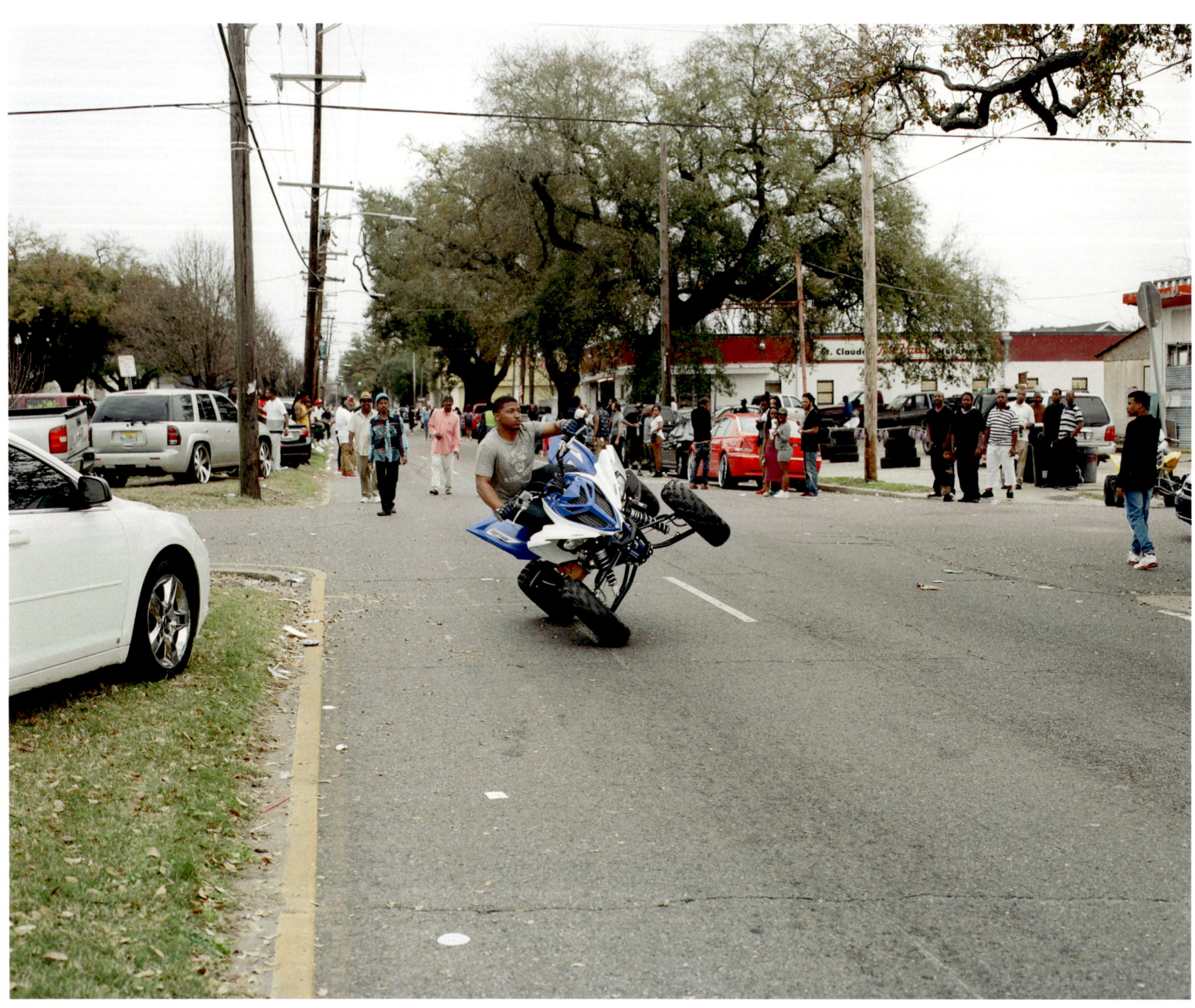

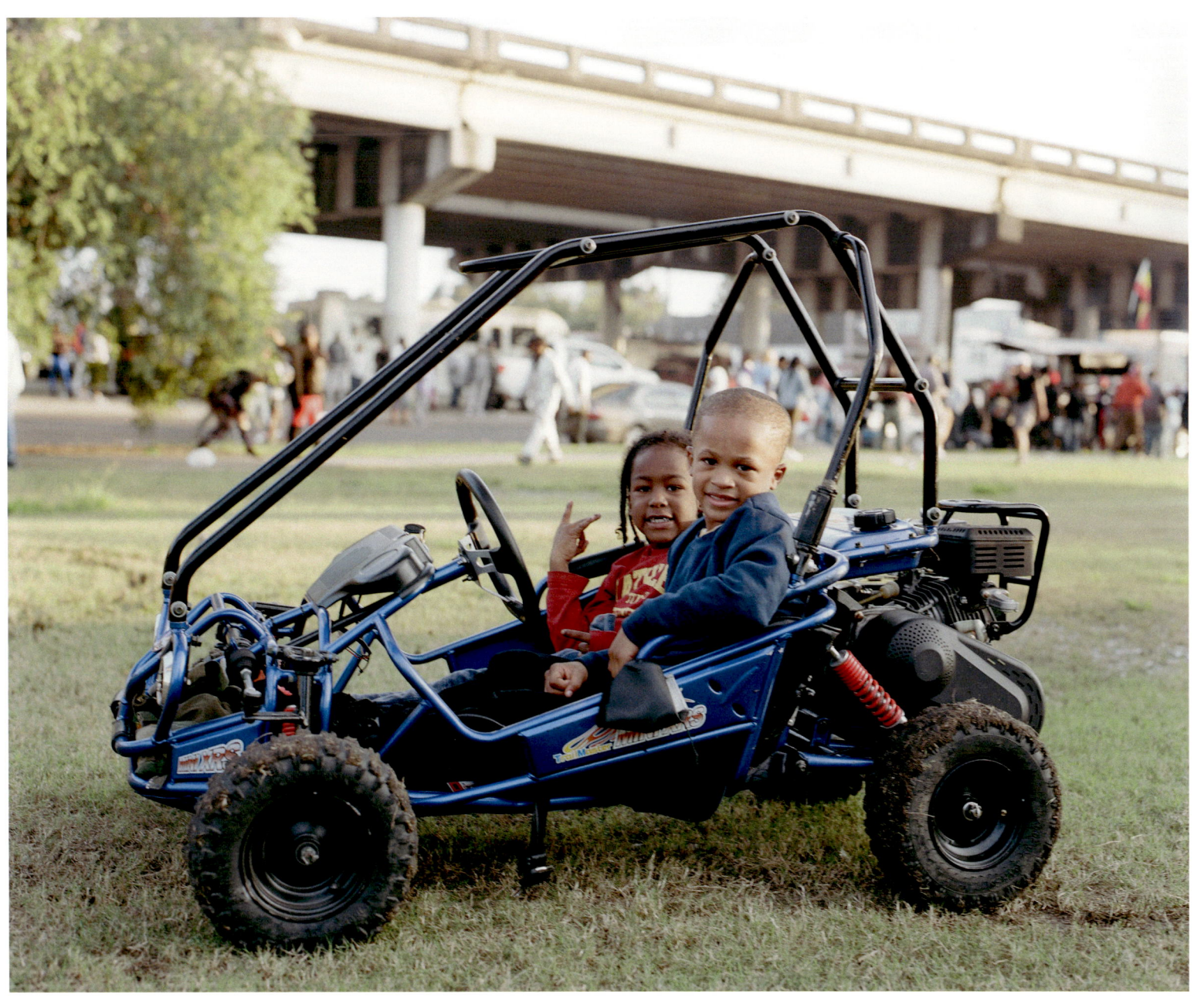

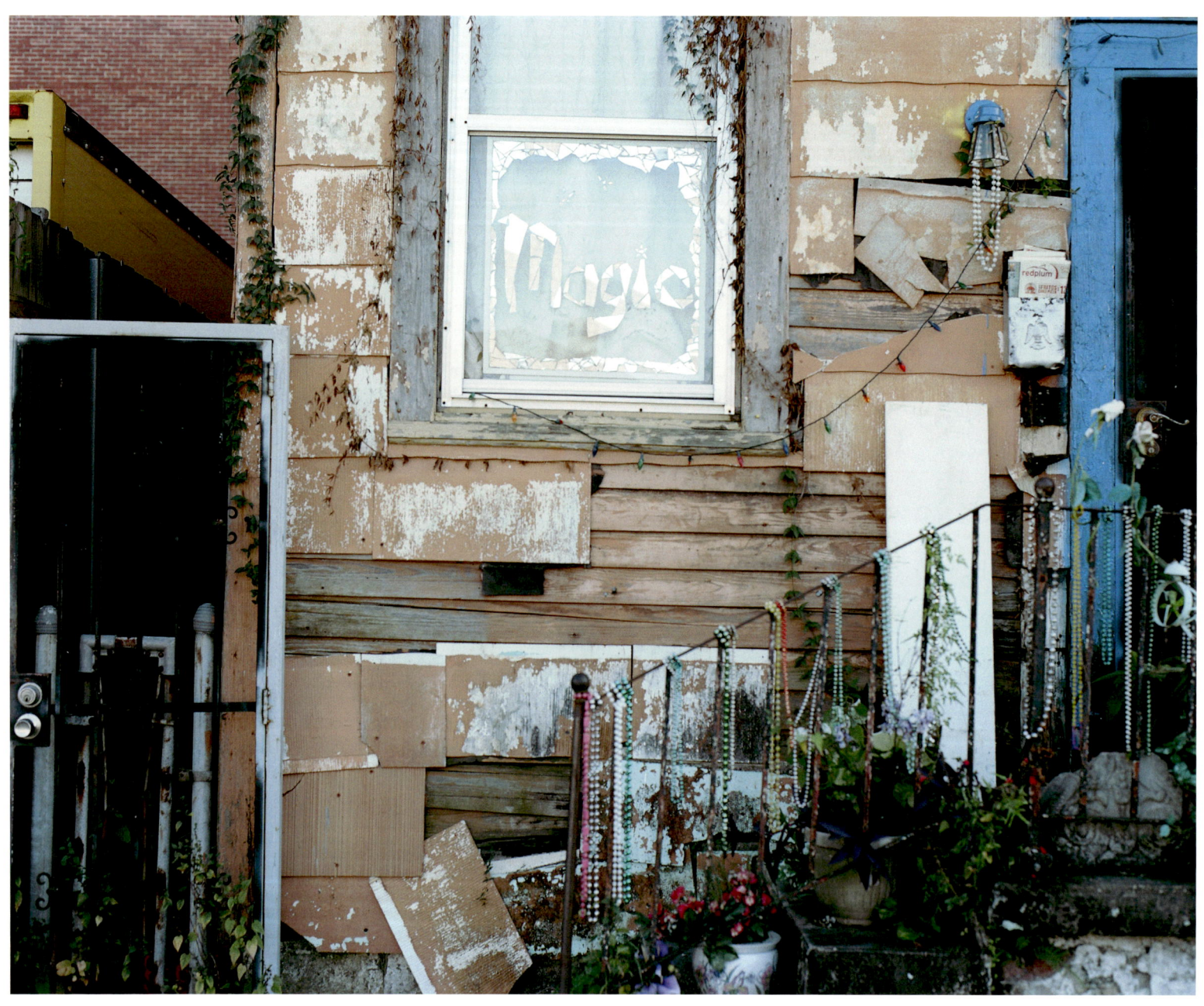

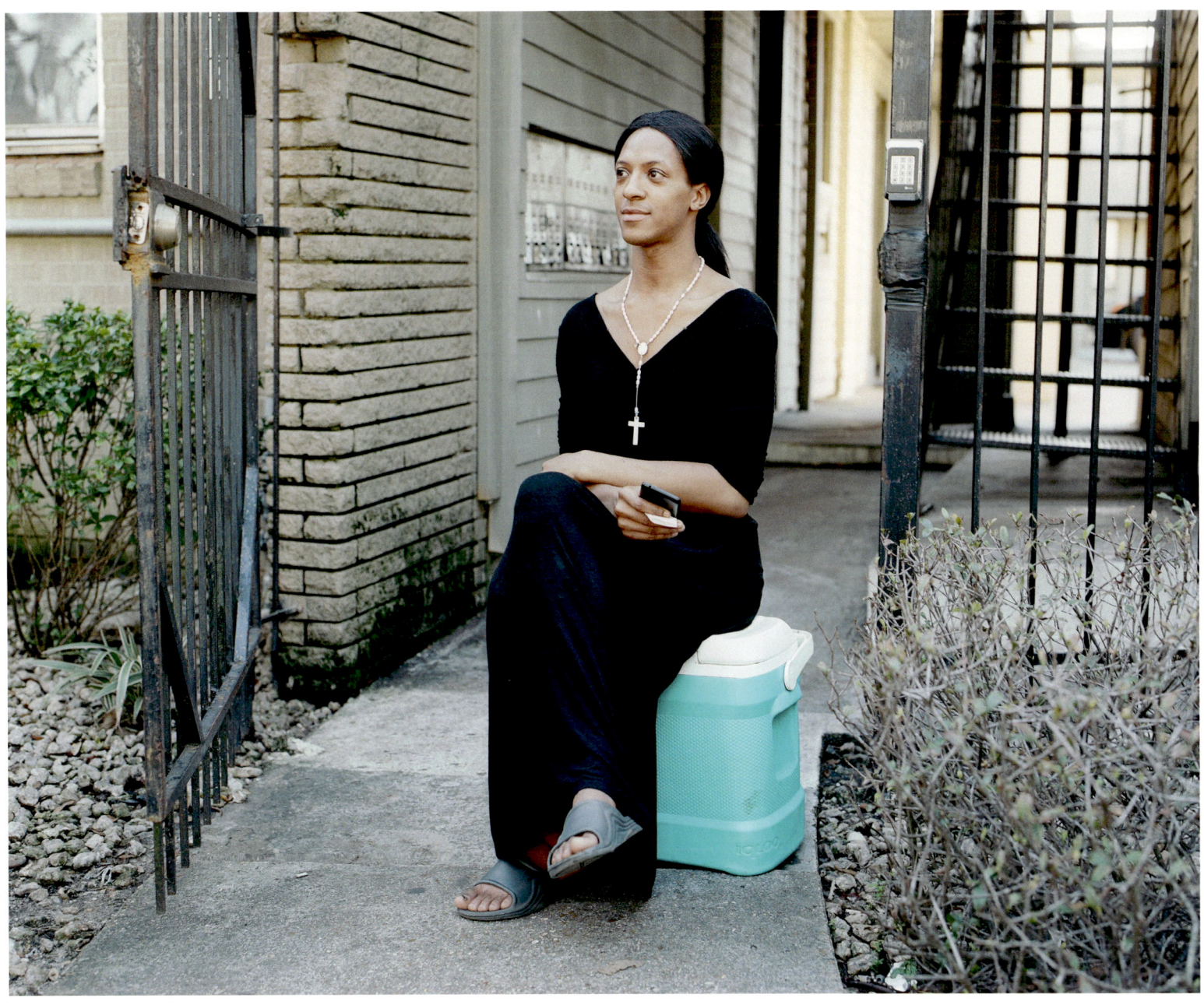

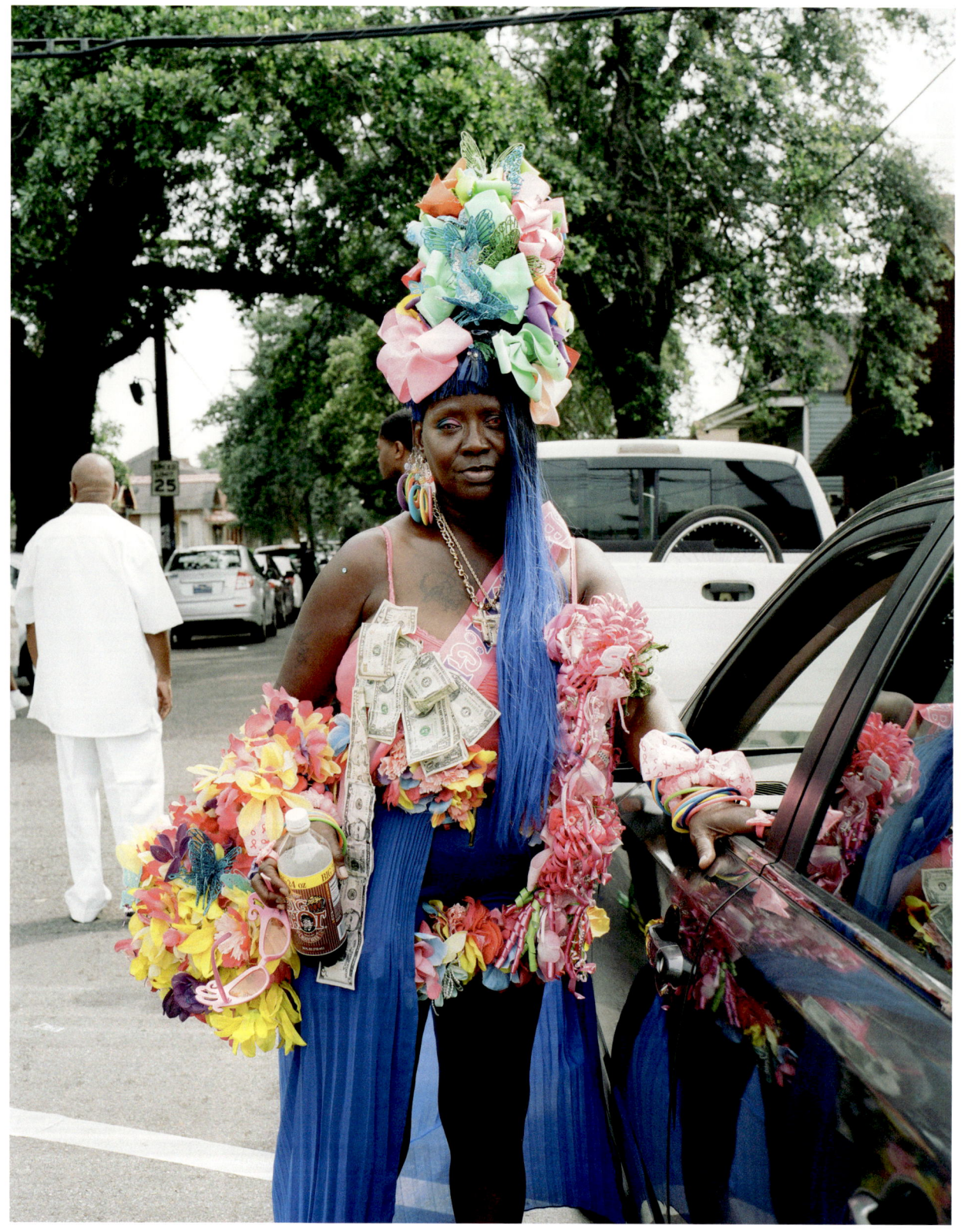

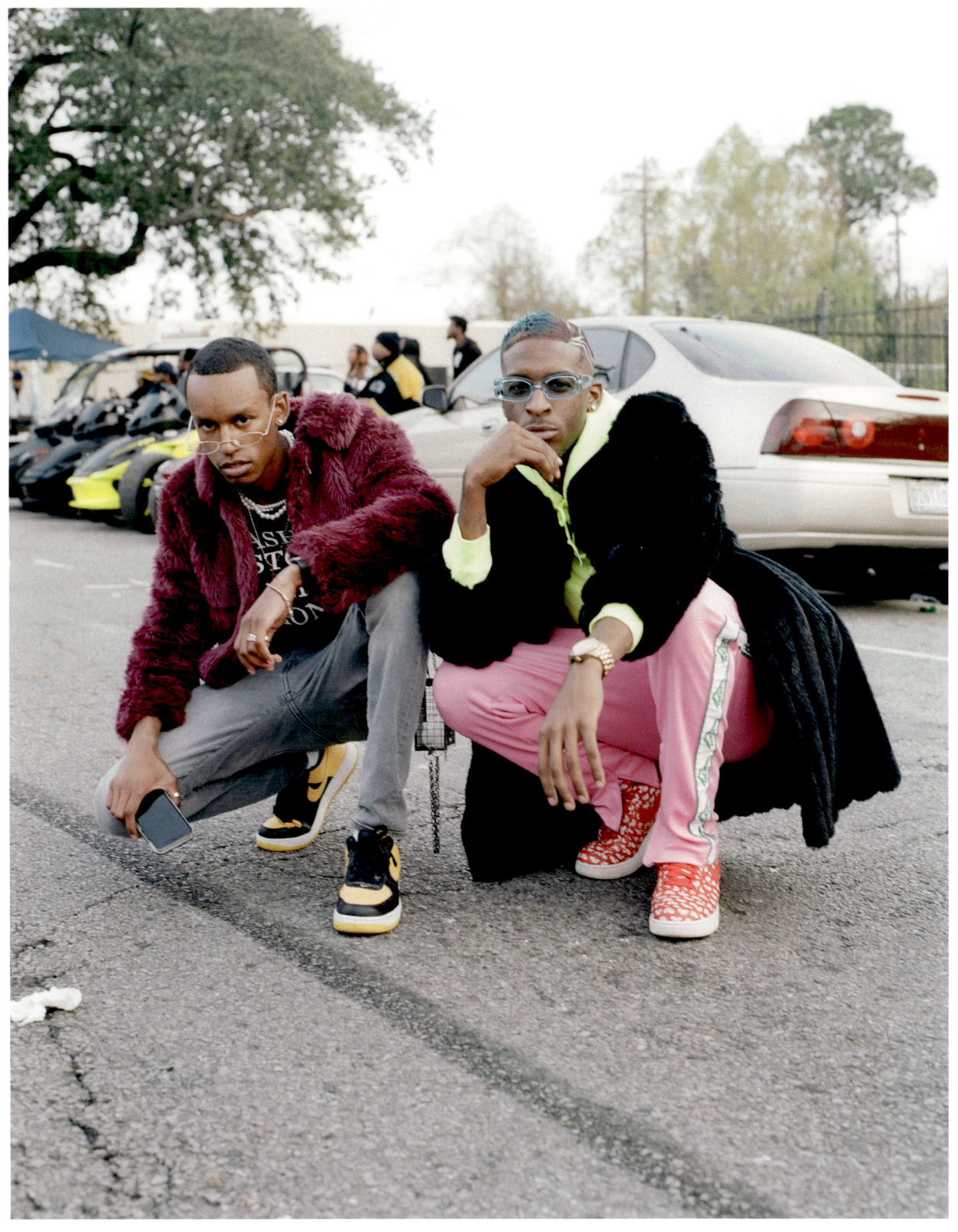

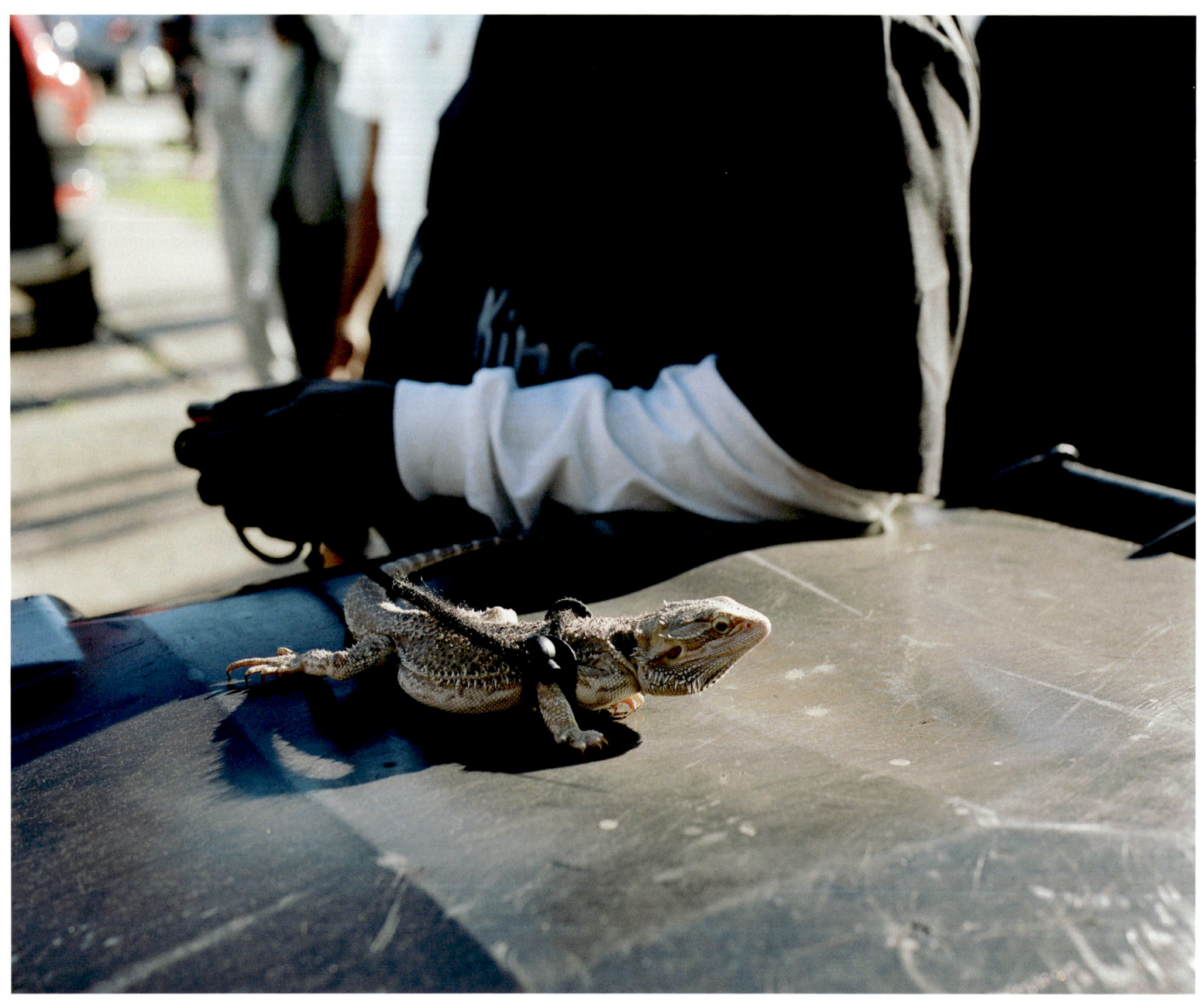

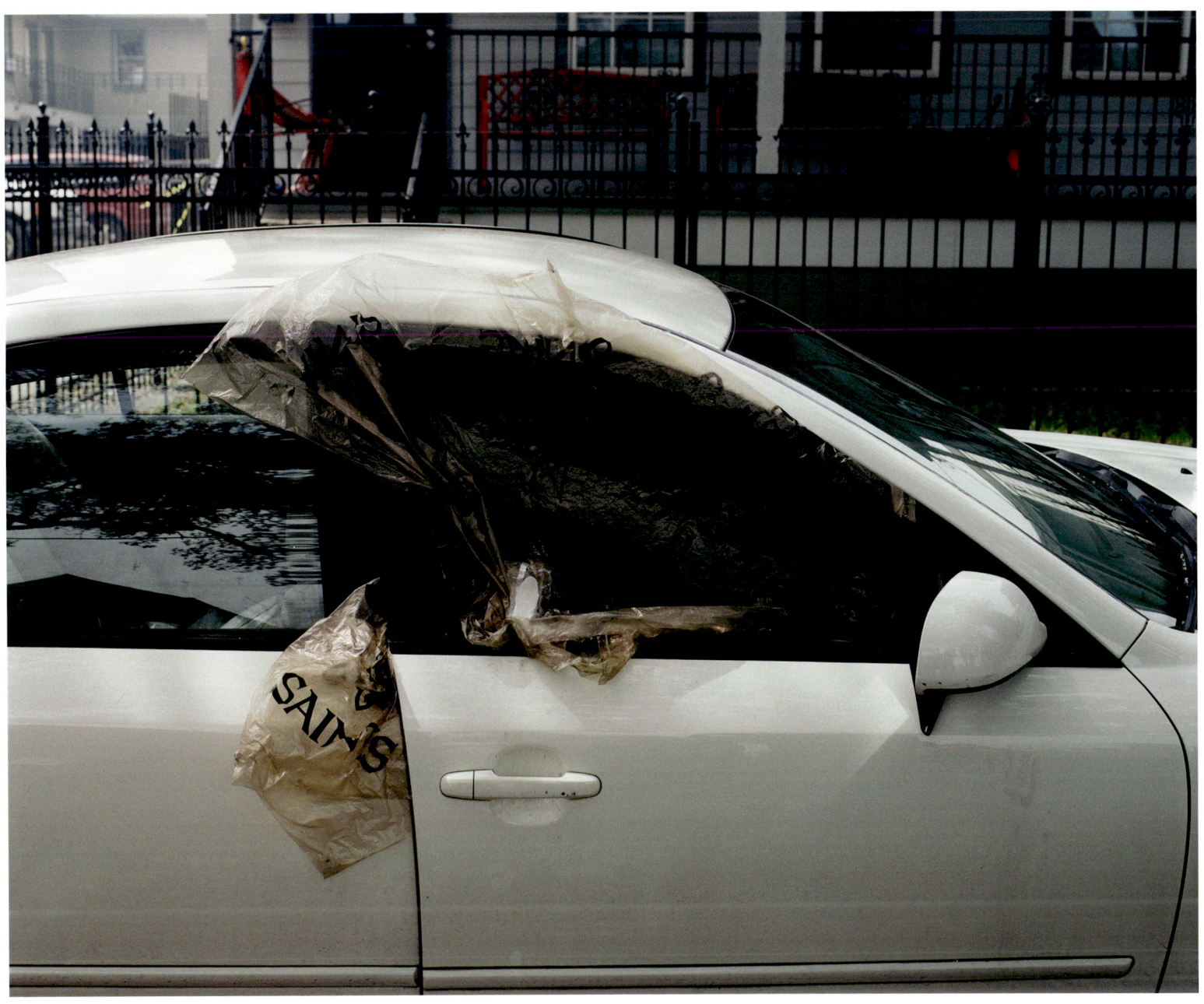

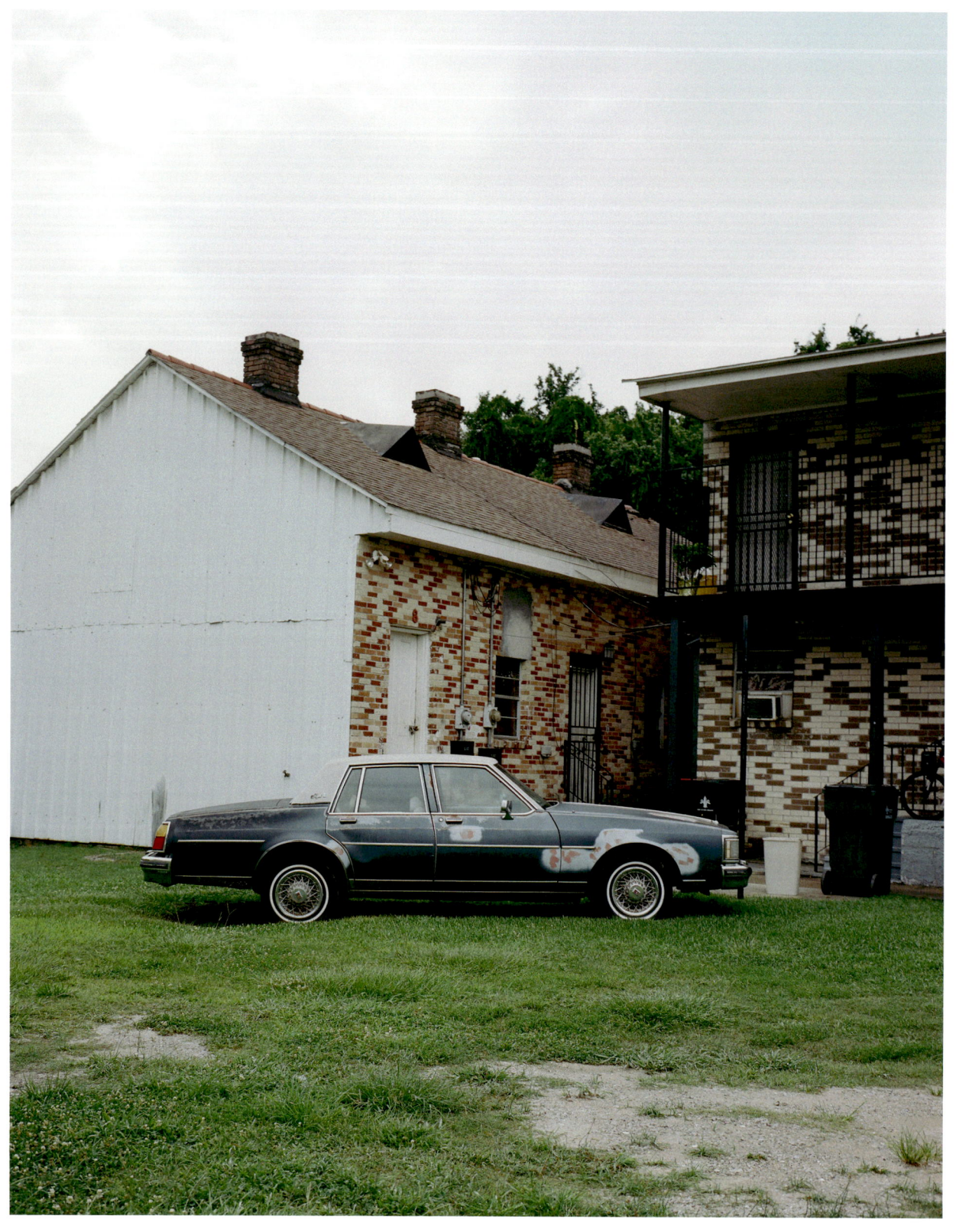

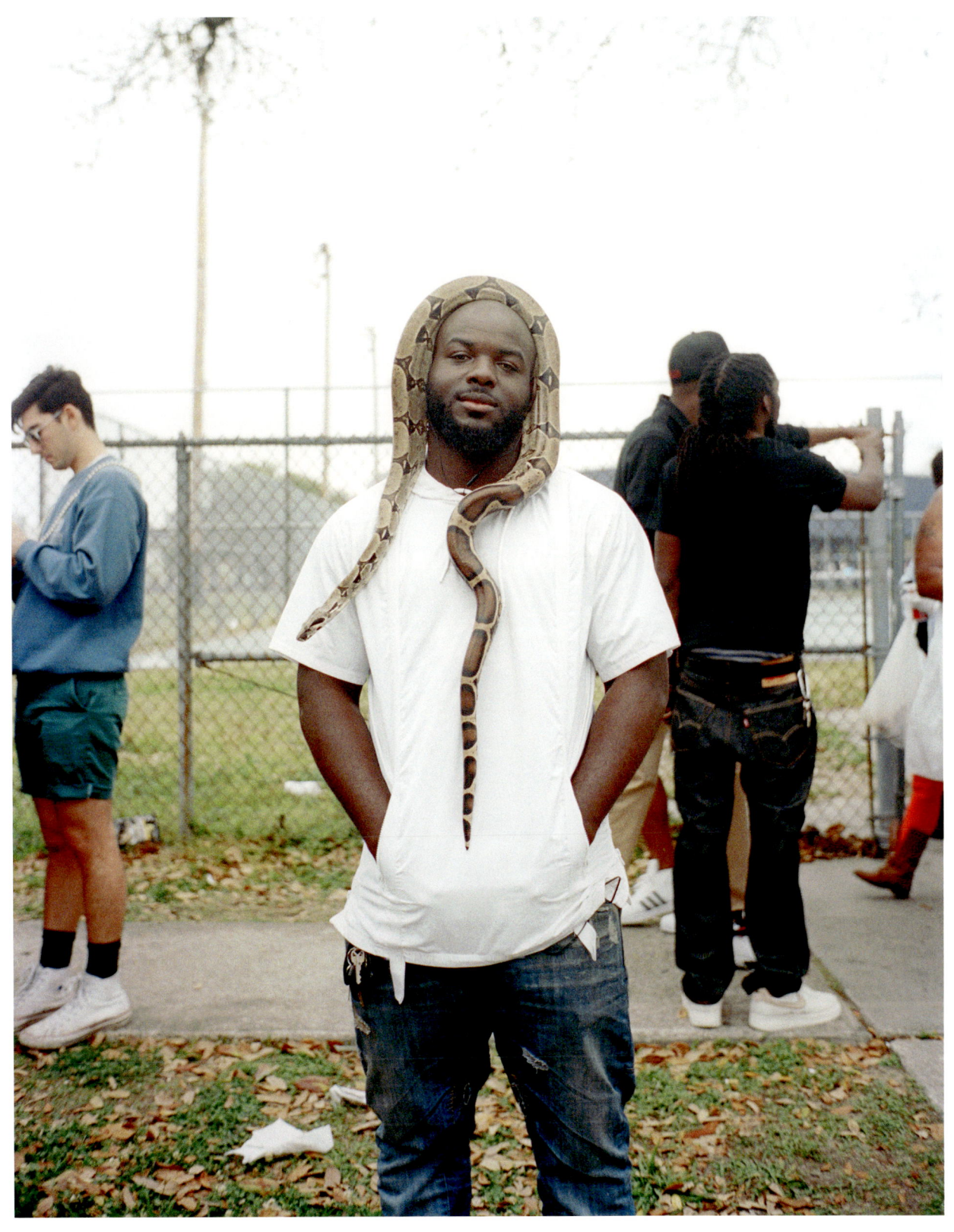

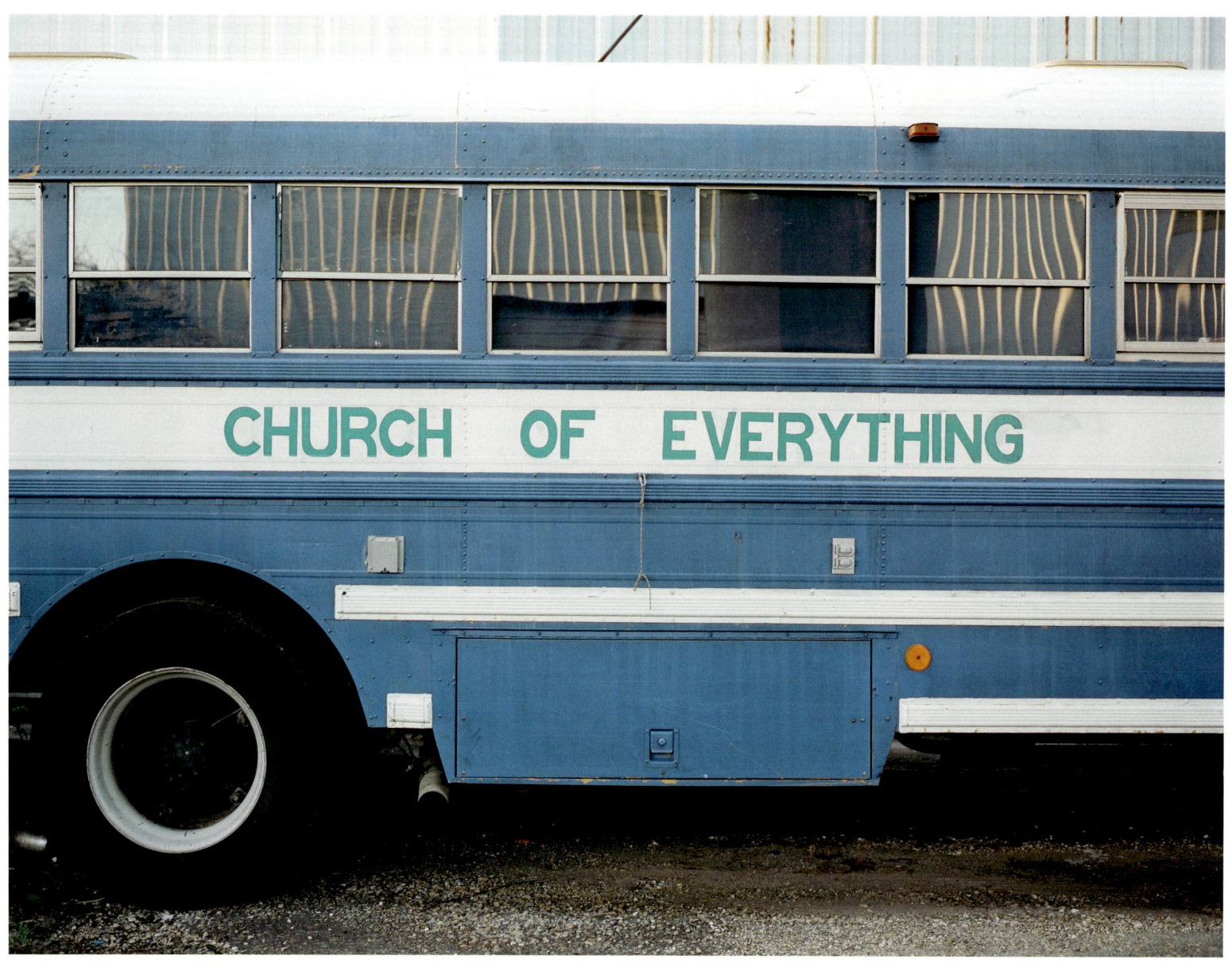

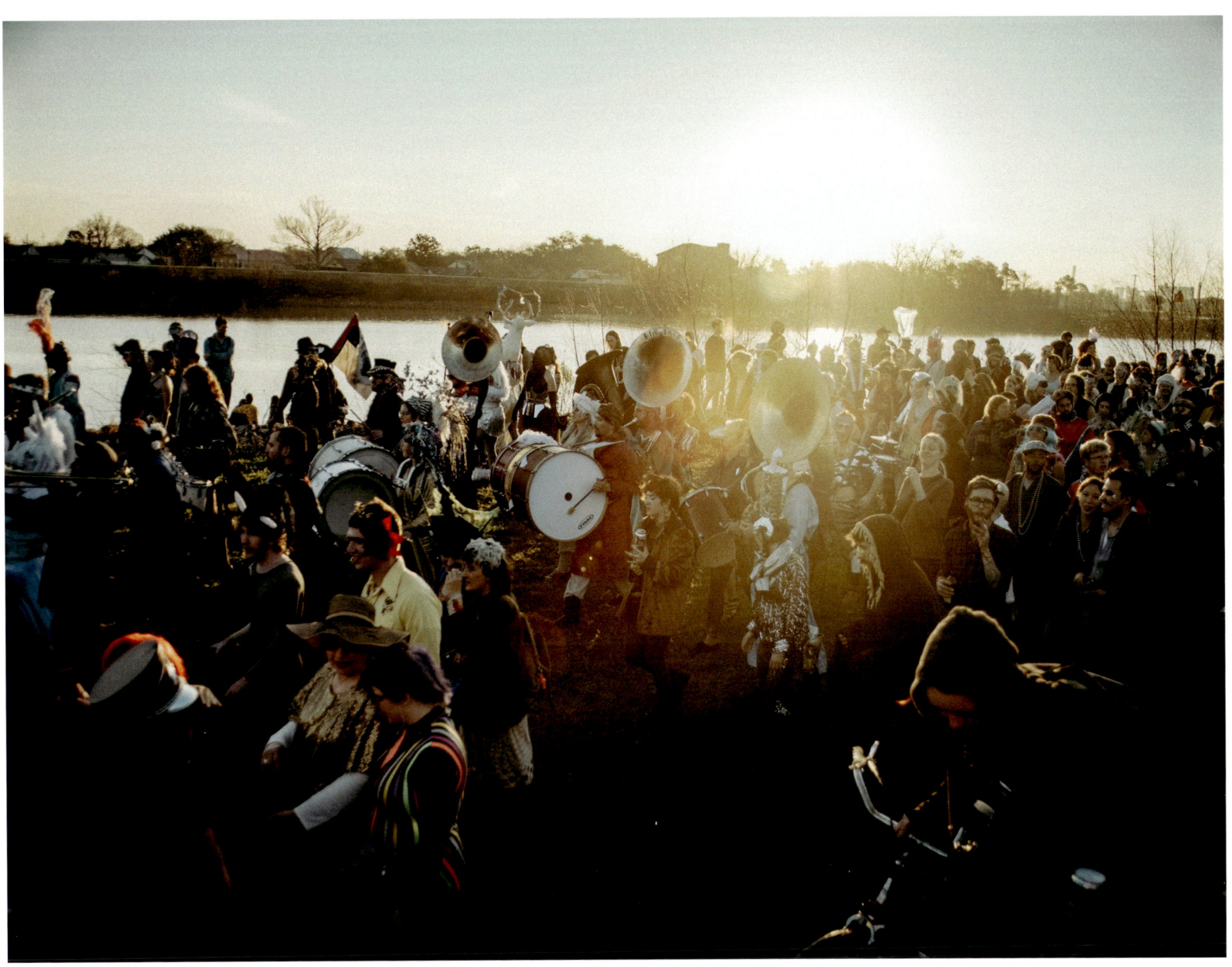

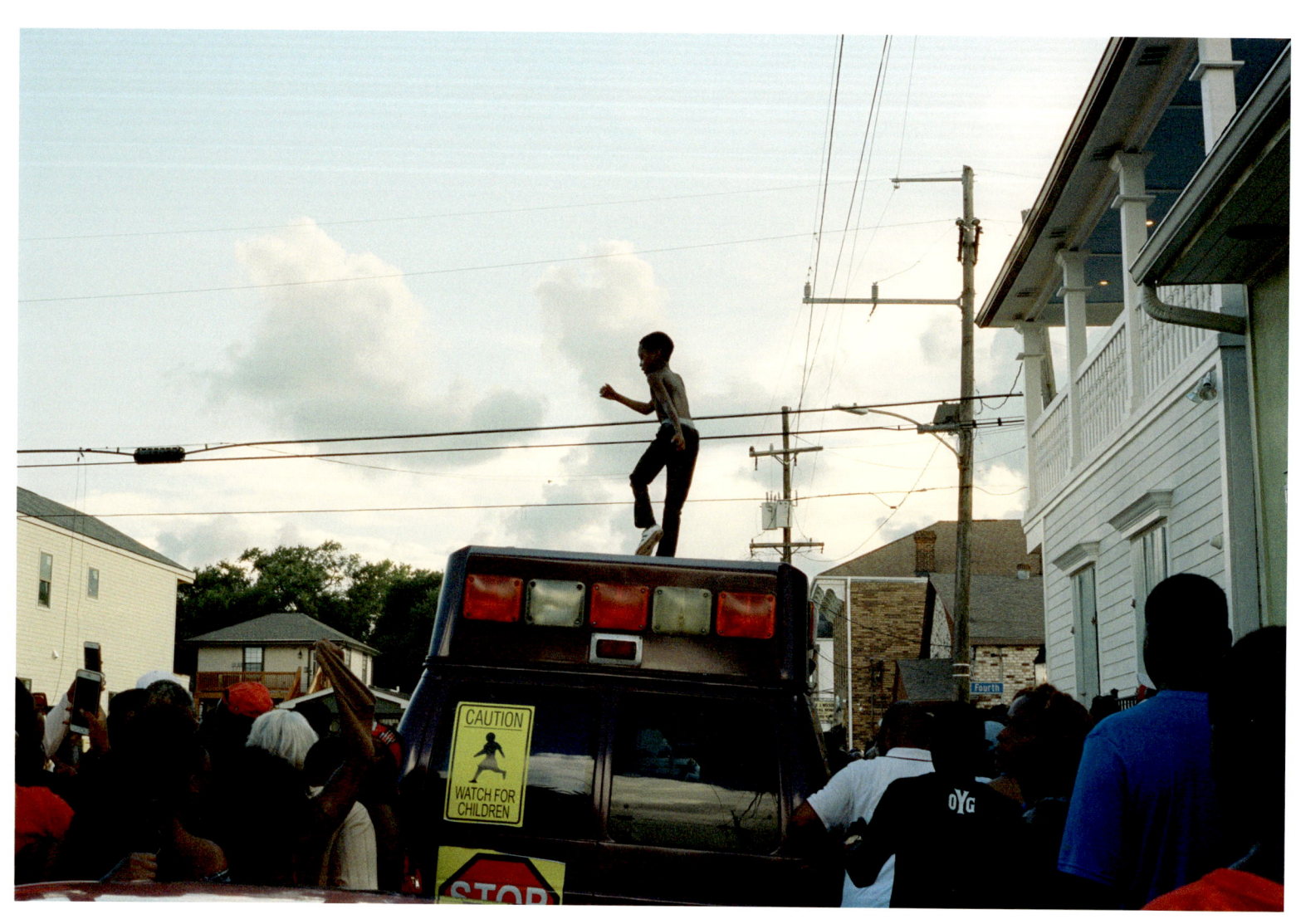

AFTERWORD

Anne Gisleson

"In other places, culture comes down from on high. In New Orleans, it bubbles up from the street." The jazz patriarch Ellis Marsalis' dictum was repeated often after Hurricane Katrina and the federal floods that followed. It articulated the depth of the relationship between the city's physical and psychic environments, and the urgency of the threats both were facing.

In mid-July 2019, these New Orleans streets are empty, blanketed by a tense quietude as yet another tropical storm approaches from the Gulf. At the moment, people fear what might bubble up from the street—floodwaters swamping homes, cars, and businesses. In an unprecedented confluence, this storm is approaching while the Mississippi River is at flood stage, inching toward the tops of the earthen levees surrounding the city.

Climate change has been blamed for this worst-case scenario: heavy spring rains to the north swell the river and warmer temperatures feed bigger storms in the Gulf. The city's buffer against the Gulf of Mexico, its wetlands, has also been degraded by climate-change-related sea level rise, as well as by overdevelopment, oil and gas industry activity, and the three-hundred-year-old management of the river, which has starved the delta of much needed sediment—land.

In New Orleans, like in coastal cities the world over, climate-driven gentrification is deepening existing inequity. Our high ground along the river, the architecturally and culturally rich historic core of the French Quarter, Marigny, and Bywater, has become increasingly coveted by, and marketed to, the affluent. Rents and property taxes are skyrocketing, but the creation of affordable housing is at a stand-still, and wages remain stagnant as city leaders double down on the low-paying, soul-depleting tourist economy.

One result of the city's rush toward overtourism is the gutting of locals from the historic core to provide short-term rentals for tourists. Security lockboxes dangling from doorknobs on entire blocks of Treme, the oldest African American neighborhood in America, have become depressing little symbols of denied access to one's heritage, to homes built by generations of people of color. Some housing advocates are calling the accelerated displacement of the city's longtime citizens a "second Katrina."

Across the pre-storm city, during this breezy moment of sandbags on stoops and drinks in hands, in a high-ground gentrifying neighborhood, there's much talk of the "new normal" of extreme weather, of embracing ways of "living with water"—new canals, urban wetlands, green infrastructure. But as cities such as Copenhagen have demonstrated, improved resilience in neighborhoods often leads to more gentrification and displacement. Any urgent call to a radical re-visioning of New Orleans' tradition-bound built environment would have to address the equally urgent question of how we help our most vulnerable communities thrive.

Before we commit to living with water, we need to confront how we live with one another.

I don't think I need to tell you what this book is about. I don't really think I could. I can't summarize Death, Magick, or Abundance. But I can show you what those words mean to me, as exemplified by the city where I've been lucky enough to spend the last decade. Witnessing how the people of New Orleans adorn themselves in a dizzying array of hallucinatory fashion, observing how music and style disseminate from the streets instead of from a supposed elite influencer class, and cultivating friendships with the people who comprise the heart of this book—these experiences have forever changed my life.

If there's one message I hope these photos convey, it must be this: More than any party, more than any song, more than any team or dome or disaster, New Orleans is her people. Take me out of the equation and you have a book about those people: the ones who persevere, the ones who survive, the ones who thrive and live to transform this city again and again, filling New Orleans with her vitality and strength.

Photography, by nature, extracts; it whittles out love, hope, horror, and treasure from the strata of our world. Sometimes, in its most potent form, photography can capture a piece of something true. That truth can be a woman's acrylic nails, a man on horseback, or the way a tree reclaims a decimated brick wall. Maybe it's because of these extractions that I sometimes question my role as a photographer amongst a community of people whom I love. It's such an immense privilege to be invited into someone's life, family, and neighborhood so I can take a few pictures. I deeply respect everyone in this book who showed up and allowed me to document who they are, who they want to be, their treasured being.

I think that when we are adorned in our most ardent splendor, we are perhaps, in fact, the most naked. I remind myself of this as I weave the kaleidoscopic streets of New Orleans. I tell myself, *This city is important. Be careful with her. Honor her people. Cherish this moment in time. It will not come again.*

Akasha Rabut

These photographs were made in collaboration with the people in this book. I could not have done any of this without you.

Thank you:

To my mom, Valerie Litvak, who always told me to follow my heart, nourished my creativity, and encouraged me to pursue art; my stepmom, Rozlyn Reiner, who taught me the importance of ethics, and how to be a strong woman; my dad, Florencio Rabut, who taught me to enjoy life; my brother Rory Rabut, who is one of the kindest hearts I have ever known; my brother Richard Reid, who is incredibly positive and supportive; my Aunt Tamara Tresenrider, who is a wonderful guide in the world; my Uncle Pat Livingston, who is forever supportive; my Great Auntie Donna Van Houghton, who has always cheered me on; my cousin Danny Babush, who has talked me through many difficult times; and my ancestors, who've guided me to where I am today;

To my soul sister, Jillian Kunysz, for keeping me grounded and for being one of the best friends that I have ever known; to Chad Kunysz, who is always available to offer wonderful advice, love and support; to Laura Kunysz, who can heal any wound;

To Logan Antill, who has spent hours offering me endless emotional support while I was making this book;

To Darcy Padilla, for your mentorship, for teaching me that people are not subjects, and of the importance of making photographs with integrity;

To Keely Merritt, who constantly reminded me that I was an artist and encouraged me to follow my dream of being a photographer;

To Darcy McKinnon, who encouraged me to be an educator—thank you for sharing your knowledge and power with me;

To Frank Espada, who loved my photography and inspired me to photograph people;

To Mr. Brooks, who allowed me to live in the darkroom in high school and spent lunch periods talking to me about how to pursue my love for photography;

To important friendships: Katie McMullin, Yudi Echevarria, Garrett Bradley, Christine Stulik, Claire Bangser, Leyla McCalla, Alex Welsh, Monika Wyndham, and Nathan Perkel;

To Chris Harrero and the Edna Karr Marching Band, Dance Team, Drum Majors, Majorettes, Flag Team, and Colorguard of 2014–2017 for sharing your incredible talent—your dance moves and music inspired me to make this body of work;

To Dirty South Ryderz Devence Hampton and Dwayne Monette, for sharing your world with me; to Jesse Murdock, for inviting me to my first trail ride; to Kristiaan Lewis-Hampton, Louis Chancellor, Chris Carr, Eric Bell, Roc Roc, and Earl, for always being down to be in a photograph;

To the Young Rollers, Original Big 7, Original Big 7 Junior Steppers, Ronald Lewis and the House of Dance & Feathers, Black Men of Labor, Wild Magnolias, Theodore Gurley and the Uptown Warriors, Red Hawk Hunters, Chief Charlie and the Comanche, Sharon "Ms. Colors" Walker, Second Chief Jeremy Stevenson, Little Queen Kaylin Cook, Queen Christine Cook and Monogram Hunters, Young Cheyenne and all of the Social Aid and Pleasure Clubs of New Orleans, Baby Dolls, Mardi Gras Indians and Culture Bearers—for keeping New Orleans' culture alive;

To the Caramel Curves: Shanika Beatty, Nellie Brooks, Nakosha Smith, Andrea Shepherd, Dezell Bell, Marquetta Daniels, Keioka Royal, Iveira Brown, Kimberly Gilbert, Tiffany Harvey, and Tierra Thomas; and to past members of the Caramel Curves: Carolyn Sterling, Daria K. Cotton, Karena James, Shalonda Lewis, Dywanna Franklin, Adrian Taylor, Tywanda Cannon, Shamika Martin, and Fay Phillips, for pushing boundaries of race and gender roles and for being positive female role models;

To Rachel Breunlin and the Neighborhood Story Project, for being a cultural liaison—your involvement with the community is deep and beautiful, and I'm forever grateful for your involvement in this project;

To Pauly Lingerfelt, who made the beautiful cover of this book;

To the team at Anthology Editions, for making this book a reality.

215

First published in the United States of America in 2020
by Anthology Editions

87 Guernsey Street
Brooklyn, NY 11222

anthologyeditions.com

Foreword by Sam Feather
Afterword by Anne Gisleson
Oral histories by Rachel Breunlin of the Neighborhood Story Project

Editors: Jesse Pollock and Akasha Rabut
Editorial Assistance: Clark Allen and Mark Iosifescu
Art Director: Bryan Cipolla
Cover Art: Pauly Lingerfelt
Cover Design: Alex Tults

First Edition
ARC 073
Printed in China

ISBN: 978-1-944860-27-1
Library of Congress Control Number: 2019951569